The complete correspondence and works of Charles Lamb; with an essay on his life and genius

Charles Lamb, Thomas Purnell, Barry Cornwall

CORRESPONDENCE AND WORKS

OF

CHARLES LAMB.

U

B)

THE COMPLETE

CORRESPONDENCE AND WORKS

OF

CHARLES LAMB;

WITH AN ESSAY ON HIS LIFE AND GENIUS BY

THOMAS PURNELL,

AIDED BY THE RECOLLECTIONS OF

THE AUTHOR'S ADOPTED DAUGHTER.

Vol. IV.

LONDON:
E. MOXON, SON AND CO., DOVER STREET.
1870.

LONDON
SWIFT AND CO., 55, KING STREET,
REGENT STREET, W

CONTENTS OF VOL. IV.

COMMENDATORY VERSES

MISCELLANEOUS POEMS.

TRANSLATIONS.

DRAMATIC WORKS.

TALES.

———

VI.

COMMENDATORY VERSES.[1]

TO J. S. KNOWLES, ESQ.

ON HIS TRAGEDY OF VIRGINIUS.[2]

TWELVE years ago I knew thee, Knowles, and then
Esteemed you a perfect specimen
Of those fine spirits warm-soul'd Ireland sends,
To teach us colder English how a friend's
Quick pulse should beat. I knew you brave, and
    plain,
Strong-sensed, rough-witted, above fear or gain:
But nothing further had the gift to espy.
Sudden you re-appear.   With wonder I

---

[1] It is to be remarked that in all former editions of Lamb, poems which had no right to come under this head were inserted. They have now been placed in their proper positions.

[2] Produced at the Glasgow Theatre, and afterwards (1820) brought out at Covent Garden. It was acted at Covent Garden, May 17, 1820; at Drury Lane, Oct. 13, 1823, and again at Covent Garden, Dec. 15, 1828.

Hear my old friend (turn'd Shakspeare) read a
    scene
Only to *his* interior in the clean
Passes of pathos : with such fence-like art—
Ere we can see the steel, 'tis in our heart.
Almost without the aid language affords,
Your piece seems wrought. That huffing medium,
    words,
(Which in the modern Tamburlaines quite sway
Our shamed souls from their bias) in your play
We scarce attend to. Hastier passion draws
Our tears on credit : and we find the cause
Some two hours after, spelling o'er again
Those strange few words at ease, that wrought the
    pain.
Proceed, old friend ; and, as the year returns,
Still snatch some new old story from the urns
Of long-dead virtue. We, that knew before
Your worth, may admire, we cannot love you more.

TO THE AUTHOR OF POEMS,

PUBLISHED UNDER THE NAME OF BARRY CORNWALL.

LET hate, or grosser heats, their foulness mask
Under the vizor of a borrow'd name ;
Let things eschew the light deserving blame :
No cause hast thou to blush for thy sweet task.

" Marcian Colonna " is a dainty book :
And thy " Sicilian Tale " may boldly pass ;
Thy " Dream " 'bove all, in which, as in a glass,
On the great world's antique glories we may look.
No longer then, as " lowly substitute,
Factor, or PROCTER, for another's gains,"
Suffer the admiring world to be deceived ,
Lest thou thyself, by self of fame bereaved,
Lament too late the lost prize of thy pains,
And heavenly tunes piped through an alien flute.

TO THE EDITOR OF THE " EVERY-DAY BOOK."

I LIKE you, and your book, ingenuous Hone !
  In whose capacious all-embracing leaves
The very marrow of tradition's shown ;
  And all that history—much that fiction—weaves.

By every sort of taste your work is graced.
  Vast stores of modern anecdote we find,
With good old story quaintly interlaced—
  The theme as various as the reader's mind.

Rome's lie-fraught legends you so truly paint—
  Yet kindly,—that the half-turn'd Catholic
Scarcely forbears to smile at his own saint,
  And cannot curse the candid heretic.

B 2

Rags, relics, witches, ghosts, fiends, crowd your page,
  Our fathers' mummeries we well-pleased behold,
And, proudly conscious of a purer age,
  Forgive some fopperies in the times of old.

Verse-honouring Phœbus, Father of bright *Days*,
  Must needs bestow on you both good and many,
Who, building trophies of his Children's praise,
  Run their rich Zodiac through, not missing any.

Dan Phœbus loves your book—trust me, friend
    Hone—
  The title only errs, he bids me say:
For while such art, wit, reading, there are shown,
  He swears, 'tis not a work of *every day*.

TO T. STOTHARD, ESQ.

ON HIS ILLUSTRATIONS OF THE POEMS OF MR. ROGERS.

CONSUMMATE Artist, whose undying name
With classic Rogers shall go down to fame,
Be this thy crowning work! In my young days
How often have I, with a child's fond gaze,
Pored on the pictur'd wonders thou hadst done:
Clarissa mournful, and prim Grandison!
All Fielding's, Smollett's heroes, rose to view;
I saw, and I believed the phantoms true.

But, above all, that most romantic tale
Did o'er my raw credulity prevail,
Where Glums and Gawries wear mysterious things,
That serve at once for jackets and for wings.
Age, that enfeebles other men's designs,
But heightens thine, and thy free draught refines.
In several ways distinct you make us feel—
Graceful as Raphael, as Watteau *genteel*.
Your lights and shades, as Titianesque, we praise,
And warmly wish you Titian's length of days.

VII.

MISCELLANEOUS POEMS.[1]

DEDICATION.[2]

TO S. T. COLERIDGE, ESQ.

My dear Coleridge,—You will smile to see the slender labours of your friend designated by the title of *Works*; but such was the wish of the gentlemen who have kindly undertaken the trouble of collecting them, and from their judgment could be no appeal.

It would be a kind of disloyalty to offer to any one but yourself a volume containing the *early pieces*, which were first published among your poems, and were fairly derivatives from you and them. My friend Lloyd and myself came into our first battle (authorship is a sort of warfare) under cover of the greater Ajax. How this association, which shall always be a dear and proud recollection to me, came to be broken,—who snapped the threefold cord,—whether yourself (but I know that was not the case) grew ashamed of your former companions,—or whether (which is by much the more probable) some ungracious bookseller was author of the separation,—I cannot tell:—but wanting the support of your friendly elm, (I speak for myself,) my vine has, since that time, put forth few or no fruits; the sap (if ever it had any) has become, in a manner, dried up and extinct; and

---

[1] Those pieces which are now first added to this collection are placed at the end between crotchets. The original dedication to Coleridge is retained.

[2] Prefixed to the Author's works published in 1818.

you will find your old associate, in his second volume, dwindled into prose and *criticism*.

Am I right in assuming this as the cause? or is it that, as years come upon us, (except with some more healthy-happy spirits,) Life itself loses much of its Poetry for us? we transcribe but what we read in the great volume of Nature; and as the characters grow dim, we turn off, and look another way You yourself write no Christabels, nor Ancient Mariners, now.

Some of the Sonnets, which shall be carelessly turned over by the general reader, may happily awaken in you remembrances, which I should be sorry should be ever totally extinct—the memory

"Of Summer days and of delightful years—"

even so far back as to those old suppers at our old [Salutation] Inn,— when life was fresh, and topics exhaustless,—and you first kindled in me, if not the power, yet the love of poetry, and beauty, and kindliness.—

"What words have I heard
Spoke at the Mermaid!"

The world has given you many a shrewd nip and gird since that time, but either my eyes are grown dimmer, or my old friend is the *same* who stood before me three-and-twenty years ago—his hair a little confessing the hand of Time, but still shrouding the same capacious brain,—his heart not altered, scarcely where it "alteration finds."

One piece, Coleridge, I have ventured to publish in its original form, though I have heard you complain of a certain over-imitation of the antique in the style If I could see any way of getting rid of the objection, without re-writing it entirely, I would make some sacrifices. But when I wrote John Woodvil, I never proposed to myself any distinct deviation from common English. I had been newly initiated in the writings of our elder dramatists Beaumont and Fletcher, and Massinger, were then a *first love*, and from what I was so freshly conversant in, what wonder if my language imperceptibly took a tinge? The very *time* which I had chosen for my story, that which immediately followed the Restoration, seemed to require, in an English play, that the English should be of rather an older cast than that of the precise year in which it happened to be written. I wish it had not some faults, which I can less vindicate than the language

I remain, my dear Coleridge,

Yours, with unabated esteem,

C LAMB

HESTER.

WHEN maidens such as Hester die,
Their place ye may not well supply,
Though ye among a thousand try,
    With vain endeavour.

A month or more hath she been dead,
Yet cannot I by force be led
To think upon the wormy bed,
    And her together.

A springy motion in her gait,
A rising step, did indicate
Of pride and joy no common rate,
    That flush'd her spirit.

I know not by what name beside
I shall it call:—if 'twas not pride,
It was a joy to that allied,
    She did inherit.

Her parents held the Quaker rule,
Which doth the human feeling cool,
But she was train'd in Nature's school,
    Nature had blest her.

A waking eye, a prying mind,
A heart that stirs, is hard to bind,
A hawk's keen sight ye cannot blind,
    Ye could not Hester.

My sprightly neighbour! gone before
To that unknown and silent shore,
Shall we not meet, as heretofore,
　　Some Summer morning,

When from thy cheerful eyes a ray
Hath struck a bliss upon the day,
A bliss that would not go away,
　　A sweet fore-warning?

THE THREE FRIENDS.

THREE young maids in friendship met,
Mary, Martha, Margaret.
Margaret was tall and fair,
Martha shorter by a hair,
If the first excell'd in feature,
Th' other's grace and ease were greater;
Mary, though to rival loth,
In their best gifts equall'd both.
They a due proportion kept:
Martha mourn'd if Margaret wept;
Margaret joy'd when any good
She of Martha understood;
And in sympathy for either
Mary was outdone by neither.
Thus far, for a happy space,
All three ran an equal race,
A most constant friendship proving,
Equally beloved and loving;

All their wishes, joys, the same ;
Sisters only not in name.

Fortune upon each one smiled,
As upon a fav'rite child ;
Well to do and well to see
Were the parents of all three ;
Till on Martha's father crosses
Brought a flood of worldly losses,
And his fortunes rich and great
Changed at once to low estate ;
Under which o'erwhelming blow
Martha's mother was laid low ;
She a hapless orphan left,
Of maternal care bereft,
Trouble following trouble fast,
Lay in a sick bed at last.

In the depth of her affliction
Martha now receiv'd conviction,
That a true and faithful friend
Can the surest comfort lend.
Night and day, with friendship tried,
Ever constant by her side
Was her gentle Mary found,
With a love that knew no bound;
And the solace she imparted
Saved her dying broken-hearted.

In this scene of earthly things
Not one good unmixèd springs.
That which had to Martha proved
A sweet consolation, moved
Different feelings of regret
In the mind of Margaret.

She, whose love was not less dear,
Nor affection less sincere
To her friend, was, by occasion
Of more distant habitation,
Fewer visits forced to pay her;
When no other cause did stay her;
And her Mary living nearer,
Margaret began to fear her.
Lest her visits day by day
Martha's heart should steal away.
That whole heart she ill could spare her,
Where till now she'd been a sharer.
From this cause with grief she pined,
Till at length her health declined.
All her cheerful spirits flew,
Fast as Martha's gather'd new;
And her sickness waxed sore,
Just when Martha felt no more.

Mary, who had quick suspicion
Of her alter'd friend's condition,
Seeing Martha's convalescence
Less demanded now her presence,
With a goodness, built on reason,
Changed her measures with the season
Turn'd her steps from Martha's door,
Went where she was wanted more;
All her care and thoughts were set
Now to tend on Margaret.
Mary living 'twixt the two,
From her home could oft'ner go,
Either of her friends to see,
Than they could together be.

Truth explain'd is to suspicion
Evermore the best physician.
Soon her visits had the effect;
All that Margaret did suspect,
From her fancy vanish'd clean;
She was soon what she had been,
And the colour she did lack
To her faded cheek came back.
Wounds which love had made her feel,
Love alone had power to heal.

Martha, who the frequent visit
Now had lost, and sore did miss it,
With impatience waxèd cross,
Counted Margaret's gain her loss:
All that Mary did confer
On her friend, thought due to her.
In her girlish bosom rise
Little foolish jealousies,
Which into such rancour wrought,
She one day for Margaret sought;
Finding her by chance alone,
She began, with reasons shown,
To insinuate a fear
Whether Mary was sincere;
Wish'd that Margaret would take heed
Whence her actions did proceed.
For herself, she'd long been minded
Not with outsides to be blinded;
All that pity and compassion,
She believed was affectation;
In her heart she doubted whether
Mary cared a pin for either.

She could keep whole weeks at distance,
And not know of their existence,
While all things remain'd the same ,
But when some misfortune came,
Then she made a great parade
Of her sympathy and aid,—
Not that she did really grieve,
It was only *make-believe*,
And she cared for nothing, so
She might her fine feelings show,
And get credit, on her part,
For a soft and tender heart.

With such speeches, smoothly made,
She found methods to persuade
Margaret (who being sore
From the doubts she'd felt before,
Was prepared for mistrust)
To believe her reasons just ;
Quite destroy'd that comfort glad,
Which in Mary late she had ;
Made her, in experience' spite,
Think her friend a hypocrite,
And resolve, with cruel scoff,
To renounce and cast her off.

See how good turns are rewarded !
She of both is now discarded,
Who to both had been so late
Their support in low estate,
All their comfort, and their stay—
Now of both is cast away.
But the league her presence cherish'd,
Losing its best prop, soon perish d :

She, that was a link to either,
To keep them and it together,
Being gone, the two (no wonder)
That were left, soon fell asunder ;—
Some civilities were kept,
But the heart of friendship slept ;
Love with hollow forms was fed,
But the life of love lay dead :—
A cold intercourse they held,
After Mary was expell'd.

Two long years did intervene
Since they'd either of them seen,
Or, by letter, any word
Of their old companion heard,—
When, upon a day once walking,
Of indifferent matters talking,
They a female figure met ;
Martha said to Margaret,
" That young maid in face does carry
A resemblance strong of Mary."
Margaret, at nearer sight,
Own'd her observation right ;
But they did not far proceed
Ere they knew 'twas she indeed.
She—but, ah ! how changed they view her
From that person which they knew her !
Her fine face disease had scarr'd,
And its matchless beauty marr'd :—
But enough was left to trace
Mary's sweetness—Mary's grace.
When her eye did first behold them,
How they blush'd !—but when she told them

How on a sick bed she lay
Months, while they had kept away,
And had no inquiries made
If she were alive or dead ;—
How, for want of a true friend,
She was brought near to her end,
And was like so to have died,
With no friend at her bed-side ;—
How the constant irritation,
Caused by fruitless expectation
Of their coming, had extended
The illness, when she might have mended,—
Then, O then, how did reflection
Come on them with recollection !
All that she had done for them,
How it did their fault condemn !

But sweet Mary, still the same,
Kindly eased them of their shame ;
Spoke to them with accents bland,
Took them friendly by the hand ;
Bound them both with promise fast,
Not to speak of troubles past ;
Made them on the spot declare
A new league of friendship there ;
Which, without a word of strife,
Lasted thenceforth long as life.
Martha now and Margaret
Strove who most should pay the debt
Which they owed her, nor did vary
Ever after from their Mary.

TO A RIVER IN WHICH A CHILD WAS DROWNED.

SMILING river, smiling river,
 On thy bosom sun-beams play ;
Though they're fleeting, and retreating,
 Thou hast more deceit than they:

In thy channel, in thy channel,
 Chok'd with ooze and grav'lly stones,
Deep immersed, and unhearsed,
 Lies young Edward's corse ; his bones

Ever whitening, ever whitening,
 As thy waves against them dash ;
What thy torrent, in the current,
 Swallow'd, now it helps to wash.

As if senseless, as if senseless
 Things had feeling in this case ,
What so blindly, and unkindly,
 It destroy'd, it now does grace.

THE OLD FAMILIAR FACES.

I HAVE had playmates, I have had companions,
In my days of childhood, in my joyful school-days,
All, all are gone, the old familiar faces.

I have been laughing, I have been carousing,
Drinking late, sitting late, with my bosom cronies,
All, all are gone, the old familiar faces.

I loved a love once,[1] fairest among women ;
Closed are her doors on me, I must not see her—
All, all are gone, the old familiar faces.

I have a friend, a kinder friend has no man ;
Like an ingrate, I left my friend abruptly ;
Left him, to muse on the old familiar faces.

Ghost-like I paced round the haunts of my child-
    hood.
Earth seem'd a desert I was bound to traverse,
Seeking to find the old familiar faces.

Friend of my bosom,[2] thou more than a brother,
Why wert not thou born in my father's dwell-
    ing ?
So might we talk of the old familiar faces—

How some they have died, and some they have left
    me,
And some are taken from me ; all are departed ;
All, all are gone, the old familiar faces.

---

[1] Miss Alice   [2] Coleridge.

A VISION OF REPENTANCE.

I SAW a famous fountain, in my dream
   Where shady path-ways to a valley led ;
A weeping willow lay upon that stream,
   And all around the fountain brink were spread
Wide-branching trees, with dark green leaf rich clad,
   Forming a doubtful twilight—desolate and sad.

The place was such, that whoso enter'd in,
   Disrobèd was of every earthly thought
And straight became as one that knew not sin,
   Or to the world's first innocence was brought ;
Enseem'd it now, he stood on holy ground,
In sweet and tender melancholy wrapt around.

A most strange calm stole o'er my soothèd sprite ;
   Long time I stood. and longer had I staid,
When lo ! I saw, saw by the sweet moon-light,
   Which came in silence o'er that silent shade,
Where, near the fountain, SOMETHING like DESPAIR
Made, of that weeping willow, garlands for her hair.

And eke with painful fingers she inwove
   Many an uncouth stem of savage thorn—
" The willow garland, *that* was for her love,
   And *these* her bleeding temples would adorn."
With sighs her heart nigh burst, salt tears fast fell,
As mournfully she bended o'er that sacred well.

ⵏ   ꝺ

To whom when I addrest myself to speak,
   She lifted up her eyes, and nothing said;
The delicate red came mantling o'er her cheek,
   And, gath'ring up her loose attire, she fled
To the dark covert of that woody shade,
And in her goings seem'd a timid gentle maid.

Revolving in my mind what this should mean,
   And why that lovely lady plained so;
Perplexed in thought at that mysterious scene,
   And doubting if 'twere best to stay or go,
I cast mine eyes in wistful gaze around,
When from the shades came slow a small and plaintive sound.

    " PSYCHE am I, who love to dwell
    In these brown shades, this woody dell,
    Where never busy mortal came,
    Till now, to pry upon my shame.

    At thy feet what thou dost see
    The waters of repentance be,
    Which, night and day, I must augment
    With tears, like a true penitent,

    If haply so my day of grace
    Be not yet past; and this lone place,
    O'er shadowy, dark, excludeth hence
    All thoughts but grief and penitence "

    " Why dost thou weep, thou gentle maid '
    And wherefore in this barren shade
    Thy hidden thoughts with sorrow feed?
    Can thing so fair repentance need?"

"O I have done a deed of shame,
And tainted is my virgin fame,
And stain'd the beauteous maiden white
In which my bridal robes were dight."

"*And who the promised spouse? declare:
And what those bridal garments were.*"

"Severe and saintly righteousness
Composed the clear white bridal dress;
JESUS, the Son of Heaven's high King,
Bought with his blood the marriage ring.

A wretched sinful creature, I
Deem'd lightly of that sacred tie,
Gave to a treacherous WORLD my heart,
And play'd the foolish wanton's part.
Soon to these murky shades I came,
To hide from the sun's light my shame.
And still I haunt this woody dell,
And bathe me in that healing well,
Whose waters clear have influence
From sin's foul stains the soul to cleanse;
And, night and day, I them augment,
With tears, like a true penitent,
Until, due expiation made,
And fit atonement fully paid,
The Lord and Bridegroom me present,
Where in sweet strains of high consent
God's throne before, the Seraphim
Shall chant the ecstatic marriage hymn."

"Now Christ restore thee soon"—I said,
And thenceforth all my dream was fled.

DIALOGUE BETWEEN A MOTHER AND CHILD.

CHILD.

"O LADY, lay your costly robes aside,
No longer may you glory in your pride."

MOTHER.

Wherefore to-day art singing in mine ear
Sad songs were made so long ago, my dear?
This day I am to be a bride, you know,
Why sing sad songs, were made so long ago?

CHILD.

O mother, lay your costly robes aside,
For you may never be another's bride.
That line I learn'd not in the old sad song.

MOTHER.

I pray thee, pretty one, now hold thy tongue,
Play with the bride-maids, and be glad, my boy,
For thou shalt be a second father's joy.

CHILD.

One father fondled me upon his knee.
One father is enough, alone, for me.

QUEEN ORIANA'S DREAM.

On a bank with roses shaded,
Whose sweet scent the violets aided,
Violets whose breath alone
Yields but feeble smell or none,

(Sweeter bed Jove ne'er reposed on
When his eyes Olympus closed on,)
While o'er head six slaves did hold
Canopy of cloth o' gold,
And two more did music keep,
Which might Juno lull to sleep,
Oriana, who was queen
To the mighty Tamerlane,
That was lord of all the land
Between Thrace and Samarchand,
While the noon-tide fervour beam'd,
Mused herself to sleep, and *dream'd*.

Thus far in magnific strain,
A young poet soothed his vein,
But he had nor prose nor numbers
To express a princess' slumbers.—
Youthful Richard had strange fancies,
Was deep versed in old romances,
And could talk whole hours upon
The Great Cham and Prester John,—
Tell the field in which the Sophi
From the Tartar won a trophy—
What he read with such delight of,
Thought he could as eas'ly write of—
But his over-young invention
Kept not pace with brave intention.
Twenty suns did rise and set,
And he could no further get ,
But unable to proceed,
Made a virtue out of need,
And, his labours wiselier deem'd of,
Did omit *what the queen dream'd of*.

A BALLAD.

NOTING THE DIFFERENCE OF RICH AND POOR, IN THE WAYS OF A RICH NOBLE'S PALACE AND A POOR WORKHOUSE.

To the tune of the "Old and Young Courtier."

In a costly palace Youth goes clad in gold ;
In a wretched workhouse Age's limbs are cold :
There they sit, the old men by a shivering fire,
Still close and closer cowering, warmth is their
    desire.

In a costly palace, when the brave gallants dine,
They have store of good venison, with old canary
    wine,
With singing and music to heighten the cheer ;
Coarse bits, with grudging, are the pauper's best
    fare.

In a costly palace Youth is still carest
By a train of attendants which laugh at my young
    Lord's jest ;
In a wretched workhouse the contrary prevails :
Does Age begin to prattle ?—no man heark'neth to
    his tales.

In a costly palace if the child with a pin
Do but chance to prick a finger, straight the doctor
    is call'd in ;
In a wretched workhouse men are left to perish
For want of proper cordials, which their old age
    might cherish.

In a costly palace Youth enjoys his lust ;
In a wretched workhouse Age, in corners thrust,
Thinks upon the former days, when he was well
    to do,
Had children to stand by him, both friends and
    kinsmen too.

In a costly palace Youth his temples hides
With a new-devised peruke'that reaches to his sides ;
In a wretched workhouse Age's crown is bare,
With a few thin locks just to fence out the cold air.

In peace, as in war, 'tis our young gallants pride,
To walk, each one 'i the streets, with a rapier by his
    side,
That none to do them injury may have pretence.
Wretched Age, in poverty, must brook offence.

HYPOCHONDRIACUS.

By myself walking
To myself talking,
When as I ruminate
On my untoward fate,
Scarcely seem I
Alone sufficiently,
Black thoughts continually
Crowding my privacy ;
They come unbidden,
Like foes at a wedding,

Thrusting their faces
In better guests' places,
Peevish and malecontent,
Clownish, impertinent,
Dashing the merriment;
So in like fashions
Dim cogitations
Follow and haunt me,
Striving to daunt me,
In my heart festering,
In my ears whispering,
" Thy friends are treacherous,
Thy foes are dangerous,
Thy dreams ominous."

Fierce Anthropophagi,
Spectra, Diaboli,
What scared St. Anthony,
Hobgoblins, Lemures,
Dreams of Antipodes,
Night-riding Incubi
Troubling the fantasy,
All dire illusions
Causing confusions;
Figments heretical,
Scruples fantastical,
Doubts diabolical,
Abaddon vexeth me,
Mahu perplexeth me,
Lucifer teareth me ——

Jesu! Maria! liberate nos ab his diris tentationibus Inimici.

A FAREWELL TO TOBACCO.

MAY the Babylonish curse
Straight confound my stammering verse,
If I can a passage see
In this word-perplexity,
Or a fit expression find,
Or a language to my mind,
(Still the phrase is wide or scant)
To take leave of thee, GREAT PLANT !
Or in any terms relate
Half my love, or half my hate:
For I hate yet love thee so,
That, whichever thing I show,
The plain truth will seem to be
A constrain'd hyperbole,
And the passion to proceed
More from a mistress than a weed.

Sooty retainer to the vine,
Bacchus' black servant, negro fine ;
Sorcerer, that mak'st us dote upon
Thy begrimed complexion,
And, for thy pernicious sake,
More and greater oaths to break
Than reclaimèd lovers take
'Gainst women : thou thy siege dost lay
Much too in the female way,
While thou suck'st the lab'ring breath
Faster than kisses or than death.

Thou in such a cloud dost bind us,
That our worst foes cannot find us,

And ill fortune, that would thwart us,
Shoots at rovers, shooting at us;
While each man, through thy height'ning steam,
Does like a smoking Etna seem,
And all about us does express
(Fancy and wit in richest dress)
A Sicilian fruitfulness.

Thou through such a mist dost show us,
That our best friends do not know us,
And, for those allowed features,
Due to reasonable creatures,
Liken'st us to fell Chimeras
Monsters that, who see us, fear us;
Worse than Cerberus or Geryon,
Or, who first loved a cloud, Ixion.

Bacchus we know, and we allow
His tipsy rites. But what art thou,
That but by reflex canst show
What his deity can do,
As the false Egyptian spell
Aped the true Hebrew miracle?
Some few vapours thou may'st raise,
The weak brain may serve to amaze,
But to the reins and nobler heart
Canst nor life nor heat impart.

Brother of Bacchus, later born,
The old world was sure forlorn
Wanting thee, that aidest more
The god's victories than before
All his panthers, and the brawls
Of his piping Bacchanals.

l   D

These, as stale, we disallow,
Or judge of *thee* meant : only thou
His true Indian conquest art ;
And, for ivy round his dart,
The reformèd god now weaves
A finer thyrsus of thy leaves.

Scent to match thy rich perfume
Chemic art did ne'er presume
Through her quaint alembic strain,
None so sov'reign to the brain.
Nature, that did in thee excel,
Framed again no second smell.
Roses, violets, but toys
For the smaller sort of boys,
Or for greener damsels meant :
Thou art the only manly scent.

Stinking'st of the stinking kind,
Filth of the mouth and fog of the mind,
Africa, that brags her foison,
Breeds no such prodigious poison,
Henbane, nightshade, both together,
Hemlock, aconite——

Nay, rather,
Plant divine, of rarest virtue ;
Blisters on the tongue would hurt you.
'Twas but in a sort I blamed thee ;
None e'er prosper'd who defamed thee ;
Irony all, and feign'd abuse,
Such as perplex'd lovers use,
At a need, when, in despair
To paint forth their fairest fair,

Or in part but to express
That exceeding comeliness
Which their fancies doth so strike,
They borrow language of dislike;
And, instead of Dearest Miss,
Jewel, Honey, Sweetheart, Bliss,
And those forms of old admiring,
Call her Cockatrice and Siren,
Basilisk, and all that's evil,
Witch, Hyena, Mermaid, Devil,
Ethiop, Wench, and Blackamoor,
Monkey, Ape, and twenty more,
Friendly Trait'ress, loving Foe,—
Not that she is truly so,
But no other way they know
A contentment to express,
Borders so upon excess,
That they do not rightly wot
Whether it be pain or not

Or, as men, constrain'd to part
With what's nearest to their heart,
While their sorrow's at the height,
Lose discrimination quite,
And their hasty wrath let fall,
To appease their frantic gall,
On the darling thing whatever
Whence they feel it death to sever,
Though it be, as they, perforce,
Guiltless of the sad divorce.

For I must (nor let it grieve thee,
Friendliest of plants, that I must) leave thee.
For thy sake, TOBACCO, I
Would do any thing but die,

And but seek to extend my days
Long enough to sing thy praise.
But, as she, who once hath been
A king's consort, is a queen
Ever after, nor will bate
Any tittle of her state,
Though a widow, or divorced,
So I, from thy converse forced,
The old name and style retain,
A right Katherine of Spain;
And a seat, too, 'mongst the joys
Of the blest Tobacco Boys;
Where, though I, by sour physician,
Am debarr'd the full fruition
Of thy favours, I may catch
Some collateral sweets, and snatch
Sidelong odours, that give life
Like glances from a neighbour's wife;
And still live in the by-places
And the suburbs of thy graces;
And in thy borders take delight,
An unconquer'd Canaanite.

T [HORNTON] L [EIGH] H [UNT].

A CHILD.

MODEL of thy parent dear,
Serious infant worth a fear
In thy unfaltering visage well
Picturing forth the son of TELL,

When on his forehead, firm and good,
Motionless mark, the apple stood,
Guileless traitor, rebel mild,
Convict unconscious, culprit child !
Gates that close with iron roar
Have been to thee thy nursery door ;
Chains that chink in cheerless cells
Have been thy rattles and thy bells ;
Walls contrived for giant sin
Have hemm'd thy faultless weakness in ;
Near thy sinless bed black Guilt
Her discordant house hath built,
And fill'd it with her monstrous brood—
Sights, by thee not understood—
Sights of fear, and of distress,
That pass a harmless infant's guess !

But the clouds, that overcast
Thy young morning, may not last ;
Soon shall arrive the rescuing hour
That yields thee up to Nature's power :
Nature, that so late doth greet thee,
Shall in o'erflowing measure meet thee.
She shall recompense with cost
For every lesson thou hast lost.
Then wandering up thy sire's loved hill,[1]
Thou shalt take thy airy fill
Of health and pastime. *Birds shall sing
For thy delight each May morning.*
Mid new-yean'd lambkins thou shalt play
Hardly less a lamb than they.

---

[1] Eldest son of Mr Leigh Hunt.

l   D

Then thy prison's lengthen'd bound
Shall be the horizon skirting round :
And while thou fillest thy lap with flowers,
To make amends for wintry hours,
The breeze, the sunshine, and the place,
Shall from thy tender brow efface
Each vestige of untimely care,
That sour restraint had graven there ;
And on thy every look impress
A more excelling childishness.

So shall be thy days beguiled,
THORNTON HUNT, my favourite child.

BALLAD.

FROM THE GERMAN.

THE clouds are blackening, the storms threatening,
   And ever the forest maketh a moan ;
Billows are breaking, the damsel's heart aching,
   Thus by herself she singeth alone,
     Weeping right plenteously.

" The world is empty, the heart is dead surely,
   In this world plainly all seemeth amiss ;
To thy breast, holy one, take now thy little one,
   I have had earnest of all earth's bliss,
     Living right lovingly."

DAVID IN THE CAVE OF ADULLAM.

DAVID and his three captains bold
Kept ambush once within a hold.
It was in Adullam's cave,
Nigh which no water they could have,
Nor spring, nor running brook was near
To quench the thirst that parch'd them there.
Then David, king of Israel,
Straight bethought him of a well,
Which stood beside the city gate,
At Bethlem; where, before his state
Of kingly dignity, he had
Oft drunk his fill, a shepherd lad;
But now his fierce Philistine foe
Encamp'd before it he does know.
Yet ne'er the less, with heat opprest,
Those three bold captains he addrest,
And wish'd that one to him would bring
Some water from his native spring.
His valiant captains instantly
To execute his will did fly.
The mighty Three the ranks broke through
Of armèd foes, and water drew
For David, their beloved king,
At his own sweet native spring.
Back through their armèd foes they haste,
With the hard-earn'd treasure graced.
But when the good king David found
What they had done, he on the ground

The water pour'd ; " Because," said he,
" That it was at the jeopardy
Of your three lives this thing ye did :
That I should drink it, God forbid !' "

SALOME.

ONCE on a charger there was laid,
And brought before a royal maid,
As price of attitude and grace,
A guiltless head, a holy face.

It was on Herod's natal day,
Who o'er Judæa's land held sway.
He married his own brother's wife,
Wicked Herodias.   She the life
Of John the Baptist long had sought,
Because he openly had taught
That she a life unlawful led,
Having her husband's brother wed.

This was he, that saintly John,
Who in the wilderness alone
Abiding, did for clothing wear
A garment made of camel's hair ;
Honey and locusts were his food,
And he was most severely good.
He preachèd penitence and tears,
And waking first the sinner's fears,
Prepared a path, made smooth a way,
For his diviner Master's day.

Herod kept in princely state
His birth-day.   On his throne he sate,
After the feast, beholding her
Who danced with grace peculiar;
Fair Salome, who did excel
All in that land for dancing well.
The feastful monarch's heart was fired,
And whatsoe'er thing she desired,
Though half his kingdom it should be,
He in his pleasure swore that he
Would give the graceful Salome.
The damsel was Herodias' daughter :
She to the queen hastes, and besought her
To teach her what great gift to name.
Instructed by Herodias, came
The damsel back : to Herod said,
" Give me John the Baptist's head ;
And in a charger let it be
Hither straightway brought to me."
Herod her suit would fain deny,
But for his oath's sake must comply.

When painters would by art express
Beauty in unloveliness,
Thee, Herodias' daughter, thee,
They fittest subject take to be.
They give thy form and features grace ;
But ever in thy beauteous face
They show a steadfast cruel gaze,
An eye unpitying ; and amaze
In all beholders deep they mark,
That thou betrayest not one spark
Of feeling for the ruthless deed,
That did thy praiseful dance succeed.

For on the head they make you look,
As if a sullen joy you took,
A cruel triumph, wicked pride,
That for your sport a saint had died.

LINES

SUGGESTED BY A PICTURE OF TWO FEMALES BY LIONARDO DA VINCI.

THE lady Blanch, regardless of all her lover's fears,
To the Urs'line convent hastens, and long the Abbess
    hears :
" O Blanch, my child, repent ye of the courtly life ye
    lead."   '
Blanch look'd on a rose-bud and little seem'd to
    heed.
She look'd on the rose-bud, she look'd round, and
    thought
On all her heart had whisper'd, and all the Nun had
    taught.
" I am worshipp'd by lovers, and brightly shines my
    fame,
" All Christendom resoundeth the noble Blanch's
    name.
" Nor shall I quickly wither like the rose-bud from
    the tree,
" My queen-like graces shining when my beauty's
    gone from me.

"But when the sculptured marble is raised o'er my
    head,
"And the matchless Blanch lies lifeless among the
    noble dead,
"This saintly lady Abbess hath made me justly fear,
"It nothing will avail me that I were worshipp'd
    here."

LINES

ON THE SAME PICTURE BEING REMOVED TO MAKE PLACE FOR A PORTRAIT OF A LADY BY TITIAN

Who art thou, fair one, who usurp'st the place
Of Blanch, the lady of the matchless grace?
Come, fair and pretty, tell to me,
Who, in thy life-time, thou might'st be.
Thou pretty art and fair,
But with the lady Blanch thou never must compare.
No need for Blanch her history to tell;
Whoever saw her face, they there did read it well.
But when I look on thee, I only know
There lived a pretty maid some hundred years ago.

LINES

ON THE CELEBRATED PICTURE BY LIONARDO DA VINCI, CALLED THE VIRGIN OF THE ROCKS.

While young John runs to greet
The greater Infant's feet.

The Mother standing by, with trembling passion
Of devout admiration,
Beholds the engaging mystic play, and pretty adora-
tion ;
Nor knows as yet the full event
Of those so low beginnings,
From whence we date our winnings,
But wonders at the intent
Of those new rites, and what that strange child
worship meant.
But at her side
An angel doth abide,
With such a perfect joy
As no dim doubts alloy,
An intuition,
A glory, an amenity,
Passing the dark condition
Of blind humanity,
As if he surely knew
All the blest wonder should ensue,
Or he had lately left the upper sphere,
And had read all the sovran schemes and divine
riddles there.

ON THE SAME.

MATERNAL lady with the virgin grace,
Heaven-born thy Jesus seemeth sure,
And thou a virgin pure.
Lady most perfect, when thy sinless face
Men look upon, they wish to be
A Catholic, Madonna fair, to worship thee.

PINDARIC ODE TO THE TREAD-MILL.

I.

INSPIRE my spirit, Spirit of De Foe,
That sang the pillory,
In loftier strains to show
A more sublime Machine
Than that, where thou wert seen,
With neck out-stretcht and shoulders ill awry,
Courting coarse plaudits from vile crowds below—
A most unseemly show !

II.

In such a place
Who could expose thy face,
Historiographer of deathless Crusoe !
That paint'st the strife
And all the naked ills of savage life,
Far above Rousseau ?
Rather myself had stood
In that ignoble wood,
Bare to the mob, on holyday or high day.
If nought else could atone
For waggish libel,
I swear on Bible,
I would have spared him for thy sake alone,
Man Friday !

III.

Our ancestors' were sour days,
Great Master of Romance !
A milder doom had fallen to thy chance
In our days :

ℓ ⟩

Thy sole assignment
Some solitary confinement,
(Not worth thy care a carrot,)
Where in world-hidden cell
Thou thy own Crusoe might have acted well,
Only without the parrot ;
By sure experience taught to know,
Whether the qualms thou mak'st him feel were truly
    such or no.

IV.

But stay ! methinks in statelier measure—
A more companionable pleasure—
I see thy steps the mighty Tread-Mill trace,
(The subject of my song,
Delay'd however long,)
And some of thine own race,
To keep thee company, thou bring'st with thee
    along.
There with thee go,
Link'd in like sentence,
With regulated pace and footing slow,
Each old acquaintance,
Rogue—harlot—thief—that live to future ages ;
Through many a labour'd tome,
Rankly embalm'd in thy too natural pages.
Faith, friend De Foe, thou art quite at home !
Not one of thy great offspring thou dost lack,
From pirate Singleton to pilfering Jack.
Here Flandrian Moll her brazen incest brags ;
Vice-stript Roxana, penitent in rags,
There points to Amy, treading equal chimes,
The faithful handmaid to her faithless crimes.

V.

Incompetent my song to raise
To its just height thy praise,
Great Mill!
Taat by thy motion proper,
(No thanks to wind, or sail, or working rill,)
Grinding that stubborn corn, the Human will,
Turn'st out men's consciences,
That were begrimed before, as clean and sweet
As flour from purest wheat,
Into thy hopper.
All reformation short of thee but nonsense is,
Or human, or divine.

VI.

Compared with thee,
What are the labours of that Jumping Sect,
Which feeble laws connive at rather than respect!
Thou dost not bump,
Or jump,
But *walk* men into virtue; betwixt crime
And slow repentance giving breathing time,
And leisure to be good;
Instructing with discretion demireps
How to direct their steps.

VII.

Thou best Philosopher made out of wood!
Not that which framed the tub,
Where sate the Cynic cub,
With nothing in his bosom sympathetic;
But from those groves derived, I deem,
Where Plato nursed his dream

l   D

Of immortality ;
Seeing that clearly
Thy system all is merely
Peripatetic.
Thou to thy pupils dost such lessons give
Of how to live
With temperance, sobriety, morality,
(A new art,)
That from thy school, by force of virtuous deeds
Each Tyro now proceeds
A " Walking Stewart !"

GOING OR GONE.

I.

FINE merry franions,
Wanton companions,
My days are ev'n banyans
    With thinking upon ye !
How Death, that last stinger,
Finis-writer, end-bringer,
Has laid his chill-finger,
    Or is laying on ye.

II.

There's rich Kitty Wheatley,
With footing it featly
That took me completely,
    She sleeps in the Kirk House ;

And poor Polly Perkin,
Whose Dad was still firking
The jolly ale firkin,
    She's gone to the Work-house ;

III.

Fine Gard'ner, Ben Carter
(In ten counties no smarter)
Has ta'en his departure
    For Proserpine's orchards :
And Lily, postilion,
With cheeks of vermilion,
Is one of a million
    That fill up the church-yards ,

IV.

And, lusty as Dido,
Fat Clemitson's widow
Flits now a small shadow
    By Stygian hid ford ;
And good Master Clapton
Has thirty years napt on,
The ground he last hapt on,
    Intomb'd by fair Widford ;

V.

And gallant Tom Dockwra,
Of Nature's finest crockery,
Now but thin air and mockery,
    Lurks by Avernus,
Whose honest grasp of hand
Still, while his life did stand,
At friend's or foe's command,
    Almost did burn us.

VI.

Roger de Coverley
Not more good man than he ,
Yet has he equally
    Push'd for Cocytus,
With drivelling Worral,
And wicked old Dorrell,
'Gainst whom I've a quarrel,
    Whose end might affright us !—

VII.

Kindly hearts have I known ;
Kindly hearts, they are flown ;
Here and there if but one
    Linger yet uneffaced,
Imbecile tottering elves,
Soon to be wreck'd on shelves,
These scarce are half themselves,
    With age and care crazed.

VIII.

But this day Fanny Hutton
Her last dress has put on ;
Her fine lessons forgotten,
    She died, as the dunce died ;
And prim Betsy Chambers,
Decay'd in her members,
No longer remembers
    Things, as she once did ;

IX.

And prudent Miss Wither
Not in jest now doth *wither*,
And soon must go—whither
    Nor I well, nor you know ;

And flaunting Miss Waller,
That soon must befall her,
Whence none can recall her,
Though proud once as Juno!

ANGEL HELP.[1]

THIS rare tablet doth include
Poverty with Sanctitude.
Past midnight this poor maid hath spun,
And yet the work is not half-done,
Which must supply from earnings scant
A feeble bed-rid parent's want.
Her sleep-charged eyes exemption ask,
And Holy hands take up the task ;
Unseen the rock and spindle ply,
And do her earthly drudgery.
Sleep, saintly poor one! sleep, sleep on ;
And, waking, find thy labours done.
Perchance she knows it by her dreams :
Her eye hath caught the golden gleams,
Angelic presence testifying,
That round her everywhere are flying :

---

[1] Suggested by a drawing in the possession of Charles Aders, Esq .
in which is represented the legend of a poor female Saint · who, having
spun past midnight, to maintain a bed-rid mother, has fallen asleep
from fatigue, and Angels are finishing her work. In another part of
the chamber an angel is tending a lily, the emblem of purity

Ostents from which she may presume,
That much of heaven is in the room.
Skirting her own bright hair they run,
And to the sunny add more sun :
Now on that aged face they fix,
Streaming from the Crucifix ;
The flesh-clogg'd spirit disabusing,
Death-disarming sleeps infusing,
Prelibations, foretastes high,
And equal thoughts to live or die.
Gardener bright from Eden's bower,
Tend with care that lily flower ,
To its leaves and root infuse
Heaven's sunshine, Heaven's dews.
'Tis a type, and 'tis a pledge,
Of a crowning privilege.
Careful as that lily flower,
This Maid must keep her precious dower ,
Live a sainted Maid, or die
Martyr to virginity.

ON AN INFANT DYING AS SOON AS BORN.

I SAW where in the shroud did lurk
A curious frame of Nature's work.
A flow'ret crushed in the bud,
A nameless piece of Babyhood,
Was in her cradle-coffin lying ;
Extinct, with scarce the sense of dying :

So soon to exchange the imprisoning womb
For darker closets of the tomb!
She did but ope an eye, and put
A clear beam forth, then straight up shut
For the long dark: ne'er more to see
Through glasses of mortality
Riddle of destiny, who can show
What thy short visit meant, or know
What thy errand here below?
Shall we say, that Nature blind
Check'd her hand, and changed her mind,
Just when she had exactly wrought
A finish'd pattern without fault?
Could she flag, or could she tire,
Or lack'd she the Promethean fire
(With her nine moons' long workings sicken'd)
That should thy little limbs have quicken'd?
Limbs so firm, they seem'd to assure
Life of health and days mature:
Woman's self in miniature!
Limbs so fair, they might supply
(Themselves now but cold imagery)
The sculptor to make Beauty by.
Or did the stern-eyed Fate descry,
That babe, or mother, one must die;
So in mercy left the stock,
And cut the branch, to save the shock
Of young years widow'd; and the pain
When Single State comes back again
To the lone man, who, 'reft of wife,
Thenceforward drags a maimed life?
The economy of Heaven is dark;
And wisest clerks have miss'd the mark,

Why Human Buds, like this, should fall,
More brief than fly ephemeral,
That has his day ; while shrivell'd crones
Stiffen with age to stocks and stones ;
And crabbed use the conscience sears
In sinners of an hundred years.
Mother's prattle, mother's kiss,
Baby fond, thou ne'er wilt miss.
Rites, which custom does impose,
Silver bells and baby clothes ;
Coral redder than those lips,
Which pale death did late eclipse ;
Music framed for infants' glee,
Whistle never tuned for thee ;
Though thou want'st not, thou shalt have them,
Loving hearts were they which gave them.
Let not one be missing ; nurse
See them laid upon the hearse
Of infant slain by doom perverse.
Why should kings and nobles have
Pictured trophies to their grave,
And we, churls, to thee deny
Thy pretty toys with thee to lie,
A more harmless vanity !

THE CHRISTENING.

ARRAY'D—a half-angelic sight—
In vests of pure Baptismal white,
The Mother to the Font doth bring
The little helpless, nameless thing,

With hushes soft and mild caressing,
At once to get—a name and blessing.
Close by the babe the Priest doth stand,
The Cleansing Water at his hand,
Which must assoil the soul within
From every stain of Adam's sin.
The Infant eyes the mystic scenes,
Nor knows what all this wonder means;
And now he smiles, as if to say
"I am a Christian made this day,"
Now frighted clings to Nurse's hold,
Shrinking from the water cold,
Whose virtues, rightly understood,
Are, as Bethesda's waters, good.
Strange' words — The World, The Flesh, The
        Devil—
Poor Babe, what can it know of Evil?
But we must silently adore
Mysterious truths, and not explore.
Enough for him, in after-times,
When he shall read these artless rhymes,
If, looking back upon this day
With quiet conscience, he can say—
"I have in part redeem'd the pledge
Of my Baptismal privilege;
And more and more will strive to flee
All which my Sponsors kind did then renounce for
        me."

THE YOUNG CATECHIST.[1]

WHILE this tawny Ethiop prayeth,
Painter, who is she that stayeth
By, with skin of whitest lustre,
Sunny locks, a shining cluster,
Saint-like seeming to direct him
To the Power that must protect him?
Is she of the Heaven-born Three,
Meek Hope, strong Faith, sweet Charity?
Or some Cherub?—

         They you mention
Far transcend my weak invention.
'Tis a simple Christian child,
Missionary young and mild,
From her stock of Scriptural knowledge,
Bible-taught without a college,
Which by reading she could gather
Teaches him to say OUR FATHER
To the common Parent, who
Colour not respects, nor hue.
White and black in Him have part,
Who looks not to the skin, but heart.

---

[1] A picture by Henry Meyer, Esq.

TO A YOUNG FRIEND,

ON HER TWENTY-FIRST BIRTHDAY.

———

CROWN me a cheerful goblet, while I pray
A blessing on thy years, young Isola;
Young, but no more a child.   How swift have flown
To me thy girlish times, a woman grown
Beneath my heedless eyes ! in vain I rack
My fancy to believe the almanack,
That speaks thee Twenty-One.   Thou shouldst have still
Remain'd a child, and at thy sovereign will
Gambol'd about our house, as in times past.
Ungrateful Emma, to grow up so fast,
Hastening to leave thy friends !—for which intent,
Fond Runagate, be this thy punishment:
After some thirty years, spent in such bliss
As this earth can afford, where still we miss
Something of joy entire, may'st thou grow old
As we whom thou hast left !   That wish was cold.
O far more aged and wrinkled, till folks say,
Looking upon thee reverend in decay,
" This Dame, for length of days, and virtues rare,
With her respected Grandsire may compare."
Grandchild of that respected Isola,
Thou shouldst have had about thee on this day
Kind looks of Parents, to congratulate
Their Pride grown up to woman's grave estate.

E 2

ι   )

But they have died, and left thee, to advance
Thy fortunes how thou may'st, and owe to chance
The friends which Nature grudged, and thou wilt
    find,
Or make such, Emma, if I am not blind
To thee and thy deservings.   That last strain
Had too much sorrow in it.   Fill again
Another cheerful goblet, while I say
"Health, and twice health, to our lost Isola!"

SHE IS GOING.

For their elder Sister's hair
Martha does a wreath prepare
Of bridal rose, ornate and gay:
To-morrow is the wedding day.
           She is going.

Mary, youngest of the three,
Laughing idler, full of glee,
Arm in arm does fondly chain her,
Thinking (poor trifler!) to detain her;
           But she's going.

Vex not, maidens, nor regret
Thus to part with Margaret.
Charms like yours can never stay
Long within doors; and one day
           You'll be going.

VII.

TRANSLATIONS.

FROM THE LATIN OF VINCENT BOURNE.

―――――

I.

THE BALLAD SINGERS.

―――――

WHERE seven fair Streets to one tall Column[1] draw,
Two Nymphs have ta'en their stand, in hats of
    straw;
Their yellower necks huge beads of amber grace,
And by their trade they're of the Sirens' race:
With cloak loose-pinn'd on each, that has been red,
But, long with dust and dirt discoloured,
Belies its hue; in mud behind, before,
From heel to middle leg becrusted o'er.
One a small infant at the breast does bear;
And one in her right hand her tuneful ware,
Which she would vend. Their station scarce is
    taken,
When youths and maids flock round. His stall for-
    saken,

―――――――――――――――――

[1] Seven Dials.

Forth comes a Son of Crispin, leathern-capt,
Prepared to buy a ballad, if one apt
To move his fancy offers.   Crispin's sons
Have, from uncounted time, with ale and buns,
Cherish'd the gift of *Song*, which sorrow quells;
And, working single in their low-rooft cells,
Oft cheat the tedium of a Winter's night
With anthems warbled in the Muses' spight.—
Who now hath caught the alarm ? the Servant Maid
Hath heard a buzz at distance, and, afraid
To miss a note, with elbows red comes out.
Leaving his forge to cool, Pyracmon stout
Thrusts in his unwash'd visage.   *He* stands by,
Who the hard trade of Porterage does ply
With stooping shoulders.   What cares he ? he sees
The assembled ring, nor heeds his tottering knees,
But pricks his ears up with the hopes of song.
So, while the Bard of Rhodope his wrong
Bewail'd to Proserpine on Thracian strings,
The tasks of Gloomy Orcus lost their stings,
And stone-vext Sysiphus forgets his load.
Hither and thither from the sevenfold road
Some cart or waggon crosses, which divides
The close-wedged audience, but as when the tides
To ploughing ships give way, the ship being past,
They re-unite, so these unite as fast.
The older Songstress hitherto hath spent
Her elocution in the argument
Of their great Song in *prose;* to wit, the woes
Which Maiden true to faithless Sailor owes—
Ah ! " *Wandering He !*"—which now in loftier *verse*
Pathetic they alternately rehearse.
All gaping wait the event.   This Critic opes
His right ear to the strain.   The other hopes

To catch it better with his left. Long trade
It were to tell, how the deluded Maid
A victim fell. And now right greedily
All hands are stretching forth the songs to buy,
That are so tragical; which She, and She,
Deals out, and *sings the while;* nor can there be
A breast so obdurate here, that will hold back
His contribution from the gentle rack
Of Music's pleasing torture. Irus' self,
The staff-propt Beggar, his thin gotten pelf
Brings out from pouch, where squalid farthings rest,
And boldly claims his ballad with the best.
An old Dame only lingers. To her purse
The penny sticks. At length, with harmless curse,
"Give me," she cries. "I'll paste it on my wall,
While the wall lasts, to show what ills befall
Fond hearts, seduced from Innocency's way;
How Maidens fall, and Mariners betray."

II.

TO DAVID COOK,

OF THE PARISH OF ST. MARGARET'S, WESTMINSTER,
WATCHMAN.

FOR much good-natured verse received from thee,
A loving verse take in return from me.
"Good morrow to my masters," is your cry,
And to our David "twice as good," say I.

l   D

Not Peter's monitor, shrill Chanticleer,
Crows the approach of dawn in notes more clear,
Or tells the hours more faithfully.   While night
Fills half the world with shadows of affright,
You with your lantern, partner of your round,
Traverse the paths of Margaret's hallow'd bound.
The tales of ghosts which old wives' ears drink up,
The drunkard reeling home from tavern cup,
Nor prowling robber, your firm soul appal :
Arm'd with thy faithful staff, thou slight'st them all.
But if the market gard'ner chance to pass,
Bringing to town his fruit, or early grass,
The gentle salesman you with candour greet,
And with reit'rated " good mornings " meet.
Announcing your approach by formal bell,
Of nightly weather you the changes tell ;
Whether the Moon shines, or her head doth steep
In rain-portending clouds.   When mortals sleep
In downy rest, you brave the snows and sleet
Of Winter ; and in alley, or in street,
Relieve your midnight progress with a verse.
What though fastidious Phœbus frown averse
On your didactic strain—indulgent Night
With caution hath seal'd up both ears of Spite,
And critics sleep while you in staves do sound
The praise of long-dead Saints, whose Days abound
In wintry months ; but Crispin chief proclaim :
Who stirs not at that Prince of Cobblers' name ?
Profuse in loyalty some couplets shine,
And wish long days to all the Brunswick line !
To youths and virgins they chaste lessons read ;
Teach wives and husbands how their lives to lead ;
Maids to be cleanly, footmen free from vice ;
How Death at last all ranks doth equalize ;

And, in conclusion, pray good years befall,
With store of wealth, your " worthy masters all."
For this and other tokens of good will,
On boxing-day may store of shillings fill
Your Christmas purse . no householder give less,
When at each door your blameless suit you press ;
And what you wish to us (it is but reason)
Receive in turn—the compliments o' th' season !

III.

ON A SEPULCHRAL STATUE OF AN INFANT SLEEPING.

BEAUTIFUL Infant, who dost keep
Thy posture here, and sleep'st a marble sleep,
May the repose unbroken be,
Which the fine Artist's hand hath lent to thee,
While thou enjoy'st along with it
That which no art, or craft, could ever hit,
Or counterfeit to mortal sense,
The heaven-infusèd sleep of Innocence !

IV.

EPITAPH ON A DOG.

POOR Irus' faithful wolf-dog here I lie,
That wont to tend my old blind master's steps.

His guide and guard , nor, while my service lasted,
Had he occasion for that staff, with which
He now goes picking out his path in fear
Over the highways and crossings, but would plant
Safe in the conduct of my friendly string,
A firm foot forward still, till he had reach'd
His poor seat on some stone, nigh where the tide
Of passers-by in thickest confluence flow'd :
To whom with loud and passionate laments
From morn to eve his dark estate he wail'd.
Nor wail'd to all in vain · some here and there,
The well-disposed and good, their pennies gave
I meantime at his feet obsequious slept ;
Not all-asleep in sleep, but heart and ear
Prick'd up at his least motion, to receive
At his kind hand my customary crumbs,
And common portion in his feast of scraps ;
Or when night warn'd us homeward, tired and
    spent
With our long day and tedious beggary.
These were my manners, this my way of life,
Till age and slow disease me overtook,
And sever'd from my sightless master's side.
But lest the grace of so good deeds should die,
Through tract of years in mute oblivion lost,
This slender tomb of turf hath Irus rear'd,
Cheap monument of no ungrudging hand,
And with short verse inscribed it, to attest,
In long and lasting union to attest,
The virtues of the Beggar and his Dog.

V.

THE RIVAL BELLS.

A Tuneful challenge rings from either side
Of Thames' fair banks. Thy twice six Bells, St.
    Bride,
Peal swift and shrill ; to which more slow reply
The deep-toned eight of Mary Overy.
Such harmony from the contention flows,
That the divided ear no preference knows ;
Betwixt them both disparting Music's State,
While one exceeds in number, one in weight,

VI.

NEWTON'S PRINCIPIA.

Great Newton's self, to whom the world's in debt,
Owed to School Mistress sage his Alphabet ;
But quickly wiser than his Teacher grown,
Discover'd properties to her unknown ;
Of A *plus* B, or *minus*, learn'd the use,
Known Quantities from unknown to educe :
And made—no doubt to that old dame's surprise—
The Christ-Cross-Row his Ladder to the skies.
Yet, whatsoe'er Geometricians say,
Her Lessons were his true Principia !

VII.

THE HOUSEKEEPER.

THE frugal snail, with fore-cast of repose,
Carries his house with him, where'er he goes;
Peeps out—and if there comes a shower of rain,
Retreats to his small domicile amain.
Touch but a tip of him, a horn—'tis well—
He curls up in his sanctuary shell.
He's his own landlord, his own tenant; stay
Long as he will, he dreads no Quarter Day.
Himself he boards and lodges; both invites,
And feasts, himself; sleeps with himself o' nights.
He spares the upholsterer trouble to procure
Chattels; himself is his own furniture,
And his sole riches.   Wheresoe'er he roam —
Knock when you will—he's sure to be at home.

VIII.

ON A DEAF AND DUMB ARTIST.[1]

AND hath thy blameless life become
A prey to the devouring tomb?
A more mute silence hast thou known,
A deafness deeper than thine own,

---

[1] Benjamin Ferrers—Died A.D. 1732.

While Time was ? and no friendly Muse,
That mark'd thy life, and knows thy dues,
Repair with quickening verse the breach,
And write thee into light and speech ?
The Power, that made the Tongue, restrain'd
Thy lips from lies, and speeches feign'd ;
Who made the Hearing, without wrong
Did rescue thine from Siren's song.
He let thee *see* the ways of men,
Which thou with pencil, not with pen,
Careful Beholder, down didst note,
And all their motley actions quote,
Thyself unstain'd the while.   From look
Or gesture reading, more than *book*,
In letter'd pride thou took'st no part,
Contented with the Silent Art,
Thyself as silent.   Might I be
As speechless, deaf, and good, as He !

IX.

THE FEMALE ORATORS.

NIGH London's famous Bridge, a Gate more famed
Stands, or once stood, from old Belinus named,
So judged Antiquity ; and therein wrongs
A name, allusive strictly to *two Tongues*.
Her School hard by the Goddess Rhetoric opes,
And *gratis* deals to Oyster-wives her Tropes.
With Nereid green, green Nereid disputes,
Replies, rejoins, confutes, and still confutes.

L

One her coarse sense by metaphors expounds,
And one in literalities abounds ;
In mood and figure these keep up the din :
Words multiply, and every word tells in.
Her hundred throats here bawling Slander strains ;
And unclothed Venus to her tongue gives reins
In terms, which Demosthenic force outgo,
And baldest jests of foul-mouth'd Cicero.
Right in the midst great Atè keeps her stand,
And from her sovereign station taints the land.
Hence Pulpits rail ; grave Senates learn to jar ;
Quacks scold ; and Billingsgate infects the Bar.

EXISTENCE, CONSIDERED IN ITSELF NO BLESSING.[1]

FROM THE LATIN OF PALINGENIUS.

The poet, after a seeming approval of suicide from a consideration of the cares and crimes of life, finally rejecting it, discusses the negative importance of existence, contemplated in itself, without reference to good or evil.

OF these sad truths consideration had,
Thou shalt not fear to quit this world so mad,
So wicked : but the tenet rather hold
Of wise Calanus and his followers old,

---

[1] From the *Athenæum*, 1832.

Who with their own wills their own freedom
    wrought,
And by self-slaughter their dismissal sought
From this dark den of crime, this horrid lair
Of men, that savager than monsters are ;
And scorning longer in this tangled mesh
Of ills, to wait on perishable flesh,
Did with their desperate hands anticipate
The too, too slow relief of lingering fate.
And if religion did not stay thine hand,
And God, and Plato's wise behests withstand,
I would in like case counsel thee to throw
This senseless burden off, of cares below.
Not wine, as wine, men choose, but as it came
From such or such a vintage : 'tis the same
With life, which simply must be understood
A blank negation, if it be not good.
But if 'tis wretched all,—as men decline
And loathe the sour lees of corrupted wine,—
'Tis so to be contemned.   Merely TO BE
Is not a boon to seek, or ill to flee ;
Seeing that every vilest little thing
Has it in common,—from a gnat's small wing,
A creeping worm, down to the moveless stone,
And crumbling bark from trees.   Unless TO BE,
And TO BE BLEST, be one, I do not see
In bare existence, *as* existence, aught
That's worthy to be loved or to be sought.

THE PARTING SPEECH OF THE CELESTIAL MESSENGER TO THE POET.

FROM THE LATIN OF PALINGENIUS, IN THE ZODIACUS VITÆ.

BUT now time warns (my mission at an end)
That to Jove's starry court I re-ascend;
From whose high battlements I take delight
To scan your earth, diminished to the sight,
Pendant and round, and, as an apple, small,
Self-propt, self-balanced, and secure from fall
By her own weight; and how with liquid robe
Blue Ocean girdles round her tiny globe,
While lesser Nereus, gliding like a snake,
Betwixt her lands his flexile course doth take,
Shrunk to a rivulet; and how the Po,
The mighty Ganges, Tanais, Ister, show
No bigger than a ditch which rains have swell'd.
Old Nilus' seven proud mouths I late beheld,
And mock'd the watery puddles.   Hosts steel-clad
Ofttimes I thence beheld; and how the sad
Peoples are punish'd by the fault of kings,
Which from the purple fiend Ambition springs.
Forgetful of mortality, they live
In hot strife for possessions fugitive,
At which the angels grieve.   Sometimes I trace
Of fountains, rivers, seas, the change of place;
By ever-shifting course, and Time's unrest,
The vale exalted, and the mount deprest

To an inglorious valley; ploughshares going
Where tall trees reared their tops, and fresh trees
　　growing
In antique postures; cities lose their site:
Old things wax new.　Oh what a rare delight
To him, who, from this vantage, can survey
At once stern Afric and soft Asia,
With Europe's cultured plains, and, in their turns.
Their scattered tribes!—those whom the hot Crab
　　burns,
The tawny Ethiops; Orient Indians;
Getulians; ever-wandering Scythians;
Swift Tartan hordes: Cilicians rapacious,
And Parthians with black-bended bow pugnacious;
Sabeans incense bring, men of Thrace;
Italian, Spaniard, Gaul; and that rough race
Of Britons, rigid as their native colds,
With all the rest the circling sun beholds.
But clouds and elemental mists deny
These visions blest to any fleshly eye.

HERCULES PACIFICATUS.

A TALE FROM SUIDAS [1]

In days of yore, ere early Greece
Had dream'd of patrols or police,
A crew of rake-hells *in terrorem*
Spread wide, and carried all before 'em,

---

[1] Contributed to the *Englishman's Magazine* for Aug 1831. It
is printed, but not very accurately, in *Eliana*.

Rifled the poultry, and the women,
And held that all things were in common ;
Till Jove's great Son the nuisance saw,
And did abate it by Club Law.
Yet not so clean he made his work,
But here and there a rogue would lurk
In caves and rocky fastnesses,
And shunn'd the strength of Hercules.

Of these, more desperate than others,
A pair of ragamuffin brothers
In secret ambuscade join'd forces,
To carry on unlawful courses.
These Robbers' names, enough to shake us,
Were, Strymon one, the other Cacus.
And, more the neighbourhood to bother,
A wicked dam they had for mother,
Who knew their craft, but not forbid it,
And whatsoe'er they nymm'd, she hid it ;
Received them with delight and wonder,
When they brought home some 'special plunder ;
Call'd them her darlings, and her white boys,
Her ducks, her dildings—all was right boys—
" Only," she said, " my lads, have care
Ye fall not into BLACK BACK's snare ;
For, if he catch, he'll maul your *corpus*,
And clapper-claw you to some purpose."
She was in truth a kind of witch,
Had grown by fortune-telling rich ;
To spells and conjurings did tackle her,
And read folks' dooms by light oracular ;
In which she saw as clear as daylight,
What mischief on her bairns would a-light ;

Therefore she had a special loathing
For all that own'd that sable clothing.

Who can 'scape fate, when we're decreed to 't ?
The graceless brethren paid small heed to 't.
A brace they were of sturdy fellows,
As we may say, that fear'd no colours,
And sneer'd with modern infidelity
At the old gipsy's fond credulity.
It proved all true tho', as she mumbled—
For on a day the varlets stumbled
On a green spot—*sit linguæ fides*—
'Tis Suidas tells it—where Alcides
Secure, as fearing no ill neighbour,
Lay fast asleep after a " Labour."
His trusty oaken plane was near—
The prowling rogues look round, and leer,
And each his wicked wits 'gan rub,
How to bear off the famous Club ;
Thinking that they, *sans* price or hire, wou'd
Carry 't strait home, and chop for fire wood.
'Twould serve their old dame half a Winter—
You stare ! but 'faith it was no splinter;
I would not for much money 'spy
Such beam in any neighbour's eye,
The villains these exploits not dull in,
Incontinently fell a pulling.
They found it heavy—no slight matter—
But tugg'd, and tugg'd, till the clatter
'Woke Hercules, who in a trice
Whipt up the knaves, and with a splice,
He kept on purpose—which before
Had served for giants many a score—

F 2

To end of Club tied each rogue's head fast,
Strapping feet too, to keep them steadfast.
And pickaback them carries townwards,
Behind his brawny back head-downwards,
(So foolish calf—for rhyme I bless X—
Comes *nolens volens* out of Essex;)
Thinking to brain them with his *dextra*,
Or string them up upon the next tree.
That Club—so equal fates condemn—
They thought to catch, has now catch'd them.

Now Hercules, we may suppose,
Was no great dandy in his clothes;
Was seldom, save on Sundays, seen
In calimanco, or nankeen;
On anniversaries would try on
A jerkin spick-span new from lion;
Went bare for the most part, to be cool,
And save the time of his Groom of the Stole;
Besides, the smoke he had been in
In Stygian gulf, had dyed his skin
To a natural sable—a right hell-fit—
That seem'd to careless eyes black velvet.

The brethren from their station scurvy,
Where they hung dangling topsy turvy,
With horror view the black costume,
And each presumes his hour is come!
Then softly to themselves 'gan mutter
The warning words their dame did utter;
Yet not so softly, but with ease
Were overheard by Hercules.
Quoth Cacus, "This is he she spoke of,
Which we so often made a joke of."

" I see," said th' other ; " thank our sin for 't,
'Tis Black Back sure enough : we're in for 't."
His godship, who, for all his brag
Of roughness, was at heart a wag,
At his new name was tickled finely,
And fell a laughing most divinely.
Quoth he, " I'll tell this jest in heaven ;
The musty rogues shall be forgiven ."
So in a twinkling did uncase them,
On mother earth once more to place them.
The varlets, glad to be unhamper'd,
Made each a leg, then fairly scamper'd.

C. L.

l   D

DRAMATIC WORKS

OF

CHARLES LAMB.

ι   )

ℓ   𝔇

JOHN WOODVIL.

A TRAGEDY.

[NEVER ACTED.[1]]

CHARACTERS.

SIR WALTER WOODVIL.	SANDFORD. *Sir Walter's old steward.*
JOHN, } *his sons.* SIMON, }	MARGARET. *Orphan Ward of Sir Walter.*
LOVEL, } *pretended friends of* GRAY, } *John.*	FOUR GENTLEMEN. *John's riotous companions.*
	SERVANTS.

SCENE—*for the most part at Sir Walter's mansion in* DEVONSHIRE; *at other times in the Forest of* SHERWOOD.

TIME—*soon after the* RESTORATION.

ACT THE FIRST.

SCENE—*A Servants' Apartment in Woodvil Hall. Servants drinking*—TIME, *the Morning.*

A Song, by DANIEL.

" When the King enjoys his own again."

Peter. A delicate song. Where didst learn it, fellow?

---

[1] Printed, and distributed among a few intimate friends, in 1800, but not published till 1801. It was originally intended to entitle it *Pride's Cure.*

Dan. Even there, where thou learnest thy oaths and thy politics—at our master's table.—Where else should a serving-man pick up his poor accomplishments ?

Mar. Well spoken, Daniel. O rare Daniel! his oaths and his politics ! excellent !

Fran. And where didst pick up thy knavery, Daniel ?

Peter. That came to him by inheritance. His family have supplied the shire of Devon, time out of mind, with good thieves and bad serving-men. All of his race have come into the world without their conscience.

Mar. Good thieves, and bad serving-men ! Better and better. I marvel what Daniel hath got to say in reply.

Dan. I marvel more when thou wilt say any thing to the purpose, thou shallow serving-man, whose swiftest conceit carries thee no higher than to apprehend with difficulty the stale jests of us thy compeers. When was't ever known to club thy own particular jest among us ?

Mar. Most unkind Daniel, to speak such biting things of me !

Fran. See—if he hath not brought tears into the poor fellow's eyes with the saltness of his rebuke !

Dan. No offence, brother Martin—I meant none. 'Tis true, Heaven gives gift, and withholds them. It has been pleased to bestow upon me a nimble invention to the manufacture of a jest ; and upon thee, Martin, an indifferent bad capacity to understand my meaning.

Mar. Is that all ? I am content. Here's my hand.

Fran. Well, I like a little innocent mirth myself, but never could endure bawdry.

Dan. *Quot homines tot sententiæ.*

Mar. And what is that!

Dan. 'Tis Greek, and argues difference of opinion.

Mar. I hope there is none between us.

Dan. Here's to thee, brother Martin. (*Drinks.*)

Mar. And to thee, Daniel. (*Drinks*)

Fran. And to thee, Peter. (*Drinks.*)

Peter. Thank you, Francis. And here's to thee. (*Drinks.*)

Mar. I shall be fuddled anon.

Dan. And drunkenness I hold to be a very despicable vice.

All. O, a shocking vice! (*They drink round.*)

Peter. In as much as it taketh away the understanding.

Dan. And makes the eyes red.

Peter. And the tongue to stammer.

Dan. And to blab out secrets.

> [*During this conversation they continue drinking.*

Peter. Some men do not know an enemy from a friend when they are drunk.

Dan. Certainly sobriety is the health of the soul.

Mar. Now I know I am going to be drunk.

Dan. How canst tell, dry-bones?

Mar. Because I begin to be melancholy. That's always a sign.

Fran. Take care of Martin, he'll topple off his seat else.   [Martin *drops asleep.*

Peter. Times are greatly altered since young master took upon himself the government of this household.

All. Greatly altered.

L   D

Fran. I think every thing be altered for the better since His Majesty's blessed restoration.

Peter. In Sir Walter's days there was no encouragement given to good house-keeping.

All. None.

Dan. For instance, no possibility of getting drunk before two in the afternoon.

Peter. Every man his allowance of ale at breakfast —his quart.

All. A quart !   (*In derision.*)

Dan. Nothing left to our own sweet discretions.

Peter. Whereby it may appear, we were treated more like beasts than what we were—discreet and reasonable serving-men.

All. Like beasts.

Mar. (*Opening his eyes*) Like beasts.

Dan. To sleep, wagtail !

Fran. I marvel all this while where the old gentleman has found means to secrete himself. It seems no man has heard of him since the day of the King's return. Can any tell why our young master, being favoured by the Court, should not have interest to procure his father's pardon ?

Dan. Marry, I think 'tis the obstinacy of the old Knight, that will not be beholden to the Court for his safety.

Mar. Now that is wilful.

Fran. But can any tell me the place of his concealment ?

Peter. That cannot I ; but I have my conjectures.

Dan. Two hundred pounds, as I hear, to the man that shall apprehend him.

Fran. Well, I have my suspicions.

Peter. And so have I.

Mar. And I can keep a secret.

Fran. (to PETER.) Warwickshire you mean ?

[*Aside.*

Peter. Perhaps not.

Fran. Nearer, perhaps ?

Peter. I say nothing.

Dan. I hope there is none in this company would be mean enough to betray him.

All. O Lord, surely not.

[*They drink to* SIR WALTER'S *safety.*

Fran. I have often wondered how our master came to be excepted by name in the late Act of Oblivion.

Dan. Shall I tell the reason ?

All. Ay, do.

Dan. 'Tis thought he is no great friend to the present happy establishment.

All. O, monstrous !

Peter. Fellow servants, a thought strikes me :— Do we, or do we not, come under the penalties of the Treason Act, by reason of our being privy to this man's concealment ?

All. Truly a sad consideration.

To them enters SANDFORD *suddenly.*

Sand. You well-fed and unprofitable grooms,
Maintain'd for state, not use ;
You lazy feasters at another's cost,
That eat like maggots into an estate,
And do as little work,
Being indeed but foul excrescences,
And no just parts in a well-order'd family :
You base and rascal imitators,
Who act up to the height your master's vices,

But cannot read his virtues in your bond :
Which of you, as I enter'd, spake of betraying?
Was it you, or you, or thin-face, was it you?

 Mar. Whom does he call thin-face?

 Sand. No prating, loon, but tell me who he
  was,
That I may brain the villain with my staff,
That seeks Sir Walter's life !
You miserable men,
With minds more slavish than your slave's estate,
Have you that noble bounty so forgot,
Which took you from the looms, and from the
  ploughs,
Which better had ye follow'd, fed ye, clothed ye,
And entertain'd ye in a worthy service,
Where your best wages was the world's repute,
That thus ye seek his life, by whom ye live.
Have you forgot too
How often in old times
Your drunken mirths have stunn'd day's sober
  ears,
Carousing full cups to Sir Walter's health ?—
Whom now ye would betray, but that he lies
Out of the reach of your poor treacheries.
This learn from me,
Our master's secret sleeps with trustier tongues
Than will unlock themselves to carls like you,
Go, get you gone, you knaves. Who stirs? this
  staff
Shall teach you better manners else.

 All. Well, we are going.

 Sand. And quickly too, ye had better, for I see
Young mistress Margaret coming this way.

       [*Exeunt all but* SANDFORD.

Enter MARGARET *as in a fright, pursued by a Gentleman, who, seeing* SANDFORD, *retires muttering a curse.*

 Sand. Good morrow to my fair mistress. 'Twas a chance
I saw you, lady, so intent was I
On chiding hence these graceless serving-men.
Who cannot break their fast at morning meals
Without debauch and mis-timed riotings.
This house hath been a scene of nothing else
But atheist riot and profane excess
Since my old master quitted all his rights here.

 Marg. Each day I endure fresh insult from the scorn
Of Woodvil's friends, the uncivil jests
And free discourses of dissolute men
That haunt this mansion, making me their mirth.

 Sand. Does my young master know of these affronts?

 Marg. I cannot tell. Perhaps he has not been told.
Perhaps he might have seen them if he would.
I have known him more quick-sighted. Let that pass.
All things seem changed, I think. I had a friend,
(I can't but weep to think him alter'd too,)
These things are best forgotten; but I knew
A man, a young man, young, and full of honour,
That would have pick'd a quarrel for a straw,
And fought it out to the extremity,
E'en with the dearest friend he had alive,
On but a bare surmise, a possibility,
That Margaret had suffer'd an affront.
Some are too tame, that were too splenetic once

 Sand. 'Twere best he should be *told* of these affronts.

Marg.   I am the daughter of his father's friend,
Sir Walter's orphan ward.
I am not his servant maid, that I should wait
The opportunity of a gracious hearing,
Inquire the times and seasons when to put
My peevish prayer up at young Woodvil's feet,
And sue to him for slow redress, who was
Himself a suitor late to Margaret.
I am somewhat proud : and Woodvil taught me
          pride.
I was his favourite once, his playfellow in infancy,
And joyful mistress of his youth.
None once so pleasant in his eyes as Margaret.
His conscience, his religion, Margaret was,
His dear heart's confessor, a heart within that heart,
And all dear things summ'd up in her alone.
As Margaret smiled or frown'd John lived or died ;
His dress, speech, gesture, studies, friendships, all
Being fashion'd to her liking.
His flatteries taught me first this self-esteem,
His flatteries and caresses, while he loved.
The world esteem'd her happy, who had won
His heart, who won all hearts ;
And ladies envied me the love of Woodvil.
    Sand.   He doth affect the courtier's life too much,
Whose art is to forget,
And that has wrought this seeming change in him,
That was by nature noble.
'Tis these court-plagues, that swarm about our house,
Have done the mischief, making his fancy giddy
With images of state, preferment, place,
Tainting his generous spirit with ambition.
    Marg.   I know not how it is ;
A cold protector is John grown to me.

The mistress and presumptive wife of Woodvil
Can never stoop so low to supplicate
A man, her equal, to redress those wrongs
Which he was bound first to prevent ;
But which his own neglect have sanctioned rather,
Both sanction'd and provok'd : a mark'd neglect,
And strangeness fastening bitter on his love,
His love, which long has been upon the wane.
For me, I am determined what to do :
To leave this house this night, and lukewarm John,
And trust for food to the earth and Providence.

 Sand. O lady, have a care
Of these indefinite and spleen-bred resolves.
You know not half the dangers that attend
Upon a life of wand'ring, which your thoughts now,
Feeling the swellings of a lofty anger,
To your abused fancy, as 'tis likely,
Portray without its terrors, painting *lies*
And representments of fallacious liberty—
You know not what it is to leave the roof that shelters
  you.

 Marg. I have thought on every possible event,
The dangers and discouragements you speak of,
Even till my woman's heart hath ceased to fear
  them,
And cowardice grows enamour'd of rare accidents ;
Nor am I so unfurnish'd, as you think,
Of practicable schemes.

 Sand. Now God forbid ; think twice of this, dear
  lady.

 Marg. I pray you spare me, Mr. Sandford.
And once for all believe, nothing can shake my purpose,

 Sand. But what course have you thought on ?

Marg. To seek Sir Walter in the forest of Sher-
     wood.
I have letters from young Simon,
Acquainting me with all the circumstances
Of their concealment, place, and manner of life,
And the merry hours they spend in the green haunts
Of Sherwood, nigh which place they have ta'en a
     house
In the town of Nottingham, and pass for foreigners,
Wearing the dress of Frenchmen.—
All which I have perused with so attent
And child-like longings, that to my doting ears
Two sounds now seem like one,
One meaning in two words, Sherwood and Liberty.
And, gentle Mr. Sandford,
'Tis you that must provide now
The means of my departure, which for safety
Must be in boy's apparel.
     Sand. Since you will have it so,
(My careful age trembles at all may happen,)
I will engage to furnish you.
I have the keys of the wardrobe, and can fit you
With garments to your size.
I know a suit
Of lively Lincoln green, that shall much grace you
In the wear, being glossy, fresh, and worn but
     seldom.
Young Stephen Woodvil wore them while he lived.
I have the keys of all this house and passages,
And ere day-break will rise and let you forth.
What things soe'er you have need of I can furnish
     you ;
And will provide a horse and trusty guide,
To bear you on your way to Nottingham.

Marg. That once this day and night were fairly
     past!
For then I'll bid this house and love farewell :
Farewell, sweet Devon ; farewell, lukewarm John ;
For with the morning's light will Margaret be gone.
Thanks, courteous Mr. Sandford.— .

                              [*Exeunt divers ways.*

ACT THE SECOND.

SCENE.—*An Apartment in Woodvil Hall*

JOHN WOODVIL—*alone.*   (*Reading parts of a letter.*)

" WHEN Love grows cold, and difference has usurped
upon old Esteem, it is no marvel if the world begin
to account *that* dependence, which hitherto has been
esteemed honourable shelter. The course I have
taken, (in leaving this house, not easily wrought
thereunto,) seemed to me best for the once-for-all
releasing of yourself (who in times past have deserved
well of me) from the now daily, and not-to-be-endured
tribute of forced love, and ill-dissembled reluctance
of affection.   ·   MARGARET."

Gone ! gone ! my girl ? so hasty, Margaret !
And never a kiss at parting ? shallow loves,
And likings of a ten days' growth, use courtesies,
And show red eyes at parting. Who bids " farewell "
In the same tone he cries " God speed you, sir ? "
Or tells of joyful victories at sea,

                              G 2

Where he hath ventures ; does not rather muffle
His organs to emit a leaden sound,
To suit the melancholy dull " farewell,"
Which they in Heaven not use ?—
So peevish, Margaret ?
But 'tis the common error of your sex
When our idolatry slackens, or grows less,
(As who of woman born can keep his faculty
Of Admiration, being a decaying faculty,
For ever strain'd to the pitch ? or can at pleasure
Make it renewable, as some appetites are,
As, namely, Hunger, Thirst !—) this being the case,
They tax us with neglect, and love grown cold,
Coin plainings of the perfidy of men,
Which into maxims pass, and apothegms
To be retail'd in ballads.—

                              I know them all.
They are jealous, when our larger hearts receive
More guests than one. (Love in a woman's heart
Being all in one.)   For me, I am sure I have room
     here
For more disturbers of my sleep than one.
Love shall have part, but love shall not have all.
Ambition, Pleasure, Vanity, all by turns,
Shall lie in my bed, and keep me fresh and waking
Yet Love not be excluded.—Foolish wench,
I could have loved her twenty years to come,
And still have kept my liking.   But since 'tis so,
Why, fare thee well, old play-fellow !   I'll try
To squeeze a tear for old acquaintance' sake.
I shall not grudge so much.——

                To him enters Lovel.

   Lovel.   Bless us, Woodvil ! what is the matter
I protest, man, I thought you had been weeping.

Wood. Nothing is the matter; only the wench has forced some water into my eyes, which will quickly disband.

Lovel. I cannot conceive you.

Wood. Margaret is flown.

Lovel. Upon what pretence?

Wood. Neglect on my part: which it seems she has had the wit to discover, maugre all my pains to conceal it.

Lovel. Then, you confess the charge?

Wood. To say the truth, my love for her has of late stopped short on this side idolatry.

Lovel. As all good Christians' should, I think.

Wood. I am sure, I could have loved her still within the limits of warrantable love.

Lovel. A kind of brotherly affection, I take it.

Wood. We should have made excellent man and wife in time.

Lovel. A good old couple, when the snows fell, to crowd about a sea-coal fire, and talk over old matters.

Wood. While each should feel, what neither cared to acknowledge, that stories oft repeated may, at last, come to lose some of their grace by the repetition.

Lovel. Which both of you may yet live long enough to discover. For, take my word for it, Margaret is a bird that will come back to you without a lure.

Wood. Never, never, Lovel. Spite of my levity, with tears I confess it, she was a lady of most confirmed honour, of an unmatchable spirit, and determinate in all virtuous resolutions; not hasty to anticipate an affront, nor slow to feel, where just provocation was given.

l

Lovel.   What made you neglect her, then ?

Wood.   Mere levity and youthfulness of blood, a malady incident to young men; physicians call it caprice.   Nothing else.   He that slighted her knew her value: and 'tis odds, but, for thy sake, Margaret, John will yet go to his grave a bachelor.

[*A noise heard, as of one drunk and singing.*

Lovel.   Here comes one, that will quickly dissipate these humours.

Enter one drunk.

Drunken Man.   Good-morrow to you, gentlemen. Mr. Lovel, I am your humble servant.   Honest Jack Woodvil, I will get drunk with you to-morrow.

Wood.   And why to-morrow, honest Mr. Freeman ?

Drunken Man.   I scent a traitor in that question : a beastly question.   Is it not his Majesty's birthday? the day of all days in the year, on which King Charles the Second was graciously pleased to be born. (*Sings.*) " Great pity 'tis such days as those should come but once a year "

Lovel.   Drunk in a morning ! foh ! how he stinks !

Drunken Man.   And why not drunk in a morning ? canst tell, bully ?

Wood.   Because, being the sweet and tender infancy of the day, methinks it should ill endure such early blightings.

Drunken Man.   I grant you, 'tis in some sort the youth and tender nonage of the day.   Youth is bashful, and I give it a cup to encourage it. (*Sings.*) " Ale that will make Grimalkin prate."—At noon I drink for thirst, at night for fellowship, but, above all, I love to usher in the bashful morning under the auspices of a freshening stoop of liquor. (*Sings.*) "Ale in a Saxon rumkin then, makes valour burgeon in tall men."—But I crave pardon. I fear I keep that gentleman from serious thoughts. There be those that wait for me in the cellar.

Wood. Who are they?

Drunken Man. Gentlemen, my good friends, Cleveland, Delaval, and Truby. I know by this time they are all clamorous for me. [*Exit singing*

Wood. This keeping of open house acquaints a man with strange companions.

Enter, at another door, Three calling for HARRY FREEMAN.

Harry Freeman, Harry Freeman!
He is not here. Let us go look for him.
Where is Freeman?
Where is Harry? [*Exeunt the Three, calling for* FREEMAN.

Wood. Did you ever see such gentry? (*laughing.*) These are they that fatten on ale and tobacco in a morning, drink burnt brandy at noon to promote digestion, and piously conclude with quart bumpers after supper, to prove their loyalty.

Lovel. Come, shall we adjourn to the Tennis Court?

Wood. No, you shall go with me into the gallery, where I will show you the *Vandyke* I have purchased: "The late King taking leave of his children."

Lovel. I will but adjust my dress, and attend you.
[*Exit* LOVEL.

John Wood. (*alone.*) Now universal England getteth drunk
For joy, that Charles, her monarch, is restored
And she, that sometime wore a saintly mask,
The stale-grown vizor from her face doth pluck,

And weareth now a suit of morris bells,
With which she jingling goes through all her towns
        and villages.
The baffled factions in their houses skulk ;
The commonwealthsman, and state machinist,
The cropt fanatic, and fifth-monarchy man,
Who heareth of these visionaries now ?
They and their dreams have ended.   Fools do sing,
Where good men yield God thanks ; but politic
        spirits,
Who live by observation, note these changes
Of the popular mind, and thereby serve their ends.
Then why not I ?   What's Charles to me, or Oliver,
But as my own advancement hangs on one of them ?
I to myself am chief.——I know,
Some shallow mouths cry out, that I am smit
With the gauds and show of state, the point of
        place,
And trick of precedence, the ducks, and nods
Which weak minds pay to rank.   'Tis not to sit
In place of worship at the royal masques,
Their pastimes, plays, and Whitehall banquetings,
For none of these,
Nor yet to be seen whispering with some great one,
Do I affect the favours of the Court.
I would be great, for greatness hath great *power*,
And that's the fruit I reach at.—
Great spirits ask great play-room.   Who could sit,
With these prophetic swellings in my breast,
That prick and goad me on, and never cease,
To the fortunes something tells me I was born to?
Who, with such monitors within to stir him,
Would sit him down, with lazy arms across,
A unit, a thing without a name in the state,

A something to be govern'd, not to govern,
A fishing, hawking, hunting, country gentleman?

[*Exit.*

SCENE.—*Sherwood Forest.*

Sir WALTER WOODVIL. SIMON WOODVIL. (*Disguised as Frenchmen.*)

Sir W. How fares my boy, Simon, my youngest
    born,
My hope, my pride, young Woodvil? speak to me;
Some grief untold weighs heavy at thy heart:
I know it by thy alter'd cheer of late.
Thinkest thy brother plays thy father false?
It is a mad and thriftless prodigal,
Grown proud upon the favours of the Court;
Court manners, and Court fashions, he affects,
And in the heat and uncheck'd blood of youth,
Harbours a company of riotous men,
All hot, and young, Court-seekers, like himself,
Most skilful to devour a patrimony;
And these have eat into my old estates,
And these have drain'd thy father's cellars dry.
But these so common faults of youth not named,
(Things which themselves outgrow, left to them-
    selves,)
I know no quality that stains his honour.
My life upon his faith and noble mind,
Son John could never play thy father false.
  Simon. I never thought but nobly of my brother,
Touching his honour and fidelity.
Still I could wish him charier of his person,
And of his time more frugal, than to spend
In riotous living, graceless society,
And mirth unpalatable, hours better employ'd

l   ꝓ

(With those persuasive graces Nature lent him)
In fervent pleadings for a father's life.

   Sir W. I would not owe my life to a jealous Court,
Whose shallow policy I know it is,
On some reluctant acts of prudent mercy,
(Not voluntary, but extorted by the times,
In the first tremblings of new-fixed power,
And recollection smarting from old wounds,)
On these to build a spurious popularity.
Unknowing what free grace or mercy mean,
They fear to punish, therefore do they pardon.
For this cause have I oft forbid my son,
By letters, overtures, open solicitings,
Or closet tamperings, by gold or fee,
To beg or bargain with the Court for my life.

   Simon. And John has ta'en you, father, at your
     word,
True to the letter of his paternal charge.

   Sir W. Well, my good cause, and my good con-
     science, boy,
Shall be for sons to me, if John prove false.
Men die but once, and the opportunity
Of a noble death is not an every-day fortune:
It is a gift which noble spirits pray for.

   Simon. I would not wrong my brother by surmise;
I know him generous, full of gentle qualities,
Incapable of base compliances,
No prodigal in his nature, but affecting
This show of bravery for ambitious ends.
He drinks, for 'tis the humour of the Court,
And drink may one day wrest the secret from him,
And pluck you from your hiding-place in the sequel.

   Sir W. Fair death shall be my doom, and foul life
     his.

Till when, we'll live as free in this green forest,
As yonder deer, who roam unfearing treason :
Who seem the aborigines of this place,
Or Sherwood theirs by tenure.

Simon. 'Tis said, that Robert Earl of Huntingdon,
Men call'd him Robin Hood, an outlaw bold,
With a merry crew of hunters here did haunt,
Not sparing the king's venison.   May one believe
The antique tale ?

Sir W.   There is much likelihood,
Such bandits did in England erst abound,
When polity was young.   I have read of the pranks
Of that mad archer, and of the tax he levied
On travellers, whatever their degree,
Baron, or knight, whoever pass'd these woods,
Layman, or priest, not sparing the bishop's mitre
For spiritual regards , nay, once, 'tis said,
He robb'd the king himself.

Simon.   A perilous man. (*smiling.*)

Sir W. How quietly we live here,
Unread in the world's business,
And take no note of all its slippery changes.
'Twere best we make a world among ourselves,
A little world,
Without the ills and falsehoods of the greater ;
We too being all the inhabitants of ours,
And kings and subjects both in one.

Simon. Only the dangerous errors, fond conceits,
Which make the business of that greater world,
Must have no place in ours .
As, namely, riches, honours, birth, place, courtesy,
Good fame and bad, rumours and popular noises,
Books, creeds, opinions, prejudices national,
Humours particular,

Soul-killing lies, and truths that work small good,
Feuds, factions, enmities, relationships,
Loves, hatreds, sympathies, antipathies,
And all the intricate stuff quarrels are made of.

MARGARET—*enters in boy's apparel.*

Sir W. What pretty boy have we here?
Marg. Bon jour, messieurs.   Ye have handsome
    English faces,
I should have ta'en thee else for other two,
I came to seek in the forest.
                      Sir W. Who are they?
Marg. A gallant brace of Frenchmen, curl'd mon-
    sieurs,
That, men say, haunt these woods, affecting privacy,
More than the manner of their countrymen.
    Simon. We have here a wonder.
The face is Margaret's face.
    Sir W. The face is Margaret's, but the dress the
    same
My Stephen sometime wore.   [*To* MARGARET.
Suppose us them; whom do men say we are?
Or know you what you seek?
    Marg. A worthy pair of exiles,
Two whom the politics of state revenge,
In final issue of long civil broils,
Have houseless driven from your native France,
To wander idle in these English woods,
    Where now ye live; most part
Thinking on home, and all the joys of France,
Where grows the purple vine.
    Sir W. These woods, young stranger,
And grassy pastures, which the slim deer loves,

Are they less beauteous than the land of France,
Where grows the purple vine?

Marg. I cannot tell.
To an indifferent eye both show alike.
'Tis not the scene,
But all familiar objects in the scene,
Which now ye miss, that constitute a difference.
Ye had a country, exiles; ye have none now;
Friends had ye, and much wealth; ye now have
    nothing;
Our manners, laws, our customs, all are foreign to
    you;
I know ye loathe them, cannot learn them readily;
And there is reason, exiles, ye should love
Our English earth less than your land of France,
Where grows the purple vine; where all delights
    grow
Old custom has made pleasant.

Sir W. You, that are read
So deeply in our story, what are you?

Marg. A bare adventurer; in brief a woman,
That put strange garments on, and came thus far
To seek an ancient friend:
And having spent her stock of idle words,
And feeling some tears coming,
Hastes now to clasp Sir Walter Woodvil's knees,
And beg a boon for Margaret,—his poor ward.

                        [*Kneeling.*

Sir W. Not at my feet, Margaret; not at my feet.
Marg. Yes, till her suit is answered.
Sir W. Name it.
Marg. A little boon, and yet so great a grace,
She fears to ask it.
Sir W. Some riddle, Margaret?

l   D

Marg.   No riddle, but a plain request.

Sir W.   Name it.

Marg.   Free liberty of Sherwood,

And leave to take her lot with you in the forest.

Sir W.   A scant petition, Margaret ; but take it,

Seal'd with an old man's tears.—

Rise, daughter of Sir Rowland.

                                   [*Addressing them both.*

                          O you most worthy,

You constant followers of a man proscribed,

Following poor misery in the throat of danger ;

Fast servitors to crazed and penniless poverty,

Serving poor poverty without hope of gain ;

Kind children of a sire unfortunate ;

Green clinging tendrils round a trunk decay'd,

Which needs must bring on you timeless decay ;

Fair living forms to a dead carcase join'd ,—

What shall I say ?

Better the dead were gather'd to the dead,

Than death and life in disproportion meet.—

Go, seek your fortunes, children.—

Simon.   Why, whither should we go ?

Sir W.   *You* to the Court, where now your brother

      John

Commits a rape on Fortune.

Simon.   Luck to John !

A light-heel'd strumpet, when the sport is done.

Sir W.   *You* to the sweet society of your equals,

Where the world's fashion smiles on youth and

      beauty.

Marg.   Where young men's flatteries cozen young

      maid's beauty.

There pride oft gets the vantage hand of duty,

There sweet humility withers.

l   *D*

Simon.   Mistress Margaret,
How fared my brother John, when you left Devon ?
Marg. John was well, sir.
Simon.   'Tis now nine months almost,
Since I saw home.   What new friends has John
    made ?
Or keeps he his first love ?—I did suspect
Some foul disloyalty.   Now do I know,
John has proved false to her, for Margaret weeps.
It is a scurvy brother.
    Sir W.   Fie upon it.
All men are false, I think.   The date of love
Is out, expired , its stories all grown stale,
O'erpast, forgotten, like an antique tale
Of Hero and Leander.
    Simon. I have known some men that are too
general-contemplative for the narrow passion.   I am
in some sort a *general* lover.
    Marg.   In the name of the boy god, who plays at
hoodman blind with the Muses, and cares not whom
he catches ; what is it *you* love ?
    Simon.   Simply, all things that live,
From the crook'd worm to man's imperial form
And God-resembling likeness ; the poor fly,
That makes short holiday in the sun-beam,
And dies by some child's hand ; the feeble bird
With little wings, yet greatly venturous
In the upper sky ; the fish in th' other element,
That knows no touch of eloquence.   What else ?
Yon tall and elegant stag,
Who paints a dancing shadow of his horns
In the water, where he drinks.
    Marg.   I myself love all these things, yet so as
with a difference :—for example, some animals better

than others, some men rather than other men ; the
nightingale before the cuckoo ; the swift and graceful
palfrey before the slow and asinine mule.   Your
humour goes to confound all qualities.   What sports
do you use in the forest ?—

 Simon.   Not many ; some few, as thus :—
To see the sun to bed, and to arise,
Like some hot amourist with glowing eyes,
Bursting the lazy bands of sleep that bound him,
With all his fires and travelling glories round him.
Sometimes the moon on soft night clouds to rest,
Like beauty nestling in a young man's breast,
And all the winking stars, her handmaids, keep
Admiring silence, while those lovers sleep.
Sometimes outstretcht, in very idleness,
Nought doing, saying little, thinking less,
To view the leaves, thin dancers upon air,
Go eddying round ; and small birds, how they fare,
When mother Autumn fills their beaks with corn,
Filch'd from the careless Amalthea's horn ;
And how the woods berries and worms provide
Without their pains, when Earth has nought beside
To answer their small wants :
To view the graceful deer come tripping by,
Then stop, and gaze, then turn, they know not why,
Like bashful younkers in society,
To mark the structure of a plant or tree,
And all fair things of Earth, how fair they be.

 Marg. (*smiling.*)   And, afterwards, them paint in
  simile.

 Sir W.   Mistress Margaret will have need of some
refreshment.   Please you, we have some poor viands
within.

 Marg.   Indeed I stand in need of them.

Sir W.   Under the shade of a thick-spreading
  tree,
Upon the grass, no better carpeting,
We'll eat our noon-tide meal; and, dinner done,
One of us shall repair to Nottingham,
To seek some safe night-lodging in the town,
Where you may sleep, while here with us you dwell
By day, in the forest, expecting better times,
And gentler habitations, noble Margaret.
  Simon   *Allons*, young Frenchman—
  Marg.   *Allons*, Sir Englishman.   The time has
  been
I've studied love-lays in the English tongue,
And been enamour'd of rare poesy
Which now I must unlearn.   Henceforth,
Sweet mother-tongue, old English speech adieu.
For Margaret has got new name and language new
                              [*Exeunt.*

ACT THE THIRD.

SCENE.—*An Apartment of State in Woodvil Hall.*
  Cavaliers drinking.

JOHN WOODVIL, LOVEL, GRAY, *and four more.*

John.   More mirth, I beseech you, gentlemen—
Mr. Gray, you are not merry —
  Gray.   More wine, say I, and mirth shall ensue in
course   What! we have not yet above three half

pints a man to answer for. Brevity is the soul of drinking, as of wit. Despatch, I say. More wine.

(*Fills.*)

1st Gent. I entreat you, let there be some order, some method, in our drinkings. I love to lose my reason with my eyes open, to commit the deed of drunkenness with forethought and deliberation. I love to feel the fumes of the liquor gathering here, like clouds.

2nd Gent. And I am for plunging into madness at once. Damn order, and method, and steps, and degrees, that he speaks of. Let confusion have her legitimate work.

Lovel. I marvel why the poets, who, of all men, methinks, should possess the hottest livers, and most empyreal fancies, should affect to see such virtues in cold water.

Gray. Virtue in cold water! ha! ha! ha!

John. Because your poet-born hath an internal wine, richer than lippara or canaries, yet uncrushed from any grapes of earth, unpressed in mortal wine-presses.

3rd Gent. What may be the name of this wine?

John. It hath as many names as qualities. It is denominated indifferently, wit, conceit, invention, inspiration, but its most royal and comprehensive name is *fancy*.

3rd Gent. And where keeps he this sovereign liquor?

John. Its cellars are in the brain, whence your true poet deriveth intoxication at will; while his animal spirits, catching a pride from the quality and neighbourhood of their noble relative, the brain, refuse to be sustained by wines and fermentations of earth.

3rd Gent. But is your poet-born always tipsy with this liquor ?

John. He hath his stoopings and reposes ; but his proper element is the sky, and in the suburbs of the empyrean.

3rd Gent. Is your wine-intellectual so exquisite ? Henceforth, I, a man of plain conceit, will, in all humility, content my mind with canaries.

4th Gent. I am for a song or a catch. When will the catches come on, the sweet wicked catches ?

John. They cannot be introduced with propriety before midnight. Every man must commit his twenty bumpers first. We are not yet well roused. Frank Lovel, the glass stands with you.

Lovel. Gentlemen, the Duke. (*Fills.*)

All. The Duke. (*They drink.*)

Gray. Can any tell, why his Grace, being a Papist—

John. Pshaw ! we will have no questions of state now. Is not this his Majesty's birthday ?

Gray. What follows ?

John. That every man should sing, and be joyful, and ask no questions.

2nd Gent. Damn politics, they spoil drinking.

3rd Gent. For certain, 'tis a blessed monarchy.

2nd Gent. The cursed fanatic days we have seen ! The times have been when swearing was out of fashion.

3rd Gent. And drinking.

1st Gent. And wenching.

Gray. The cursed yeas and forsooths, which we have heard uttered, when a man could not rap out an innocent oath, but straight the air was thought to be infected.

H 2

Lovel. 'Twas a pleasant trick of the saint, which that trim puritan *Swear-not-at-all Smooth-speech* used, when his spouse chid him with an oath for committing with his servant maid, to cause his house to be fumigated with burnt brandy, and ends of scripture, to disperse the devil's breath, as he termed it.

All. Ha! ha! ha!

Gray. But 'twas pleasanter, when the other saint *Resist-the-devil-and-he-will-flee-from-thee Pure-man* was overtaken in the act, to plead an illusio visûs, and maintain his sanctity upon a supposed power in the adversary to counterfeit the shapes of things.

All. Ha! ha! ha!

John. Another round, and then let every man devise what trick he can in his fancy for the better manifesting our loyalty this day.

Gray. Shall we hang a puritan?

John. No, that has been done already in Coleman Street.

2nd Gent. Or fire a conventicle?

John. That is stale too.

3rd Gent. Or burn the Assembly's Catechism?

4th Gent. Or drink the king's health, every man standing upon his head naked?

John (to Lovel). We have here some pleasant madness.

3rd Gent. Who shall pledge me in a pint bumper, while we drink to the king upon our knees?

Lovel. Why on our knees, Cavalier?

John (smiling). For more devotion, to be sure. *(To a servant.)* Sirrah, fetch the gilt goblets.

[*The goblets are brought. They drink the King's health, kneeling. A shout of general approbation following the first appearance of the goblets.*

l   *D*

John. We have here the unchecked virtues of the grape. How the vapours curl upwards! It were a life of gods to dwell in such an element: to see, and hear, and talk brave things. Now fie upon these casual potations!—that a man's most exalted reason should depend upon the ignoble fermenting of a fruit, which sparrows pluck at as well as we!

Gray (aside to Lovel). Observe how he is ravished!

Lovel. Vanity and gay thoughts of wine do meet in him and engender madness.

[*While the rest are engaged in a wild kind of talk,* JOHN *advances to the front of the stage, and soliloquizes*

John. My spirits turn to fire, they mount so fast.
My joys are turbulent, my hopes show like fruition.
These high and gusty relishes of life, sure,
Have no allayings of mortality in them.
I am too hot now, and o'ercapable,
For the tedious processes, and creeping wisdom,
Of human acts, and enterprises of a man.
I want some seasonings of adversity,
Some strokes of the old mortifier Calamity,
To take these swellings down, divines call vanity.

1st Gent. Mr. Woodvil, Mr. Woodvil.

2nd Gent. Where is Woodvil?

Gray. Let him alone. I have seen him in these lunes before. His abstractions must not taint the good mirth.

John (continuing to soliloquize.) O for some friend
    now,
To conceal nothing from, to have no secrets.
How fine and noble a thing is confidence,
How reasonable too, and almost godlike!
Fast cement of fast friends, band of society,

Old natural go-between in the world's business,
Where civil life and order, wanting this cement,
Would presently rush back
Into the pristine state of singularity,
And each man stand alone.

(A servant enters.)

Servant. Gentlemen, the fireworks are ready.

1st Gent. What be they?

Lovel. The work of London artists, which our host has provided in honour of this day.

2nd Gent. 'Sdeath, who would part with his wine for a rocket?

Lovel. Why truly, gentlemen, as our kind host has been at the pains to provide this spectacle, we can do no less than be present at it.   It will not take up much time.   Every man may return fresh and thirsting to his liquor.

3rd Gent. There's reason in what he says.

2nd Gent. Charge on then, bottle in hand.   There's husbandry in that.

[*They go out, singing.   Only* Lovel *remains, who observes* Woodvil.

John (still talking to himself.) This Lovel here's
    of a tough honesty,
Would put the rack to the proof.   He is not of that
    sort
Which haunt my house, snorting the liquors,
And when their wisdoms are afloat with wine,
Spend vows as fast as vapours, which go off
Even with the fumes, their fathers.   He is one,
Whose sober morning actions
Shame not his o'ernight's promises;
Talks little, flatters less, and makes no promises;

Why this is he, whom the dark-wisdom'd fate
Might trust her counsels of predestination with,
And the world be no loser.
Why should I fear this man?   [*Seeing* LOVEL.
Where is the company gone?

Lovel. To see the fireworks, where you will be
expected to follow. But I perceive you are better
engaged.

John. I have been meditating this half-hour
On all the properties of a brave friendship,
The mysteries that are in it, the noble uses,
Its limits withal, and its nice boundaries.
Exempli gratiâ, how far a man
May lawfully forswear himself for his friend;
What number of lies, some of them brave ones,
He may lawfully incur in a friend's behalf;
What oaths, blood-crimes, hereditary quarrels,
Night brawls, fierce words, and duels in the morning,
He need not stick at, to maintain his friend's honour,
     or his cause.

     Lovel. I think many men would die for their
     friends.

     John. Death! why 'tis nothing. We go to it for
     sport,
To gain a name, or purse, or please a sullen humour,
When one has worn his fortune's livery threadbare,
Or his spleen'd mistress frowns. Husbands will
     venture on it,
To cure the hot fits and cold shakings of jealousy.
A friend, sir, must do more.

     Lovel. Can he do more than die?

     John. To serve a friend this he may do. Pray
     mark me.
Having a law within (great spirits feel one)

l   )

He cannot, ought not, to be bound by any
Positive laws or ord'nances extern,
But may reject all these : by the law of friendship
He may do so much, be they, indifferently,
Penn'd statutes, or the land's unwritten usages,
As public fame, civil compliances,
Misnamed honour, trust in matter of secrets,
All vows and promises, the feeble mind's religion,
(Binding our morning knowledge to approve
What last night's ignorance spake ;)
The ties of blood withal, and prejudice of kin.
Sir, these weak terrors
Must never shake me.   I know what belongs
To a worthy friendship.   Come, you shall have my
    confidence.

 Lovel. I hope you think me worthy.

 John. You will smile to hear now—
Sir Walter never has been out of the island.

 Lovel. You amaze me.

 John. That same report of his escape to France
Was a fine tale, forged by myself—
Ha ! ha !
I knew it would stagger him.

 Lovel.   Pray, give me leave.
Where has he dwelt, how lived, how lain conceal'd ?
Sure I may ask so much.

 John. From place to place, dwelling in no place long,
My brother Simon still hath borne him company,
('Tis a brave youth, I envy him all his virtues)
Disguised in foreign garb, they pass for Frenchmen,
Two Protestant exiles from the Limousin
Newly arrived.   Their dwelling's now at Nottingham,
Where no soul knows them.

 Lovel. Can you assign any reason why a gentle-

man of Sir Walter's known prudence should expose
his person so lightly ?

John. I believe, a certain fondness,
A child-like cleaving to the land that gave him birth,
Chains him like fate.

Lovel.   I have known some exiles thus
To linger out the term of the law's indulgence,
To the hazard of being known.

John. You may suppose sometimes
They use the neighb'ring Sherwood for their sport,
Their exercise and freer recreation.—
I see you smile.   Pray now, be careful.

Lovel. I am no babbler, sir ; you need not fear me.

John. But some men have been known to talk in
   their sleep,
And tell fine tales that way.

Lovel. I have heard so much.   But, to say truth,
   I mostly sleep alone.

John. Or drink, sir ? do you never drink too
   freely ?
Some men will drink, and tell you all their secrets.

Lovel. Why do you question me, who know my
   habits ?

John. I think you are no sot,
No tavern-troubler, worshipper of the grape ;
But all men drink sometimes,
And veriest saints at festivals relax,
The marriage of a friend, or a wife's birthday.

Lovel. How much, sir, may a man with safety
   drink ?   [*Smiling.*

John. Sir, three half-pints a day is reasonable ,
I care not if you never exceed that quantity.

Lovel. I shall observe it ;
On holidays two quarts.

John. Or stay, you keep no wench ?

Lovel. Ha !

John.   No painted mistress for your private
    hours ?
You keep no whore, sir ?

Lovel.   What does he mean ?

John. Who for a close embrace, a toy of sin,
And amorous praising of your worship's breath,
In rosy junction of four melting lips,
Can kiss out secrets from you ?

Lovel. How strange this passionate behaviour
    shows in you !
Sure you think me some weak one.

John. Pray pardon me some fears.
You have now the pledge of a dear father's life.
I am a son—would fain be thought a loving one ;
You may allow me some fears : do not despise
    me,
If, in a posture foreign to my spirit,
And by our well-knit friendship I conjure you,
Touch not Sir Walter's life.   [*Kneels.*
You see these tears.   My father's an old man,
Pray let him live.

Lovel. I must be bold to tell you, these new
    freedoms
Show most unhandsome in you.

John (rising.)   Ha ! do you say so ?
Sure, you are not grown proud upon my secret !
Ah ! now I see it plain.   He would be babbling.
No doubt a garrulous and hard-faced traitor—
But I'll not give you leave.   [*Draws.*

Lovel.   What does this madman mean ?

John.   Come, sir ; here is no subterfuge :
You must kill me, or I kill you.

Lovel (drawing.) Then self-defence plead my ex-
cuse.
Have at you, sir.   [*They fight.*
John.   Stay, sir.
I hope you have made your will.
If not, 'tis no great matter.
A broken cavalier has seldom much
He can bequeathe : an old worn peruke,
A snuff-box with a picture of Prince Rupert,
A rusty sword he'll swear was used at Naseby,
Though it ne'er came within ten miles of the place ;
And, if he's very rich,
A cheap edition of the *Icon Basilike*,
Is mostly all the wealth he dies possess'd of.
You say few prayers, I fancy,—
So to it again. [*They fight again.* LOVEL *is disarmed.*
  Lovel. You had best now take my life I guess
   you mean it.
  John (musing). No :—Men will say I fear'd him
   if I kill'd him.
Live still, and be a traitor in thy wish,
But never act thy thought, being a coward.
That vengeance, which thy soul shall nightly thirst
   for,
And this disgrace I've done you cry aloud for,
Still have the will without the power to execute.
So now I leave you,
Feeling a sweet security. No doubt
My secret shall remain a virgin for you !—
       [*Goes out smiling, in scorn.*
  Lovel (rising.) For once you are mistaken in your
   man.
The deed you wot of shall forthwith be done.
A bird let loose, a secret out of hand,

l   D

Returns not back. Why, then 'tis baby policy
To menace him who hath it in his keeping.
I will go look for Gray;
Then, northward ho! such tricks as we shall play
Have not been seen, I think, in merry Sherwood,
Since the days of Robin Hood, that archer good.

ACT THE FOURTH.

SCENE.—*An Apartment in Woodvil Hall.*

JOHN WOODVIL. *(Alone.)*

A weight of wine lies heavy on my head,
The unconcocted follies of last night.
Now all those jovial fancies, and bright hopes,
Children of wine, go off like dreams.
This sick vertigo here
Preacheth of temperance, no sermon better.
These black thoughts, and dull melancholy,
That stick like burrs to the brain, will they ne'er
    leave me?
Some men are full of choler when they are drunk;
Some brawl of matter foreign to themselves;
And some, the most resolved fools of all,
Have told their dearest secrets in their cups.

SCENE —*The Forest.*

SIR WALTER. SIMON. LOVEL. GRAY.

Lovel. Sir, we are sorry we cannot return your
French salutation.

Gray. Nor otherwise consider this garb you trust to than as a poor disguise.

Lovel. Nor use much ceremony with a traitor.

Gray. Therefore, without much induction of superfluous words, I attach you, Sir Walter Woodvil, of High Treason, in the King's name.

Lovel. And of taking part in the great Rebellion against our late lawful Sovereign, Charles the First.

Simon. John has betrayed us, father

Lovel. Come, sir, you had best surrender fairly. We know you, sir.

Simon. Hang ye, villains, ye are two better known than trusted. I have seen those faces before ;—are ye not two beggarly retainers, trencher-parasites, to John ? I think ye rank above his footmen ;—a sort of bed and board worms—locusts that infest our house , a leprosy that long has hung upon its walls and princely apartments, reaching to fill all the corners of my brother's once noble heart.

Gray. We are his friends.

Simon Fie, sir, do not weep. How these rogues will triumph ! Shall I whip off their heads, father ?

　　　　　　　　　　　　　　　　　　[Draws.

Lovel. Come, sir, though this show handsome in you, being his son, yet the law must have its course.

Simon. And if I tell ye the law shall not have its course, cannot ye be content ? Courage, father; shall such things as these apprehend a man ? Which of ye will venture upon me ?—Will you, Mr. Constable self-elect ? or you, sir, with a pimple on your nose, got at Oxford by hard drinking, your only badge of loyalty ?

Gray. 'Tis a brave youth—I cannot strike at him.

Simon. Father, why do you cover your face with

your hands? Why do you fetch your breath so hard?
See, villains, his heart is burst! O villains, he
cannot speak! One of you run for some water;
quickly, ye knaves; will ye have your throats cut?

[*They both slink off.*

How is it with you, Sir Walter? Look up, sir, the
villains are gone. He hears me not, and this deep
disgrace of treachery in his son hath touched him
even to the death. O most distuned and distempered
world, where sons talk their aged fathers into their
graves! Garrulous and diseased world, and still
empty, rotten and hollow *talking* world, where good
men decay, states turn round in an endless mutability,
and still for the worse; nothing is at a stay, nothing
abides but vanity, chaotic vanity.—Brother, adieu!

There lies the parent stock which gave us life,
Which I will see consign'd with tears to earth.
Leave thou the solemn funeral rites to me,
Grief and a true remorse abide with thee.

[*Bears in the body.*

SCENE.—*Another part of the Forest.*

Marg. (*alone.*) It was an error merely, and no
    crime,
An unsuspecting openness in youth,
That from his lips the fatal secret drew,
Which should have slept like one of Nature's mys-
    teries,
Unveil'd by any man.
Well, he is dead!
And what should Margaret do in the forest?
O ill-starr'd John!
O Woodvil, man enfeoff'd to despair!
Take thy farewell of peace.

O never look again to see good days,
Or close thy lids in comfortable nights,
Or ever think a happy thought again,
If what I have heard be true —
Forsaken of the world must Woodvil live,
If he did tell these men.
No tongue must speak to him, no tongue of man
Salute him, when he wakes up in a morning;
Or bid "good night" to John. Who seeks to live
In amity with thee, must for thy sake
Abide the world's reproach. What then?
Shall Margaret join the clamours of the world
Against her friend? O undiscerning world,
That cannot from misfortune separate guilt,
No, not in thought! O never, never, John.
Prepared to share the fortunes of her friend
For better or for worse thy Margaret comes,
To pour into thy wounds a healing love,
And wake the memory of an ancient friendship.
And pardon me, thou spirit of Sir Walter,
Who, in compassion to the wretched living,
Have but few tears to waste upon the dead.

SCENE.—*Woodvil Hall.*

SANDFORD. MARGARET. *(As from a journey.)*

Sand. The violence of the sudden mischance hath
so wrought in him, who by nature is allied to nothing
less than a self-debasing humour of dejection, that
I have never seen any thing more changed and
spirit-broken. He hath, with a peremptory resolution, dismissed the partners of his riots and late
hours, denied his house and person to their most
earnest solicitings, and will be seen by none. He

keeps ever alone, and his grief (which is solitary) does not so much seem to possess and govern in him, as it is by him, with a wilfulness of most manifest affection, entertained and cherished.

Marg. How bears he up against the common rumour?

Sand. With a strange indifference, which whosoever dives not into the niceness of his sorrow might mistake for obdurate and insensate Yet are the wings of his pride for ever clipt; and yet a virtuous predominance of filial grief is so ever uppermost, that you may discover his thoughts less troubled with conjecturing what living opinions will say, and judge of his deeds, than absorbed and buried with the dead, whom his indiscretion made so.

Marg. I knew a greatness ever to be resident in him, to which the admiring eyes of men should look up even in the declining and bankrupt state of his pride. Fain would I see him, fain talk with him; but that a sense of respect, which is violated, when without deliberation we press into the society of the unhappy, checks and holds me back. How, think you, he would bear my presence?

Sand. As of an assured friend, whom in the forgetfulness of his fortunes he pass'd by. See him you must; but not to-night. The newness of the sight shall move the bitterest compunction and the truest remorse; but afterwards, trust me, dear lady, the happiest effects of a returning peace, and a gracious comfort, to him, to you, and all of us.

Marg. I think he would not deny me. He hath ere this received farewell letters from his brother, who hath taken a resolution to estrange himself, for a time, from country, friends, and kindred, and to seek occupation for his sad thoughts in travelling in foreign places, where sights remote and extern to himself may draw from him kindly and not painful ruminations.

Sand. I was present at the receipt of the letter. The contents seemed to affect him, for a moment, with a more lively passion of grief than he has at any time outwardly shown. He wept with many tears, (which I had not before noted in him,) and appeared to be touched with the sense as of some unkindness; but the cause of their sad separation and divorce quickly recurring, he presently returned to his former inwardness of suffering.

Marg. The reproach of his brother's presence at this hour would have been a weight more than could be sustained by his already oppressed and sinking spirit.—Meditating upon these intricate and wide-spread sorrows, hath brought a heaviness upon me, as of sleep. How goes the night?—

Sand. An hour past sun-set. You shall first refresh your limbs (tired with travel) with meats and some cordial wine, and then betake your no less wearied mind to repose.

Marg. A good rest to us all.

Sand. Thanks, lady.

ACT THE FIFTH.

JOHN WOODVIL (*dressing*).

John. How beautiful (*handling his mourning*)
And comely do these mourning garments show!

Sure Grief hath set his sacred impress here,
To claim the world's respect ! they note so feelingly
By outward types the serious man within.—
Alas ! what part or portion can I claim
In all the decencies of virtuous sorrow,
Which other mourners use ? as namely,
This black attire, abstraction from society,
Good thoughts, and frequent sighs, and seldom
      smiles,
A cleaving sadness native to the brow,
All sweet condolements of like-grieved friends,
(That steal away the sense of loss almost)
Men's pity, and good offices
Which enemies themselves do for us then,
Putting their hostile disposition off,
As we put off our high thoughts and proud looks.

                    [*Pauses, and observes the pictures.*
These pictures must be taken down :
The portraitures of our most ancient family
For nigh three hundred years !   How have I listen'd,
To hear Sir Walter, with an old man's pride,
Holding me in his arms, a prating boy,
And pointing to the pictures where they hung,
Repeat by course their worthy histories,
(As Hugh de Widville, Walter, first of the name,
And Anne the handsome, Stephen, and famous John
Telling me, I must be his famous John.)
But that was in old times.
Now, no more
Must I grow proud upon our house's pride.
I rather, I, by most unheard-of crimes,
Have backward tainted all their noble blood,
Rased out the memory of an ancient family,
And quite reversed the honours of our house.

Who now shall sit and tell us anecdotes?
The secret history of his own times,
And fashions of the world when he was young:
How England slept out three-and-twenty years,
While Carr and Villiers ruled the baby king .
The costly fancies of the pedant's reign,
Balls, feastings, huntings, shows in allegory,
And Beauties of the Court of James the First.

MARGARET *enters.*

John.   Comes Margaret here to witness my dis-
    grace?
O lady, I have suffer'd loss,
And diminution of my honour's brightness.
You bring some images of old times, Margaret,
That should be now forgotten.
   Marg.   Old times should never be forgotten,
    John,
I came to talk about them with my friend.
   John.   I did refuse you, Margaret, in my pride.
   Marg.   If John rejected Margaret in his pride,
(As who does not, being splenetic, refuse
Sometimes old playfellows,) the spleen being gone,
The offence no longer lives.
O Woodvil, those were happy days,
When we two first began to love,—when first,
Under pretence of visiting my father,
(Being then a stripling nigh upon my age,)
You came a wooing to his daughter, John.
Do you remember,
With what a coy reserve and seldom speech,
(Young maidens must be chary of their speech,)
I kept the honours of my maiden pride?
I was your favourite then.

John.   O Margaret, Margaret !
These your submissions to my low estate,
And cleavings to the fates of sunken Woodvil,
Write bitter things 'gainst my unworthiness.
Thou perfect pattern of thy slander'd sex,
Whom miseries of mine could never alienate,
Nor change of fortune shake ; whom injuries,
And slights (the worst of injuries) which moved
Thy nature to return scorn with like scorn,
Then when you left in virtuous pride this house,
Could not so separate, but now in this
My day of shame, when all the world forsake me,
You only visit me, love, and forgive me.
    Marg.   Dost yet remember the green arbour,
        John,
In the south gardens of my father's house,
Where we have seen the summer sun go down,
Exchanging true love's vows without restraint ?
And that old wood, you call'd your wilderness,
And vow'd in sport to build a chapel in it,
There dwell

> " Like hermit poor
>   In pensive place obscure,"

And tell your Ave Marias by the curls
(Dropping like golden beads) of Margaret's hair ;
And make confession seven times a day
Of every thought that stray'd from love and Margaret ;
And I your saint the penance should appoint—
Believe me, Sir, I will not now be laid
Aside, like an old fashion.
    John.   O lady, poor and abject are my thoughts ;
My pride is cured, my hopes are under clouds,
I have no part in any good man's love,

l   *D*

In all earth's pleasures portion have I none ;
I fade and wither in my own esteem ;
This earth holds not alive so poor a thing as I am.
I was not always thus.   [*Weeps*

   Marg.   Thou noble nature,
Which lion-like didst awe the inferior creatures,
Now trampled on by beasts of basest quality,
My dear heart's lord, life's pride, soul-honour'd
    John !
Upon her knees (regard her poor request)
Your favourite, once beloved Margaret, kneels.

   John. What would'st thou, lady, ever honour'd
    Margaret ?

   Marg. That John would think more nobly of him-
    self,
More worthily of high Heaven ;
And not for one misfortune, child of chance,
No crime, but unforeseen, and sent to punish
The less offence with image of the greater,
Thereby to work the soul's humility,
(Which end hath happily not been frustrate quite,)
O not for one offence mistrust Heaven's mercy,
Nor quit thy hope of happy days to come—
John yet has many happy days to live ;
To live and make atonement.

   John.   Excellent lady,
Whose suit hath drawn this softness from my
    eyes,
Not the world's scorn, nor falling off of friends,
Could ever do. Will you go with me, Margaret ?

   Marg. (*rising.*) Go whither, John ?

   John.   Go in with me,
And pray for the peace of our unquiet minds ?

   Marg. That I will, John.   [*Exeunt.*

L   D

SCENE —*An inner Apartment.*

JOHN *is discovered kneeling.*—MARGARET *standing over him.*

John. (*rises.*) I cannot bear
To see you waste that youth and excellent beauty,
('Tis now the golden time of the day with you,)
In tending such a broken wretch as I am.
   Marg. John will break Margaret's heart if he
     speak so.
O sir, sir, sir, you are too melancholy,
And I must call it caprice. I am somewhat bold
Perhaps in this. But you are now my patient,
(You know you gave me leave to call you so,)
And I must chide these pestilent humours from you.
   John. They are gone.—
Mark, love, how cheerfully I speak!
I can smile too, and I almost begin
To understand what kind of creature Hope is.
   Marg. Now this is better; this mirth becomes you,
     John.
   John. Yet tell me, if I over-act my mirth.
(Being but a novice, I may fall into that error.)
That were a sad indecency, you know.
   Marg. Nay, never fear.
I will be mistress of your humours,
And you shall frown or smile by the book.
And herein I shall be most peremptory,
Cry, " This shows well, but that inclines to levity;
This frown has too much of the Woodvil in it,
But that fine sunshine has redeem'd it quite."
   John. How sweetly Margaret robs me of myself!
   Marg. To give you in your stead a better self!
Such as you were, when these eyes first beheld
You mounted on your sprightly steed, White Margery,

Sir Rowland my father's gift,
And all my maidens gave my heart for lost.
I was a young thing then, being newly come
Home from my convent education, where
Seven years I had wasted in the bosom of France:
Returning home true Protestant, you call'd me
Your little heretic nun. How timid-bashful
Did John salute his love, being newly seen!
Sir Rowland term'd it a rare modesty,
And praised it in a youth.

    John. Now Margaret weeps herself.

(A noise of bells heard.)

    Marg. Hark!—the bells, John!
    John. Those are the church bells of St. Mary
      Ottery.
    Marg. I know it.
    John. St. Mary Ottery, my native village
In the sweet shire of Devon.
Those are the bells.
    Marg.   Wilt go to church, John?
    John. I have been there already.
    Marg. How canst say thou hast been there
already? The bells are only now ringing for
morning service, and hast thou been at church
already?
    John. I left my bed betimes, I could not sleep,
And when I rose, I look'd (as my custom is)
From my chamber window, where I can see the sun
      rise;
And the first object I discern'd
Was the glistering spire of St. Mary Ottery.
    Marg. Well, John.
    John. Then I remember'd 'twas the Sabbath Day.

Immediately a wish arose in my mind,
To go to church and pray with Christian people.
And then I check'd myself, and said to myself,
" Thou hast been a heathen, John, these two years
    past,
(Not having been at church in all that time,)
And is it fit, that now for the first time
Thou should'st offend the eyes of Christian people
With a murderer's presence in the house of prayer?
Thou would'st but discompose their pious thoughts,
And do thyself no good : for how could'st thou pray
With unwash'd hands, and lips unused to the
    offices ?"
And then I at my own presumption smiled ;
And then I wept that I should smile at all,
Having such cause of grief ! I wept outright ;
Tears like a river flooded all my face,
And I began to pray, and found I could pray ;
And still I yearn'd to say my prayers in the church.
" Doubtless (said I) one might find comfort in it."
So stealing down the stairs, like one that fear'd
    detection,
Or was about to act unlawful business
At that dead time of dawn,
I flew to the church, and found the doors wide open.
(Whether by negligence I knew not,
Or some peculiar grace to me vouchsafed,
For all things felt like mystery.)
   Marg. Yes.
   John. So entering in, not without fear,
I pass'd into the family pew,
And covering up my eyes for shame,
And deep perception of unworthiness,
Upon the little hassock knelt me down,

Where I so oft had kneel'd,
A docile infant by Sir Walter's side ;
And, thinking so, I wept a second flood
More poignant than the first,
But afterwards was greatly comforted.
It seem'd, the guilt of blood was passing from me
Even in the act and agony of tears,
And all my sins forgiven.

MR. H—[1]

A FARCE IN TWO ACTS.

AS IT WAS PERFORMED AT DRURY LANE THEATRE,

DECEMBER, 1806.

"Mr. H——, thou wert DAMNED. Bright shone the morning on the play-bills that announced thy appearance, and the streets were filled with the buzz of persons asking one another if they would go to see Mr. H——, and answering that they would certainly, but before night the gaiety, not of the author, but of his friends and the town, was eclipsed, for thou wert DAMNED! Hadst thou been anonymous, thou haply mightst have lived. But thou didst come to an untimely end for thy tricks, and for want of a better name to pass them off——" *Theatrical Examiner.*

CHARACTERS.

Mr. H——. . . *Mr. Elliston*	MELESINDA . . . *Miss Mellon*
BELVIL . . *Mr. Bartley.*	MAID TO MELESINDA *Mrs. Harlowe*
LANDLORD PRY . *Mr. Wewitzer.*	Gentlemen, Ladies, Waiters, Servants, &c.

Scene—BATH.

PROLOGUE, SPOKEN BY MR. ELLISTON.

IF we have sinn'd in paring down a name,
All civil, well bred authors do the same.
Survey the columns of our daily writers—
You'll find that some initials are great fighters.

---

[1] Performed at Drury Lane, December 10, 1806, for one night only. It was *damned.* See Haslitt's *Table-Talk,* ii. 159. It was understood

How fierce the shock, how fatal is the jar,
When Ensign W meets Lieutenant R.
With two stout seconds, just of their own gizzard,
Cross Captain X. and rough old General Izzard!
Letter to Letter spreads the dire alarms,
Till half the Alphabet is up in arms.
Nor with less lustre have Initials shone,
To grace the gentler annals of Crim Con
Where the dispensers of the public lash
Soft penance give; a letter and a dash—
Where Vice reduced in size shrinks to a failing,
And loses half her grossness by curtailing.
Faux pas are told in such a modest way,—
"The affair of Colonel B— with Mrs. A—"
You must forgive them—for what is there, say,
Which such a pliant Vowel must not grant
To such a very pressing Consonant?
Or who poetic justice dares dispute,
When, mildly melting at a lover's suit,
The wife's a Liquid, her good man a Mute?
Even in the homelier scenes of honest life,
The coarse-spun intercourse of man and wife,
Initials I am told have taken place
Of Deary, Spouse, and that old-fashion'd race,
And Cabbage, ask'd by brother Snip to tea,
Replies "I'll come—but it don't rest with me—
I always leaves them things to Mrs. C"
O should this mincing fashion ever spread
From names of living heroes to the dead,
How would Ambition sigh, and hang the head,
As each loved syllable should melt away—
Her Alexander turn'd into Great A—

---

that one cause of failure was a want of sufficient resolution in piling up the horrors Hogsflesh was not bad enough The name should have been something more decidedly sensational; it was drawn too mild "Mr. H" was a success in America. Mr. Daniel, in his Recollections of Lamb, says that Lamb himself joined in the hissing Horace Smith, on the first night of the performance of his comedy *First Impressions*, at Drury Lane in 1813, is said to have done the same.

A single C. her Cæsar to express—
Her Scipio shrunk into a Roman S—
And nick'd and dock'd to these new modes of speech,
Great Hannibal himself a Mr. H——.

MR. H——,

A FARCE IN TWO ACTS.

ACT I.

SCENE—*A Public Room in an Inn.   Landlord, Waiters,
Gentlemen, &c.*

Enter MR. H.

Mr. H.   Landlord, has the man brought home my
boots ?

Landlord.   Yes, Sir.

Mr. H.   You have paid him ?

Landlord.   There is the receipt, Sir, only not quite
filled up, no name, only blank—"Blank, Dr. to
Zekiel Spanish for one pair of best hessians." Now,
Sir, he wishes to know what name he shall put in,
who he shall say " Dr."

Mr. H.   Why, Mr. H. to be sure.

Landlord.   So I told him, Sir; but Zekiel has
some qualms about it. He says he thinks that Mr.
H. only would not stand good in law.

Mr. H.   Rot his impertinence ! Bid him put in
Nebuchadnezzar, and not trouble me with his
scruples.

Landlord.   I shall, Sir.   [*Exit.*

Enter a Waiter.

Waiter.   Sir, Squire Level's man is below, with a
hare and a brace of pheasants for Mr. H.

Mr. H. Give the man half-a-crown, and bid him return my best respects to his master. Presents, it seems, will find me out, with any name or no name.

Enter 2nd Waiter.

2nd Waiter. Sir, the man that makes up the Directory is at the door.

Mr. H. Give him a shilling; that is what these fellows come for.

2nd Waiter. He has sent up to know by what name your Honour will please to be inserted.

Mr. H. Zounds, fellow, I give him a shilling for leaving out my name, not for putting it in. This is one of the plaguy comforts of going anonymous,

[*Exit 2nd Waiter.*

Enter 3rd Waiter.

3rd Waiter. Two letters for Mr. H. [*Exit.*

Mr. H. From ladies (*opens them*). This from Melesinda, to remind me of the morning call I promised; the pretty creature positively languishes to be made Mrs H. I believe I must indulge her (*affectedly*). This from her cousin, to bespeak me to some party, I suppose (*opening it*).—Oh, "this evening"—"Tea and cards"—(*surveying himself with complacency*). Dear H., thou art certainly a pretty fellow. I wonder what makes thee such a favourite among the ladies · I wish it may not be owing to the concealment of thy unfortunate——pshaw !

Enter 4th Waiter.

4th Waiter. Sir, one Mr. Printagain is inquiring for you.

Ma H. Oh, I remember, the poet: he is publishing by subscription   Give him a guinea, and tell him he may put me down.

4th Waiter.   What name shall I tell him, Sir ?

Mr. H.   Zounds, he is a poet; let him fancy a name.   [*Exit 4th Waiter.*

Enter 5th Waiter

5th Waiter.   Sir, Bartlemy the lame beggar, that you sent a private donation to last Monday, has by some accident discovered his benefactor, and is at the door waiting to return thanks.

Mr. H.   Oh, poor fellow, who could put it into his head ?   Now I shall be teased by all his tribe, when once this is known.   Well, tell him I am glad I could be of any service to him, and send him away.

5th Waiter.   I would have done so, Sir; but the object of his call now, he says, is only to know who he is obliged to.

Mr. H.   Why, me.

5th Waiter.   Yes, Sir.

Mr. H.   Me, me, me : who else, to be sure ?

5th Waiter.   Yes, Sir; but he is anxious to know the name of his benefactor.

Mr. H.   Here is a pampered rogue of a beggar, that cannot be obliged to a gentleman in the way of his profession, but he must know the name, birth, parentage, and education of his benefactor !   I warrant you, next he will require a certificate of one's good behaviour, and a magistrate's licence in one's pocket, lawfully empowering so and so to—give an alms.   Any thing more ?

5th Waiter.   Yes, Sir; here has been Mr. Patriot, with the county petition to sign; and Mr. Failtime, that owes so much money, has sent to remind you of your promise to bail him.

l   )

Mr. H. Neither of which I can do, while I have no name. Here is more of the plaguy comforts of going anonymous, that one can neither serve one's friend nor one's country. Damn it, a man had better be without a nose than without a name. I will not live long in this mutilated, dismembered state ; I will to Melesinda this instant, and try to forget these vexations. Melesinda ! there is music in the name ; but then (hang it !) there is none in mine to answer to it. [*Exit.*

(*While* MR. H *has been speaking, two Gentlemen have been observing him curiously*)

1st Gent. Who the devil is this extraordinary personage ?

2nd Gent. Who ? Why 'tis Mr. H.

1st Gent. Has he no more name ?

2nd Gent. None that has yet transpired. No more ! why that single letter has been enough to inflame the imaginations of all the ladies in Bath. He has been here but a fortnight, and is already received into all the first families.

1st Gent. Wonderful ! yet nobody know who he is, or where he comes from !

2nd Gent. He is vastly rich, gives away money as if he had infinity ; dresses well, as you see , and for address, the mothers are all dying for fear the daughters should get him ; and for the daughters, he may command them as absolutely as——. Melesinda the rich heiress, 'tis thought, will carry him.

1st Gent. And is it possible that a mere anonymous——

2nd Gent. Poh ! that is the charm.—Who is he ? and what is he ? and what is his name ?——The man with the great nose on his face never excited more of the gaping passion of wonderment in the dames of Strasburg than this new-comer, with the single letter to his name, has lighted up among the wives and maids of Bath · his simply having lodgings here, draws more visitors to the house than an election. Come with me to the Parade, and I will show you more of him.

SCENE *in the Street.* MR. H. *walking,* BELVIL *meeting him.*

Belvil. My old Jamaica schoolfellow, that I have not seen for so many years? it must—it can be no other than Jack (*going up to him*). My dear Ho——

Mr. H. (*Stopping his mouth*). Ho——! the devil, hush.

Belvil. Why sure it is—

Mr. H. It is, it is your old friend Jack, that shall be nameless.

Belvil. My dear Ho——

Mr. H. (*Stopping him*). Don't name it.

Belvil. Name what?

Mr. H. My curst unfortunate name. I have reasons to conceal it for a time.

Belvil. I understand you—Creditors, Jack?

Mr. H. No, I assure you.

Belvil. Snapp'd up a ward, peradventure, and the whole Chancery at your heels?

Mr. H. I don't use to travel with such cumbersome luggage.

Belvil. You ha'n't taken a purse?

Mr. H. To relieve you at once from all disgraceful conjecture, you must know, 'tis nothing but the sound of my name.

Belvil. Ridiculous! 'tis true yours is none of the

most romantic; but what can that signify in a man?

Mr. H. You must understand that I am in some credit with the ladies.

Belvil. With the ladies !

Mr. H And truly I think not without some pretensions. My fortune—

Belvil. Sufficiently splendid, if I may judge from your appearance.

Mr. H. My figure—

Belvil Airy, gay, and imposing.

Mr. H. My parts—

Belvil. Bright.

Mr. H. My conversation—

Belvil. Equally remote from flippancy and taciturnity.

Mr. H. But then my name—damn my name !

Belvil. Childish !

Mr. H. Not so. Oh Belvil, you are blest with one which sighing virgins may repeat without a blush, and for it change the paternal. But what virgin of any delicacy (and I require some in a wife) would endure to be called Mrs.——— ?

Belvil. Ha, ha, ha ! most absurd. Did not Clementina Falconbridge, the romantic Clementina Falconbridge, fancy Tommy Potts ? and Rosabella Sweetlips sacrifice her mellifluous appellative to Jack Deady ? Matilda her cousin married a Gubbins, and her sister Amelia a Clutterbuck

Mr. H. Potts is tolerable, Deady is sufferable, Gubbins is bearable, and Clutterbuck is endurable, but Ho——

Belvil. Hush, Jack, don't betray yourself. But you are really ashamed of the family name ?

Mr. H. Ay, and of my father that begot me, and my father's father, and all their forefathers that have borne it since the Conquest.

Belvil But how do you know the women are so squeamish ?

Mr. H. I have tried them. I tell you there is neither maiden of sixteen nor widow of sixty but would turn up their noses at it. I have been refused by nineteen virgins, twenty-nine relicts, and two old maids.

Belvil. That was hard indeed, Jack.

Mr. H. Parsons have stuck at publishing the bans, because they averred it was a heathenish name ; parents have lingered their consent, because they suspected it was a fictitious name, and rivals have declined my challenges, because they pretended it was an ungentlemanly name.

Belvil. Ha, ha, ha ! but what course do you mean to pursue ?

Mr. H. To engage the affections of some generous girl, who will be content to take me as Mr. H.

Belvil. Mr. H ?

Mr. H. Yes, that is the name I go by here ; you know one likes to be as near the truth as possible.

Belvil. Certainly. But what then ? to get her to consent—

Mr. H. To accompany me to the altar without a name—in short, to suspend her curiosity (that is all) till the moment the priest shall pronounce the irrevocable charm, which makes two names one.

Belvil. And that name——and then she must be pleased, ha, Jack ?

Mr. H. Exactly such a girl it has been my fortune

to meet with ; hark'e (*whispers*)——(*musing*). Yet, hang it ! 'tis cruel to betray her confidence.

Belvil. But the family name, Jack ?

Mr. H. As you say, the family name must be perpetuated.

Belvil. Though it be but a homely one.

Mr. H. True ; but come, I will show you the house where dwells this credulous melting fair.

Belvil Ha, ha ! my old friend dwindled down to one letter. [*Exeunt.*

SCENE.—*An Apartment in* MELESINDA'S *House.* MELESINDA *sola, as if musing.*

Melesinda. H, H, H. Sure it must be something precious by its being concealed. It can't be Homer, that is a Heathen's name , nor Horatio, that is no surname ; what if it be Hamlet ? the Lord Hamlet— pretty, and I his poor distracted Ophelia ! No, 'tis none of these : 'tis Harcourt or Hargrave, or some such sounding name, or Howard, high-born Howard. that would do ; may be it is Harley, methinks my H. resembles Harley, the feeling Harley. But I hear him ! and from his own lips I will once for ever be resolved.

Enter MR H

Mr. H. My dear Melesinda.

Melesinda. My dear H. that is all you give me power to swear allegiance to,—to be enamoured of inarticulate sounds, and call with sighs upon an empty letter. But I will know

Mr. H. My dear Melesinda, press me no more for the disclosure of that, which in the face of day so soon must be revealed. Call it whim, humour, caprice, in me. Suppose I have sworn an oath, never, till the ceremony of our marriage is over, to disclose my true name.

l *D*

Melesinda. Oh H, H, H ! I cherish here a fire of restless curiosity which consumes me. 'Tis appetite, passion, call it whim, caprice, in me. Suppose I have sworn, I must and will know it this very night.

Mr. H. Ungenerous Melesinda ! I implore you to give me this one proof of your confidence. The holy vow once past, your H. shall not have a secret to withhold.

Melesinda. My H. has overcome : his Melesinda shall pine away and die before she dare express a saucy inclination ; but what shall I call you till we are married ?

Mr. H. Call me ? call me any thing, call me Love, Love ! ay Love : Love will do very well.

Melesinda. How many syllables is it, Love ?

Mr. H. How many ? ud, that is coming to the question with a vengeance ! One, two, three, four,—what does it signify how many syllables ?

Melesinda. How many syllables, Love ?

Mr. H. My Melesinda's mind, I had hoped, was superior to this childish curiosity.

Melesinda. How many letters are there in it ?

[*Exit* MR. H. *followed by* MELESINDA, *repeating the question.*

SCENE.—*A Room in the Inn. Two Waiters disputing.*

1st Waiter. Sir Harbottle Hammond, you may depend upon it.

2nd Waiter. Sir Harry Hardcastle, I tell you.

1st Waiter. The Hammonds, of Huntingdonshire.

2nd Waiter. The Hardcastles, of Hertfordshire.

1st Waiter. The Hammonds.

2nd Waiter. Don't tell me : does not Hardcastle begin with an H ?

1st Waiter.   So does Hammond for that matter.

2nd Waiter.   Faith, so it does if you go to spell it. I did not think of that.   I begin to be of your opinion; he is certainly a Hammond.

1st Waiter.   Here comes Susan Chambermaid: may be she can tell.

Enter Susan.

Both.   Well, Susan, have you heard any thing who the strange gentleman is ?

Susan.   Haven't you heard ?   'tis all come out ! Mrs. Guesswell, the parson's widow, has been here about it.   I overheard her talking in confidence to Mrs. Setter and Mrs. Pointer, and she says they were holding a sort of a *cummitty* about it.

Both.   What ?   What ?

Susan.   There can't be a doubt of it, she says, what from his *figger* and the appearance he cuts, and his *sumpshous* way of living; and, above all, from the remarkable circumstance that his surname should begin with an H, that he must be—

Both.   Well, well—

Susan.   Neither more nor less than the Prince.

Both.   Prince !

Susan.   The Prince of Hessey-Cassel in disguise.

Both.   Very likely, very likely.

Susan.   Oh, there can't be a doubt on it.   Mrs. Guesswell says she knows it.

1st Waiter.   Now if we could be sure that the Prince of Hessey what-do-you-call-him was in England on his travels.

2nd Waiter.   Get a newspaper.   Look in the newspapers.

Susan. Fiddle of the newspapers! who else can it be?

Both. That is very true (*gravely*).

Enter LANDLORD.

Landlord. Here, Susan, James, Philip, where are you all? The London coach is come in, and there is Mr. Fillaside, the fat passenger, has been bawling for somebody to help him off with his boots.

[*The Chambermaid and Waiters slip out.*

(*Solus.*) The house is turned upside down since the strange gentleman came into it. Nothing but guessing and speculating, and speculating and guessing; waiters and chambermaids getting into corners and speculating; ostlers and stable-boys speculating in the yard; I believe the very horses in the stable are speculating too, for there they stand in a musing posture, nothing for them to eat, and not seeming to care whether they have any thing or no; and, after all, what does it signify? I hate such curious——odso, I must take this box up into his bed-room—he charged me to see to it myself;—I hate such inquisitive——I wonder what is in it—it feels heavy; (*reads*) " Leases, title-deeds, wills." Here now a man might satisfy his curiosity at once. Deeds must have names to them, so must leases and wills. But I wouldn't—no I wouldn't——it is a pretty box too—prettily dovetailed—I admire the fashion of it much. But I'd cut my fingers off before I'd do such a dirty—what have I to do—curse the keys, how they rattle !—rattle in one's pockets—the keys and the halfpence! (*Takes out a bunch and plays with them.*) I wonder if any of these would fit; one might just try them, but I wouldn't lift up the lid if

l   *Ɽ* they did. Oh no, what should I be the richer for knowing ? *(All this time he tries the keys one by one).* What's his name to me ? a thousand names begin with an H.   I hate people that are alway prying, poking and prying into things,—thrusting their finger into one place, (a mighty little hole this,) and their keys into another.   Oh Lord ! little rusty fits it ! but what is that to me ?   I wouldn't go to—no, no—but it is odd little rusty should just happen— *(While he is turning up the lid of the box* MR. H. *enters behind him, unperceived.)*

Mr. H.   What are you about, you dog ?

Landlord.   Oh Lord, Sir ! pardon ; no thief, as I hope to be saved.   Little Pry was always honest.

Mr. H.   What else could move you to open that box ?

Landlord.   Sir, don't kill me, and I will confess the whole truth.   This box happened to be lying—that is, I happened to be carrying this box, and I happened to have my keys out, and so—little rusty happened to fit——

Mr. H.   So little rusty happened to fit !—and would not a rope fit that rogue's neck ?   I see the papers have not been moved : all is safe, but it was as well to frighten him a little *(aside).*   Come, Land-lord, as I think you honest, and suspect you only intended to gratify a little foolish curiosity——

Landlord.   That was all, Sir, upon my veracity.

Mr. H.   For this time I will pass it over.   Your name is Pry, I think ?

Landlord.   Yes, Sir, Jeremiah Pry, at your service.

Mr. H.   An apt name : you have a prying temper— I mean, some little curiosity—a sort of inquisitive-ness about you.

Landlord. A natural thirst after knowledge you may call it, Sir. When a boy, I was never easy but when I was thrusting up the lids of some of my school-fellows' boxes,—not to steal any thing, upon my honour, Sir,—only to see what was in them; have had pens stuck in my eyes for peeping through key-holes after knowledge; could never see a cold pie with the legs dangling out at top, but my fingers were for lifting up the crust,—just to try if it were pigeon or partridge,—for no other reason in the world. Surely I think my passion for nuts was owing to the pleasure of cracking the shell to get at something concealed, more than to any delight I took in eating the kernel. In short, Sir, this appetite has grown with my growth.

Mr. H. You will certainly be hanged some day for peeping into some bureau or other, just to see what is in it.

Landlord. That is my fear, Sir. The thumps and kicks I have had for peering into parcels, and turning of letters inside out,—just for curiosity! The blankets I have been made to dance in for searching parish registers for old ladies' ages,—just for curiosity! Once I was dragged through a horse-pond, only for peeping into a closet that had glass doors to it, while my Lady Bluegarters was undressing,—just for curiosity!

Mr. H. A very harmless piece of curiosity, truly; and now, Mr. Pry, first have the goodness to leave that box with me, and then do me the favour to carry your curiosity so far as to inquire if my servants are within.

Landlord. I shall, Sir. Here, David, Jonathan,— I think I hear them coming,—shall make bold to leave you, Sir.   [*Exit.*

Mr. H. Another tolerable specimen of the comforts of going anonymous !

Enter Two Footmen.

1st Footman. You speak first.

2nd Footman. No, you had better speak.

1st Footman. You promised to begin.

Mr. H. They have something to say to me. The rascals want their wages raised, I suppose ; there is always a favour to be asked when they come smiling. Well, poor rogues, service is but a hard bargain at the best. I think I must not be close with them. Well, David—well, Jonathan.

1st Footman. We have served your honour faithfully——

2nd Footman. Hope your honour won't take offence——

Mr. H. The old story, I suppose—wages ?

1st Footman. That's not it, your honour.

2nd Footman. You speak.

1st Footman. But if your honour would just be pleased to——

2nd Footman. Only be pleased to——

Mr. H. Be quick with what you have to say, for I am in haste.

1st Footman. Just to——

2nd Footman. Let us know who it is——

1st Footman. Who it is we have the honour to serve.

Mr. H. Why me, me, me ; you serve me.

2nd Footman. Yes, Sir ; but we do not know who you are.

Mr. H. Childish curiosity ! do not you serve a rich master, a gay master, an indulgent master ?

1st Footman. Ah, Sir! the figure you make is to us, your poor servants, the principal mortification.

2nd Footman. When we get over a pot at the public-house, or in a gentleman's kitchen, or elsewhere, (as poor servants must have their pleasures,) when the question goes round, who is your master? and who do you serve? and one says, I serve Lord So-and-so, and another, I am Squire Such-a-one's footman——

1st Footman. We have nothing to say for it, but that we serve Mr. H.

2nd Footman. Or Squire H.

Mr. H. Really you are a couple of pretty modest, reasonable personages! but I hope you will take it as no offence, gentlemen, if, upon a dispassionate review of all that you have said, I think fit not to tell you any more of my name than I have chosen, for especial purposes, to communicate to the rest of the world.

1st Footman. Why, then, Sir, you may suit your-self.

2nd Footman. We tell you plainly, we cannot stay.

1st Footman. We don't choose to serve Mr. H.

2nd Footman. Nor any Mr. or Squire in the alphabet——

1st. Footman. That lives in Chris-cross Row.

Mr. H. Go, for a couple of ungrateful, inquisitive, senseless rascals! Go hang, starve, or drown!— Rogues, to speak thus irreverently of the alphabet—I shall live to see you glad to serve old Q—to curl the wig of great S—adjust the dot of little i—stand behind the chair of X, Y, Z—wear the livery of Etcætera—and ride behind the sulky of And-by-itself-and!   [*Exit in a rage.*

ACT II.

Scene.—*A handsome Apartment well lighted, Tea, Cards, &c.— A large party of Ladies and Gentlemen; among them* Melesinda.

1st Lady. I wonder when the charming man will be here.

2nd Lady. He is a delightful creature! Such a polish———

3rd Lady. Such an air in all that he does or says———

4th Lady. Yet gifted with a strong understanding———

5th Lady. But has your ladyship the remotest idea of what his true name is?

1st Lady. They say his very servants do not know it. His French valet, that has lived with him these two years———

2nd Lady. There, Madam, I must beg leave to set you right . my coachman———

1st Lady. I have it from the very best authority: my footman———

2nd Lady. Then, Madam, you have set your servants on———

1st Lady. No, Madam, I would scorn any such little mean ways of coming at a secret. For my part, I don't think any secret of that consequence.

2nd Lady. That's just like me , I make a rule of troubling my head with nobody's business but my own.

Melesinda. But then, she takes care to make every body's business her own, and so to justify herself that way——— (*Aside.*)

l   D

1st Lady.   My dear Melesinda, you look thoughtful.

Melesinda.   Nothing.

2nd Lady.   Give it a name.

Melesinda.   Perhaps it is nameless.

1st Lady.   As the object——Come, never blush, nor deny it, child.   Bless me, what great ugly thing is that, that dangles at your bosom ?

Melesinda.   This ?   it is a cross :   how do you like it ?   ˙

2nd Lady.   A cross !   Well, to me it looks for all the world like a great staring H.

(Here a general laugh.

Melesinda.   Malicious creatures !   Believe me it is a cross, and nothing but a cross.

1st Lady.   A cross, I believe, you would willingly hang at.

Melesinda.   Intolerable spite !

[Mr. H. is announced.

Enter Mr. H.

1st Lady.   O, Mr. H., we are so glad—

2d Lady.   We have been so dull——

3d Lady.   So perfectly lifeless——You owe it to us, to be more than commonly entertaining.

Mr. H.   Ladies, this is so obliging——

4th Lady.   O, Mr. H., those ranunculas you said were dying, pretty things, they have got up——

5th Lady   I have worked that sprig you commended—I want you to come——

Mr. H.   Ladies——

6th Lady.   I have sent for that piece of music from London.

Mr. H.   The   Mozart — (*seeing* Melesinda) — Melesinda !

Several Ladies at once. Nay, positively, Melesinda, you shan't engross him all to yourself.

[*While the Ladies are pressing about* MR. H., *the gentlemen show signs of displeasure.*

1st Gent. We shan't be able to edge in a word, now this coxcomb is come.

2d Gent. Damn him, I will affront him.

1st Gent. Sir, with your leave, I have a word to say to one of these ladies.

2d Gent. If we could be heard——

　　　　[*The ladies pay no attention but to* MR. H.

Mr. H. You see, gentlemen, how the matter stands. (*Hums an air.*) I am not my own master: positively I exist and breathe but to be agreeable to these—Did you speak?

1st Gent. And affects absence of mind—Puppy!

Mr. H. Who spoke of absence of mind ?—did you, Madam ? How do you do, Lady Wearwell—how do ? I did not see your ladyship before—what was I about to say ?—O—absence of mind. I am the most unhappy dog in that way, sometimes spurt out the strangest things—the most mal-a-propos—without meaning to give the least offence, upon my honour—sheer absence of mind—things I would have given the world not to have said.

1st Gent. Do you hear the coxcomb?

1st Lady. Great wits, they say——

2d Lady. Your fine geniuses are most given——

3d Lady. Men of bright parts are commonly too vivacious——

Mr. H. But you shall hear. I was to dine the other day at a great Nabob's that must be nameless, who, between ourselves, is strongly suspected of—being very rich, that's all. John, my valet, who

knows my foible, cautioned me, while he was dressing
me, as he usually does where he thinks there's a
danger of my committing a *lapsus*, to take care in
my conversation how I made any allusion direct or
indirect to presents—you understand me? I set out
double charged with my fellow's consideration and
my own; and, to do myself justice, behaved with
tolerable circumspection for the first half-hour or so
—till at last a gentleman in company, who was indulging a free vein of raillery at the expense of the
ladies, stumbled upon that expression of the poet,
which calls them " fair defects."

1st Lady. It is Pope, I believe, who says it.

Mr. H. No, Madam; Milton. Where was I?
Oh, " fair defects." This gave occasion to a critic in
company to deliver his opinion on the phrase—that
led to an enumeration of all the various words which
might have been used instead of " defect," as want,
absence, poverty, deficiency, lack. This moment I,
who had not been attending to the progress of the
argument, (as the denouement will show,) starting
suddenly up out of one of my reveries, by some unfortunate connection of ideas, which the last fatal
word had excited, the Devil put it into my head to
turn round to the Nabob, who was sitting next me,
and in a very marked manner (as it seemed to the
company) to put the question to him, Pray, Sir, what
may be the exact value of a lack of rupees? You
may guess the confusion which followed.

1st Lady. What a distressing circumstance!

2d Lady. To a delicate mind——

3d Lady. How embarrassing——

4th Lady. I declare, I quite pity you.

1st Gent. Puppy!

Mr. H. A Baronet at the table, seeing my dilemma, jogged my elbow, and a good-natured Duchess, who does every thing with a grace peculiar to herself, trod on my toes at that instant : this brought me to my-self, and—covered with blushes, and pitied by all the ladies—I withdrew.

1st Lady. How charmingly he tells a story !

2d Lady. But how distressing !

Mr. H. Lord Squandercounsel, who is my particular friend, was pleased to rally me in his inimitable way upon it next day. I shall never forget a sensible thing he said on the occasion—speaking of absence of mind, my foible—says he, my dear Hogs——

Several Ladies. Hogs——what—ha—

Mr. H. My dear Hogsflesh—my name—(*here a universal scream*)—O my cursed unfortunate tongue ! —H. I mean—where was I ?

1st Lady. Filthy—abominable !

2d Lady. Unutterable !

3d Lady. Hogs——foh !

4th Lady. Disgusting !

5th Lady. Vile !

6th Lady. Shocking !

1st Lady. Odious !

2d Lady. Hogs——pah !

3d Lady. A smelling bottle—look to Miss Mele-sinda. Poor thing ! it is no wonder. You had better keep off from her, Mr. Hogsflesh, and not be pressing about her in her circumstances.

1st Gent. Good time of day to you, Mr. Hogsflesh.

2d Gent The compliments of the season to you, Mr. Hogsflesh.

Mr. H. This is too much—flesh and blood cannot endure it.

l   *D*

1st Gent.   What flesh ?—hog's-flesh ?

2d Gent.   How he sets up his bristles !

Mr. H.   Bristles !

1st Gent.   He looks as fierce as a hog in armour.

Mr. H.   A hog !——Madam !——(*here he severally accosts the Ladies, who by turns repel him.*)

1st Lady.   Extremely obliged to you for your attentions ; but don't want a partner.

2d Lady.   Greatly flattered by your preference ; but believe I shall remain single.

3d Lady.   Shall always acknowledge your politeness ; but have no thoughts of altering my condition.

4th Lady.   Always be happy to respect you as a friend ; but you must not look for any thing further.

5th Lady.   No doubt of your ability to make any woman happy ; but have no thoughts of changing my name.

6th Lady.   Must tell you, Sir, that if, by your insinuations, you think to prevail with me, you have got the wrong sow by the ear.   Does he think any lady would go to pig with him ?

Old Lady.   Must beg you to be less particular in your addresses to me.   Does he take me for a Jew, to long after forbidden meats ?

Mr. H.   I shall go mad !—to be refused by old Mother Damnable—she that's so old, nobody knows whether she was ever married or no, but passes for a maid by courtesy ; her juvenile exploits being beyond the farthest stretch of tradition !—old Mother Damnable !

[*Exeunt all, either pitying or seeming to avoid him.*

SCENE —*The street.*

BELVIL *and another Gentleman.*

Belvil. Poor Jack, I am really sorry for him. The account which you give me of his mortifying change of reception at the assembly, would be highly diverting, if it gave me less pain to hear it. With all his amusing absurdities, and amongst them not the least, a predominant desire to be thought well of by the fair sex, he has an abundant share of good-nature, and is a man of honour. Notwithstanding all that has happened, Melesinda may do worse than take him yet. But did the women resent it so deeply as you say?

Gent. O, intolerably—they fled him as fearfully when 'twas once blown, as a man would be avoided, who was suddenly discovered to have marks of the plague, and as fast; when before they had been ready to devour the foolishest thing he could say.

Belvil. Ha! ha! so frail is the tenure by which these women's favourites commonly hold their envied pre-eminence. Well, I must go find him out and comfort him. I suppose, I shall find him at the inn.

Gent. Either there or at Melesinda's—Adieu!

[*Exeunt.*

SCENE.—Mr H———'s *Apartment*

Mr. H. (*solus.*) Was ever anything so mortifying? to be refused by old Mother Damnable!—with such parts and address,—and the little squeamish devils, to dislike me for a name, a sound.—Oh my cursed name! that it was something I could be revenged on! if it were alive, that I might tread upon it, or crush it, or pummel it, or kick it, or spit it out—for it sticks in my throat, and will choke me.

My plaguy ancestors! if they had left me but a Van, or a Mac, or an Irish O', it had been something to qualify it.—Mynheer Van Hogsflesh,—or Sawney MacHogsflesh,—or Sir Phelim O'Hogsflesh,—but downright blunt ————. If it had been any other name in the world, I could have borne it. If it had been the name of a beast, as Bull, Fox, Kid, Lamb, Wolf, Lion; or of a bird, as Sparrow, Hawk, Buzzard, Daw, Finch, Nightingale; or of a fish, as Sprat, Herring, Salmon; or the name of a thing, as Ginger, Hay, Wood; or of a colour, as Black, Grey, White, Green; or of a sound, as Bray; or the name of a month, as March, May; or of a place, as Barnet, Baldock, Hitchen; or the name of a coin, as Farthing, Penny, Twopenny; or of a profession, as Butcher, Baker, Carpenter, Piper, Fisher, Fletcher, Fowler, Glover; or a Jew's name, as Solomons, Isaacs, Jacobs; or a personal name, as Foot, Leg, Crook-shanks, Heaviside, Sidebottom, Longbottom, Rams-bottom, Winterbottom; or a long name, as Blanchen-hagen, or Blanchenhausen; or a short name, as Crib, Crisp, Crips, Tag, Trot, Tub, Phips, Padge, Papps, or Prig, or Wig, or Pip, or Trip; Trip had been some-thing, but Ho————. (*Walks about in great agitation —recovering his calmness a little, sits down.*)

Farewell the most distant thoughts of marriage; the finger-circling ring, the purity-figuring glove, the envy-pining bridemaids, the wishing parson, and the simpering clerk. Farewell the ambiguous blush-raising joke, the titter-provoking pun, the morning-stirring drum.—No son of mine shall exist, to bear my ill-fated name. No nurse come chuckling, to tell

me it is a boy. No midwife, leering at me from under
the lids of professional gravity. I dreamed of caudle.
(*Sings in a melancholy tone.*) Lullaby, Lullaby,—
Hush-a-by-baby—how like its papa it is !—(*Makes
motions as if he was nursing.*—And then, when grown
up, " Is this your son, Sir ?" " Yes, Sir, a poor copy
of me, a sad young dog,—just what his father was
at his age,—I have four more at home." Oh ! oh !
oh !

Enter LANDLORD.

Mr. H. Landlord, I must pack up to-night ; you
will see all my things got ready.

Landlord. Hope your Honour does not intend to
quit the Blue Boar,—sorry anything has happened.

Mr. H. He has heard it all.

Landlord. Your Honour has had some mortification, to be sure, as a man may say; you have brought
your pigs to a fine market.

Mr. H. Pigs !

Landlord. What then ? take old Pry's advice, and
never mind it. Don't scorch your crackling for 'em,
Sir.

Mr. H. Scorch my crackling ! a queer phrase , but
I suppose he don't mean to affront me.

Landlord. What is done can't be undone ; you
can't make a silken purse out of a sow's ear.

Mr. H. As you say, Landlord, thinking of a thing
does but augment it.

Landlord. Does but *hogment* it, indeed, Sir.

Mr. H. *Hogment* it ! damn it, I said augment it.

Landlord. Lord, Sir, 'tis not everybody has such
gift of fine phrases as your Honour, that can lard his
discourse——

Mr. H. Lard!

Landlord. Suppose they do smoke you—

Mr. H. Smoke me!

Landlord. One of my phrases; never mind my words, Sir, my meaning is good. We all mean the same thing, only you express yourself one way, and I another, that's all. The meaning's the same; it is all pork.

Mr. H. That's another of your phrases, I presume.   [*Bell rings and the Landlord called for*

Landlord. Anon, anon.

Mr. H. Oh, I wish I were anonymous.

[*Exeunt several ways.*

Scene.—*Melesinda's Apartment.*

Melesinda *and* Maid.

Maid. Lord, Madam! before I'd take on as you do about a foolish—what signifies a name? Hogs—Hogs—what is it—is just as good as any other, for what I see.

Melesinda. Ignorant creature! yet she is perhaps blest in the absence of those ideas, which, while they add a zest to the few pleasures which fall to the lot of superior natures to enjoy, doubly edge the——

Maid. Superior natures! a fig! If he's hog by name, he's not hog by nature, that don't follow—his name don't make him anything, does it? He don't grunt the more for it, nor squeak, that ever I hear; he likes his victuals out of a plate, as other Christians do; you never see him go to the trough——

Melesinda. Unfeeling wretch! yet possibly her intentions ——

Maid. For instance, Madam, my name is Finch—Betty Finch. I don't whistle the more for that, nor

l   *D*

long after canary-seed while I can get good wholesome mutton—no, nor you can't catch me by throwing salt on my tail.   If you come to that, hadn't I a
young man used to come after me, they said courted
me—his name was Lion, Francis Lion, a tailor , but
though he was fond enough of me, for all that he
never offered to eat me.

Melesinda.   How fortunate that the discovery has
been made before it was too late ʼ   Had I listened to
his deceits, and, as the perfidious man had almost
persuaded me, precipitated myself into an inextricable
engagement before ——

Maid.   No great harm if you had.   You'd only
have bought a pig in a poke—and what then ?   Oh,
here he comes creeping ——

Enter Mr. H. *abject*

Go to her, Mr. Hogs—Hogs—Hogsbristles, what's
your name ?   Don't be afraid, man—don t give it
up—she's not crying—only *summat* has made her
eyes red—she has got a sty in her eye, I believe—
(*going*).

Melesinda.   You are not going, Betty ?

Maid.   O, Madam, never mind me—I shall be
back in the twinkling of a pig's whisker, as they
say.   [*Exit.*

Mr. H.   Melesinda, you behold before you a wretch
who would have betrayed your confidence—but it
was love that prompted him ; who would have tricked
you, by an unworthy concealment, into a participation of that disgrace which a superficial world has
agreed to attach to a name—but with it you would
have shared a fortune not contemptible, and a heart—
but 'tis over now.   That name he is content to bear

alone—to go where the persecuted syllables shall be no more heard, or excite no meaning—some spot where his native tongue has never penetrated, nor any of his countrymen have landed, to plant their unfeeling satire, their brutal wit, and national ill manners—where no Englishmen—(*Here* MELESINDA, *who has been pouting during this speech, fetches a deep sigh*). Some yet undiscovered Otaheite, where witless, unapprehensive savages shall innocently pronounce the ill-fated sounds, and think them not inharmonious.

Melesinda. Oh!

Mr. H. Who knows but among the female natives might be found ——

Melesinda. Sir! [*raising her head.*]

Mr. H. One who would be more kind than—some Oberea—Queen Oberea.

Melesinda. Oh!

Mr. H. Or what if I were to seek for proofs of reciprocal esteem among unprejudiced African maids, in Monomotopa?

Enter Servant.

Servant. Mr. Belvil.   [*Exit.*

Enter BELVIL.

Mr. H. Monomotopa [*musing*].

Belvil Heyday, Jack! what means this mortified face? nothing has happened, I hope, between this lady and you? I beg pardon, Madam, but understanding my friend was with you, I took the liberty of seeking him here. Some little difference possibly which a third person can adjust—not a word. Will you, Madam, as this gentleman's friend, suffer me to be the arbitrator—strange—hark'ee, Jack, nothing

has come out, has there ? you understand me. Oh,
I guess how it is—somebody has got at your secret ,
you haven't blabbled it yourself, have you ? ha ! ha !
ha ! I could find in my heart—Jack, what would you
give me if I should relieve you ?

Mr. H.   No power of man can relieve me [*sighs*] ;
but it must lie at the root, gnawing at the root—here
it will lie.

Belvil.   No power of man ? not a common man, I
grant you . for instance, a subject—it's out of the
power of any subject.

Mr. H.   Gnawing at the root—there it will lie.

Belvil.   Such a thing has been known as a name to
be changed ; but not by a subject—[*shows a Gazette*].

Mr. H.   Gnawing at the root—[*suddenly snatches
the paper out of* BELVIL'S *hand*]—ha ! pish ! nonsense ! give it me—what ! [*reads*] promotions, bankrupts—a great many bankrupts this week—there it
will lie.   [*Lays it down, takes it up again, and reads.*]
" The King has been graciously pleased "—gnawing
at the root—" graciously pleased to grant unto John
Hogsflesh,"—the devil—" Hogsflesh, Esq., of Sty
Hall, in the county of Hants, his royal licence and
authority "—O Lord ! O Lord !—" that he and his
issue "—me and my issue—" may take and use the
surname and arms of Bacon "—Bacon, the surname
and arms of Bacon—" in pursuance of an injunction
contained in the last will and testament of Nicholas
Bacon, Esq., his late uncle, as well as out of grateful
respect to his memory :"—grateful respect ! poor old
soul—— here's more—" and that such arms may be
first duly exemplified "—they shall, I will take care
of that—" according to the laws of arms, and recorded
in the Herald's Office "

Belvil. Come, Madam, give me leave to put my own interpretation upon your silence, and to plead for my friend, that now that only obstacle which seemed to stand in the way of your union is removed, you will suffer me to complete the happiness which my news seems to have brought him, by introducing him with a new claim to your favour, by the name of Mr. Bacon. (*Takes their hands and joins them, which* MELESINDA *seems to give consent to with a smile.*)

Mr. H. Generous Melesinda ! my dear friend —" he and his issue," me and my issue !—O Lord !——

Belvil. I wish you joy, Jack, with all my heart.

Mr. H. Bacon, Bacon, Bacon—how odd it sounds! I could never be tired of hearing it. There was Lord Chancellor Bacon. Methinks I have some of the Verulam blood in me already.—Methinks I could look through Nature—there was Friar Bacon, a conjuror, —I feel as if I could conjure too ——

Enter a Servant.

Servant. Two young ladies and an old lady are at the door, inquiring if you see company, Madam.

Mr. H. " Surname and arms "——

Melesinda. Show them up.—My dear Mr. Bacon, moderate your joy.

Enter three Ladies, being part of those who were at the Assembly.

1st Lady. My dear Melesinda, how do you do?

2nd Lady. How do you do? We have been so concerned for you ——

Old Lady. We have been so concerned—(*seeing him*)—Mr. Hogsflesh ——

Mr. H. There's no such person—nor there never was—nor 'tis not fit there should be—" surname and arms " ——

Belvil. It is true what my friend would express; we have been all in a mistake, ladies. Very true, the name of this gentleman was what you call it, but it is so no longer. The succession to the long-contested Bacon estate is at length decided, and with it my friend succeeds to the name of his deceased relative.

Mr. H. " His Majesty has been graciously pleased "—

1st Lady. I am sure we all join in hearty congratulation—(*sighs*)

2nd Lady. And wish you joy with all our hearts —(*heigh ho!*)

Old Lady. And hope you will enjoy the name and estate many years—(*cries*)

Belvil. Ha ! ha ! ha ! mortify them a little, Jack.

1st Lady. Hope you intend to stay ——

2nd Lady. With us some time ——

Old Lady. In these parts ——

M. H. Ladies, for your congratulations I thank you ; for the favours you have lavished on me, and in particular, for this lady's (*turning to the old Lady*) good opinion, I rest your debtor. As to any future favours (*accosts them severally in the order in which he was refused by them at the assembly*)—Madam, shall always acknowledge your politeness ; but at present, you see, I am engaged with a partner. Always be happy to respect you as a friend, but you must not look for anything further. Must beg of you

to be less particular in your addresses to me.   Ladies
all, with this piece of advice, of Bath and you

Your ever grateful servant takes his leave.
Lay your plans surer when you plot to grieve ;
See, while you kindly mean to mortify
Another, the wild arrow do not fly,
And gall yourself.   For once you've been mistaken ;
Your shafts have miss'd their aim—Hogsflesh has
      saved his Bacon.

COMIC OPERA.

APPENDIX TO VOL. I. OF "MY FRIENDS AND ACQUAINT-
ANCE. BY P. G. PATMORE." 8vo. 1854.

I am in possession of an unpublished drama (qy. tragedy) by Charles
Lamb, which, as it is unquestionably his first substantive production,
and dates at a very early period of his life, may claim to rank among
the most interesting and valuable of our " Curiosities of Literature."

It is a complete Opera, in three acts, and the numerous songs and
concerted pieces are written expressly to popular melodies of the time, in
the manner afterwards adopted with such brilliant success by Moore.

Of the existence of this drama not one of Lamb's friends (myself
included) was aware until after his death. Unfortunately, I am not
able to account, even by remote conjecture, for this latter circumstance,
though Lamb was the last person in the world to keep a secret,
especially his own. This, however, only renders the drama still
more an object of literary interest and curiosity, considering that its
authenticity is placed beyond question, by every portion of it, even
to the minutest alterations, erasures, &c., being in his own handwriting[1]—a hand that is too peculiar to be mistaken by any one who
has once seen a page of it. Moreover, though this drama is entirely
different in its general style, as well as in the character of the materials
employed in its construction, from anything in Lamb's other writings,
there are passages in it which would confirm, if necessary, by internal
evidence, the unimpeachable testimony of the handwriting.

I have used every means at my disposal, but in vain, for ascertaining
the early history of this autograph. I have searched in vain for any

---

[1] See the facsimile at the commencement of this volume.

l   D

direct glimpse of such history in the "Life and Letters" and the "Final Memorials" of Mr. Justice Talfourd. But I find a passage in the last-named work, in a letter from Miss Lamb to Mrs. Hazlitt, which will, perhaps, leave as little doubt in the reader's mind as it does in mine, as to the true origin of this production. The passage I allude to is as follows —

"The Skeffington is quite out now, my brother having got merry with claret and Tom Sheridan *This visit, and the occasion of it, is a profound secret,* and therefore I tell it to nobody but you and Mrs. Reynolds. Through the medium of Wroughton,[1] there came an invitation and proposal from T. S that C L should write some scenes in a speaking pantomime, the other parts of which Tom now, and his father formerly, have manufactured between them So in the Christmas holidays my brother and his two great associates, we expect, will all three be damned together, that is, I mean, if Charles's share, which is done and sent in, is accepted "—(*Final Memorials,* 129, 130)

This passage, though it has evidently no direct reference to the drama now in question, establishes beyond doubt a personal as well as a professional connection between Lamb and the Sheridans ; and it is well known to those familiar with the dramatic history of the time, that they (the Sheridans) were in the habit occasionally, in the case of dramas that they did not like to part with, yet could not produce at the moment, of either purchasing such dramas at a small price, or giving small sums in advance on them, when their authors became inconveniently pressing for a decision Coupling the above with the facts,—first, that this drama belongs to a period precisely corresponding in date with that at which Lamb is described by his biographer, as struggling to better the condition of his aged parents and his sister, by any and every literary exertion and resource that he could call into play, and that at the period in question the drama was "the be-all and the end-all" of his literary ambition ;—these circumstances being taken into consideration, little doubt will remain as to the early history of this curious MS I have given the first leaf of this drama in fac-simile The MS. was shown to the late Mr Justice Talfourd (one of Lamb's executors) immediately on its discovery by me. and also to Mr. Moxon, (his friend and publisher,) neither of whom raised the smallest doubt as to the handwriting

---

1 At that time stage manager of Drury Lane Theatre

L   )

CHARACTERS OF THE OPERA.

LOVELACE   *A man of fortune, refused by Violeta—enlists for a Soldier and goes to Gibraltar.*

MAJOR APTJONES   *A Welchman* } *Officers of the Garrison.*
CAPTAIN LOTHIAN   *A Scotsman* }

BLOOMER.   *Aide de Camp to the Governor, an admirer of Caroline, but a flatterer of Mrs. Lapelle.*

CAPTAIN LAPELLE   *An Officer, who comes with his lady from England to join the garrison.*

GOVERNOR
HALBERT   *A Sergeant*
DRUMMER
JUDGE ADVOCATE.
CLERK, SOLDIERS, &c

LADIES

MRS LAPELLE   *Wife of Captain Lapelle, who encourages the addresses of Bloomer*

CAROLINE   *A young lady in love with Bloomer*

VIOLETA   *In the character of an Officer—follows Lovelace to Gibraltar*

JESSE   *Her servant—habited as her foot-boy*

TURKS, &c

SCENE—*Gibraltar.*

ACT THE FIRST.

SCENE THE FIRST—A PARADE.
Sergeant HALBERT *and a* DRUMMER *meeting as by chance.*

Hal. What news in the garrison to-day—thou'rt a very Harlequin messenger—and of as many colours.

Drum. Yes, our young *aide-de-camp* keeps me wagging; there is not a drum in the army that is rattled about like me.

Hal. A drummer's profession is a pimp, and if thou mind'st it, boy, it is a certain road to preferment. it has always succeeded in the army, and will ever raise a man to situation: thou hast ten rounds of

Love-cartridges to fire off there. What, is there anything new arrived?

Drum. Only four transports stuff'd with recruits, their wives and wenches. But among them is a Madame Lapelle, who is married—a certain reason why all the garrison should be mad after her, she is the finest piece of red-and-white flesh that ever England trusted on salt water. She is as straight as a halbert, and tight as a new braid tunic.

Hal. The husband, then, is a lucky fellow; for she'll be besieged like a frontier town; and if she don't surrender, she is the first that ever defied the assailants of Gibraltar.

Drum. Believe I have ammunition enough about me to ensure a capitulation; but there is no fear of conquest, while our young ensigns keep the cartouche-box of Cupid.

Hal. A platoon of hair-powder and washball will bring her down. The strangers make fine work for you; you finger the pistareens, my little rather-of-sheep-skin.

Drum. No poor pay, when you consider I ran twenty times a day from Europa Point to the Convent, bearing packets of sighs to red lips and bright black eyes. But this Madam outstrips everything that appeared before. She has a skin fairer than Spanish milk; a cheek like a Barbary orange; and so delicate, that a puff of rocambole from the Spanish lines would kill her dead as a rifleman. The Governor is ten years younger at the sight of her; and the *aides-de-camps* were up before the sun to be powdered to do her honour. I am now on the wings of Love, to invite all the world to bid her welcome, by the sound of drum.

Air First—*The Reveillé to fife and drum.*

Now Beauty's up. the Army's gay,
And ev'ry heart beats reveillé;
A brighter flame can ne'er inspire
A soldier's breast with martial fire.

When *that* Beauty takes the field,
Generals and Captains yield;
Rank and file must all give way,
And to Beauty yield the day.   [*Exit.*

Hal. This Drummer will beat himself into bread,
while I shall remain here 'till I am fit for nothing—
but Chelsea. The God of War be praised, I never
yet was enlisted by the parson, nor will I resign the
name of bachelor Halbert, while there is a comrade's
wife to take pity on me: but now to reconnoitre.
The new comers—may I never make another speech
at the drum-head, but I will have a wench out of this
new draught: what should we do in this stone hen-
coop if little England did not send us fresh provision?
The life of a bachelor soldier is an honour to the army;
but he that has a wife for a knapsack is his own
baggage waggon.

Air Second.   Sergeant Halbert—*Bachelor Bluff.*

He that is single is free from all care.
  Cæsar and Pompey were horned,
Tho' Sampson was strong, he was shorn of his hair,
  And like a weak husband was scorned,
Bachelor Bluff, heigh! for a heart that is tougher than bluff.

Soldiers and sailors should never be wed,
  But follow with rapture the wenches;
Let wives and their cuckolds go scolding to bed,
  They sleep undisturbed in the trenches
      Bachelor Bluff, &c.

SCENE THF SECOND—*A Saloon.*

GOVERNOR BASTION *and Aide-de-Camp* BLOOMER.

Gov. Ay, Bloomer, ay, by all accounts she is a gorgeous paragon of beauty, the very salient angle of Venus of Medicis. Zounds, the husband must mount guard night and day, or we shall carry her by a coup-de-main.

Blo. The garrison was never besieged before: she would make a saint for the Spanish army, and they would follow her as a guardian angel. (When she left the boat, and press'd her velvet foot to the earth, Jews, Turks, Christians, and Infidels, stood, with their mouths expanded, in amazement, as if she commanded the opening and the shutting.)

Gov. Ay, Bloomer, ay, this is a pretty description of her powers, and our softness. No, no, Bloomer, she should undo my soldiers. I'd put out their eyes, and make them grope and grapple with the Spaniards in the dark: zounds, we'd beat them blindfold.

Blo. That indeed, Sir, would be making Cupids of them all.

AIR. BLOOMER.

How can the man in love go right,
    When Folly is his guide;
With Cupid 'tis eternal night,
    And mischief's all his pride.

Who can foretell for what high cause,
    This darling of the gods was born;
For he who doth obey his laws
    Is sure of misery and scorn.

Ah Cupid, did it prove thee wise,
When Folly put out both thy eyes.

Enter SERVANT.

Serv. Captain Lothian and Major Aptjones, wait on the Governor.

Gov. Gentlemen, good morning to you. Have you seen the new recruits from England, with Ensign Etheridge, who is strongly recommended to me as a youth of family and fortune.

Major Yes, hur has been down to the Lant-port-gate, and they are as pretty fellows as the sun ever shone upon. I have ordered the Sergeant to march them to the parade.

Lothian. The Major's partial; the lads are in general from the rugged mountains of Merioneth-shire.

Major. Ay, this is to be a Scotman. Hur has no ragged mountains to be sure in hur fertile country of Argyleshire. The Welch lads are brave, and so are the Scot lads too, but let hur praise her men for their toings and not for their kirtles; they are poor enough porn in Wales and in Scotland too.

Lothian. 'Tis the pride of your land, is your up-setting, Major.

Major Cot knows hur countrymen are prout enough, but they make coot soldiers, and a coot soldier is not afraid of a pullet or the pelly-ache.

Lothian. There is no character like a soldier, nor no death like the bed of honour, but were twa bullets hurled through my *whem*, Sir, I must speak my mind, and praise the bonny lads of North Britain.

Gov. A truce to your nationality; I shall soon have occasion to expend some brave lads of all countries. The Welsh and Scotch are equally poetical. The English makes a friendship; he never defends the claims of his own country, but bravely stands by the honest man, be he Turk, Jew, or Infidel. But now, gentlemen, I shall have the honour of feasting your eyes with a new beauty, the wife of Captain Lapelle.

Major. The eyes of peauty were ever more fatal to the Aptjones than swort or gun.

Lothian. Hoot, major, hoot. What, mon, at these years to be trapp'd by a blind boy?

Major. It is peauty that will vanquish the proudest victor. It was Cæsar of Rome, and Alexander of Macedon, that felt the plow of love; and so did King David, and Catwallater of Wales.

Blo. True, my gallant major, the Welsh have ever been susceptible to the power of love. The clime of Scotland is too cold for so pure and light a flame, and the diet too barren to feed Arcadian shepherds.

Lothian. What, Sir, do you ridicule the Land o'cakes. Are there not the Pastorals of Allan Ramsay, and the elegiac tears of Ossian?

AIR THE THIRD—LOTHIAN. *"Sherry wine."*

The soldier and tar should be cherished by war,
  And not vanquished by sighs, tears, or Beauty;
What is Love and his Laws to the national cause,
  And the glory of doing our duty.

Chorus.

Let honour and glory then lead on before ye,
  If you wish to be famed in story,

What is Cupid and Venus, but fit to bemean us
Of life the mere squibs and the rockets.
There are no ambuscades, so fatal as jades,
To our credits as well as our pockets.

Chorus.

Let honour, &c.

Gov. Come, gentlemen! this is not a time for disputants. Fall into the rear, and make room for love and beauty!

Enter CAPTAIN *and* MRS. LAPELLE. VIOLETA *as an Ensign, her servant* JESSE *as her man-servant.*

Gov Mrs. Lapelle, I give you joy on your arrival. Gibraltar never was made so happy before. Captain Lapelle—Mr. Etheridge, you are welcome, you are welcome. (*Going severally to them, and bowing in the manner of reception and congratulation.*) I hope, Ma'am, your passage was pleasant.

Mrs. Lap. Indeed, Governor, there are no thanks due from me to the God of the Ocean. That turbulent Bay of Biscay made me often repent that I had undertaken so long a voyage.

Gov. It is the general complaint of all passengers; but the contrast gives a lustre to the Spanish climate.

Blo. Beauty gives brilliancy to every climate; but what most surprises me, is how the sea could be so rude when bearing her own Venus.

Mrs. Lap. Upon my word, I do not lament the fatigue of the voyage, since I have gained the shore of compliments and hospitality.

Viol. Compliments, Ma'am, are birds of passage ; and then springes catch woodcocks in all climes

Blo. Woodcocks, Sir!

Viol. Yes, Sir, woodcocks! And you might be ginn'd were your nose longer.

M 2

Blo. I don't know whatever you were springing;
but if you don't mind your flight you will be a good
shot here.

Viol. I came here for the purpose, Sir, nor mean
I to return until I have winged a dozen cockatoos.

Gov. Come, come, young soldier, this snip-snap,
running fire won't do here. I have seen many young
fellows wear their cockades as high as you, and
repent of their follies.

Blo. Stick me on a *chevaux de frise* if it won't be
his case too.

Viol. Sir!

Blo. Sir! What news have you, Mr. Etheridge,
in England.

Viol. Nothing very new, sir. They speak
English at the play-houses and Italian at the operas.
Fornication is at the summit, and as a pretty fellow
you might get into keeping at the advertising
office in Dover Street, for ladylike gentlemen are all
the ton.

Blo. Indeed! I'm surprised, then, how they
came to spare you.

Gov. A truce to these squibs and crackers, I must
find better entertainment for Mrs. Lapelle.

Viol. I believe you or your aide-de-camp may.

Mrs. Lap. Etheridge, are you sober?

Viol. Alas! dear worthy Lapelle, thou wilt have
the hottest campaign here that ever soldier went
through . won't he, my Lady Lapelle?

Mrs. Lap. You are an impertinent coxcomb.

Viol. You are a very pretty woman.

AIR.—Mrs. LAPELLE *and* VIOLETA.

She.—A coxcomb's the plague of my life.
He.— The plague of each pretty wife.

She.—I hate and detest all their airs.

He.— They kill and dispel all your cares.

She.—They are mockers of men.

He.— Which you cannot condemn.

She.—They are blockheads and fools.

He.— But they are made in your schools.

[*Exeunt the* LAPELLES, GOVERNOR,
BLOOMER, *who hands the lady off.*

LOTHIAN, APTJONES, *and* JESSE *come forward.*

Viol. Well, Will, how do you like the scorching sun, and this tremendous ragged rock?

Jesse. It promises to spoil all your faces and garden stuff: everything must be burnt to a cinder but virtue,—and that lays so in the shade it can't be scorch'd.

Viol. Thank you, Will, for the simile.

Loth. He is a smart child, ensign, that you have brought over.

Viol. Well enough, as food for your powder goes He will serve to expend, and fill up a hole as well as a better man.

Maj. Cot's plessing upon hur—hur is as smart as a carrot, and pites like a raddish.

Viol. My dear taffy, where is hur peard?

[*mocking him.*

Maj. Hur peard, what does hur mean?

Viol. I never saw a goat on a rock without one before.

Maj. Splutter and pudding, does hur mean to offend hur.　　[*putting his hand to his sword.*

Loth. Zounds, major, will ye never be coil; thou'rt as quick as bruised powder.

Viol. Put up your cheese-toaster, it will serve to spit larks on half-pay.

l　　　　　　　　　　　　　　　　　　　ᴅ

Loth. I am stun'd, an auld fellow as sore as a minister.

Viol. To be sure the blood in the Caledonian barometer does not mount so quick: 'tis as lazy as the case that contains it.

Loth. You are a perfect snap-dragon ; but we shall tame you.

Maj. That is cholerick as a turkey cock.

Viol. Come, come, ye are veterans of service. and will forgive the folly of a young man.

Maj. O, when hur confesses hur errors, hur is ready to forgive.

Loth. And now, Sir, what, what have you ganging forward in London ?

Viol. I left all the Common Council of the City with as good stomachs as ever you knew them ; and the Mansion House——

Maj. How !

Viol. In the same place. I paid my tailor, too, to make him stare.

Loth. This is nothing to the purpose—get on.

Viol. First then, I left their Majesties in a good state of health, reigning in the hearts of their subjects ; and the Lords and Commons doing wonders ; and, by their patriot zeal and large supplies, they mean to convince the world that England is a match for the four quarters.

Loth. Yas, yas, this is the auld spirit.

Maj. It is like Vesuvius, it smothers awhile, and then blazes.

Viol. The Park is filled with beaux of the maids, who wear bloody stocks, to make the world believe they are cut-throats. George's is cramm'd with honest soldiers, who have every advantage in life but one.

Maj. What is that?

Viol. Credit for what they want.

Maj. Yes, it is an old sore in the army, but the war will get over it.

Viol. Not if they don't get over the war.

Maj. Now let hur come to particulars.

Viol. Why! almost four months ago, I had a rencounter with a woman of the first fashion, and received a deep wound—

Maj. In hur heart.

Viol. No, in her constitution.

Loth. That's a worse place: a soldier only wants a heart to scale a parapet. Well, younker gang your gait.

Viol. I rak'd—was not black-balled at Renny's, where I won money without false dice—I fought a dozen duels without a wound on any side—I fell in love with every woman I saw without marrying—and I am now here to fight, toast, and drink with the bravest and the best. I am just going down to the ragged staff to see my party landed, where I will be happy to have your company, if you will do me the honour to meet me there.

Loth. Yas, we will receive your bonny boys, and then introduce you to the regiment.

[*Exeunt* MAJOR *and* LOTHIAN.

Viol. Alas! dear, generous Lovelace! what have I suffer'd for thee! Tedious journeys, tempestuous seas, and every other distress that even men might shrink at. May not this atone for my neglect and usage of thee? O let me read again the dismal letter, the cause of all my woes.—

"False, cruel, perjured Violeta,—

"With suffering constancy I bore your cruelty, your

l   *D*

neglect, your cold disdain; but now I've conquer'd, and have torn your image from my heart. I am this moment embarking as a private soldier for Gibraltar, where I hope some kind bullet will possess that heart once designed for you. Farewell eternally,

"LOVELACE."

How I upbraid my cruelty, and blame the folly of my mind—flattered with the idle idea of securing every heart at my pleasure. O Lovelace, Lovelace, how unjustly I have treated thee!

Jess. Dear, dear gentleman, where is he, for in vain have I inquired of every creature since he landed.

Viol. Break, stubborn heart, break.

Jess. O, dear madam, remember with how many tears and entreaties I begg'd of you not to leave England; indeed now, I blame myself for yielding to your solicitations, for nothing but misery and starvation stare us in the face.

Viol Then you had for ever forfeited my esteem; all my care is now for what you may endure, my dear Jessica.

Jess. O, dearest mistress, fear not me. If you can bear up under the difficulties that threaten us, I will support them with pleasure.

Viol. Come on; and since Lovelace has so highly resented the fickleness of my sex, I will be revenged on his, and quarrel with every fellow that I meet; now will I shake all female weakness from my heart, assume the airs of a real male maccaroni, and make every coxcomb in the Army stand clear of me.

AIR VIOLETA.

I'll cock my head, and draw my sword,
   And be so fierce a blade,
As ever swore or pawn'd his word,
   Or woo'd a willing maid.

I'll swear, I'll drink, I'll rake, I'll fight,
   Talk nonsense by the hour.
Sonnets to every Beauty write,
   And riot in amour.   *[Exeunt*

SCENE.—*A beach. A transport ship lying near the shore. Soldiers coming from aboard. Women, children, etc. landed.*

LOVELACE, *as a Grenadier, sitting in a disconsolate manner*

DRUMMER *beating his drum to the fife and surrounded with Trulls.*

AIR —DRUMMER.—*Maggie Lauder.*

Is there a life, pray tell me girls,
   That beats the bonny Drummer
The maidens' smiles make all the year,
   To him, perpetual summer !
Eightpence per day,
Tho' all his pay,
   It powders him for duty :
To love and you,
He beats tattoo,
   And quarters with his Beauty

Enter HALBERT.

Hal. So my sheep and mess fiddler, I find you are never out of your way while there's a wench in the garrison, or a bottle of black strap going about

Drum. Since it's my business to make a report of the baggage waggon, I must taste, sergeant, before I recommend.

Hal. Ah, thou'rt a sensible boy, and know when to support the Commanding Officer's quarters. But now comrades for duty. Come—fall into the rank there.

Love. O for the day of battle—that I might rush amid the thickest war—and end this hated life. O cruel Violeta.   [*Aside.*

Hal. Silence. Fall back. You women hold your red rags still or you will cross the hot sands of Spain to Saint à Rocque. What, louder! Then the devil a one of you enter a barrack in Gibraltar.

1st Trull. Why, sergeant, do you know that this here cribbage-face hussey here, says that she's as much my husband's lawful wife as I am.

2nd Trull. Your husband—that's good camp impudence! Did I not carry his knapsack, all the last German war, when the horse galloped away, and left us to take our chance with the French, on foot. Besides, can there be so good a proof as his beating me every day of his life.

Hal. The strongest proof of marriage love ; and, therefore, Mrs. Scrub-tub, let me advise you to leave him, and hire yourself out to a company of grenadiers to wash their linen.

2nd Trull. Then, if you please, sergeant, I'll take up with Formal here. (*to* LOVELACE.)

Love. Away—strumpet.

2nd Trull. What, you shabby dog, to dare to strike a woman you're not married to—or refuse such a comely woman as me, that every officer of the regiment has said civil things to.

Drum. Yes: " pioneers and all."

Hal. No more ; this is a young recruit, and if he wants to jump across a sword with you, let him ; but no bullying a man into his matrimonial leap.

AIR.—HALBERT

A wench who dare follow the camp,
No danger her spirit should damp.
In the midst of the thunder,
Her part is to plunder
And after her labour and toils
  She's to crown,
  She's to crown
The brow of her hero with spoils.

2nd Trull. No, no, let it come of itself, for, poor man, I shall never forget it, that very thing killed my sixth husband.

Drum. Ay, sixth and your seventh too.

2nd Trull. No, indeed, Drummer; he, poor man, was hang'd for sheep stealing.

Love. Ye gods, what afflictions have I now brought upon me—what a banditti's here!   [*Aside.*

Hal. Come, order! to the right about—march.

    [*They go off to a cotillon—with drums and fifes—round the stage, and the scene closes on the women, &c., &c.*

ACT THE SECOND.

SCENE—*A grove and bower.*—BLOOMER AND CAROLINE.

Car. Is it possible I can observe your partial attentions and not be affected? Do you not watch every motion of her features, and study her very frowns and smiles? Have you, since the hour she arrived, ever paid me the least attention? but ever studious to observe her inclinations and to obey them. Is this the love and constancy you have sworn; is this the firm and everlasting testimony of your affections?

Blo. Upon my word, Miss Caroline, you really are so quick in your jealousies, and so prim'd and loaded with unjust resentments, that you go off, smack bang, before one has touched the trigger. I—I—I have noticed Mrs. Lapelle with that civility so natural to my breeding, and which no well-bred man can avoid to a pretty woman, but that I have any idea of dishonour about me towards the lady, is as false, as that my affection to you are as true, and as my rifled barrel-pistols to the touch of my finger.

Car. O such preposterous rhodomontade is more insulting than your behaviour.

Blo. What, in the name of Mars and Mercury, am I to do or say. Upon my virtue, my sacred virtue, Miss Caroline, I do most sincerely love you, and every officer in the garrison has observed it, and called me——

Car. Call'd you, Mr. Bloomer—called you what!

Blo. Only, happy dog; and indeed I began to think so till this new fracas broke out.

Car. And do you really think so?

Blo. Upon my word I not only think so, but I feel myself so enamoured and wedded to your affections.

Car. If your conduct convinces me, Bloomer, I may endeavour to believe it.

Blo. Upon my word I am very well pleased to find that you have recover'd your faith. It is a curs'd troublesome thing, that whenever people are in love, they are sure to be eternally quarrelling and pouting, to prove the ardour of their passions.

Air. Bloomer.

Nature had long a treasure made
  Of all her choicest store
Fearing when she should be decay'd
  To beg in vain for more.

Love wisely had of long foreseen
 That he must once grow old,
And, therefore, stor'd a magazine
 To keep him from the cold.

Thus all his powers did unite
 To make a fire divine.
None ever burn'd so hot, so bright,
 As mine for Caroline

So we alone the happy rest,
 While all the world is poor,
And have within ourselves preserv'd
 All love's and nature's store.

Car. And pray, Bloomer, where did you leave Mrs. Lapelle?

Blo. At the convent, where we are to have a Ball al-fresco, and for which I purpose I am come to invite my fair Caroline. I am to have the management of the whole business, and I flatter myself I shall dispose of the variegated lamps with more taste than the Cornelly's, and throw her garden into the sere leaf, with my perpetual Spring.

Car. You're an agreeable creature when you please.

Blo. Yes, little Caroline, I am that: and Mrs. Lapelle has found it out, too.

Car. Oh your vanity, Bloomer, is your deformity —she has too much taste. But who or what is she, Bloomer, for you're in every family secret?

Blo. Who is she, Caroline? why, a lady—who has been—a lady.

Car. What, what, dear Bloomer, a lady—a lady of what?

Blo. Her husband is, without exception, the most sensible, worthy, gallant fellow that ever drew sword.

Car. But what's that to her: a fiddlestick of her husband?

Blo. Surely, my dear inquisitive little girl; it is a great deal; for the virtues of a husband, like a mirror, reflect the virtues of his wife.

Car. But do you know who she was? Or where she was born? Or where she comes from? Or where he got her? Come, tell me, for I am dying to know.

Blo. Yes, I daresay you are. She was long his mistress, and for her exemplary behaviour he made her his wife; and a damn'd generous action it was.

Car. His mistress! what, a kept mistress—good heavens!

Blo. Yes, identically; not that I approve of the metamorphosis, for I never knew an instance of a good mistress making a good wife, unless for the garrison of Gibraltar. But do now, my sweet little orange flower, do now prepare for the Ball.

AIR.—CAROLINE.—*Through the Wood Laddie.*

O BLOOMER ne'er seek thy dear Caro to tease,
   For thou'rt all my pleasure,
   My joy, and my treasure.
And yet thou delight'st not thy maiden to please,
   Who robb'd of her lovers, depriv'd of her ease.
     Fare thee well, Rover, &c.

'Tis thine to reflect and some caution to take,
   Nor thus like a feather,
   The caprice of weather,
Be blown to and fro, like a common town Rake,
But think of the maiden who lives for thy sake.
     Fare thee well, Rover, &c.

[*Exit.*

Blo. Yes, my little Caroline, to be sure you love me, and I love you, and we have plighted vows;

and if I continue in the same mind, I may marry you. But yet I confess, this Madam Lapelle hath altered the disposition of my army—constancy and fidelity, those steady sentinels of my heart, are disbanded. Truth and sincerity were my body guards, but they are march'd into Winter-quarters : and as for love and opportunity, they are out on a recruiting party. But there is no reasoning on love, and it takes every thing by storm. Now for this al-fresco. I must not sacrifice taste for the want of cash, and, therefore, two Jews are to supply the garrison with five hundred moidores immediately Yes, yes, the Jews must supply the garrison, there is no being without ammunition, when a serious siege is laid against a man's taste, and a lady like Lapelle is to be won.

Enter DRUMMER

Drum. Sir, here's the last young ensign from England without, who says he will see you, whether you'll be seen or not. I told him you were engaged with a lady ; he said that was still a greater reason why he would come in ; egad, such a fellow, your honour, would be in the courtway before you could make a rally. But here he is.

Enter VIOLETA

Viol. Your servant, Sir.
Blo. Your servant, Sir.
Viol. You had a lady here, Sir.
Blo. I had, Sir ; what might you want with her ?
Viol. To make love to her.
Blo. 'Tis my concern, Sir.
Viol. 'Tis a way I have, Sir.

Blo. You seem, Sir, to be a spark of the true celestial fire; did you ever cudgel a scoundrel?

Viol. Twenty.

Blo. Without an effort of resistance.

Viol. Peaceable as martyrs.

Blo. Then, Sir, I have a job at hand shall make your list of flagellation twenty-two.

Viol. Come on—blow rencounters are the joy of my soul.

Blo. You must know I have borrowed five hundred moidores of the scoundrels of usurious Jews.

Viol. Not a word more; I am used to the work; I was white-washed, the last act of grace, for four thousand, half-pay and all.

Blo. Drummer, bid the Jews Pottifar and Absolom come in.

Enter Jews.

Drum. Here gentlemen—these are the Jerusalem cucumbers. (I wish I had thy wife 'potechary, and Absolom was hung on a tree.   [*Aside.*

Pot. Your servants, Captains; here be little Absolom and I with de moneys, which I have——

Blo. It is no matter if you had it from the Devil, I must have it.

Pot. Ten per cents. and twenty moidores, presents, my good Captain.

Blo. Yes, yes, I don't object, it is a forc'd march with me.

Pot. You wants de silk stockings; Absolom has good ones?

Blo. No, damn me, if I want a stocking.

Pot. Yes, you must take ten pounds in stockings; gentlemen always wants stockings.

Viol. But Jew, how do you know they will fit? Bloomer, I say you shan't take a stocking.

Pot. Yes, he must take the stockings, or I takes away de moneys.

Blo. Damn his stockings; I'll take them—fit or no fit.

Viol. You shan't draw one of them on.

Blo. I will; Drummer, take the cash.

Drum. Yes, and I'll keep it as safe as the Jew of Venice.

Blo. Now, sir, I'll try the length of your sword—whether I shall or shall not wear his stockings.

Viol. With all my heart! Come on. [*They draw and push.* POTTIFAR *falls down between them on his knees.*

Pot. Oh, for the sakes of the Great Gods—don't fight till I have insur'd your lifes.

Viol. Away—Dives—I'll kill him dead as Nebuchadnezzar.

Enter MAJOR APTJONES *suddenly.*

Maj. Plood and confusion; is hur always a fighting? 'Tis pity hur was not in America. A few guards on Punker's Hill would cool hur plood for hur. What is the cause of hur drawing hur sworts?

Blo. These Judæan scoundrels, Major, wanted to pick my pocket of twenty pieces.

Maj. They are de thieves of the earth—from an old pair of preeches to a pound—hur is sure to be a knave—I'll have them drum'd out the garrison.

Pot. For the Great God's sake, Major, spare little Pottifar, and drum out Absolom, who wanted to cheat the gentleman.

Maj. Get hur to hur synagogue, or I will get hur to a jail.

Pot. The tribe of Israel pray for the Major and the Governor.   [*Exeunt.*

Maj. Well, what has hur to say for hurself now?

Viol. I have been ill-treated by this feather of a soldier, and unless he makes the amende honorable, I can't put up with the affront.

Maj. In all quarrels every party is in fault; and, therefore, you must beg one another's partons, 'tis the best excuse to save hur lives; shake hands—kiss, and be friends—and I will then introduce hur to the mess.

Viol. On your account, Major. I will look it over. But let every man take care how he affronts Ensign Etheridge.

Enter Jessie.

Jes. I am desir'd to inform you, gentlemen, the drum hath beat to dinner.

AIR.

Drinking and fighting, gaming and cheering,
Wooing, seducing, deceiving, caressing:
  Are the amusements a soldier desires.
  For dancing and wenching
  Surpass all entrenching:
  If they're ta'en by surprise
  'Tis by Beauty's bright eyes,
And not by the sword or the enemy's fires.

[*Exeunt* Bloomer, Violeta, and Major.

Drummer *and* Jessie *come forward.*

Jes. These are hard times, comrade.

Drum. Only with those who choose to make 'em so, my little smock-faced blade.

Jes. Drummer, can you keep a secret?

Drum. 'Tis part of my profession ; but more difficult to keep than my money.

Jes. That I believe; but you are not entrusted with enough of either to give you any consequence.

Drum There's your mistake, my little cream colour'd plate, for my knapsack has all the intrigues of the garrison in it, and my supplies for pimping enable me to keep a bevy of beauties. I am the next man in the place to the Governor.

Jes. How so?

Drum. By being in the Cabinet Council of all intrigues. I am received at all hours, in all rooms. O, like the true God of Love. I shut my eyes, nor look at that which I brought together with my own hands.

Jes. Then you hear all, see nothing, and say less.

Drum. Truffle's the word.

Jes. Do you know my Master means to make love to Miss Caroline ?

Drum. He may, the quarters are clear.

Jes Does not Bloomer kneel there ?

Drum. No; he's after Madam Lapelle, and Caroline's after him. Love's like hunting, when one flies t'other pursues.

Jes. So I believe ; and we have experienced that most miserably in our family.

Drum. In what manner ?

Jes. My master left England for love, and I too.

Drum. 'Tis a curs'd disorder , and seems to have sweated you down to the size of a drumstick. Drink black-strap and get into flesh; not snivel away your time like a whining Italian.

N 2

Jes.   I have lost my brother.

Drum.   Well, if he died like a soldier in battle, a prince might envy him his fall.

Jes.   No, he is not dead, he is in this garrison: would you help me to find him?

Drum.   That I will, if love has not disguised him as much as you.   What's his name?

Jes.   Lovelace, and a handsome youth he is.

Drum.   Yes; a family ought to be handsome with so much love in it.   Well, I'll pick him out, and turn that dismal face into smiles.

AIR.—DRUMMER *and* JESSIE.

DRUMMER.

Ye gods, what a plague to the soul of a man,
  Is that trickling urchin of love.
If the life of the longest is only a span,
  How short must a soldier then prove.

JESSIE.

What contests has he with the seas and the war
  A prey to the sword and the gun:
His fame is increas'd by his number of scars;
  By peace he is only undone.

Both.

Ye heroes of arms—whether soldier or tar,
  Attend, and this maxim approve,
The soldier's bright star is the great God of War,
  And he is the true God of Love.

[Exeunt.

SCENE.—*An apartment, discovering* MRS. LAPELLE *and* CAPTAIN LAPELLE *seated.*

Cap. Lap.   Dear lady, I flatter myself, that universal tenderness which I have shown you for a series of years, has made so happy an impression on your mind, that any admonitions or cautions which I may find necessary to give you, will meet with that approbation your good sense entitles it to. I have observed——

Mrs. Lap. Well, what have you observed? Bless me, Mr. Lapelle, you are a-going to preach, and you know how much I hate it.

Capt. Lap. Preach, Madam! is it preaching to tell a wife of her danger, when she is giving liberties that may do her great discredit?

Mrs. Lap. Liberties! I should not have thought of that. Liberties!

Capt. Lap. Yes, liberties, Madam; and such as neither your reputation nor my honour will permit.

Mrs. Lap. Reputation! honour! I don't understand you, Sir,

Capt. Lap. Then, Madam, you shall The freedom, Mrs. Lapelle, which you have suffered that insignificant coxcomb, Bloomer, to take with you, neither becomes the dignity of a wife to suffer, nor a husband to bear.

Mrs Lap. What! a woman is not to suffer the polite addresses of a pretty fellow, truly, lest it is to throw a husband into a fit of jealous vapours!

Capt. Lap. Do you call such addresses warrantable?

Mrs. Lap. Warrantable! Yes, very much so.

Capt. Lap. Is it, Madam, consistent with the character of my wife to suffer an impertinent pretty fop to kiss her at his will.

Mrs Lap. Kiss her! and where's the harm of that. What can be more innocent than a simple kiss?

Capt. Lap. So, Mrs. Lapelle, you laugh at it—you laugh at it, Madam?

Mrs. Lap. My dear, doting *caro sposo*, would you have me cry at it?

Capt. Lap. But—but—but, Madam, I am sorry, very sorry to mention it; but—but—he eat some comfits out of your mouth, and that is a liberty no lady should permit, and it is what my nature will not bear. Madam, you have been here a short time, and your head has been turned with a deluge of flattery; and if, Madam, you cannot so conduct yourself, as to reflect honour to yourself and me, I shall be under the disagreeable predicament of taking a step that may be very disagreeable to you.

Mrs. Lap. You may take such steps as you please, Sir. I have no illmeaning in my behaviour, and I shall be very attentive to those who are polite and attentive to me.

AIR —Mrs. LAPELLE

Ye belles and ye flirts, pray who'd be a wife,
If the whims of a husband so torture her life.
For surely these days a new fashion approve,
And all, but her husband, a lady may love.

Wedlock's now a release from mammas and old aunts,
A spouse must supply all a fair lady wants:
A husband is but the convenience of life,
He may be the friend, not the flirt of a wife.

Enter CAROLINE. BLOOMER *with a fine bouquet.*

CAPT. AND MRS. LAPELLE, CAROLINE, AND BLOOMER,

Blo. (Walking hastily to Mrs. Lapelle, presents her with a nosegay.) I have ransack'd every garden in Gibraltar to compose this bouquet for your acceptance, and for the high gratification of presenting it on my bended knee.

Mrs. Lap. Dear me, Bloomer, you do me infinite honour.

Car. I suppose the garrison, Sir, would not afford two nosegays?

Blo. Platoon me to death with puns, Miss Caroline, if it would.

Mrs. Lap. Poor girl, it is a pity to teaze her, for she's in love with the fellow, and yet a Turk, may as well part with the favourite of his harem, as a pretty woman with an agreeable flatterer. Miss Caroline, will you accept the bouquet?

Blo. Now there's a piece of complaisance.

Car. O ma'am, by no means, I must beg your pardon.

Blo. That's better on her side than I expected. O dear, Lady Lapelle, you are the real Flora it belongs to; Nature produced it for your bosom, and blush'd that it was not better.

Capt. Lap. Upon my word, Sir, your compliments are so very flowery and ready, that the hot-bed of your imagination must be well supplied.

Blo. Supplied, Sir! Supplied with what, Sir?

Capt. Lap. With materials for raising mushrooms

Mrs. Lap. I am astonished, Captain Lapelle, at your indelicacy; such false notions, and abusive prejudices, make you ridiculous.

Capt. Lap. I am more astonished, Mrs. Lapelle, at the encouragement you give to every meteor of a spark that wishes to borrow fire at your eyes.

AIR.—MRS. LAPELLE

When maids we tease our mothers' hearts
  Perpetually in love;
And use a thousand little arts,
  Their jealousies to move.

A husband is our only care,
    And when the man we've got,
Like game entangl'd in a snare,
    We toil to break the knot

[MRS. LAPELLE *handed off by* BLOOMER.

MR. LAPELLE *and* CAROLINE.

Capt. Lap. I would not have believed it possible, that so amiable, so sensible a woman, who, for a series of years, has been a pattern of domestic virtue, could have been so unguarded. O insupportable infatuation!

Car. Alas, I fear that it is but true—I have with deepest sorrow mark'd it and bewail'd it. O fickle, false, insidious Bloomer.

Capt. Lap. Ah, fair lady! and—and—has the attachment been so palpable?

Car. Indeed, Captain Lapelle, it would be the height of perfidy in me to alarm your mind with any ungenerous suspicions—but I have seen——

Capt. Lap. O, madam, I have seen enough already to make advancing dangerous; I entreat you to proceed.

Car. It is too plain that I am miserable. Bloomer false, and she untrue

Capt. Lap. O base degenerate Enchantress; not content with the ruin of her own reputation, the world's opinion, and my peace—but to rob so fair a lady of her love, is adding crime to crime. What is become of conjugal honour, once the bright radiant star of England? Have vice and folly, and a lewd intercourse with frippery France, perverted all our honourable manners to the most paltry foppery of folly. O England, England! While the salt sea confined thy nature's home, thy sons were valiant and thy daughters virtuous. By all the gods, he shall experience the force of my resentment.

Car. I do beseech you, Sir, to bear awhile this tide of inquiry; some lucky moment may destroy the tie, and snatch her from the brink of ruin that she braves. O my fond credulity, what hast thou betray'd me to?

Capt. Lap. Alas, fair maid, the injury is double, she knew too well the love you bore to Bloomer, and gloried in the captivation. Ungrateful woman! Did I not love her, then I might be happy, but she is twin'd so close about my yielding heart that death alone can shake her off.

Car. Be moderate, Sir; we both may be deceived. Perhaps it's but a sudden sense of giddiness, which your calm admonitions may adjust, and bring her back to him, and calm reflection. More women are influenc'd by little beauties, and the hope of conquest over their admirers, than stirr'd by passions to commit an error.

Capt. Lap. What unequalled tenderness! Alas, fair maid, our lots are mutually unfortunate—might not some stratagem awake her virtue—and his love to you. Suppose this eve at the Ball we assume a more lively air than usual. I'll pay a constant attention to some other lady, and do you encourage the addresses of Etheridge; thus playing off the one against the other, you may recover the inconstant soldier, and I bring back the wandering dove.

Car. With all my heart. But yet how difficult a task to dress a face in smiles, and wear a heavy heart; but to regain the wanton flower, there's not a thing in life I would not do to constitute your felicity and prevent her *shame*.

AIR.—CAROLINE.—*Kate of Aberdeen.*

Should the fond dove a wanton grow,
   And sigh to change her grove;
By sad experience she may know
   The loss of mutual love.

For which she leaves her brooding mate
   And tries the varying scene;
How hard may be her hapless fate,
   What woes may intervene.

If tir'd of constancy and truth,
   The country she explores,
May not her inexperienc'd youth
   Wreck her on Syren shores.

May she not in her varied range,
   Each sad disaster prove:
And wounded grieve the fatal change—
   The loss of mutual love.

[Exeunt.

*Scene opens and discovers a Regimental Mess—*MAJOR APTJONES *at the head of the table—*LOTHIAN *and* VIOLETA, *sitting next the audience, and opposite with other officers, " Chorus as after a song,"—*

   " When ye come to Gibraltar,
     Your notes will soon alter,
       With plenty of claret and bumper, Squire Jones."

Aptjones. Come, here's a pumper to the healths of hur Majesties, and may the trade and arms of Great Britain flourish for ever.

Viol. With all my heart—fill round.   *[Sings.*

   " With claret a bumper, Squire Jones,"

Aptjones. Come, Ensign Etheridge—as hur is a stranger—give hur a toast.

Viol. May he that flinches at a breast-work, fall in the covert-way.

Loth. 'Tis a guid military sentiment, and gives a smack to the liquor.

Maj. Let us have a peauty; 'tis love and wine that makes a soldier's fair as good a scarlet as his coat, for a soldier should look fierce, as well as be fierce.

Viol. True, Major; courage becomes a soldier, but there is no occasion to hang out the sign of the Red Lyon of Brentford. Come give us a Spanish Demi-rep—a Duenna, if you will—for fashion has made an old woman all the mode now. Lothian have you no lass with thick classic legs, that has danced a reel on her linen by the side of some rapid bourne?

Loth. Yas, yas, Maister Etheridge, those are the bonnie things of the North—I'll gave you the Highland Queen.

Viol. [*bursts into laughter.*] What, Mary Queen of Scots?

Enter HALBERT

Hal. I have the Governor's orders to inform the Gentlemen of the Regiment that he will be happy to have their company at the ball.

Ensign Etheridge, your party, Sir, will be ready to review to-morrow morning.

Viol. Very well, Sergeant—I will beat the ground —but I must first reconnoitre the recruits at the Convent.

Major. Sergeant Halbert is an orderly, good man, and does hur duty like a soldier—give hur a glass of wine, and the Sergeant will give us a new song made by a prave fellow of the 24th. Come, Sergeant, sing to hur Regiment.

AIR.—HALBERT.

While the vine's balmy juices my troubles destroy,
  O Bacchus thy bounty dispense,
But ne'er mighty God let the liquor of joy,
  Like Lither deprive me of sense.

When Love's tender passion my bosom alarms,
  Grant, Venus, some beautiful fair !
But O never make me a slave to her charms,
  Nor poison my pleasure with care !

These cordials of Heaven by fools are abus'd,
  And turn'd to the fountains of strife;
'Tis by wise men alone, when rightly they're us'd,
  Love and wine are the blessings of life.

Scene closes on the Company, but VIOLETA *and* HALBERT *advance.*

Viol. Well, Sergeant, what do you think of my party ?

Hal. They are fine fresh lads, Sir, and will drill into smart fellows.

Viol. I believe, Halbert, I shall want a little practice with you, for my experience has not extended further than the bows of a page, and drinking Enazet at the St. James's Coffee House.

Hal. O, Sir, what I have seen of you already, convinces me that you are infinitely superior to the Borough-Election Officers we have daily remitted here.

Viol. Well, I will be punctually at the exercising ground in the morning, and as good a soldier, as mounting guard at the Opera House can make a pretty fellow.   [*Exit.*

DRUMMER *passing the Stage.*

Hal. Halt ! where so fast my little striped Zebra ?

Drum. That's making me no better than an ass, Sergeant.

Hal. But thou'lt allow it to be a fine ass; it is an ass of the Court.

Drum. An ass, is an ass, whether of Court or country. I don't think the reflection less, whether a man's an ass in rags or lace; and therefore, Sergeant, send your ass into Spain; for the Spanish King is fond of their services. [*Going.*

Hal. But why in such a hurry?

Drum. I have business enough, and more than haste and honesty can fulfil.

Hal. You'll advance to-night, I shall be there with the guard; don't you forget to smuggle a bottle with a little good peek to close the orifice of the stomach. Great men, Drum, play into one another's hands: always imitate your superiors.

AIR.—HALBERT.

Who the devil, pray, would be a sergeant,
For to drill and attend on these war gents!
 To turn out their toes,
 Cock their hats, clean their clothes,
And with pockets without the true argent
 Thine's a trade to make the great,
 Pimping in a mode of state.
 'Tis, my boy, the leading star
 Mars, the mighty god of war.
 This, is only now between us;
 How the plague did he get Venus?
 How did he adorn the skull-pan,
 Of the limping Blacksmith Vulcan?
  But by pimping—but by pimping,

[*Exeunt.*

Chorus,

How did he adorn the skull-pan,
Of the limping Blacksmith Vulcan?
But by pimping, but by pimping.

*Scene unfolds and displays a superb garden, with variegated
lamps—A great company of Officers and Ladies—At the upper
end of the Stage two palm trees to be distinguished The sea to
extend beyond the garden, and across the water the coast of
Spain to be observed at a considerable distance—Music to finish,
as after dancing.*

CAROLINE *and* VIOLETA *come forward.*

Car Upon my word, Sir, you are very free and
familiar in your opinion of us and our place; it must
be down-right prejudice, Mr. Etheridge, you can have
no real knowledge of either our modes or our
manners.

Viol. In a moment, my pretty sprig of Spanish
jessamine, I can squint through the manners of a
town; it is my trade, I served as regular an apprenticeship to it, as a lump of a country boy to weigh
sugar and rice in the city.

Car. An apprenticeship; where, Sir?

Viol. At Court.

Car. That is the last place, Mr. Etheridge, to learn
any vicious habits in, it is the Asylum of Innocence
and Conjugal Love.

AIR.—CAROLINE.

Viol. Madam, you're mistaken; the circle is a
magic ring, where I had the honour of being a page,
and where I learnt the language of looks and sighs,
or I had not so soon discovered those little Cupids
dancing in your bright eyes.

Car. Upon my word, you are very plain, very flattering, and very insincere.

Viol. Yes, we have dropp'd all form, and stiffness; ceremony is the worst mark of ill breeding. Paris has taught us better, we come slap dash to the question at once, and carry off a woman, before she has time to reflect.

Car. Any new fashions, Etheridge? you seem to be a fop of the Ton.

Viol. This is the last polonese frock—after Beau Battartly—this is the last smart cock—this the new genteel walking air—we bow thus and ogle thus—and run away with a beauty thus.

[*Takes her round the waist and mixes with the crowd.*

CAPTAIN LAPELLE *is seen to take very particular notice of a lady.* BLOOMER *and* MRS. LAPELLE *come forward.*

Mrs. Lap. Didn't you observe Lapelle's attention of Mrs. Wilmot?

Blo. And didn't you observe Etheridge's addresses to Caroline?

Mrs. Lap. Yes, yes, yes; I see how it is. But I will never suffer or support it.

Blo. Nor I. Damn the coxcomb! I hate a coxcomb: I'll challenge him.

Mrs. Lap. And I will instantly put an end to their flirtation.

Blo. And I'll put an end to him, or myself. Damn the coxcomb!

[*They mix with the crowd.*

Gover. Ladies and gentlemen, make room for the new group of elegant Italian dancers, and then for supper. Music strike up. A grand Ballet finishes.

l   *D*

ACT THE THIRD.

SCFNE.—*The Drill Ground.*

Soldiers with their firelocks, carelessly dispersed. SERGEANT *and* DRUMMER *talking to each other* LOVELACE *comes forward, leaning on his firelock.*

Love. Despair and grief must end my hated life. What have I left for the false, disdainful Violeta? Fortune, friends, and everything that made life pleasing and society endearing. O could my conscience admit a thought of suicide, I would hasten death. But no laws, human or divine, can reconcile self-murder Ah, Violeta, thou yet must reign my sharp tormentor.

AIR.—LOVELACE.

Tho' ruin'd my fortune, my peace, and my fame,
I cannot against her unkindly exclaim,
    And yet wear the willow, the badge of my shame;
    O the green willow, the badge of my shame.

Tho' she scorned my love, yet her name I adore!
And her beauties I'll praise, tho' I ne'er see them more;
    Yet wear the sad willow, and sigh down the shore,
    O wear the green willow, and sigh down the shore.

Ah, maiden, to rend a poor heart with despair,
Whose love and sincerity caus'd all its care,
    And brought the possessor the willow to wear.
    Ah, lack-a-day me, the green willow to wear.

Ah, well may ye blame me thus madly to rove,
And for one that's so false still continue to love,
    And for her wear the willow, whom plaints cannot move,
    The garland of sorrow, which Beauty has wove

HALBERT *and* DRUMMER *coming up to him.*

Hal. What, comrade, still in the dumps? Won't Spanish wine and new beauties enliven thee? Thou'rt a dull mixture for a soldier.

Love. I have had misfortunes, and was trepann'd to 'list by some merciless monsters who ply about Charing Cross to devour the innocent and unwary.

Drum. What! you were not fairly beat up—the volunteer to a sheep's skin. It is a shame in a free country that such kidnappers should be suffered, or that the Savoy should receive the bones of an honest fellow.

Hal. Come, come, my brave boy, we shall soon get rid of these qualms for you, and make you as light and gay as a grenadier's feather. It is well those kidnapping alligators didn't strip you for the East Indies, where you had not been a champ for a crocodile. Here's Drummer will show you what life is, and how a gentleman soldier makes sixpence go farther than a vulgar fellow can half-a-crown.

Drum. Showing will not signify anything, unless you can get a little priming into him. Wet powder won't go off.

Hal. I like the looks of the lad—and so I'll teach him his exercise myself, and the joys of the army.

AIR.—HALBERT.

Do poets record
A dull tradesman, or lord?
   They're not worth the dip of their pen:
'Tis the soldier of glory
That's famed in story,
   For they are the heroes of men, brave boys

They're the pride of each wench,
And the fear of the French,
   The dread of all Old England's foes:

They have no cares to vex,
  No bad debts to perplex,
    The King finds them money and clothes, brave boys.

Drum. Now for tossing the brown musket; here comes our officer.

Hal. Order, there—fall back—stand to your arms.   [*The party form a line.*

Drum. Now for my rub-ba-dub—(*takes and slings his drum*)—how sounds may be produced! The skin of the sheep which makes this music—(*striking the drum*)—when alive, only cried ba; and though the most harmless animal of the creation, yet when manufactured into parchment, supplies lawyers with deeds and armies with drums, the certain instruments of fraud and murder.

Enter VIOLETA *and* JESSE *with the spontoon.*

Viol. Well, Sergeant, are we are all here, and sober——   [*Takes the spontoon.*

Hal. Yes, your honour, perfectly sober.

Viol. Come, Halbert, give me a few hints. [*Aside.*

Hal. Remember, Sir, to take long strides, and every now and then look round with an air of contempt. Stick your spontoon in the ground, shake your head, and with a loud voice command silence.

Viol. Silence, I say.

Hal. Now give your spontoon to your boy, take snuff affectedly, flourish your cane, swear as you please, and these are as many qualities as a gentleman requires to make a tolerable soldier.

Viol. Is that an attitude for a soldier, sirrah? (*To a second*)—Who cock'd your hat, dog? (*To another.*) I'll teach you to wear such a stock, villain. (*To another*)—How came you into the field, scoundrel, with a dirty shirt? Do you think his Majesty allows you the luxury of sixpence a-day to stuff vulgar meat and drink? (*To* LOVELACE)— What a boor of a clown have we here—carry your firelock thus—and your head thus—or I'll knock it off your shoulders, monster.

Love. Oh, my unlucky stars, what a coxcomb's here.

Hal. A major of twenty years' standing could not have done better.

Jesse. What a spirit she has. Were she known in the City, she would puzzle the brokers more about the quality of her sex than the most artful chevalier of the kingdom of France. Now for't.

Hal. Now, Sir, for the word of command.

Viol. What shall I do for the words. (*Aside to* HALBERT.)

Hal O, Sir, an officer wants no words—only speak as if your mouth was full of pudding—they'll know the motion by the drill corporal.

Viol. If you don't mind the word given, I'll knock you down, scoundrel.

Hal. O, that passion is very graceful, Sir, and the true quality of a martinet.

Viol Ready—bo—boo. Scoundrels, rascals, mongrel dogs. (*strikes* LOVELACE.) I'll have the villain tied to the halbert directly.

Love. My soul's above a blow. Rascal as thou art, have at thy life

> [*attempts to stab* VIOLETA *with his bayonet. The* SERGEANT *knocks the piece out of his hand, and seizes him.*

Hal. This is mutiny. The court-martial's sitting, drag him to the court. Thou wilt be shot immediately.

Love. I don't care how soon, for I am sick of life.

Jesse. Oh, ye gods, what an escape was this.

Viol. Away with the bloody-minded villain; I'll see him executed.

Love. Were I at liberty, I would first execute thee.

Jesse. Pray secure the wretch, that he don't get loose!

Hal. Corporal, march in front, and two in the rear. If he attempts to break from you, kill him dead.

Drum. Shall I beat the funeral?

Hal. March.

[*Exeunt all but* JESSE *and* VIOLETA.

Jesse. O dearest lady, what risks do you run? I am all in a tremor. What could inspire you with such intrepidity? or what could provoke you to venture such a danger?

Viol. Revenge for the loss of my unhappy Lovelace, and for his injuries. I'll persecute all the sex, lose my own life, or find the hapless wanderer.

Jesse. O, for the sake of pity, drop these violent resolutions; throw yourself at the Governor's feet, declare yourself a woman, and solicit his protection.

Viol. No, no, I'll have the rank of colonel first, and show the ———— breed of soldiers that the softer sex is not so soft as them. I'll have a regiment, and make thee a captain. Thou wilt not discredit thy colours, wench?

Jesse. I declare, Madam, your spirit gives me courage.

Air.—Jesse.—Daniel Cooper.

No wonder girls in country towns
 With soldiers gay are smitten ;
No wonder, too, that country clowns
 By them so oft are bitten.
  The smart cockade,
  The gay parade,
May well allure the farmer,
  'Twill lead him on,
  To sword and gun,
And make him quit his charmer.

Who can resist the scarlet coat,
 Or turn on sons of glory?
'Twas Paris the fair Helen brought
 To Troy, as told in story.
  From that to this,
  Each blooming miss,
Hath help'd the hero's duty :
  And sons of arms
  Have own'd our charms,
The pow'r of love and beauty.

Enter Bloomer

Blo. So, Etheridge, you have been out with your party. I am weary with the business of last night. It was a cursed bore.

Viol. It did not appear so ; or it is an ill compliment to Mrs. Lapelle.

Blo. A very dull bore indeed. But one must sacrifice to the whims of a fine woman. You danced with Caroline, I think?

Viol. I had that honour, Sir.

Blo. Yes, she is a pleasing girl

Viol. A most accomplished woman.

Blo. I am glad our sentiments cotton together. Do you like Caroline Etheridge?

Viol. Yes, she has it about her that will capti-vate.

Blo. O yes, she has it about her; the girl's well enough.

Viol. Yes, in general ; they make 'em so now.

Blo. Do you think of her further than a flirt or two ?

Viol. That depends upon her attentions—and my virtue.

Blo. I thought you were sweet upon her; she is a pretty pouter.

Viol. I flattered her a little—and you flattered Lapelle not a little.

Blo. A gentleman's under an obligation of atten-tion to these neglected wives !

Viol. Neglected wives ! Come, come, Mr. Bloomer, I must throw aside the mask, and assure you that no lady in the land is so little neglected as Mrs. Lapelle, who possesses a husband one of the first ornaments of the army and society ; nor does your particular attentions, Sir, to that lady become your situation or her character. Husbands, Mr. Bloomer, are too often so critically situated, that they cannot take up these matters properly ; so you must desist, Sir, in your bows and attentions to her, or I shall inform him who will add your bones to the petrifactions at Europa Point.

Blo. What the devil's the matter with you now ? you're as full of fire as the electrical eel.

Viol. I am, Sir ; and will touch the torpid spark of your disposition, or any man's disposition, who dare to invade the peace and felicity of a worthy family. I am going to attend the court-martial, and then, Sir, I shall send Captain Lapelle to attend you.

AIR.—VIOLETA.

Would wives consult their dignity and fame,
The price of honour and a virtuous name,
They'd never sacrifice to fools,
And throw themselves away;
But follow virtue's hallow'd rules,
Nor let such meteors lead astray

[*Exit* VIOLETA.

Blo. Gunpowder! I must mind the manœuvres of this youth, or he'll rescue Lapelle, and walk off with Caroline. Here, you fellow, your master's servant Where the devil does your master come from? where was he born? for he's the hottest spark——

Jesse. Yes, Sir, he is of a very hot quality. I very often feel the fever of his fury. His mother was a very passionate woman, Sir; and his father a very tiger

Blo. O, I find, then, he has it on both sides. I can tell you one thing, boy, and if you regard him you may tell him also, that if he does not lower his rail a little, he will be whipp'd through the lungs as sure as he is alive.

Jesse. That will not be an easy matter, Sir, for he is a special swordsman, and is supposed to thrust better than any man in the county of Galway.

[*Puts herself in a fencing attitude.*

Blo. Galway! and I suppose a member of Lucas's. Coventry must be his residence, and soliloquies his amusement.

AIR —BLOOMER

There's not a place around the world,
Where fate or chance hath soldiers hurl'd,
At once to cool, to tame, and settle,
The boiling blood in sparks of mettle,
Like a trip to Coventry

l   *D*

Though masters, books, and moral rules,
The lash and lumber of the schools,
May fail—yet still we oft discover
Amendment in the Buck and Lover
        By a trip to Coventry.

SCENE.—*A room.*

MR. *and* MRS. LAPELLE.

Mr. Lap. I am determined, Mrs. Lapelle, to move you from this place. The career you are driving with this young fop is a dishonour to your age, your character, and fame.

Mrs. Lap. Age, Sir?

Mr. Lap. Yes, age, Madam! Your native bloom, by the hand of time, is swept from your pallid cheek, which you have supplied with art. I blush to mention this, Madam; but fashion has establish'd this disgraceful custom, which, tho' it once discredited the courtesan, is adopted by the married ladies. O fie, fie, to hang out false colours, like a common syren, to allure an unworthy character.

Mrs. Lap. This, Sir, is a rudeness I am unused to, and which I will not bear.

Mr. Lap. This you shall bear, Madam, nay, and ten times more, unless you will alter this eccentric conduct. The honour of my house, Madam, is equal to the honour of my character. Nor shall either be sullied while I've a hand to defend one and a mind to support the other.

Mrs. Lap. You have, indeed, Sir, thrown yourself into a violent rage, and for what I am at a loss to explain.

Mr. Lap. Madam, I will not be trifled with. I have seen enough to convince me that a looseness of your behaviour has discredited me, and drawn the reflection of the world upon you.

Mrs. Lap. The world! I despise the world—the bugbear you always introduce to awe me. I have done nothing, Sir, that can reflect dishonour. I feel my innocence; and I defy the public calumny—the world

Mr. Lap. Without the countenance of the world you so contemptuously despise, a situation in society, Madam, is narrow and irksome. Remember, madam, the pains I took to raise you to a situation and the world's opinion; and will you, Mrs Lapelle, in a few days destroy and ruin what I have laboured for years to accomplish? Is this your gratitude?

Mrs. Lap. My gratitude, never; but as my intentions are innocent in regard to Mr. Bloomer, (and perfectly arising from a platonic friendship,) there is nothing you can do, Sir, shall make me alter my opinion or my behaviour.

Mr. Lap Platonic friendship!—platonic nonsense!—the idle romantic frenzy of a false philosopher, who, to prove his ability, has aimed at reconciling all the absurd contradictions of nature. The system, Madam, may do in the leaf of life, but not with youth and beauty—'tis incompatible and unnatural.

Mrs. Lap. Heavens! what a man, to attempt to designate the fame of the inimitable Eloisa. Sir, the friend of that school you so condemn, is what I have ever wished to find in life.

Mr. Lap. That friend you have in me without that school.

Mrs. Lap. No, Sir; the friendships are distinct; to you I owe in duty, love; but sure I may have a pure and virtuous friendship for another, without abating my affections for you.

Mr. Lap. This, Madam, is trifling with me. To prove the strength of this friendship, see, see Mrs. Lapelle, your own letter.

Mrs. Lap. (*Falls on her knees.*) O, I confess my error. O pardon and forgive me; with the humblest contrition, I now beseech it.

Mr. Lap. Rise, dear lady; there is not a favour you can ask, I can refuse. Be this the future beacon to your conduct, and now avoid the coast you were so nearly wreck'd on.

Mrs. Lap. O exemplary goodness! Never from this moment will I sport with the affections of him to whom I owe every blessing and honour: forgive me, dear Lapelle.

Mr. Lap. I do. Dry those tears, which I have made to flow, and which I hope may never stream again.

AIR—MRS. LAPELLE.

Would ye, ye wives, this lesson prove,
Ye ne'er would sink in shame.
Make pride, the sentinel of love,
And guardian of your fame.

The pride of every female breast,
Should be reproach to shun
She that is pure in mind, is blest!
If false, she is undone.

[*Exeunt.*

Scene changes to the Street before the Court-Martial Room.

Enter HALBERT, DRUMMER, LOVELACE *as a prisoner. Guard, etc.*

Hal. I never felt my heart relax for a comrade before, when he had committed a capital offence.

but there is something about thee, that moves the hardness of my disposition, because I fear there is no hope of serving thee, thine is the most capital crime in the army.

Love. Your concern for me betrays the humanity of thine heart I thank you for your affection, but death is more to me than life.

Drum. It would be a long time before I would persuade myself to think so: but I fear there is no more chance for thee, than the head of my drum against the point of a sharp knife. Mutiny to an officer is a deadly stroke. I remember I received four hundred lashes once for a sort of a speech I made on a march once

Hal. How so, Drummer?

Drum. We were padding the hoof, all over dirt, and sweat, at the retreat of St. Cas, where a good pair of heels was of vast service to a man: so says a comrade to me, seeing the officers ride, let's pull them off their horses; zounds, shall they ride and we walk? Be quiet, replies I; if they don't ride horses they'll ride us. Egad, as soon as we had escaped the bayonet they tickled my back, with the hands of two brother chums. Four hundred; and laid it in as close as wax.

Love. Thou'rt a cheerful, happy lad, and may prosper. I am pleased with my condition; nor do I repine at the expected fate.

AIR —LOVELACE.

The world hath lost its charms for me;
Beauty and truth's no more
My mirth is chang'd for misery,
She's false whom I adore.

l *)*

> Angels are not more fair above,
>   In each exterior part:
> But angels are more true in love,
>   And wear a purer heart.

Drum. Zounds, my brave fellow, don't let the idea of a bullet kill thee before thou'rt shot. If the breath of life is so irksome, the sooner it's let out the better. Come, come, I hate to see a fine fellow chap-fallen—bear up my buck, there's good sound in thee yet.

DRUMMER —AIR —*There was a Mouse liv'd in a Mill*

(Kettle-drum and two flutes)

> We've bright blue eyes about the town,
>   Whose rigdum will decoy ye
> And buxom damsels fair and brown,
>   With a rigdum, bonny blue, decoy me.
> Decoy me, Mary, decoy me, Jenny, decoy me, Sarah, decoy me.
> Humstrum, shittle-dum, rum-dum, beauty, decoy me.

[*Exeunt.*

Scene opens and discovers a Regimental Court-Martial—JUDGE-ADVOCATE, CLERK, MAJOR APTJONES, LOTHIAN, BLOOMER, *and other officers*

Loth. Come, Mr. Judge, let us proceed to business.

Clerk. Gentlemen of the Court—by virtue of a warrant signed by His Excellency the Governor, you are to inform yourselves of all complaints and misdemeanours that may be brought before ye—and upon evidence and confession of the criminal party, you are to proceed in judgment according to the established Articles of War and the custom of the army. Being sworn, gentlemen, you may open the Court.

Maj. Well; let hur call in the parties.

l   D

Judge. Call in the prisoner and the witnesses against him.

Enter Lovelace, Violeta, Jesse, Halbert, *and* Drummer

Judge. (*to* Violeta.) Stand where you are, Sir—what have you to advance against the prisoner?

Viol. I was exercising my party early in the morning, and this recruit being more awkward than the rest, I corrected him for it, when he called me rascal, and endeavoured to stab me with his bayonet, which he certainly had effected, but the Sergeant prevented.

Hal It is certainly true as my officer reports.

Loth. Such a bloody dug should have been cut to mince collops on the spot.

Maj. Hur is a clouded knave—nor has the fear of Cot before hur eyes—hur shall be advanced to a gibbet.

Blo. Yes; he should hang in the wind to cool his fiery spirit.

Drum. (*to* Lovelace) Ah, comrade, I thought that you would be no more in their hands than a drumstick in mine.

Love. Gentlemen, I know your power, and submit to my sentence: life has been long a burthen to me, I had rather paid the debt in the field—but I die contented. A blow is what I never received before, and which my pride will never suffer me to bear.

Blo. 'Tis an insolent dog to resent a stroke from an officer. I always think I do a fellow an honour when I cane him.

Love. But, permit me to inform this honourable court before I die, that I am a gentleman of the County of York, but being cruelly treated by the woman I adored, I sought the battle to relieve my woes—and as a soldier left my country—now lead me to my fate. Ah, ungrateful Violeta.

[*Turning as to go off.*

Viol. O, save me, Heaven!

[*Faints in* HALBERT'S *arms,* JESSIE *rushes to her.*

Blo. What, does our fighting spark faint at the name of death?

Jes. O help, help! O save my mistress.

Love. Mistress!

Viol. [*recovering.*] Hold—hold—hold! Ah, injured Lovelace—wretched Violeta.

Love. Ah ye protecting powers, I know that tuneful voice. She lives, she lives—the dear deluded Violeta

Blo. 'Tis a woman, egad I must make a pretty figure here to have set my wits to a woman.

Loth. Warriors: if women begin to turn soldiers, and only lady-like officers got promotion—'tis time I was home in quarters for life.

FINALE.

MRS LAPELLE

It should be the study of mistress and wife,
To smooth by her smiles the rough journey of life
For happiness truly the fair must attend,
Who makes virtue her guide, and her husband her friend.

LOVELACE.

All heroes of arms since the day of old Troy
Have been scratch'd more or less with the dart of the boy,
It is beauty the standard that bears to the field,
And to beauty alone 'tis that Englishmen yield

Caroline

The fop may reform and the rake may repent,
For vice when corrected, brings pleasing content ,
And ev'ry Virgin so vain of her charms
That thinks the Reformation's confin'd to her arms.

Violeta.

The spirit I've shown, I hope will inspire,
Our lady-like soldiers with courage and fire :
He cannot wear scarlet, or fight with the French,
Who won't surpass me for the love of his wench.

Halbert and Chorus

'Tis valour's the star, irradiates on earth,
Not titles and things, the mere fungus of birth.
By courage our fathers defended this Isle,
Nor her sons will retreat while her daughters will smile.

Chorus

'Tis valour, &c

THE PAWNBROKER'S DAUGHTER.

A FARCE.

BY C. LAMB, ESQ.[1]

CHARACTERS.

FLINT, *a Pawnbroker*	BEN, CUTLET's *Boy.*
DAVENPORT, *in love with* MARIAN	
PENDULOUS, *a Reprieved Gentleman.*	MISS FLYN
CUTLET, *a Sentimental Butcher*	BETTY, *her Maid*
GOLDING, *a Magistrate*	MARIAN, *Daughter to* FLINT
WILLIAM, *Apprentice to* FLINT.	LUCY, *her Maid.*

ACT I.

SCENE I.—*An Apartment at* FLINT's *house.*

FLINT.   WILLIAM.

Flint. Carry those umbrellas, cottons, and wearing-apparel, up stairs. You may send that chest of tools to Robins's.

Wil. That which you lent six pounds upon to the journeyman carpenter that had the sick wife?

Flint. The same.

Wil. The man says, if you can give him till Thursday——

---

1 From *Blackwood's Magazine* for 1830. It was never acted. The text in *Eliana* is not very faithful.

Flint. Not a minute longer. His time was out yesterday. These improvident fools !

Wil. The finical gentleman has been here about the seal that was his grandfather's.

Flint. He cannot have it. Truly our trade will be brought to a fine pass if we were bound to humour the fancies of our customers. This man would be taking a liking to a snuff box that he had inherited : and that gentlewoman might conceit a favourite chemise that had descended to her.

Wil The lady in the carriage has been here crying about those jewels. She says, if you cannot let her have them at the advance she offers, her husband will come to know that she has pledged them.

Flint. I have uses for those jewels. Send Marian to me. (*Exit* WILLIAM.) I know no other trade that is expected to depart from its fair advantages but ours. I do not see the baker, the butcher, the shoemaker or, to go higher, the lawyer, the physician, the divine give up any of their legitimate gains, even when the pretences of their art had failed , yet *we* are to be branded with an odious name, stigmatized discountenanced even by the administrators of those laws which acknowledge us ; scowled at by the lower sort of people, whose needs we serve !

Enter MARIAN.

Come hither, Marian. Come, kiss your father. The report runs that he is full of spotted crime. What is your belief, child ?

Mar. That never good report went with our calling, father. I have heard you say, the poor look only to the advantages which we derive from them.

and overlook the accommodations which they receive
from us. But the poor *are* the poor, father, and have
little leisure to make distinctions. I wish we could
give up this business.

Flint. You have not seen that idle fellow, Davenport?

Mar. No, indeed, father, since your injunction.

Flint. I take but my lawful profit. The law is
not over-favourable to us.

Mar. Marian is no judge of these things

Flint. They call me oppressive, grinding, — I
know not what——

Mar. Alas!

Flint Usurer, extortioner. Am I these things?

Mar. You are Marian's kind and careful father
That is enough for a child to know.

Flint. Here, girl, is a little box of jewels, which
the necessities of a foolish woman of quality have
transferred into our true and lawful possession. Go,
place them with the trinkets that were your mother's.
They are all yours, Marian, if you do not cross me in
your marriage. No gentry shall match into this
house, to flout their wife hereafter with her parentage.
I will hold this business with convulsive grasp to my
dying day. I will plague these *poor*, whom you speak
so tenderly of

Mar. You frighten me, father. Do not frighten
Marian.

Flint. I have heard them say, There goes Flint—
Flint, the cruel pawnbroker!

Mar. Stay at home with Marian. You shall hear
no ugly words to vex you.

Flint. You shall ride in a gilded chariot upon the
necks of these *poor*, Marian. Their tears shall drop

pearls for my girl Their sighs shall be good wind for us. They shall blow good for my girl. Put up the jewels, Marian. [*Exit.*

Enter LUCY.

Lucy. Miss, miss, your father has taken his hat, and is stept out, and Mr. Davenport is on the stairs; and I came to tell you——

Mar. Alas! who let him in?

Enter DAVENPORT.

Dav. My dearest girl——

Mar. My father will kill me if he finds you have been here.

Dav. There is no time for explanations. I have positive information that your father means, in less than a week, to dispose of you to that ugly Saunders. The wretch has bragged of it to his acquaintance, and already calls you *his.*

Mar. O heavens!

Dav. Your resolution must be summary, as the time which calls for it. Mine or his you must be without delay. There is no safety for you under this roof.

Mar. My father——

Dav. Is no father, if he would sacrifice you.

Mar. But he is unhappy. Do not speak hard words of my father

Dav. Marian must exert her good sense.

Lucy (*as if watching at the window*) O miss, your father has suddenly returned. I see him with Mr. Saunders, coming down the street. Mr Saunders, ma'am !

Mar. Begone, begone, if you love me, Davenport.

P 2

Dav. You must go with me then, else here I am fixed

Lucy. Ay, miss, you must go, as Mr. Davenport says. Here is your cloak, miss, and your hat, and your gloves. Your father, ma'am——

Mar. O, where, where? Whither do you hurry me, Davenport?

Dav. Quickly, quickly, Marian. At the back door. [*Exit* MARIAN, *with* DAVENPORT, *reluctantly : in her flight still holding the jewels.*

Lucy. Away—away. What a lucky thought of mine to say her father was coming! he would never have got her off else. Lord, Lord, I do love to help lovers. [*Exit, following them.*

SCENE II.—*A Butcher's Shop.*

CUTLET. BEN.

Cut. Reach me down that book off the shelf, where the shoulder of veal hangs.

Ben. Is this it?

Cut. No—this is "Flowers of sentiment"—the other—ay, this is a good book: "An Argument against the Use of Animal Food. By J. R." *That* means Joseph Ritson. I will open it anywhere, and read just as it happens. One cannot dip amiss in such books as these. The motto, I see, is from Pope. I dare say, very much to the purpose. (*Reads.*)

" The lamb thy riot dooms to bleed to-day,
    Had he thy reason, would he skip and play?
    Pleas'd to the last, he crops his flowery food,
    And licks the hand——"

Bless us, is that saddle of mutton gone home to Mrs. Simpson's? It should have gone an hour ago.

Ben. I was just going with it.

Cut. Well go. Where was I ? Oh !

"And licks the hand just raised to shed his blood."

What an affecting picture ! [*turns over the leaves, and reads.*] " It is probable that the long lives which are recorded of the people before the flood were owing to their being confined to a vegetable diet."

Ben. The young gentleman in Pullen's Row, Islington, that has got the consumption, has sent to know if you can let him have a sweetbread.

Cut. Take two,—take all that are in the shop. What a disagreeable interruption ! [*reads again.*] " Those fierce and angry passions, which impel man to wage destructive war with man, may be traced to the ferment in the blood produced by an animal diet."

Ben. The two pound of rump steaks must go home to Mr. Molyneux's He is in training to fight Cribb

Cut. Well, take them ; go along, and do not trouble me with your disgusting details. [*Exit Ben.*

Cut. [*Throwing down the book.*] Why was I bred to this detestable business ? Was it not plain, that this trembling sensibility, which has marked my character from earliest infancy, must for ever disqualify me for a profession which——what do you want ? what do you buy ? O, it is only somebody going past. I thought it had been a customer.—Why was not I bred a glover, like my cousin Langston ? to see him poke his two little sticks into a delicate pair of real Woodstock——" A very little stretching, ma'am, and they will fit exactly"——Or a haberdasher, like my next-door neighbour—" not a better bit of lace in all town, my lady—Mrs Breakstock took the last of it last Friday, all but this bit, which I can afford to let your ladyship have a bargain— reach down that drawer on your left hand, Miss Fisher."

Enter in haste, Davenport, Marian, *and* Lucy.

Lucy. This is the house I saw a bill up at, ma'am; and a droll creature the landlord is.

Dav. We have no time for nicety.

Cut. What do ye want? what do ye buy? O, it is only you, Mrs. Lucy. [Lucy *whispers* Cutlet.] I have a set of apartments at the end of my garden. They are quite detached from the shop. A single lady at present occupies the ground floor.

Mar. Ay, ay, anywhere.

Dav. In, in.——

Cut. Pretty lamb,—she seems agitated.

[Davenport *and* Marian *go in with* Cutlet.

Lucy. I am mistaken if my young lady does not find an agreeable companion in these apartments. Almost a namesake   Only the difference of Flyn and Flint. I have some errands to do, or I would stop and have some fun with this droll butcher.

Cutlet *returns.*

Cut. Why, how odd this is ! *Your* young lady knows *my* young lady. They are as thick as flies.

Lucy. You may thank me for your new lodger, Mr. Cutlet.—But bless me, you do not look well !

Cut. To tell you the truth, I am rather heavy about the eyes. Want of sleep, I believe.

Lucy. Late hours, perhaps. Raking last night.

Cut. No, that is not it, Mrs. Lucy. My repose was disturbed by a very different cause from what you may imagine. It proceeded from too much thinking.

Lucy. The deuce it did ! And what, if I may be so bold, might be the subject of your Night Thoughts ?

Cut. The distresses of my fellow creatures I never lay my head down on my pillow but I fall a thinking how many at this very instant are perishing ; some with cold——

Lucy. What, in the midst of Summer ?

Cut Ay. Not here, but in countries abroad, where the climate is different from ours. Our Summers are their Winters, and *vice versâ*, you know Some with cold——

Lucy What a canting rogue it is ! I should like to trump up some fine story to plague him. [*Aside.*

Cut. Others with hunger—some a prey to the rage of wild beasts——

Lucy. He has got this by rote, out of some book.

Cut. Some drowning, crossing crazy bridges in the dark—some by the violence of the devouring flame——

Lucy. I have it.—For that matter, you need not send your humanity a travelling, Mr. Cutlet. For instance, last night——

Cut Some by fevers, some by gun-shot wounds—

Lucy. Only two streets off——

Cut Some in drunken quarrels——

Lucy. [*Aloud.*] The butcher's shop at the corner

Cut. What were you saying about poor Cleaver ?

Lucy He has found his ears at last. [*Aside*] That he has had his house burnt down.

Cut. Bless me !

Lucy. I saw four small children taken in at the greengrocer's.

Cut. Do you know if he is insured ?

Lucy. Some say he is, but not to the full amount.

l   *P*

Cut. Not to the full amount—how shocking! He killed more meat than any of the trade between here and Carnaby market. And the poor babes—four of them you say—what a melting sight! He served some good customers about Marybone. I always think more of the children in these cases than of the fathers and mothers. Lady Lovebrown liked his veal better than any man's in the market I wonder whether her ladyship is engaged. I must go and comfort poor Cleaver, however.   [*Exit.*

Lucy. Now is this pretender to humanity gone to avail himself of a neighbour's supposed ruin to inveigle his customers from him. Fine feelings!—pshaw!   [*Exit.*

Re-enter CUTLET.

Cut. What a deceitful young hussy! there is not a word of truth in her There has been no fire. How can people play with one's feelings so!—[*sings*] —"For tenderness formed"—No, I'll try the air I made upon myself. The words may compose me. —[*sings.*]

A weeping Londoner I am,
A washer-woman was my dam,
She bred me up in a cock-loft,
And fed my mind with sorrows soft.

For when she wrung with elbows stout
From linen wet the water out,—
The drops so like to tears did drip,
They gave my infant nerves the hyp.

Scarce three clean muckingers a week
Would dry the brine that dew'd my cheek.
So, while I gave my sorrows scope,
I almost ruin'd her in soap.

My parish learning I did win
In ward of Farringdon-Within;
Where, after school, I did pursue
My sports, as little boys will do.

Cockchafers—none like me was found
To set them spinning round and round.
O, how my tender heart would melt,
To think what those poor varmin felt!

I never tied tin-kettle, clog,
Or salt-box to the tail of dog,
Without a pang more keen at heart,
Than he felt at his outward part.

And when the poor thing clattered off,
To all the unfeeling mob a scoff,
Thought I, "What that dumb creature feels,
With half the parish at his heels!"

Arrived, you see, to man's estate,
The butcher's calling is my fate,
Yet still I keep my feeling ways,
And leave the town on slaughtering days.

At Kentish Town, or Highgate Hill,
I sit, retired, beside some rill;
And tears bedew my glistening eye,
To think my playful lambs must die!

But when they're dead I sell their meat,
On shambles kept both clean and neat;
Sweet-breads also I guard full well,
And keep them from the blue-bottle

Envy, with breath, sharp as my steel,
Has ne'er yet blown upon my veal,
And mouths of dames, and daintiest fops,
Do water at my nice lamb-chops.

        [Exit, half-laughing, half-crying

L   D

SCENE, *a Street.*'

DAVENPORT, *solus.*

Dav. Thus far have I secured my charming prize. I can appreciate, while I lament, the delicacy which makes her refuse the protection of my sister's roof But who comes here?

Enter PENDULOUS, *agitated.*

It must be he. That fretful animal motion—that face working up and down with uneasy sensibility, like new yeast. Jack—Jack Pendulous!

Pen. It is your old friend, and very miserable.

Dav. Vapours, Jack. I have not known you fifteen years to have to guess at your complaint. Why, they troubled you at school. Do you remember when you had to speak the speech of Buckingham, where he is going to execution?

Pen. Execution!—he has certainly heard it.

(*Aside.*)

Dav. What a pucker you were in overnight!

Pen. May be so, may be so, Mr. Davenport. That was an imaginary scene. I have had real troubles since.

Dav. Pshaw! so you call every common accident.

Pen. Do you call my case so common, then?

Dav. What case?

Pen. You have not heard, then?

Dav. Positively not a word.

Pen. You must know I have been—(*whispers*)—tried for a felony since then.

Dav. Nonsense!

Pen. No subject for mirth, Mr. Davenport. A confounded short-sighted fellow swore that I stopped him, and robbed him, on the York race-ground at nine on a fine moonlight evening, when I was two hundred miles off in Dorsetshire. These hands have been held up at a common bar.

Dav. Ridiculous ! it could not have gone so far

Pen A great deal farther, I assure you, Mr. Davenport. I am ashamed to say how far it went. You must know, that in the first shock and surprise of the accusation, shame—you know I was always susceptible—shame put me upon disguising my *name*, that, at all events, it might bring no disgrace upon my family. I called myself *James Thomson.*

Dav. For heaven's sake, compose yourself.

Pen. I will. An old family ours, Mr. Davenport —never had a blot upon it till now—a family famous for the jealousy of its honour for many generations— think of that, Mr Davenport—that felt a stain like a wound.

Dav. Be calm, my dear friend.

Pen This served the purpose of a temporary concealment well enough ; but when it came to the— *alibi*—I think they call it—excuse these technical terms, they are hardly fit for the mouth of a gentleman, the *witnesses*—that is another term—that I had sent for up from Melcombe Regis, and relied upon for clearing up my character, by disclosing my real name, *John Pendulous*—so discredited the cause which they came to serve, that it had quite a contrary effect to what was intended. In short, the usual forms passed, and you behold me here the miserablest of mankind.

Dav. (*aside.*) He must be light-headed.

Pen. Not at all, Mr. Davenport. I hear what you

say, though you speak it all on one side, as they do at the playhouse.

Dav. The sentence could never have been carried into—pshaw!—you are joking—the truth must have come out at last

Pen. So it did, Mr. Davenport—just two minutes and a second too late by the Sheriff's stop-watch. Time enough to save my life—my wretched life—but an age too late for my honour. Pray change the subject—the detail must be as offensive to you.

Dav. With all my heart, to a more pleasing theme The lovely Maria Flyn—are you friends in that quarter, still? Have the old folks relented?

Pen They are dead, and have left her mistress of her inclinations. But it requires great strength of mind to ——

Dav. To what?

Pen. To stand up against the sneers of the world. It is not every young lady that feels herself confident against the shafts of ridicule, though aimed by the hand of prejudice. Not but in her heart, I believe, she prefers me to all mankind. But think what the world would say, if, in defiance of the opinions of mankind, she should take to her arms a reprieved man!

Dav. Whims! You might turn the laugh of the world upon itself in a fortnight. These things are but nine days' wonders.

Pen. Do you think so, Mr. Davenport?

Dav. Where does she live?

Pen. She has lodgings in the next street, in a sort of garden-house, that belongs to one Cutlet. I have not seen her since the affair. I was going there at her request.

Dav. Ha, ha, ha!

Pen. Why do you laugh?

Dav. The oddest fellow! I will tell you—— But here he comes.

Enter CUTLET.

Cut. (*to Davenport.*) Sir, the young lady at my house is desirous you should return immediately. She has heard something from home.

Pen. What do I hear?

Dav. 'Tis her fears, I dare say My dear Pendulous, you will excuse me?—I must not tell him our situation at present, though it cost him a fit of jealousy. We shall have fifty opportunities for explanation

[*Exit.*

Pen Does that gentleman visit the lady at your lodgings?

Cut. He is quite familiar there, I assure you He is all in all with her, as they say.

Pen It is but too plain. Fool that I have been, not to suspect that, while she pretended scruples, some rival was at the root of her infidelity?

Cut. You seem distressed. Sir? Bless me!

Pen. I am, friend, above the reach of comfort.

Cut. Consolation, then, can be to no purpose?

Pen None.

Cut. I am so happy to have met with him!

Pen. Wretch, wretch, wretch!

Cut. There he goes! How he walks about biting his nails! I would not exchange this luxury of unavailing pity for worlds.

Pen. Stigmatised by the world——

Cut. My case exactly. Let us compare notes.

Pen For an accident which——

Cut. For a profession which——

Pen. In the eye of reason has nothing in it——

Cut. Absolutely nothing in it——

Pen. Brought up at a public bar——

Cut   Brought up to an odious trade——

Pen. With nerves like mine——

Cut. With nerves like mine——

Pen. Arraigned, condemned——

Cut   By a foolish world——

Pen. By a judge and jury——

Cut. By an invidious exclusion disqualified for sitting on a jury at all——

Pen. Tried, cast, and——

Cut. What ?

Pen   HANGED, Sir, HANGED by the neck, till I was——

Cut. Bless me !

Pen   Why should not I publish it to the whole world, since she, whose prejudice alone I wished to overcome, deserts me ?

Cut. Lord have mercy upon us ! not so bad as that comes to, I hope ?

Pen. When she joins in the judgment of an illiberal world against me——

Cut. You said HANGED, Sir—that is, I mean, perhaps I mistook you. How ghastly he looks !

Pen   Fear me not, my friend. I am no ghost—though I heartily wish I were one.

Cut. Why, then, ten to one, you were——

Pen. *Cut down.* The odious word shall out, though it choke me.

Cut. Your case must have some things in it very curious. I dare say you kept a journal of your sensations.

Pen. Sensations !

Cut. Ay, while you were being—you know what I mean. They say persons in your situation have lights dancing before their eyes—blueish. But then the worst of all is coming to one's self again.

Pen. Plagues, furies, tormentors! I shall go mad! [*Exit.*

Cut. There, he says he shall go mad. Well, my head has not been very right of late. It goes with a whirl and a buz somehow I believe I must not think so deeply. Common people that don't reason know nothing of these aberrations.

> Great wits go mad, and small ones only dull;
> Distracting cares vex not the empty skull
> They seize on heads that think, and hearts that feel,
> As flies attack the better sort of veal.

[*Exit.*

ACT II.

___

SCENE, *at* FLINT'S.
FLINT WILLIAM.

Flint. I have over-walked myself, and am quite exhausted. Tell Marian to come and play to me.

Wil. I will, Sir. [*Exit.*

Flint. I have been troubled with an evil spirit of late; I think an evil spirit. It goes and comes, as my daughter is with or from me. It cannot stand before her gentle look, when, to please her father, she takes down her music-book.

Enter WILLIAM.

Wil. Miss Marian went out soon after you, and is not returned

Flint. That is a pity—That is a pity. Where can the foolish girl be gadding?

Wil. The shopmen say she went out with Mr. Davenport.

Flint. Davenport? Impossible.

Wil. They say they are sure it was he, by the same token that they saw her slip into his hand, when she was past the door, the casket which you gave her.

Flint. Gave her, William? I only intrusted it to her. She has robbed me. Marian is a thief. You must go to the Justice, William, and get out a warrant against her immediately. Do you help them in the description. Put in "Marian Flint," in plain words—no remonstrances, William—"daughter of Reuben Flint,"—no remonstrances, but do it——

Wil. Nay, sir——

Flint. I am rock, absolute rock, to all that you can say—A piece of solid rock.—What is it that makes my legs to fail, and my whole frame to totter thus? It has been my over-walking. I am very faint. Support me in, William.   [*Exeunt.*

SCENE—*The Apartment of* MISS FLYN.

MISS FLYN.   BETTY.

Miss F. 'Tis past eleven. Every minute I expect Mr. Pendulous here. What a meeting do I anticipate!

Betty. Anticipate, truly! what other than a joyful meeting can it be between two agreed lovers who have been parted these four months?

Miss F. But in that cruel space what accidents

have happened!—(aside.) As yet I perceive she is ignorant of this unfortunate affair.

Betty. Lord, Madam, what accidents? He has not had a fall or a tumble, has he? He is not coming upon crutches?

Miss F. Not exactly a fall—(aside)—I wish I had courage to admit her to my confidence.

Betty. If his neck is whole, his heart is so too, I warrant it.

Miss F. His neck!—(aside)—She certainly mistrusts something. He writes me word that this must be his last interview.

Betty. Then I guess the whole business. The wretch is unfaithful. Some creature or other has got him into a noose.

Miss F. A noose!

Betty And I shall never more see him hang——

Miss F. Hang, did you say, Betty?

Betty. About that dear, fond neck, I was going to add, Madam, but you interrupted me.

Miss F. I can no longer labour with a secret that oppresses me thus. Can you be trusty?

Betty. Who, I, Madam?—(aside)—Lord, I am so glad! Now I shall know all.

Miss F. This letter discloses the reason of his unaccountable long absence from me. Peruse it, and say if we have not reason to be unhappy.

[BETTY *retires to the window to read the letter,*
Mr. PENDULOUS *enters.*

Miss F. My dear Pendulous!

Pen. Maria!—nay, shun the embraces of a disgraced man, who comes but to tell you that you must renounce his society for ever.

Miss F. Nay, Pendulous, avoid me not.

VOL IV.   Q

Pen.—(*aside*) That was tender. I may be mistaken. Whilst I stood on honourable terms, Maria might have met my caresses without a blush.

[BETTY, *who has not attended to the entrance of* PENDULOUS, *through her eagerness to read the letter, comes forward.*

Betty. Ha! ha! ha! What a funny story, Madam! and is this all you make such a fuss about? I should not care if twenty of my lovers had been——(*seeing* PENDULOUS)—Lord, Sir, I ask pardon.

Pen. Are we not alone, then?

Miss F. 'Tis only Betty—my old servant. You remember Betty?

Pen. What letter is that?

Miss F. O! something from her sweetheart, I suppose.

Betty. Yes, Ma'am, that is all. I shall die of laughing.

Pen. You have not surely been showing her——

Miss F. I must be ingenuous. You must know, then, that I was just giving Betty a hint—as you came in.

Pen. A hint!

Miss F. Yes, of our unfortunate embarrassment.

Pen. My letter!

Miss F. I thought it as well that she should know it at first.

Pen. 'Tis mighty well, Madam. 'Tis as it should be. I was ordained to be a wretched laughing-stock to all the world; and it is fit that our drabs and our servant wenches should have their share of the amusement

Betty. Marry come up! Drabs and servant wenches! and this from a person in his circumstances!

[BETTY *flings herself out of the room, muttering.*

Miss F. I understand not this language. I was prepared to give my Pendulous a tender meeting. To assure him, that however in the eyes of the superficial and the censorious he may have incurred a partial degradation, in the esteem of one, at least, he stood as high as ever; that it was not in the power of a ridiculous *accident*, involving no guilt, no shadow of imputation, to separate two hearts, cemented by holiest vows, as ours have been. This untimely repulse to my affections may awaken scruples in me, which hitherto, in tenderness to you, I have suppressed.

Pen. I very well understand what you call tenderness, Madam; but in some situations, pity—pity—is the greatest insult.

Miss F. I can endure no longer. When you are in a calmer mood you will be sorry that you have wrung my heart so. [*Exit.*

Pen. Maria!—She is gone—in tears—Yet it seems she has had her scruples. She said she had tried to smother them. Her maid Betty intimated as much.

Re-enter BETTY.

Betty. Never mind Betty, Sir; depend upon it she will never 'peach.

Pen. 'Peach!

Betty. Lord, Sir, these scruples will blow over. Go to her again when she is in a better humour You know we must stand off a little at first, to save appearances.

Pen. Appearances! *we !*

Betty. It will be decent to let some time elapse.

Pen. Time elapse !

Q 2

Lost, wretched Pendulous! to scorn betray'd,
The scoff alike of mistress and of maid!
What now remains for thee, forsaken man,
But to complete thy fate's abortive plan,
And finish what the feeble law began?

[Exeunt.

Re-enter MISS FLYN, *with* MARIAN

Miss F. Now both our lovers are gone, I hope my friend will have less reserve. You must consider this apartment as yours while you stay here. 'Tis larger and more commodious than your own.

Mar. You are kind, Maria. My sad story I have troubled you with. I have some jewels here, which I unintentionally brought away. I have only to beg that you will take the trouble to restore them to my father; and, without disclosing my present situation, to tell him, that my next step—with or without the concurrence of Mr. Davenport—shall be to throw myself at his feet, and beg to be forgiven. I dare not see him till you have explored the way for me. I am convinced I was tricked into this elopement.

Miss F. Your commands shall be obeyed implicitly.

Mar. You are good. (*agitated.*)

Miss F. Moderate your apprehensions, my sweet friend. I too have known my sorrows—(*smiling.*)— You have heard of the ridiculous affair.

Mar. Between Mr. Pendulous and you? Davenport informed me of it, and we both took the liberty of blaming the over-niceness of your scruples.

Miss F. You mistake. The refinement is entirely on the part of my lover. He thinks me not nice enough. I am obliged to feign a little reluctance, that he may not take quite a distaste to me. Will you believe it, that he turns my very constancy into a reproach, and declares that a woman must be devoid of all delicacy, that, after a thing of that sort, could endure the sight of her husband in——

Mar. In what?

Miss F. The sight of a man at all in——

Mar. I comprehend you not.

Miss F. In—in a—(*whispers*)—night-cap, my dear; and now the mischief is out.

Mar. Is there no way to cure him?

Miss F. None, unless I were to try the experiment, by placing myself in the hands of justice for a little while, how far an equality in misfortune might breed a sympathy in sentiment. Our reputations would be both upon a level then, you know. What think you of a little innocent shop-lifting, in sport?

Mar. And by that contrivance to be taken before a magistrate? the project sounds oddly.

Miss F. And yet I am more than half persuaded it is feasible.

Enter BETTY.

Betty. Mr. Davenport is below, Ma'am, and desires to speak with you.

Mar. You will excuse me—(*going—turning back.*) You will remember the casket?   [*Exit.*

Miss F. Depend on me.

Betty. And a strange man desires to see you, Ma'am. I do not half like his looks

Miss F. Show him in.

    (*Exit* BETTY, *and returns with a Police Officer.*
        BETTY *goes out*)

Officer. Your servant, Ma'am. Your name is——

Miss F. Flyn, Sir. Your business with me?

L   *D*

Off. (*Alternately surveying the lady and his paper of instructions*)—Marian Flint.

Miss F. Maria Flyn

Off. Ay, ay, Flyn or Flint. 'Tis all one. Some write plain Mary, and some put *ann* after it. I come about a casket.

Miss F. I guess the whole business. He takes me for my friend. Something may come out of this. I will humour him.

Off. (*aside.*)—Answers the description to a tittle. " Soft, grey eyes, pale complexion,"——

Miss F. Yet I have been told by flatterers that my eyes were blue—(*takes out a pocket-glass.*)—I hope I look pretty tolerably to-day.

Off. Blue !—they are a sort of blueish-grey, now I look better ; and as for colour, that comes and goes. Blushing is often a sign of a hardened offender. Do you know any thing of a casket ?

Miss F. Here is one which a friend has just delivered to my keeping.

Off. And which I must beg leave to secure, together with your ladyship's person. " Garnets, pearls, diamond-bracelet," — here they are, sure enough.

Miss F. Indeed, I am innocent.

Off. Every man is presumed so till he is found otherwise.

Miss F. Police wit ! Have you a warrant.

Off. Tolerably cool that. Here it is, signed by Justice Golding, at the requisition of Reuben Flint, who deposes that you have robbed him.

Miss F. How lucky this turns out !—(*aside*)— Can I be indulged with a coach ?

Off. To Marlborough Street ? certainly—an old

offender—(*aside*)—The thing shall be conducted with as much delicacy as is consistent with security.

Miss F. Police manners! I will trust myself to your protection then. [*Exeunt.*

SCENE—*Police Office.*

JUSTICE, FLINT, OFFICERS, &c.

Just. Before we proceed to extremities, Mr. Flint, let me entreat you to consider the consequences. What will the world say to your exposing your own child?

Flint. The world is not my friend. I belong to a profession which has long brought me acquainted with its injustice. I return scorn for scorn, and desire its censure above its plaudits.

Just. But in this case delicacy must make you pause.

Flint. Delicacy—ha! ha!—pawnbroker—how fitly these words suit! Delicate pawnbroker—delicate devil—let the law take its course.

Just. Consider, the jewels are found.

Flint. 'Tis not the silly baubles I regard. Are you a man? are you a father? and think you I could stoop so low, vile as I stand here, as to make money—filthy money—of the stuff which a daughter's touch had desecrated? Deep in some pit first I would bury them.

Just. Yet pause a little. Consider. An only child.

Flint. Only, only,—there it is that stings me, makes me mad. She was the only thing I had to love me—to bear me up against the nipping injuries

l   D

of the world.   I prate when I should act.   Bring in your prisoner.

> (*The* JUSTICE *makes signs to an Officer, who goes out, and returns with* MISS FLYN.

Flint.   What mockery of my sight is here?   This is no daughter.

Off.   Daughter, or no daughter, she has confessed to this casket.

Flint (handling it.)—The very same.   Was it in the power of these pale splendours to dazzle the sight of honesty—to put out the regardful eye of piety and daughter-love?   Why, a poor glow-worm shows more brightly.   Bear witness how I valued them—*(tramples on them.)*—Fair lady, know you aught of my child?

Miss F.   I shall here answer no questions.

Just.   You must explain how you came by these jewels, Madam.

Miss F. (aside)   Now confidence assist me!—— A gentleman in the neighbourhood will answer for me——

Just.   His name——

Miss F.   Pendulous——

Just.   That lives in the next street?

Miss F.   The same——now I have him sure.

Just.   Let him be sent for.   I believe the gentleman to be respectable, and will accept his security.

Flint.   Why do I waste my time, where I have no business?   None—I have none any more in the world—none.

Enter PENDULOUS.

Pen.   What is the meaning of this extraordinary summons?—Maria here?

Flint. Know you any thing of my daughter, Sir?

Pen Sir, I neither know her nor yourself, nor why I am brought hither; but for this lady, if you have any thing against her, I will answer it with my life and fortunes.

Just Make out the bail-bond.

Off. (*surveying Pendulous.*) Please, your Worship, before you take that gentleman's bond, may I have leave to put in a word?

Pen. (*agitated.*) I guess what is coming.

Off. I have seen that gentleman hold up his hand at a criminal bar.

Just. Ha!

Miss F (*aside.*) Better and better

Off My eyes cannot deceive me. His lips quivered about, while he was being tried, just as they do now. His name is not Pendulous.

Miss F. Excellent!

Off. He pleaded to the name of Thomson at York Assizes.

Just. Can this be true?

Miss F. I could kiss the fellow!

Off He was had up for a footpad.

Miss F. A dainty fellow!

Pen. My iniquitous fate pursues me everywhere.

Just. You confess, then

Pen. I am steeped in infamy.

Miss F. I am as deep in the mire as yourself.

Pen. My reproach can never be washed out.

Miss F. Nor mine.

Pen. I am doomed to everlasting shame.

Miss F. We are both in a predicament

Just. I am in a maze where all this will end.

Miss F. But here comes one who, if I mistake not, will guide us out of all our difficulties.

Enter Marian *and* Davenport.

Mar. (*kneeling.*)   My dear father !
Flint.   Do I dream ?
Mar.   I am your Marian.
Just.   Wonders thicken !
Flint.   The casket—
Miss F.   Let me clear up the rest.
Flint.   The casket—
Miss F.   Was inadvertently in your daughter's hand, when, by an artifice of her maid Lucy,—set on, as she confesses, by this gentleman here,—
Dav.   I plead guilty.
Miss F.   She was persuaded that you were in a hurry going to marry her to an object of her dislike ; nay, that he was actually in the house for the purpose. The speed of her flight admitted not of her depositing the jewels ; but to me, who have been her inseparable companion since she quitted your roof, she intrusted the return of them ; which the precipitate measures of this gentleman (*pointing to the Officer*) alone prevented. Mr. Cutlet, whom I see coming, can witness this to be true.

Enter Cutlet, *in haste.*

Cut.   Ay, poor lamb! poor lamb ! I can witness. I have run in such a haste, hearing how affairs stood, that I have left my shambles without a protector. If your Worship had seen how she cried (*pointing to* Marian,) and trembled, and insisted upon being brought to her father. Mr. Davenport here could not stay her.

Flint. I can forbear no longer. Marian, will you play once again, to please your old father?

Mar. I have a good mind to make you buy me a new grand piano for your naughty suspicions of me.

Dav. What is to become of me.

Flint. I will do more than that. The poor lady shall have her jewels again.

Mar. Shall she?

Flint. Upon reasonable terms. (*smiling.*) And now, I suppose, the court may adjourn.

Dav Marian!

Flint. I guess what is passing in your mind, Mr. Davenport, but you have behaved upon the whole so like a man of honour, that it will give me pleasure, if you will visit at my house for the future, but (*smiling*) not clandestinely, Marian.

Mar. Hush, father!

Flint. I own I had prejudices against gentry. But I have met with so much candour and kindness among my betters this day—from this gentleman in particular—(*turning to the Justice*)—that I begin to think of leaving off business, and setting up for a gentleman myself

Just. You have the feelings of one.

Flint. Marian will not object to it.

Just. But (*turning to Miss Flyn*) what motive could induce this lady to take so much disgrace upon herself, when a word's explanation might have relieved her?

Miss F. This gentleman (*turning to Pendulous*) can explain.

Pen. The devil!

Miss F. This gentleman, I repeat it, whose backwardness in concluding a long and honourable suit from a mistaken delicacy—

Pen. How!

Miss F. Drove me upon the expedient of involving myself in the same disagreeable embarrassments with himself, in the hope that a more perfect sympathy might subsist between us for the future.

Pen. I see it—I see it all.

Just (*To Pendulous.*) You were then tried at York?

Pen. I was———CAST—

Just. Condemned—

Pen. EXECUTED.

Just. How!

Pen. CUT DOWN, and CAME TO LIFE AGAIN. False delicacy, adieu! The true sort, which this lady has manifested—by an expedient which at first sight might seem a little unpromising, has cured me of the other. We are now on even terms.

Miss F. And may—

Pen. Marry,—I know it was your word.

Miss F. And make a very quiet—

Pen. Exemplary—

Miss F. Agreeing pair of—

Pen. ACQUITTED FELONS.

Flint. And let the prejudiced against our profession acknowledge that a money-lender may have the heart of a father. and that in the casket, whose loss grieved him so sorely, he valued nothing so dear as (*turning to Marian*) one poor domestic jewel.

THE WITCH.

A DRAMATIC SKETCH OF THE SEVEN-TEENTH CENTURY.

CHARACTERS.

OLD SERVANT *in the Family of* SIR FRANCIS FAIRFORD.   STRANGER

Servant. ONE summer night Sir Francis, as it
    chanced,
Was pacing to and fro in the avenue
That westward fronts our house,
Among those aged oaks, said to have been planted
Three hundred years ago,
By a neighb'ring prior of the Fairford name
Being o ertask'd in thought, he heeded not
The importunate suit of one who stood by the gate,
And begg'd an alms.
Some say he shoved her rudely from the gate
With angry chiding, but I can never think
(Our master's nature hath a sweetness in it)
That he could use a woman, an old woman,
With such discourtesy, but he refused her—
And better had he met a lion in his path
Than that old woman that night ·
For she was one who practised the black arts,
And served the devil, being since burnt for witch-
    craft.

l   *)*

She look'd at him as one that meant to blast him,
And with a frightful noise,
('Twas partly like a woman's voice,
And partly like the hissing of a snake,)
She nothing said but this
(Sir Francis told the words) :—

A mischief, mischief, mischief,
And a nine-times killing curse,
By day and by night, to the caitiff wight,
Who shakes the poor like snakes from his door,
And shuts up the womb of his purse.

And still she cried—
A mischief,
And a nine fold withering curse
For that shall come to thee that will undo thee,
Both all that thou fearest and worse.

So saying, she departed,
Leaving Sir Francis like a man, beneath
Whose feet a scaffolding was suddenly falling ;
So he described it
    Stranger.   A terrible curse !   What follow'd ?
    Servant.   Nothing immediate, but some two months
        after,
Young Philip Fairford suddenly fell sick,
And none could tell what ail'd him ; for he lay,
And pined, and pined, till all his hair fell off,
And he, that was full-flesh'd, became as thin
As a two-months' babe that has been starved in the
        nursing.
And sure I think
He bore his death-wound like a little child ;
With such rare sweetness of dumb melancholy
He strove to clothe his agony in smiles,
Which he would force up in his poor pale cheeks,

Like ill-time guests that had no proper dwelling
    there ;
And when they ask'd him his complaint, he laid
His hand upon his heart to show the place,
Where Susan came to him a-nights, he said,
And prick'd him with a pin.—
And thereupon Sir Francis call'd to mind
The beggar witch that stood by the gateway
And begg'd an alms.
    Stranger.   But, did the witch confess ?
    Servant. All this and more at her death.
    Stranger. I do not love to credit tales of magic.
Heaven's music, which is Order, seems unstrung,
And this brave world
(The mystery of God) unbeautified,
Disorder'd, marr'd, where such strange things are
    acted.

l   D

IX.

TALES.

.

R

l   D

ROSAMUND GRAY.

[FIRST PRINTED IN 1798.] [1]

CHAPTER I.

IT was noontide. The sun was very hot. An old gentlewoman sat spinning in a little arbour at the door of her cottage. She was blind ; and her grand-daughter was reading the Bible to her. The old

---

[1] This tale, printed in 1798, and favourably criticized in the *Monthly Review* for August, 1800, was republished with some other of Lamb's Essays, &c. It contained, on its appearance, the following dedication to Martin Burney—the M. B. of the Letters.

MARTIN CHARLES BURNEY, ESQ.

Forgive me, BURNEY, if to thee these late
And hasty products of a critic pen,
Thyself no common judge of books and men,
In feeling of thy worth I dedicate.
My *verse* was offered to an older friend ;*
The humbler *prose* has fallen to thy share:
Nor could I miss the occasion to declare,
What spoken in thy presence must offend—
That, set aside some few caprices wild,
Those humorous clouds that dit o'er brightest days,
In all my threadings of this worldly maze,
(And I have watch'd thee almost from a child,)
Free from self-seeking, envy, low design,
I have not found a whiter soul than thine.

lady had just left her work, to attend to the story of
Ruth.

"Orpah kissed her mother-in-law; but Ruth clave
unto her." It was a passage she could not let pass
without a *comment*. The moral she drew from it was
not very *new*, to be sure. The girl had heard it a
hundred times before; and a hundred times more
she could have heard it, without suspecting it to be
tedious. Rosamund loved her grandmother.

The old lady loved Rosamund too; and she had
reason for so doing. Rosamund was to her at once
a child and a servant. She had only *her* left in the
world. They two lived together

They had once known better days. The story of
Rosamund's parents, their failure, their folly, and
distresses, may be told another time. Our tale hath
grief enough in it.

It was now about a year and a half since old
Margaret Gray had sold off all her effects, to pay the
debts of Rosamund's father—just after the mother
had died of a broken heart; for her husband had fled
his country to hide his shame in a foreign land. At
that period the old lady retired to a small cottage in
the village of Widford, in Hertfordshire.

Rosamund, in her thirteenth year, was left destitute, without fortune or friends; she went with her
grandmother. In all this time she had served her
faithfully and lovingly.

Old Margaret Gray, when she first came into these
parts, had eyes, and could see. The neighbours
said, they had been dimmed by weeping be that
as it may, she was latterly grown quite blind. "God
is very good to us. child; I can *feel* you yet."
This she would sometimes say; and we need not

wonder to hear that Rosamund clave unto her grandmother.

Margaret retained a spirit unbroken by calamity. There was a principle *within*, which it seemed as if no outward circumstances could reach. It was a *religious* principle, and she had taught it to Rosamund, for the girl had mostly resided with her grandmother from her earliest years. Indeed she had taught her all that she knew herself, and the old lady's knowledge did not extend a vast way.

Margaret had drawn her maxims from observation, and a pretty long experience in life had contributed to make her, at times, a little *positive* but Rosamund never argued with her grandmother.

Their library consisted chiefly in a large family Bible, with notes and expositions by various learned expositors, from Bishop Jewell downwards.

This might never be suffered to lie about like other books, but was kept constantly wrapt up in a handsome case of green velvet, with gold tassels—the only relic of departed grandeur they had brought with them to the cottage—every thing else of value had been sold off for the purpose above mentioned.

This Bible Rosamund, when a child, had never dared to open without permission, and even yet, from habit, continued the custom. Margaret had parted with none of her *authority*. indeed it was never exerted with much harshness, and happy was Rosamund, though a girl grown, when she could obtain leave to read her Bible. It was a treasure too valuable for an indiscriminate use; and Margaret still pointed out to her grand-daughter *where to read*.

Besides this, they had the " Complete Angler ; or,

Contemplative Man's Recreation," with cuts ; " Pil-grim's Progress," the first Part ; a Cookery Book, with a few dry sprigs of rosemary and lavender stuck here and there between the leaves, (I suppose to point to some of the old lady's most favourite receipts,) and there was " Wither's Emblems," an old book, and quaint. The old-fashioned pictures in this last book were among the first exciters of the infant Rosamund's curiosity. Her contemplation had fed upon them in rather older years.

Rosamund had not read many books besides these ; or if any, they had been only occasional companions : these were to Rosamund as old friends, that she had long known. I know not whether the peculiar cast of her mind might not be traced, in part, to a tinc-ture she had received, early in life, from Walton and Wither, from John Bunyan and her Bible.

Rosamund's mind was pensive and reflective, rather than what passes usually for *clever or acute*. From a child she was remarkably shy and thoughtful ; this was taken for stupidity and want of feeling ; and the child has been sometimes whipt for being a *stubborn thing*, when her little heart was almost burst-ing with affection.

Even now her grandmother would often reprove her when she found her too grave or melancholy ; give her sprightly lectures about good-humour and rational mirth, and not unfrequently fall a-crying herself, to the great discredit of her lecture Those tears endeared her the more to Rosamund.

Margaret would say, " Child, I love you to cry, when I think you are only remembering your poor dear father and mother. I would have you think about them sometimes : it would be strange if you did not; but I fear, Rosamund,—I fear, girl, you sometimes think too deeply about your own situation and poor prospects in life. When you do so, you do wrong. Remember the naughty rich man in the parable. He never had any good thoughts about God, and his religion: and that might have been your case."

Rosamund, at these times, could not reply to her; she was not in the habit of *arguing* with her grandmother; so she was quite silent on these occasions; or else the girl knew well enough herself that she had only been sad to think of the desolate condition of her best friend, to see her, in her old age, so infirm and blind. But she had never been used to make excuses when the old lady said she was doing wrong.

The neighbours were all very kind to them. The veriest rustics never passed them without a bow, or a pulling off of the hat—some show of courtesy, awkward indeed, but affectionate—with a " Goodmorrow, madam," or " young madam," as it might happen.

Rude and savage natures, who seem born with a propensity to express contempt for any thing that looks like prosperity, yet felt respect for its declining lustre.

The farmers, and better sort of people, (as they are called,) all promised to provide for Rosamund when her grandmother should die. Margaret trusted in God and believed them.

She used to say, " I have lived many years in the world, and have never known people, *good people*, to be left without some friend; a relation, a benefactor, a *something*. God knows our wants—that it is not good for man or woman to be alone ; and he always sends us a helpmate, a leaning place, a *somewhat*." Upon this sure ground of experience did Margaret build her trust in Providence.

CHAPTER II.

ROSAMUND had just made an end of her story, (as I was about to relate,) and was listening to the application of the moral, (which said application she was old enough to have made herself, but her grandmother still continued to treat her, in many respects, as a child, and Rosamund was in no haste to lay claim to the title of womanhood,) when a young gentleman made his appearance and interrupted them.

It was young Allan Clare, who had brought a present of peaches, and some roses, for Rosamund.

He laid his little basket down on a seat of the arbour ; and in a respectful tone of voice, as though he were addressing a parent, inquired of Margaret " how she did."

The old lady seemed pleased with his attentions— answered his inquiries by saying, that " her cough was less troublesome a-nights, but she had not yet got rid of it, and probably she never might ; but she did not like to tease young people with an account of her infirmities."

A few kind words passed on either side, when young Clare, glancing a tender look at the girl, who had all this time been silent, took leave of them with saying, " I shall bring *Elinor* to see you in the evening."

When he was gone, the old lady began to prattle

" That is a sweet dispositioned youth, and I *do* love him dearly, I must say it—there is such a modesty in all he says or does. He should not come here so often, to be sure, but I don't know how to help it; there is so much goodness in him, I can't find it in my heart to forbid him. But, Rosamund, girl, I must tell you beforehand,—when you grow older, Mr. Clare must be no companion for *you*. while you were both so young it was all very well: but the time is coming, when folks will think harm of it, if a rich young gentleman, like Mr. Clare, comes so often to our poor cottage.—Dost hear, girl? Why don't you answer? Come, I did not mean to say any thing to hurt you. Speak to me, Rosamund. Nay, I must not have you be sullen. I don't love people that are sullen."

And in this manner was this poor soul running on, unheard and unheeded, when it occurred to her, that possibly the girl might not be *within hearing*.

And true it was, that Rosamund had slunk away at the first mention of Mr. Clare's good qualities · and when she returned, which was not till a few minutes after Margaret had made an end of her fine harangue, it is certain her cheeks *did* look very *rosy*. That might have been from the heat of the day or from exercise, for she had been walking in the garden.

Margaret, we know, was blind , and, in this case. it was lucky for Rosamund that she was so, or she might have made some not unlikely surmises.

I must not have my reader infer from this, that I

l   *p*

at all think it likely a young maid of fourteen would fall in love without asking her grandmother's leave: the thing itself is not to be conceived.

To obviate all suspicions, I am disposed to communicate a little anecdote of Rosamund.

A month or two back her grandmother had been giving her the strictest prohibitions, in her walks, not to go near a certain spot, which was dangerous from the circumstance of a huge overgrown oak-tree spreading its prodigious arms across a deep chalk-pit, which they partly concealed.

To this fatal place Rosamund came one day—female curiosity, we know, is older than the flood—let us not think hardly of the girl, if she partook of the sexual failing.

Rosamund ventured further and further, climbed along one of the branches, approached the forbidden chasm. Her foot slipped: she was not killed: but it was by a mercy she escaped. Other branches intercepted her fall, and with a palpitating heart she made her way back to the cottage.

It happened that evening that her grandmother was in one of her best humours, caressed Rosamund, talked of old times, and what a blessing it was they two found a shelter in their little cottage, and in conclusion told Rosamund " she was a good girl, and God would one day reward her for her kindness to her old blind grandmother."

This was more than Rosamund could bear. Her morning's disobedience came fresh into her mind ; she felt she did not deserve all this from Margaret, and at last burst into a fit of crying, and made confession of her fault. The old gentlewoman kissed and forgave her.

Rosamund never went near that naughty chasm again

Margaret would never have heard of this if Rosamund had not told of it herself But this young maid had a delicate moral sense, which would not suffer her to take advantage of her grandmother, to deceive her, or conceal any thing from her, though Margaret was old, and blind, and easy to be imposed upon.

Another virtuous *trait* I recollect of Rosamund, and now I am in the vein will tell it

Some, I know, will think these things trifles ; and they are so , but if these *minutiæ* make my reader better acquainted with Rosamund, I am content to abide the imputation.

These promises of character, hints, and early indications of a *sweet nature*, are to me more dear and choice in the selection than any of those pretty wild flowers which this young maid, this virtuous Rosamund, has ever gathered in a fine May morning, to make a posy to place in the bosom of her old blind friend.

Rosamund had a very just notion of drawing, and would often employ her talent in making sketches of the surrounding scenery.

On a landscape, a larger piece than she had ever yet attempted, she had now been working for three or four months. She had taken great pains with it, given much time to it, and it was nearly finished. For *whose* particular inspection it was designed I will not venture to conjecture. We know it could not have been for her grandmother's.

One day she went out on a short errand, and left her landscape on the table. When she returned she found it *gone*.

Rosamund from the first suspected some mischief,
but held her tongue. At length she made the fatal
discovery. Margaret, in her absence, had laid violent
hands on it : not knowing what it was, but taking it
for some waste-paper, had torn it in half, and with
one half of this elaborate composition had twisted
herself up a thread-paper !

Rosamund spread out her hands at sight of the
disaster, gave her grandmother a roguish smile, but
said not a word. She knew the poor soul would only
fret if she told her of it, and when once Margaret
was set a fretting for other people's misfortunes the
fit held her pretty long.

So Rosamund that very afternoon began another
piece of the same size and subject ; and Margaret,
to her dying day, never dreamed of the mischief she
had unconsciously done.

CHAPTER III.

ROSAMUND GRAY was the most beautiful young
creature that eyes ever beheld. Her face had the
sweetest expression in it, a gentleness, a modesty,
a timidity, a certain charm,—a grace without a
name.

There was a sort of melancholy mingled in her
smile. It was not the thoughtless levity of a girl ;
it was not the restrained simper of premature womanhood : it was something which the poet Young might
have remembered when he composed that perfect
line—

> " Soft, modest, melancholy, female, fair."

She was a mild eyed maid, and every body loved her. Young Allan Clare, when but a boy, sighed for her.

Her yellow hair fell in bright and curling clusters, like

"Those hanging locks
Of young Apollo"

Her voice was trembling and musical. A graceful diffidence pleaded for her whenever she spake; and if she said but little, that little found its way to the heart.

Young, and artless, and innocent, meaning no harm, and thinking none; affectionate as a smiling infant—playful, yet inobtrusive, as a weaned lamb— every body loved her. Young Allan Clare, when but a boy, sighed for her.

The moon is shining in so brightly at my window, where I write, that I feel it a crime not to suspend my employment awhile to gaze at her.

See how she glideth, in maiden honour, through the clouds, who divide on either side to do her homage.

Beautiful vision!—as I contemplate thee, an internal harmony is communicated to my mind, a moral brightness, a tacit analogy of mental purity, a calm like *that* we ascribe in fancy to the favoured inhabitants of thy fairy regions, "argent fields"

I marvel not, O moon, that heathen people, in the "olden times," did worship thy deity — Cynthia, Diana, Hecate. Christian Europe invokes thee not by these names now: her idolatry is of a blacker stain. Belial is her God: she worships Mammon.

False things are told concerning thee, fair planet,

for I will ne'er believe that thou canst take a perverse
pleasure in distorting the brains of us, poor mortals.
Lunatics ! moonstruck ! Calumny invented, and folly
took up, these names. I would hope better things
from thy mild aspect and benign influences.

Lady of Heaven, thou lendest thy pure lamp to
light the way to the virgin mourner, when she goes .
to seek the tomb where her warrior lover lies.

Friend of the distressed, thou speakest only *peace*
to the lonely sufferer, who walks forth in the placid
evening, beneath thy gentle light, to chide at fortune,
or to complain of changed friends, or unhappy loves.

Do I dream, or doth not even now a heavenly calm
descend from thee into my bosom, as I meditate on
the chaste loves of Rosamund and her Clare !

CHAPTER IV.

ALLAN CLARE was just two years older than Rosamund. He was a boy of fourteen when he first
became acquainted with her it was soon after she
had come to reside with her grandmother at Widford.

He met her by chance one day, carrying a pitcher
in her hand, which she had been filling from a neighbouring well. The pitcher was heavy, and she
seemed to be bending with its weight.

Allan insisted on carrying it for her ; for he thought
it a sin that a delicate young maid, like her, should
be so employed, and he stand idle by.

Allan had a propensity to do little kind offices for
every body ; but at the sight of Rosamond Gray his

first fire was kindled. His young mind seemed to have found an object, and his enthusiasm was from that time forth awakened. His visits from that day were pretty frequent at the cottage.

He was never happier than when he could get Rosamund to walk out with him. He would make her admire the scenes he admired—fancy the wild flowers he fancied—watch the clouds he was watching —and not unfrequently repeat to her poetry which he loved, and make her love it.

On their return, the old lady, who considered them yet as but children, would bid Rosamund fetch Mr. Clare a glass of her currant wine, a bowl of new milk, or some cheap dainty which was more welcome to Allan than the costliest delicacies of a prince s court.

The boy and girl, for they were no more at that age, grew fond of each other, more fond than either of them suspected.

> "They would sit, and sigh,
> And look upon each other, and conceive
> Not what they ail'd, yet something they did ail,
> And yet were well; and yet they were not well,
> And what was their disease they could not tell."

And thus,

> "In this first garden of their simpleness
> They spent their childhood"

A circumstance had lately happened, which in some sort altered the nature of their attachment.

Rosamund was one day reading the tale of "Julia de Roubigne"—a book which young Clare had lent her.

Allan was standing by looking over her, with one

l   )

arm thrown round her neck, and a finger of the other pointing to a passage in Julia's third letter.

" Maria ! in my hours of visionary indulgence, I have sometimes painted to myself a *husband*—no matter whom—comforting me amidst the distresses which Fortune had laid upon us. I have smiled upon him through my tears , tears, not of anguish, but of tenderness Our children were playing around us, unconscious of misfortune ; we had taught them to be humble, and to be happy : our little shed was reserved to us, and their smiles to cheer it. I have imagined the luxury of such a scene, and affliction became a part of my dream of happiness."

The girl blushed as she read, and trembled. She had a sort of confused sensation that Allan was noticing her , yet she durst not lift her eyes from the book, but continued reading, scarce knowing what she read.

Allan guessed the cause of her confusion, Allan trembled too · his colour came and went ; his feelings became impetuous—and flinging both arms round her neck, he kissed his young favourite.

Rosamund was vexed and pleased, soothed and frightened All in a moment a fit of tears came to her relief.

Allan had indulged before in these little freedoms, and Rosamund had thought no harm of them ; but from this time the girl grew timid and reserved— distant in her manner, and careful of her behaviour in Allan's presence ; not seeking his society as before, but rather shunning it ; delighting more to feed upon his idea in absence.

Allan too, from this day, seemed changed : his manner became, though not less tender, yet more respectful and diffident; his bosom felt a throb it had till now not known, in the society of Rosamund; and, if he was less familiar with her than in former times, that charm of delicacy had superadded a grace to Rosamund, which, while he feared, he loved.

There is a *mysterious character*, heightened indeed by fancy and passion, but not without foundation in reality and observation, which true lovers have eve' imputed to the object of their affections. This cha racter Rosamund had now acquired with Allan— something *angelic, perfect, exceeding nature*.

Young Clare dwelt very near to the cottage. He had lost his parents, who were rather wealthy early in life, and was left to the care of a sister some ten years older than himself.

Elinor Clare was an excellent young lady—discreet, intelligent, and affectionate. Allan revered her as a parent, while he loved her as his own familiar friend He told all the little secrets of his heart to her; but there was *one*, which he had hitherto unaccountably concealed from her—namely, the extent of his regard for Rosamund.

Elinor knew of his visits to the cottage, and was no stranger to the persons of Margaret and her grand-daughter. She had several times met them, when she had been walking with her brother—a civility usually passed on either side—but Elinor avoided troubling her brother with any unseasonable ques-tions.

Allan's heart often beat, and he has been going to tell his sister *all*, but something like shame (false or true, I shall not stay to inquire) has hitherto kept him back; still the secret, unrevealed, hung upon his conscience like a crime—for his temper had a sweet and noble frankness in it, which bespake him yet a virgin from the world.

There was a fine openness in his countenance; the character of it somewhat resembled Rosamund's, except that more fire and enthusiasm were discernible in Allan's; his eyes were of a darker blue than Rosamund's; his hair was of a chestnut colour; his cheeks were ruddy, and tinged with brown. There was a cordial sweetness in Allan's smile, the like to which I never saw in any other face.

Elinor had hitherto connived at her brother's attachment to Rosamund. Elinor I believe was something of a physiognomist, and thought she could trace in the countenance and manner of Rosamund qualities which no brother of hers need be ashamed to love.

The time was now come when Elinor was desirous of knowing her brother's favourite more intimately— an opportunity offered of breaking the matter to Allan.

The morning of the day in which he carried his present of fruit and flowers to Rosamund, his sister had observed him more than usually busy in the garden, culling fruit with a nicety of choice not common to him.

She came up to him, unobserved, and taking him by the arm, inquired, with a questioning smile— "What are you doing, Allan? and who are those peaches designed for?"

"For Rosamund Gray," he replied; and his heart seemed relieved of a burthen which had long oppressed it.

"I have a mind to become acquainted with your handsome friend. Will you introduce me, Allan?

I think I should like to go and see her this afternoon "

" Do go, do go, Elinor ; you don't know what a good creature she is ; and old blind Margaret, you will like *her* very much."

His sister promised to accompany him after dinner ; and they parted. Allan gathered no more peaches, but hastily cropping a few roses to fling into his basket, went away with it half-filled, being impatient to announce to Rosamund the coming of her promised visitor.

CHAPTER V.

WHEN Allan returned home he found an invitation had been left for him, in his absence, to spend that evening with a young friend, who had just quitted a public school in London, and was come to pass one night in his father's house at Widford, previous to his departure the next morning for Edinburgh University.

It was Allan's bosom friend ; they had not met for some months ; and it was probable a much longer time must intervene before they should meet again.

Yet Allan could not help looking a little blank when he first heard of the invitation This was to have been an important evening. But Elinor soon relieved her brother by expressing her readiness to go alone to the cottage

" I will not lose the pleasure I promised myself, whatever you may determine upon, Allan , I will go by myself rather than be disappointed."

" Will you, will you, Elinor ? "

Elinor promised to go ; and I believe, Allan, on a second thought, was not very sorry to be spared the awkwardness of introducing two persons to each other, both so dear to him, but either of whom might happen not much to fancy the other.

At times, indeed, he was confident that Elinor *must* love Rosamund, and Rosamund *must* love Elinor ; but there were also times in which he felt misgivings : it was an event he could scarce hope for very joy !

Allan's *real presence* that evening was more at the cottage than at the house, where his *bodily semblance* was visiting—his friend could not help complaining of a certain absence of mind, a *coldness* he called it

It might have been expected, and in the course of things predicted, that Allan would have asked his friend some questions of what had happened since their last meeting, what his feelings were on leaving school, the probable time when they should meet again, and a hundred natural questions which friendship is most lavish of at such times ; but nothing of all this ever occurred to Allan , they did not even settle the method of their future correspondence.

The consequence was, as might have been expected, Allan's friend thought him much altered, and, after his departure, sat down to compose a doleful sonnet about a " faithless friend."—I do not find that he ever finished it ; indignation, or a dearth of rhymes, causing him to break off in the middle.

l   *)*

CHAPTER VI.

In my catalogue of the little library at the cottage, I forgot to mention a Book of Common Prayer. My reader's fancy might easily have supplied the omission. Old ladies of Margaret's stamp (God bless them!) may as well be without their spectacles, or their elbow chair, as their prayer-book. I love them for it.

Margaret's was a handsome octavo, printed by Baskerville, the binding red, and fortified with silver at the edges. Out of this book it was their custom every afternoon to read the Proper Psalms appointed for the day.

The way they managed was this: they took verse by verse—Rosamund *read* her little portion, and Margaret repeated hers in turn, from memory—for Margaret could say all the Psalter by heart, and a good part of the Bible besides. She would not unfrequently put the girl right when she stumbled or skipped. This Margaret imputed to giddiness—a quality which Rosamund was by no means remarkable for, but old ladies, like Margaret, are not in all instances alike discriminative.

They had been employed in this manner just before Miss Clare arrived at the cottage. The Psalm they had been reading was the hundred and fourth. Margaret was naturally led by it into a discussion of the works of creation.

There had been *thunder* in the course of the day—an occasion of instruction which the old lady never let pass. She began—

" Thunder has a very awful sound : some say God Almighty is angry whenever it thunders,—that it is the voice of God speaking to us; for my part, I am not afraid of it"——

And in this manner the old lady was going on to particularize, as usual, its beneficial effects in clearing the air, destroying vermin, &c., when the entrance of Miss Clare put an end to her discourse.

Rosamund received her with respectful tenderness, and, taking her grandmother by the hand, said, with great sweetness,—" Miss Clare is come to see you, grandmother."

" I beg pardon, lady; I cannot *see* you, but you are heartily welcome. Is your brother with you, Miss Clare ? I don't hear him."

" He could not come, Madam, but he sends his love by me."

" You have an excellent brother, Miss Clare ; but pray do us the honour to take some refreshment. Rosamund "——

And the old lady was going to give directions for a bottle of her currant wine—when Elinor, smiling, said, " she was come to take a cup of tea with her, and expected to find no ceremony."

" After tea I promise to take a walk with *you*, Rosamund, if your grandmother can spare you." Rosamund looked at her grandmother.

" Oh, for that matter, I should be sorry to debar the girl from any pleasure I am sure 'tis lonesome enough for her to be with *me* always ; and if Miss Clare will take you out, child, I shall do very well by myself till you return. It will not be the first time, you know, that I have been left here alone. Some of the neighbours will be dropping in by and by ; or, if *not*, I shall take no harm."

Rosamund had all the simple manners of a child : she kissed her grandmother, and looked happy.

All tea time the old lady's discourse was little more than a panegyric on young Clare's good qualities. Elinor looked at her young friend and smiled. Rosamund was beginning to look grave ; but there was a cordial sunshine in the face of Elinor, before which any clouds of reserve that had been gathering on Rosamund's soon brake away.

"Does your grandmother ever go out, Rosamund ?"

Margaret prevented the girl's reply by saying— "My dear young lady, I am an old woman, and very infirm. Rosamund takes me a few paces beyond the door sometimes ; but I walk very badly ; I love best to sit in our little arbour when the sun shines. I can yet feel it warm and cheerful ; and if I lose the beauties of the season, I shall be very happy if you and Rosamund can take delight in this fine Summer evening."

"I shall want to rob you of Rosamund's company now and then, if we like one another. I had hoped to have seen *you*, Madam, at our house. I don't know whether we could not make room for you to come and live with us. What say you to it ? Allan would be proud to tend you, I am sure ; and Rosamund and I should be nice company "

Margaret was all unused to such kindnesses, and wept. Margaret had a great spirit, yet she was not above accepting an obligation from a worthy person. There was a delicacy in Miss Clare's manner : she could have no interest but pure goodness to induce her to make the offer. At length the old lady spake from a full heart.

" Miss Clare, this little cottage received us in our distress : it gave us shelter when we had *no home*. We have praised God in it ; and, while life remains, I think I shall never part from it. Rosamund does every thing for me "——

" And will do, grandmother, as long as I live ,"— and then Rosamund fell a-crying.

" You are a good girl, Rosamund ; and if you do but find friends when I am dead and gone, I shall want no better accommodation while I live ; but God bless you, lady, a thousand times, for your kind offer."

Elinor was moved to tears, and, affecting a sprightliness, bade Rosamund prepare for her walk. The girl put on her white silk bonnet : and Elinor thought she never beheld so lovely a creature.

They took leave of Margaret, and walked out together , they rambled over all Rosamund's favourite haunts—through many a sunny field—by secret glade or wood-walk, where the girl had wandered so often with her beloved Clare.

Who now so happy as Rosamund ? She had oft-times heard Allan speak with great tenderness of his sister. She was now rambling, arm in arm, with that very sister, the " vaunted sister " of her friend, her beloved Clare.

Not a tree, not a bush, scarce a wild-flower in their path, but revived in Rosamund some tender recollection, a conversation perhaps, or some chaste endearment. Life, and a new scene of things, were now opening before her : she was got into a fairy land of uncertain existence.

Rosamund was too happy to talk much ; but Elinor was delighted with her when she *did* talk. The girl's remarks were suggested, most of them, by the passing scene ; and they betrayed, all of them, the liveliness of present impulse. Her conversation did not consist in a comparison of vapid feeling, an interchange of sentiment lip-deep : it had all the freshness of young sensation in it.

Sometimes they talked of Allan.

"Allan is very good," said Rosamund, "very good *indeed* to my grandmother. He will sit with her, and hear her stories, and read to her, and try to divert her a hundred ways. I wonder sometimes he is not tired. She talks him to death!"

"Then you confess, Rosamund, that the old lady *does* tire *you* sometimes ?"

"Oh no, I did not mean *that* · 'tis very different. I am used to all her ways, and I can humour her. and please her ; and I ought to do it, for she is the only friend I ever had in the world."

The new friends did not conclude their walk till it was late, and Rosamund began to be apprehensive about the old lady, who had been all this time alone.

On their return to the cottage they found that Margaret had been somewhat impatient Old ladies, *good old ladies*, will be so at times. Age is timorous, and suspicious of danger, where no danger is.

Besides, it was Margaret's bed-time, for she kept very good hours. Indeed, in the distribution of her meals, and sundry other particulars, she resembled the livers in the antique world, more than might well beseem a creature of this.

So the new friends parted for that night—Elinor having made Margaret promise to give Rosamund leave to come and see her the next day.

l   *ᴅ*

CHAPTER VII.

Miss Clare, we may be sure, made her brother very happy when she told him of the engagement she had made for the morrow, and how delighted she had been with his handsome friend.

Allan, I believe, got little sleep that night. I know not whether joy be not a more troublesome bed-fellow than grief. hope keeps a body very wakeful, I know.

Elinor Clare was the best good creature—the least selfish human being I ever knew—always at work for other people's good, planning other people's happiness—continually forgetful to consult for her own personal gratifications, except indirectly, in the welfare of another;—while her parents lived, the most attentive of daughters—since they died, the kindest of sisters. I never knew but *one* like her. It happens that I have some of this young lady's *letters* in my possession. I shall present my reader with one of them. It was written a short time after the death of her mother, and addressed to a cousin, a dear friend of Elinor's, who was then on the point of being married to Mr. Beaumont, of Staffordshire, and had invited Elinor to assist at her nuptials. I will transcribe it with minute fidelity.

ELINOR CLARE TO MARIA LESLIE.

Widford, July the —, 17—.

Health, Innocence, and Beauty, shall be thy bridemaids, my sweet cousin. I have no heart to undertake the office. Alas! what have I to do in the house of feasting?

Maria, I fear lest my griefs should prove obtrusive, yet bear with me a little. I have recovered already a share of my former spirits.

I fear more for Allan than myself. The loss of two such parents, within so short an interval, bears very heavy on him. The boy *hangs* about me from morning till night. He is perpetually forcing a smile into his poor pale cheeks. You know the sweetness of his smile, Maria.

To-day, after dinner, when he took his glass of wine in his hand he burst into tears, and would not, or could not then, tell me the reason ; afterwards he told me. " He had been used to drink Mamma's health after dinner, and *that* came into his head and made him cry " I feel the claims the boy has upon me I perceive that I am living to *some end ;* and the thought supports me.

Already I have attained to a state of complacent feelings My mother's lessons were not thrown away upon her Elinor.

In the visions of last night her spirit seemed to stand at my bed side ; a light, as of noonday, shone upon the room. She opened my curtains ; she smiled upon me with the same placid smile as in her lifetime. I felt no fear. " Elinor," she said, " for my sake take care of young Allan ;" and I awoke with calm feelings.

Maria, shall not the meeting of blessed spirits, think you, be something like this ? I think, I could even now behold my mother without dread I would ask pardon of her for all my past omissions of duty, for all the little asperities in my temper, which have so often grieved her gentle spirit when living. Maria, I think she would not turn away from me.

Oftentimes a feeling, more vivid than memory, brings her before me. I see her sit in her old elbow chair—her arms folded upon her lap—a tear upon her cheek, that seems to upbraid her unkind daughter for some inattention. I wipe it away and kiss her honoured lips.

Maria, when I have been fancying all this, Allan will come in, with his poor eyes red with weeping, and taking me by the hand, destroy the vision in a moment.

I am prating to you, my sweet cousin, but it is the prattle of the heart, which Maria loves. Besides, whom have I to talk to of these things but you?— You have been my counsellor in times past, my companion and sweet familiar friend. Bear with me a little. I mourn the " cherishers of my infancy."

I sometimes count it a blessing that my father did not prove the *survivor*. You know something of his story. You know there was a foul tale current: it was the busy malice of that bad man, S———, which helped to spread it abroad. You will recollect the active good-nature of our friends W—— and T——; what pains they took to undeceive people. With the better sort their kind labours prevailed; but there was still a party who shut their ears. You know the issue of it. My father's great spirit bore up against it for some time. My father never was a *bad* man ; but that spirit was broken at the last, and the greatly-injured man was forced to leave his old paternal dwelling in Staffordshire, for the neighbours had begun to point at him. Maria, I have *seen* them *point* at him, and have been ready to drop.

In this part of the country, where the slander had not reached, he sought a retreat, and he found a still more grateful asylum in the daily solicitudes of the best of wives.

"An enemy hath done this," I have heard him say, and at such times my mother would speak to him so soothingly of forgiveness, and long-suffering, and the bearing of injuries with patience, would heal all his wounds with so gentle a touch;—I have seen the old man weep like a child.

The gloom that beset his mind, at times betrayed him into scepticism he has doubted if there be a Providence! I have heard him say, "God has built a brave world, but methinks he has left his creatures to bustle in it *how they may*."

At such times he could not endure to hear my mother talk in a religious strain He would say, "Woman, have done! You confound, you perplex me, when you talk of these matters, and for one day at least unfit me for the business of life."

I have seen her look at him (O God, Maria!) such a *look!* It plainly spake that she was willing to have shared her precious hope with the partner of her earthly cares; but she found a repulse.

Deprived of such a wife, think you, the old man could long have endured his existence? Or what consolation would his wretched daughter have had to offer him, but silent and imbecile tears?

My sweet cousin, you will think me tedious—and I am so—but it does me good to talk these matters over. And do not you be alarmed for me: my sorrows are subsiding into a deep and sweet resignation. I shall soon be sufficiently composed, I know it, to participate in my friend's happiness.

Let me call her, while yet I may, my own Maria Leslie. Methinks I shall not like you by any other name. Beaumont! Maria Beaumont! it hath a strange sound with it. I shall never be reconciled to this name, but do not you fear; Maria Leslie shall plead with me for Maria Beaumont.

And now, my sweet Friend,

God love you, and your

ELINOR CLARE.

I find in my collection several letters, written soon after the date of the preceding, and addressed all of them to Maria Beaumont. I am tempted to make some short extracts from these; my tale will suffer interruption by them, but I was willing to preserve whatever memorials I could of Elinor Clare.

FROM ELINOR CLARE TO MARIA BEAUMONT.

(AN EXTRACT)

"——I HAVE been strolling out for half an hour in the fields; and my mind has been occupied by thoughts which Maria has a right to participate. I have been bringing my *mother* to my recollection. My heart ached with the remembrance of infirmities, that made her closing years of life so sore a trial to her.

"I was concerned to think that our family differences have been one source of disquiet to her. I am sensible that *this last* we are apt to exaggerate after a person's death; and surely, in the main, there was considerable harmony among the members of our little family; still I was concerned to think that we ever gave her gentle spirit disquiet.

"I thought on years back—on all my parents'

friends—the H——s, the F——s, on D—— S——,
and on many a merry evening, in the fire-side circle,
in that comfortable back parlour. It is never used
now.—

"O ye *Matravises*[1] of the age, ye know not what ye
lose in despising these petty topics of endeared remembrance, associated circumstances of past times.
Ye know not the throbbings of the heart, tender
yet affectionately familiar, which accompany the dear
and honoured names of *father* or of *mother*.

"Maria, I thought on all these things; my heart
ached at the review of them, it yet aches, while I
write this; but I am never so satisfied with my train
of thoughts as when they run upon these subjects.
The tears they draw from us meliorate and soften the
heart, and keep fresh within us that memory of dear
friends dead, which alone can fit us for a readmission
to their society hereafter."

FROM ANOTHER LETTER.

"—— I HAD a bad dream this morning—that Allan
was dead; and who, of all persons in the world do
you think, put on mourning for him? Why—*Matravis*.
This alone might cure me of superstitious thoughts
if I were inclined to them; for why should Matravis
mourn for us, or our family? *Still* it was pleasant to
awake, and find it but a dream. Methinks something
like an awaking from an ill dream shall the Resurrec-
tion from the Dead be. Materially different from our
accustomed scenes, and ways of life, the *World to
come* may possibly not be; still it is represented to us
under the notion of a *Rest*, a *Sabbath*, a state of bliss."

---

[1] This name will be explained presently

l   *D*

FROM ANOTHER LETTER.

"—— METHINKS you and I should have been born under the same roof, sucked the same milk, conned the same horn-book, thumbed the same Testament, together; for we have been more than sisters, Maria.

"Something will still be whispering to me, that I shall one day be inmate of the same dwelling with my cousin, partaker with her in all the delights which spring from mutual good offices. kind words, attentions in sickness and in health,—conversation, sometimes innocently trivial, and at others profitably serious;—books read and commented on, together; meals ate, and walks taken, together,—and conferences, how we may best do good to this poor person or that, and wean our spirits from the world's *cares*, without divesting ourselves of its *charities*. What a picture I have drawn, Maria! and none of all these things may ever come to pass."

FROM ANOTHER LETTER.

"—— CONTINUE to write to me, my sweet cousin. Many good thoughts, resolutions, and proper views of things, pass through the mind in the course of the day, but are lost for want of committing them to paper. Seize them, Maria, as they pass, these Birds of Paradise, that show themselves and are gone,— and make a grateful present of the precious fugitives to your friend.

"To use a homely illustration, just rising in my fancy,—shall the good housewife take such pains in pickling and preserving her worthless fruits, her walnuts, her apricots, and quinces—and is there not much *spiritual housewifery* in treasuring up our mind's best fruits—our heart's meditations in its most favoured moments?

" This sad simile is much in the fashion of the old Moralisers, such as I conceive honest Baxter to have been, such as Quarles and Wither were with their curious, serio-comic, quaint emblems. But they sometimes reach the heart, when a more elegant simile rests in the fancy.

" Not low and mean, like these, but beautifully familiarized to our conceptions, and condescending to human thoughts and notions, are all the discourses of our LORD. Conveyed in parable, or similitude, what easy access do they win to the heart, through the medium of the delighted imagination! speaking of heavenly things in fable, or in simile, drawn from earth, from objects *common, accustomed.*

" Life's business, with such delicious little interruptions as our correspondence affords, how pleasant it is! Why can we not paint on the dull paper our whole feelings, exquisite as they rise up?"

FROM ANOTHER LETTER.

" —— I HAD meant to have left off at this place; but looking back. I am sorry to find too gloomy a cast tincturing my last page—a representation of life false and unthankful. Life is *not* all vanity and disappointment. It hath much of evil in it, no doubt; but to those who do not misuse it, it affords comfort, *temporary* comfort, much—much that endears us to it, and dignifies it—many true and good feelings, I trust, of which we need not be ashamed—hours of tranquillity and hope. But the morning was dull and overcast, and my spirits were under a cloud. I feel my error.

" Is it no blessing that we two love one another so dearly—that Allan is left me—that you are settled in life—that worldly affairs go smooth with us both—above all, that our lot hath fallen to us in a Christian country ? Maria, these things are not little. I will consider life as a long feast, and not forget to say grace."

FROM ANOTHER LETTER.

" —— ALLAN has written to me. You know he is on a visit at his old tutor's in Gloucestershire : he is to return home on Thursday. Allan is a dear boy. He concludes his letter, which is very affectionate throughout, in this manner—

" Elinor, I charge you to learn the following stanza by heart—

> The monarch may forget his crown,
>   That on his head an hour hath been ;
> The bridegroom may forget his bride
>   Was made his wedded wife yestreen ;
> The mother may forget her child,
>   That smiles so sweetly on her knee :
> But I'll remember thee, Glencairn,
>   And all that thou hast done for me

" The lines are in Burns. You know, we read him for the first time together at Margate ; and I have been used to refer them to you, and to call you, in my mind, *Glencairn*,—for you were always very good to me. I had a thousand failings, but you would love me in spite of them all. I am going to drink your health."

I shall detain my reader no longer from the narrative.

CHAPTER VIII

THEY had but four rooms in the cottage. Margaret slept in the biggest room up-stairs, and her grand-daughter in a kind of closet adjoining, where she could be within hearing if her grandmother should call her in the night

The girl was often disturbed in that manner. Two or three times in a night she has been forced to leave her bed, to fetch her grandmother's cordials, or do some little service for her; but she knew that Margaret's ailings were *real* and pressing, and Rosamund never complained,—never suspected, that her grandmother's requisitions had any thing unreasonable in them.

The night she parted with Miss Clare she had helped Margaret to bed, as usual; and after saying her prayers, as the custom was, kneeling by the old lady's bed side, kissed her grandmother, and wished her a good night. Margaret blessed her, and charged her to go to bed directly. It was her customary injunction, and Rosamund had never dreamed of disobeying.

So she retired to her little room. The night was warm and clear—the moon very bright; her window commanded a view of *scenes* she had been tracing in the day-time with Miss Clare.

All the events of the day past, the occurrences of their walk arose in her mind. She fancied she should like to retrace those scenes; but it was now nine o'clock, a late hour in the village.

Still she fancied it would be very charming: and then her grandmother's injunction came powerfully

T 2

to her recollection. She sighed, and turned from the window, and walked up and down her little room.

Ever, when she looked at the window, the wish returned. It was not so *very late*. The neighbours were yet about, passing under the window to their homes. She thought, and thought again, till her sensations became vivid, even to painfulness: her bosom was aching to give them vent.

The village clock struck ten!—the neighbours ceased to pass under the window. Rosamund, stealing down stairs, fastened the latch behind her, and left the cottage.

One, that knew her, met her, and observed her with some surprise. Another recollects having wished her a good night. Rosamund never returned to the cottage.

An old man, that lay sick in a small house adjoining to Margaret's, testified the next morning that he had plainly heard the old creature calling for her grand-daughter. All the night long she made her moan, and ceased not to call upon the name of Rosamund. But no Rosamund was there; the voice died away, but not till near daybreak.

When the neighbours came to search in the morning, Margaret was missing! She had *straggled* out of bed, and made her way into Rosamund's room. Worn out with fatigue and fright, when she found the girl not there, she had laid herself down to die—and, it is thought, she died *praying*—for she was discovered in a kneeling posture, her arms and face extended on the pillow, where Rosamund had slept the night before. A smile was on her face in death.

CHAPTER IX.

FAIN would I draw a veil over the transactions of that night; but I cannot: grief and burning shame forbid me to be silent. Black deeds are about to be made public, which reflect a stain upon our common nature.

Rosamund, enthusiastic and improvident, wandered unprotected to a distance from her guardian doors—through lonely glens, and wood walks, where she had rambled many a *day* in safety—till she arrived at a shady copse, out of the hearing of any human habitation.

Matravis met her.——" Flown with insolence and wine," returning home late at night, he passed that way!

Matravis was a very ugly man,—sallow complexioned; and if hearts can wear that colour, his heart was sallow-complexioned also.

A young man with *grey* deliberation! cold and systematic in all his plans: and all his plans were evil. His very lust was systematic.

He would brood over his bad purposes for such a dreary length of time, that it might have been expected some solitary check of conscience must have intervened to save him from commission. But that *Light from Heaven* was extinct in his dark bosom.

Nothing that is great, nothing that is amiable, existed for this unhappy man. He feared, he envied, he suspected; but he never loved. The sublime and beautiful in nature, the excellent and becoming in morals, were things placed beyond the capacity of his sensations. He loved not poetry—nor ever took a lonely walk to meditate—never beheld virtue, which he did not try to disbelieve, or female beauty and innocence, which he did not lust to contaminate.

A sneer was perpetually upon his face, and malice *grinning* at his heart. He would say the most ill-natured things, with the least remorse, of any man I ever knew. This gained him the reputation of a wit, other *traits* got him the reputation of a villain.

And this man formerly paid his court to Elinor Clare!—with what success I leave my readers to determine. It was not in Elinor's nature to despise any living thing ; but in the estimation of this man, to be rejected was to be *despised ,* and Matravis *never forgave.*

He had long turned his eyes upon Rosamund Gray. To steal from the bosom of her friends the jewel they prized so much, the little ewe lamb they held so dear, was a scheme of delicate revenge, and Matravis had a two-fold motive for accomplishing this young maid's ruin.

Often had he met her in her favourite solitudes, but found her ever cold and inaccessible. Of late the girl had avoided straying far from her home, in the fear of meeting him ; but she had never told her fears to Allan.

Matravis had, till now, been content to be a villain within the limits of the law ; but, on the present occasion, hot fumes of wine, co-operating with his deep desire of revenge, and the insolence of an unhoped-for meeting, overcame his customary prudence, and Matravis rose, at once, to an audacity of glorious mischief.

Late at night he met her, a lonely unprotected virgin—no friend at hand—no place near of refuge.

Rosamund Gray, my soul is exceeding sorrowful for thee. I loathe to tell the hateful circumstances of thy wrongs. Night and silence were the only witnesses of this young maid's disgrace Matravis fled.

Rosamund, polluted and disgraced, wandered an abandoned thing, about the fields and meadows till day-break. Not caring to return to the cottage, she sat herself down before the gate of Miss Clare's house—in a stupor of grief.

Elinor was just rising, and had opened the windows of her chamber, when she perceived her desolate young friend. She ran to embrace her: she brought her into the house—she took her to her bosom—she kissed her—she spake to her; but Rosamund could not speak.

Tidings came from the cottage. Margaret's death was an event which could not be kept concealed from Rosamund. When the sweet maid heard of it, she languished, and fell sick; she never held up her head after that time.

If Rosamund had been a *sister*, she could not have been kindlier treated than by her two friends.

Allan had prospects in life—might, in time, have married into any of the first families in Hertfordshire: but Rosamund Gray, humbled though she was, and put to shame, had yet a charm for *him*; and he would have been content to share his fortunes with her yet, if Rosamund would have lived to be his companion.

But this was not to be; and the girl soon after died. She expired in the arms of Elinor—quiet, gentle, as she lived—thankful that she died not among strangers—and expressing, by signs rather than words, a gratitude for the most trifling services, the common offices of humanity. She died uncomplaining; and this young maid, this untaught Rosamund, might have given a lesson to the grave philopher in death.

CHAPTER X.

I WAS but a boy when these events took place. All the village remember the story, and tell of Rosamund Gray, and old blind Margaret.

I parted from Allan Clare on that disastrous night, and set out for Edinburgh the next morning, before the facts were commonly known. I heard not of them; and it was four months before I received a letter from Allan.

"His heart," he told me, "was gone from him, for his sister had died of a frenzy fever!" Not a word of Rosamund in the letter. I was left to collect her story from sources which may one day be explained.

I soon after quitted Scotland, on the death of my father, and returned to my native village. Allan had left the place, and I could gain no information, whether he were dead or living.

I passed the *cottage*. I did not dare to look that way, or to inquire *who* lived there. A little dog that had been Rosamund's, was yelping in my path. I laughed aloud like one mad, whose mind had suddenly gone from him. I stared vacantly around me, like one alienated from common perceptions.

But I was young at that time, and the impression became gradually weakened as I mingled in the business of life. It is now *ten years* since these events took place, and I sometimes think of them as unreal. Allan Clare was a dear friend to me, but there are times when Allan and his sister, Margaret and her grand-daughter, appear like personages of a dream,—an idle dream.

CHAPTER XI.

STRANGE things have happened unto me. I seem scarce awake; but I will recollect my thoughts, and try to give an account of what has befallen me in the few last weeks.

Since my father's death our family have resided in London. I am in practice as a surgeon there. My mother died two years after we left Widford.

A month or two ago I had been busying myself in drawing up the above narrative, intending to make it public. The employment had forced my mind to dwell upon *facts*, which had begun to fade from it. The memory of old times became vivid, and more vivid. I felt a strong desire to revisit the scenes of my native village—of the young loves of Rosamund and her Clare.

A kind of dread had hitherto kept me back, but I was restless now, till I had accomplished my wish. I set out one morning to walk. I reached Widford about eleven in the forenoon. After a slight breakfast

ι

Ɗ

at my inn, where I was mortified to perceive the old
landlord did not know me again—(old Thomas Billet,
he has often made angle-rods for me when a child)—
I rambled over all my accustomed haunts.

Our old house was vacant, and to be sold. I
entered, unmolested, into the room that had been my
bedchamber. I kneeled down on the spot where my
little bed had stood. I felt like a child I prayed like
one. It seemed as though old times were to return
again. I looked round involuntarily, expecting to see
some face I knew ; but all was naked and mute. The
bed was gone. My little pane of painted window,
through which I loved to look at the sun when I
awoke in a fine Summer morning, was taken out,
and had been replaced by one of common glass.

I visited, by turns, every chamber : they were all
desolate and unfurnished, one excepted, in which the
owner had left a harpsichord, probably to be sold. I
touched the keys. I played some old Scottish tunes,
which had delighted me when a child. Past asso-
ciations revived with the music, blended with a
sense of *unreality*, which at last became too powerful. I rushed out of the room to give vent to my
feelings.

I wandered, scarce knowing where, into an old
wood, that stands at the back of the house we
called it the *Wilderness*. A well-known *form* was
missing, that used to meet me in this place. It was
thine. Ben Moxam,—the kindest, gentlest, politest of
human beings, yet was he nothing higher than a
gardener in the family Honest creature ! thou
didst never pass me in my childish rambles without
a soft speech and a smile. I remember thy good-
natured face. But there is one thing, for which I

can never forgive thee, Ben Moxam—that thou didst
join with an old maiden aunt of mine in a cruel
plot, to lop away the hanging branches of the
old fir-trees. I remember them sweeping to the
ground.

I have often left my childish sports to ramble in
this place. Its gloom and its solitude had a mysterious charm for my young mind, nurturing within me
that love of quietness and lonely thinking, which has
accompanied me to maturer years.

In this *Wilderness* I found myself, after a ten
years' absence. Its stately fir-trees were yet standing, with all their luxuriant company of underwood.
The squirrel was there, and the melancholy cooings
of the woodpigeon. All was as I had left it. My heart
softened at the sight. It seemed as though my character had been suffering a *change* since I forsook
these shades.

My parents were both dead. I had no counsellor
left, no experience of age to direct me, no sweet
voice of reproof. The Lord had taken away my
friends, and I knew not where he had laid them.
I paced round the wilderness, seeking a comforter.
I prayed that I might be restored to that *state of
innocence* in which I had wandered in those shades.

Methought my request was heard, for it seemed as
though the stains of manhood were passing from me,
and I were relapsing into the purity and simplicity
of childhood. I was content to have been moulded
into a perfect child. I stood still, as in a trance. I
dreamed that I was enjoying a personal intercourse
with my heavenly Father—and, extravagantly, put
off the shoes from my feet—for the place where I
stood was, I thought, holy ground.

This state of mind could not last long, and I returned with languid feelings to my inn. I ordered my dinner—green pease and a sweetbread. It had been a favourite dish with me in my childhood I was allowed to have it on my birth-days. I was impatient to see it come upon table ; but when it came I could scarce eat a mouthful: my tears choked me. I called for wine. I drank a pint and a half of red wine , and not till then had I dared to visit the churchyard, where my parents were interred.

The *cottage* lay in my way. Margaret had chosen it for that very reason, to be near the church, for the old lady was regular in her attendance on public worship. I passed on, and in a moment found myself among the tombs.

I had been present at my father's burial, and knew the spot again. My mother's funeral I was prevented by illness from attending. A plain stone was placed over the grave, with their initials carved upon it, for they both occupied one grave.

I prostrated myself before the spot. I kissed the earth that covered them. I contemplated, with gloomy delight, the time when I should mingle my dust with theirs, and kneeled, with my arms incumbent on the grave stone, in a kind of mental prayer, for I could not speak.

Having performed these duties. I arose with quieter feelings, and felt leisure to attend to indifferent objects. Still I continued in the churchyard, reading the various inscriptions, and moralizing on them with that kind of levity, which will not unfrequently spring up in the mind, in the midst of deep melancholy.

l   )

I read of nothing but careful parents, loving husbands, and dutiful children. I said, jestingly, Where be all the *bad* people buried? Bad parents, bad husbands, bad children—what cemeteries are appointed for these? Do they not sleep in consecrated ground? or is it but a pious fiction, a generous oversight, in the survivors, which thus tricks out men's epitaphs when dead, who in their life-time discharged the offices of life, perhaps, but lamely? Their failings, with their reproaches, now sleep with them in the grave. *Man wars not with the dead.* It is a *trait* of human nature, for which I love it.

I had not observed, till now, a little group assembled at the other end of the churchyard; it was a company of children, who were gathered round a young man, dressed in black, sitting on a grave-stone.

He seemed to be asking them questions—probably, about their learning—and one little dirty ragged-headed fellow was clambering up his knees to kiss him. The children had been eating black cherries, for some of the stones were scattered about, and their mouths were smeared with them.

As I drew near them, I thought I discerned in the stranger a mild benignity of countenance, which I had somewhere seen before. I gazed at him more attentively.

It was Allan Clare, sitting on the grave of his sister.

I threw my arms about his neck. I exclaimed "Allan!" He turned his eyes upon me he knew me. We both wept aloud. It seemed as though the interval since we parted had been as nothing. I cried out, "Come and tell me about these things"

I drew him away from his little friends. He parted

with a show of reluctance from the churchyard. Margaret and her grand-daughter lay buried there, as well as his sister. I took him to my inn—secured a room, where we might be private—ordered fresh wine. Scarce knowing what I did, I danced for joy.

Allan was quite overcome, and taking me by the hand, he said, "This repays me for all."

It was a proud day for me. I had found the friend I thought dead. Earth seemed to me no longer valuable than as it contained *him*, and existence a blessing no longer than while I should live to be his comforter.

I began, at leisure, to survey him with more attention. Time and grief had left few traces of that fine *enthusiasm*, which once burned in his countenance. His eyes had lost their original fire, but they retained an uncommon sweetness; and whenever they were turned upon me, their smile pierced to my heart.

"Allan, I fear you have been a sufferer?" He replied not, and I could not press him further. I could not call the dead to life again.

So we drank and told old stories, and repeated old poetry, and sang old songs, as if nothing had happened. We sat till very late. I forgot that I had purposed returning to town that evening. To Allan all places were alike. I grew noisy, he grew cheerful. Allan's old manners, old enthusiasm, were returning upon him. We laughed, we wept, we mingled our tears, and talked extravagantly.

Allan was my chamber-fellow that night, and lay awake planning schemes of living together under the same roof, entering upon similar pursuits, and praising GoD that we had met.

I was obliged to return to town the next morning, and Allan proposed to accompany me. " Since the death of his sister," he told me, " he had been a wanderer."

In the course of our walk he unbosomed himself without reserve—told me many particulars of his way of life for the last nine or ten years, which I do not feel myself at liberty to divulge.

Once, on my attempting to cheer him, when I perceived him over-thoughtful, he replied to me in these words :

" Do not regard me as unhappy when you catch me in these moods. I am never more happy than at times when, by the cast of my countenance, men judge me most miserable.

" My friend, the events which have left this sadness behind them are of no recent date. The melancholy which comes over me with the recollection of them is not hurtful, but only tends to soften and tranquillize my mind, to detach me from the restlessness of human pursuits.

" The stronger I feel this detachment, the more I find myself drawn heavenward to the contemplation of spiritual objects.

" I love to keep old friendships alive and warm within me, because I expect a renewal of them in the *World of Spirits.*

" I am a wandering and unconnected thing on the earth. I have made no new friendships that can compensate me for the loss of the old ; and the more I know mankind, the more does it become necessary for me to supply their loss by little images, recollections, and circumstances of past pleasures.

" I am sensible that I am surrounded by a multitude of very worthy people, plain-hearted souls, sincere and kind ; but they have hitherto eluded my pursuit, and will continue to bless the little circle of their families and friends, while I must remain a stranger to them.

"Kept at a distance by mankind, I have not ceased to love them ; and could I find the cruel persecutor, the malignant instrument of God's judgments on me and mine, I think I would forgive, and try to love him too.

"I have been a quiet sufferer. From the beginning of my calamities it was given to me, not to see the hand of man in them. I perceived a mighty arm, which none but myself could see, extended over me. I gave my heart to the Purifier, and my will to the Sovereign Will of the Universe. The irresistible wheels of destiny passed on in their everlasting rotation, and I suffered myself to be carried along with them without complaining."

CHAPTER XII.

ALLAN told me that for some years past, feeling himself disengaged from every personal tie, but not alienated from human sympathies, it had been his taste, his *humour* he called it, to spend a great portion of his time in *hospitals* and *lazar-houses*.

He had found a *wayward pleasure*, he refused to name it a virtue, in tending a description of people, who had long ceased to expect kindness or friendliness from mankind, but were content to accept the reluctant services which the oftentimes unfeeling instruments and servants of these well-meant institutions deal out to the poor sick people under their care.

It is not medicine, it is not broths and coarse meats, served up at a stated hour with all the hard formalities of a prison—it is not the scanty dole of a bed to die on—which dying man requires from his species.

Looks, attentions, consolations,—in a word, *sympathies*, are what a man most needs in this awful close of mortal sufferings. A kind look, a smile, a drop of cold water to the parched lip—for these things a man shall bless you in death.

And these better things than cordials did Allan love to administer—to stay by a bed side the whole day, when something disgusting in a patient's distemper has kept the very nurses at a distance—to sit by, while the poor wretch got a little sleep—and be there to smile upon him when he awoke—to slip a guinea, now and then, into the hands of a nurse or attendant: these things have been to Allan as *privileges*, for which he was content to live, choice marks, and circumstances of his Maker's goodness to him.

And I do not know whether occupations of this kind be not a spring of purer and nobler delight (certainly instances of a more disinterested virtue) than arises from what are called Friendships of Sentiment.

Between two persons of liberal education, like opinions, and common feelings, oftentimes subsists a Variety of Sentiment, which disposes each to look upon the other as the only being in the universe worthy of friendship, or capable of understanding it,—themselves they consider as the solitary receptacles

of all that is delicate in feeling, or stable in attachment: when the odds are, that under every green
hill, and in every crowded street, people of equal
worth are to be found, who do more good in their
generation, and make less noise in the doing of it.

It was in consequence of these benevolent propensities, I have been describing, that Allan oftentimes
discovered considerable inclinations in favour of my
way of life, which I have before mentioned as being
that of a surgeon. He would frequently attend me
on my visits to patients; and I began to think that
he had serious intentions of making my profession
his study.

He was present with me at a scene—a *death-bed
scene*. I shudder when I do but think of it

CHAPTER XIII.

I WAS sent for the other morning to the assistance
of a gentleman who had been wounded in a duel,
and his wounds by unskilful treatment had been
brought to a dangerous crisis.

The uncommonness of the name, which was
Matravis, suggested to me, that this might possibly
be no other than Allan's old enemy. Under this
apprehension I did what I could to dissuade Allan
from accompanying me; but he seemed bent upon
going, and even pleased himself with the notion that
it might lie within his ability to do the unhappy man
some service. So he went with me.

When we came to the house, which was in Soho
Square, we discovered that it was indeed the man,—

the identical Matravis, who had done all that mischief in times past, but not in a condition to excite any other sensation than pity in a heart more hard than Allan's.

Intense pain had brought on a delirium—we perceived this on first entering the room—for the wretched man was raving to himself—talking idly in mad unconnected sentences, that yet seemed, at times, to have a reference to *past facts*.

One while he told us his dream. " He had lost his way on a great heath, to which there seemed no end ; it was cold, cold, cold,—and dark, very dark. An old woman in leading-strings, *blind*, was groping about for a guide ; " and then he frightened me,—for he seemed disposed to be *jocular*, and sang a song about " an old woman clothed in grey," and said " he did not believe in a devil."

Presently he bid us " not tell Allan Clare."—Allan was hanging over him at that very moment, sobbing. I could not resist the impulse, but cried out, " *This is Allan Clare : Allan Clare is come to see you, my dear Sir.*"—The wretched man did not hear me, I believe, for he turned his head away, and began talking of *charnel-houses*, and *dead men*, and " whether they knew any thing that passed in their coffins."

Matravis died that night.

MARIA HOWE;

OR, THE EFFECT OF WITCH STORIES.[1]

I was brought up in the country. From my infancy
I was always a weak and tender-spirited girl, subject
to fears and depressions. My parents, and particularly my mother, were of a very different disposition.
They were what is usually called gay. They loved
pleasure and parties and visiting; but, as they found
the turn of my mind to be quite opposite, they gave
themselves little trouble about me, but upon such
occasions generally left me to my choice, which was
much oftener to stay at home, and indulge myself in
my solitude, than to join in their rambling visits. I
was always fond of being alone, yet always in a
manner afraid. There was a book-closet which led
into my mother's dressing-room. Here I was extremely fond of being shut up by myself, to take
down whatever volumes I pleased, and pore upon
them,—no matter whether they were fit for my years
or no, or whether I understood them. Here, when
the weather would not permit my going into the dark
walk (*my walk*, as it was called) in the garden,—
here, when my parents have been from home, I have
stayed for hours together, till the loneliness, which

---

[1] This and the next two stories were Lamb's contributions to his
sister's work, *Mrs. Leicester's School*, originally published in 1807.
There was a fourth edition in 1814.

ι   Ɗ

pleased me so at first, has at length become quite
frightful, and I have rushed out of the closet into the
inhabited parts of the house, and sought refuge in
the lap of some one of the female servants, or of my
aunt, who would say, seeing me look pale, that Maria
had been frightening herself with some of those *nasty*
books: so she used to call my favourite volumes,
which I would not have parted with, no, not with one
of the least of them, if I had had the choice to be
made a fine princess, and to govern the world. But
my aunt was no reader. She used to excuse herself,
and say that reading hurt her eyes. I have been
naughty enough to think that this was only an excuse;
for I found that my aunt's weak eyes did not prevent
her from poring ten hours a day upon her Prayer
Book, or her favourite Thomas à Kempis. But this
was always her excuse for not reading any of the
books I recommended. My aunt was my father's
sister. She had never been married. My father was
a good deal older than my mother, and my aunt was
ten years older than my father. As I was often left
at home with her, and as my serious disposition so
well agreed with hers, an intimacy grew up between
the old lady and me ; and she would often say that
she loved only one person in the world, and that was
me. Not that she and my parents were on very bad
terms ; but the old lady did not feel herself respected
enough. The attention and fondness which she
showed to me, conscious as I was that I was almost
the only being she felt any thing like fondess to,
made me love her, as it was natural · indeed, I am
ashamed to say, that I fear I almost loved her better
than both my parents put together. But there was
an oddness, a silence, about my aunt, which was

l   *)*

never interrupted but by her occasional expressions
of love to me, that made me stand in fear of her. An
odd look from under her spectacles would sometimes
scare me away, when I had been peering up in her
face to make her kiss me. Then she had a way of
muttering to herself, which, though it was good
words and religious words that she was mumbling,
somehow I did not like. My weak spirits, and the
fears I was subject to, always made me afraid of any
personal singularity or oddness in any one. I am
ashamed, ladies, to lay open so many particulars of
our family ; but indeed it is necessary to the understanding of what I am going to tell you of a very great
weakness, if not wickedness, which I was guilty of
towards my aunt. But I must return to my studies,
and tell you what books I found in the closet, and
what reading I chiefly admired. There was a great
"Book of Martyrs," in which I used to read, or
rather I used to spell out meanings ; for I was too
ignorant to make out many words : but there it was
written all about those good men who chose to be
burned alive, rather than forsake their religion and
become naughty Papists. Some words I could make
out, some I could not, but I made out enough to
fill my little head with vanity ; and I used to think I
was so courageous I could be burned too, and I
would put my hands upon the flames which were
pictured in the pretty pictures which the book had,
and feel them. But you know, ladies, there is a
great difference between the flames in a picture and
real fire : and I am now ashamed of the conceit
which I had of my own courage, and think how
poor a martyr I should have made in those days.
Then there was a book not so big, but it had pictures

in it. It was called "Culpepper's Herbal." It was
full of pictures of plants and herbs; but I did
not much care for that. There was Salmon's
"Modern History," out of which I picked a good
deal It had pictures of Chinese gods, and the great
hooded serpent, which ran strangely in my fancy.
There were some law books too ; but the old English
frightened me from reading them. But, above all,
what I relished was "Stackhouse's History of the
Bible," where there was the picture of the ark, and
all the beasts getting into it. This delighted me,
because it puzzled me : and many an aching head
have I got with poring into it, and contriving how it
might be built, with such and such rooms, to hold
all the world, if there should be another flood ; and
sometimes settling what pretty beasts should be
saved, and what should not ; for I would have no
ugly or deformed beasts in my pretty ark. But this
was only a piece of folly and vanity, that a little
reflection might cure me of. Foolish girl that I was,
to suppose that any creature is really ugly, that has
all its limbs contrived with heavenly wisdom, and
was doubtless formed to some beautiful end, though
a child cannot comprehend it Doubtless a frog or
a toad is not uglier in itself than a squirrel or a
pretty green lizard, but we want understanding to
see it

These fancies, ladies, were not so very foolish or
naughty, perhaps, but they may be forgiven in a child
of six years old ; but what I am going to tell, I shall
be ashamed of, and repent, I hope, as long as I live.
It will teach me not to form rash judgments. Besides
the picture of the ark, and many others which I have
forgot, Stackhouse contained one picture which made

more impression upon my childish understanding than all the rest; it was the picture of the raising-up of Samuel, which I used to call the Witch-of-Endor picture. I was always very fond of picking up stories about witches. There was a book called "Glanvil on Witches," which used to lie about in this closet: it was thumbed about, and showed it had been much read in former times. This was my treasure. Here I used to pick out the strangest stories. My not being able to read them very well, probably made them appear more strange and out of the way to me. But I could collect enough to understand that witches were old women, who gave themselves up to do mischief; how, by the help of spirits as bad as themselves, they lamed cattle, and made the corn not grow; and how they made images of wax to stand for people that had done them any injury, or they thought had done them injury; and how they burned the images before a slow fire, and stuck pins in them; and the persons which these waxen images represented, however far distant, felt all the pains and torments in good earnest which were inflicted in show upon these images: and such a horror I had of these wicked witches, that though I am now better instructed, and look upon all these stories as mere idle tales, and invented to fill people's heads with nonsense, yet I cannot recall to mind the horrors which I then felt, without shuddering, and feeling something of the old fit return.

This foolish book of witch-stories had no pictures in it; but I made up for them out of my own fancy, and out of the great picture of the raising-up of Samuel, in Stackhouse. I was not old enough to understand the difference there was between these

silly, improbable tales, which imputed such powers to
poor old women, who are the most helpless things in
the creation, and the narrative in the Bible, which
does not say that the witch, or pretended witch, raised
up the dead body of Samuel by her own power, but,
as it clearly appears, he was permitted by the divine
will to appear, to confound the presumption of Saul;
and that the witch herself was really as much frightened and confounded at the miracle as Saul himself,
not expecting a real appearance, but probably having
prepared some juggling, sleight-of hand tricks, and
sham appearance, to deceive the eyes of Saul;
whereas neither she, nor any one living, had ever the
power to raise the dead to life, but only He who made
them from the first. These reasons I might have
read in Stackhouse itself, if I had been old enough,
and have read them in that very book since I was
older; but, at that time, I looked at little beyond
the picture.

These stories of witches so terrified me, that my
sleeps were broken; and, in my dreams, I always
had a fancy of a witch being in the room with me.
I know now that it was only nervousness; but though
I can laugh at it now as well as you, ladies, if you
knew what I suffered you would be thankful that
you have had sensible people about you to instruct
you, and teach you better. I was let grow up wild,
like an ill weed; and thrived accordingly One
night, that I had been terrified in my sleep with my
imaginations, I got out of bed, and crept softly to
the adjoining room. My room was next to where
my aunt usually sat when she was alone. Into her
room I crept for relief from my fears. The old lady
was not yet retired to rest, but was sitting with her

eyes half open, half closed ; her spectacles tottering
upon her nose ; her head nodding over her Prayer
Book ; her lips mumbling the words as she read them,
or half read them, in her dozing posture ; her grotesque appearance, her old-fashioned dress, resembling
what I had seen in that fatal picture in Stackhouse.
All this, with the dead time of night, as it seemed to
me, (for I had gone through my first sleep,) joined to
produce a wicked fancy in me, that the form which
I had beheld was not my aunt, but some witch. Her
mumbling of her prayers confirmed me in this shocking idea. I had read in Glanvil of those wicked
creatures reading their prayers *backwards;* and I
thought that this was the operation which her lips
were at this time employed about. Instead of flying
to her friendly lap for that protection which I had
so often experienced when I have been weak and
timid, I shrunk back, terrified and bewildered, to my
bed, where I lay, in broken sleeps and miserable
fancies, till the morning. which I had so much reason
to wish for, came. My fancies a little wore away
with the light ; but an impression was fixed, which
could not for a long time be done away. In the day-
time, when my father and mother were about the
house, when I saw them familiarly speak to my aunt,
my fears all vanished : and when the good creature
has taken me upon her knees, and shown me any
kindness more than ordinary, at such times I have
melted into tears, and longed to tell her what naughty,
foolish fancies I had had of her. But when night
returned, that figure which I had seen recurred,—the
posture, the half-closed eyes, the mumbling and
muttering which I had heard. A confusion was in
my head, *who* it was I had seen that night : it was

my aunt, and it was not my aunt; it was that good
creature, who loved me above all the world, engaged
at her good task of devotions,—perhaps praying for
some good to me. Again, it was a witch, a creature
hateful to God and man, reading backwards the good
prayers; who would perhaps destroy me In these
conflicts of mind I passed several weeks, till, by a
revolution in my fate, I was removed to the house of
a female relation of my mother's in a distant part of
the country, who had come on a visit to our house,
and observing my lonely ways, and apprehensive of
the ill effect of my mode of living upon my health,
begged leave to take me home to her house to reside
for a short time. I went, with some reluctance at
leaving my closet, my dark walk, and even my aunt,
who had been such a source of both love and terror
to me. But I went, and soon found the grand effects
of a change of scene. Instead of melancholy closets
and lonely avenues of trees, I saw lightsome rooms
and cheerful faces I had companions of my own
age. No books were allowed me but what were rational
and sprightly,—that gave me mirth, or gave me instruction. I soon learned to laugh at witch-stories ;
and when I returned, after three or four months'
absence, to our own house, my good aunt appeared
to me in the same light in which I had viewed her
from my infancy, before that foolish fancy possessed
me , or rather, I should say, more kind, more fond,
more loving than before. It is impossible to say
how much good that lady (the kind relation of my
mother's that I spoke of) did to me by changing the
scene. Quite a new turn of ideas was given to me.
I became sociable and companionable. My parents
soon discovered a change in me , and I have found

a similar alteration in them. They have been plainly more fond of me since that change, as from that time I learned to conform myself more to their way of living. I have never since had that aversion to company, and going out with them, which used to make them regard me with less fondness than they would have wished to show. I impute all that I had to complain of in their neglect to my having been a little unsociable, uncompanionable mortal. I lived in this manner for a year or two, passing my time between our house and the lady's who so kindly took me in hand, till, by her advice, I was sent to this school where I have told you, ladies, what, for fear of ridicule, I never ventured to tell any person besides,—the story of my foolish and naughty fancy.

SUSAN YATES;

OR, FIRST GOING TO CHURCH.

I WAS born and brought up in a house in which my parents had all their lives resided, which stood in the midst of that lonely tract of land called the Lincolnshire Fens. Few families besides our own lived near the spot; both because it was reckoned an unwholesome air, and because its distance from any town or market made it an inconvenient situation. My father was in no very affluent circumstances; and it was a sad necessity which he was put to, of having to go many miles to fetch any thing from the nearest village, which was full seven miles distant, through a sad, miry way, that at all times made it heavy walking, and, after rain, was almost impassable. But he had no horse or carriage of his own.

The church, which belonged to the parish in which our house was situated, stood in this village; and its distance being, as I said before, seven miles from our house, made it quite an impossible thing for my mother or me to think of going to it. Sometimes, indeed, on a fine dry Sunday, my father would rise early, and take a walk to the village, just to see how *goodness thrived*, as he used to say; but he would generally return tired, and the worse for his walk. It is scarcely possible to explain to any one who has not lived in the Fens what difficult and dangerous

walking it is. A mile is as good as four, I have
heard my father say, in those parts. My mother,
who in the early part of her life had lived in a more
civilized spot, and had been used to constant church-
going, would often lament her situation. It was
from her I early imbibed a great curiosity and anxiety
to see that thing which I had heard her call a church,
and so often lament that she could never go to. I
had seen houses of various structures, and had seen
in pictures the shapes of ships and boats, and palaces
and temples, but never rightly any thing that could
be called a church, or that could satisfy me about its
form. Sometimes I thought it must be like our
house; and sometimes I fancied it must be more
like the house of our neighbour, Mr. Sutton, which
was bigger and handsomer than ours. Sometimes I
thought it was a great hollow cave, such as I have
heard my father say the first inhabitants of the earth
dwelt in. Then I thought it was like a waggon or a
cart, and that it must be something moveable. The
shape of it ran in my mind strangely; and one day I
ventured to ask my mother, what was that foolish
thing she was always longing to go to, and which
she called a church. Was it any thing to eat or
drink? or was it only like a great huge plaything, to
be seen and stared at? I was not quite five years of
age when I made this inquiry.

This question, so oddly put, made my mother
smile but in a little time she put on a more grave
look, and informed me that a church was nothing
that I had supposed it; but it was a great building,
far greater than any house which I had seen, where
men and women and children came together twice a
day, on Sundays, to hear the Bible read, and make

good resolutions for the week to come. She told me
that the fine music which we sometimes heard in the
air came from the bells of St. Mary's Church, and
that we never heard it but when the wind was in a
particular point. This raised my wonder more than
all the rest , for I had somehow conceived that the
noise which I heard was occasioned by birds up in
the air, or that it was made by the angels, whom (so
ignorant I was till that time) I had always considered
to be a sort of birds : for, before this time. I was
totally ignorant of any thing like religion , it being a
principle of my father, that young heads should not
be told too many things at once, for fear they should
get confused ideas, and no clear notions of any thing.
We had always, indeed, so far observed Sundays,
that no work was done upon that day; and upon
that day I wore my best muslin frock, and was not
allowed to sing or to be noisy but I never understood why that day should differ from any other.
We had no public meetings. indeed, the few
straggling houses which were near us would have
furnished but a slender congregation : and the loneliness of the place we lived in, instead of making us
more sociable, and drawing us closer together, as my
mother used to say it ought to have done, seemed
to have the effect of making us more distant, and
averse to society, than other people. One or two
good neighbours, indeed, we had, but not in numbers
to give me an idea of church attendance.

But now my mother thought it high time to give
me some clearer instruction in the main points of
religion : and my father came readily into her plan.
I was now permitted to sit up half an hour later on
Sunday evening, that I might hear a portion of

l   *D*

Scripture read, which had always been their custom; though by reason of my tender age, and my father's opinion on the impropriety of children being taught too young, I had never till now been an auditor. I was taught my prayers, and those things which you, ladies, I doubt not, had the benefit of being instructed in at a much earlier age.

The clearer my notions on these points became, they only made me more passionately long for the privilege of joining in that social service from which it seemed that we alone, of all the inhabitants of the land, were debarred; and when the wind was in that point which enabled the sound of the distant bells of St. Mary's to be heard over the great moor which skirted our house, I have stood out in the air to catch the sounds, which I almost devoured: and the tears have come into my eyes, when sometimes they seemed to speak to me, almost in articulate sounds, to *come to church*, and because of the great moor which was between me and them I could not come; and the too tender apprehensions of these things have filled me with a religious melancholy. With thoughts like these, I entered into my seventh year.

And now the time was come when the great moor was no longer to separate me from the object of my wishes and of my curiosity. My father having some money left him by the will of a deceased relation, we ventured to set up a sort of carriage: no very superb one, I assure you, ladies; but in that part of the world it was looked upon with some envy by our poorer neighbours. The first party of pleasure which my father proposed to take in it was to the village where I had so often wished to go; and my mother and I were to accompany him : for it was very fit, my father observed, that little Susan should go to church, and learn how to behave herself; for we might sometime or other have occasion to live in London, and not always be confined to that out-of-the-way spot.

It was on a Sunday morning that we set out, my little heart beating with almost breathless expectation. The day was fine, and the roads as good as they ever are in those parts. I was so happy and so proud! I was lost in dreams of what I was going to see. At length, the tall steeple of St. Mary's Church came in view. It was pointed out to me by my father as the place from which that music had come which I had heard over the moor, and fancied to be angels singing. I was wound up to the highest pitch of delight at having visibly presented to me the spot from which had proceeded that unknown friendly music; and when it began to peal, just as we approached the village, it seemed to speak, " *Susan is come !*" as plainly as it used to invite me *to come* when I heard it over the moor. I pass over our alighting at the house of a relation, and all that passed till I went with my father and mother to church.

St. Mary's Church is a great church for such a small village as it stands in. My father said it had been a cathedral, and that it had once belonged to a monastery; but the monks were all gone. Over the door there was stone-work representing the saints and bishops; and here and there, along the sides of the church, there were figures of men's heads, made in a strange, grotesque way. I have since seen the same sort of figures in the round tower of the Temple

Church in London.   My father said they were very
improper ornaments for such a place; and so I now
think them : but it seems the people who built these
great churches, in old times, gave themselves more
liberties than they do now; and I remember that
when I first saw them, and before my father had
made this observation, though they were so ugly and
out of shape, and some of them seemed to be grinning, and distorting their features with pain or with
laughter, yet being placed upon a church to which I
had come with such serious thoughts, I could not
help thinking they had some serious meaning; and
I looked at them with wonder, but without any
temptation to laugh.   I somehow fancied they were
the representation of wicked people, set up as a
warning.

When we got into the church the service was not
begun; and my father kindly took me round to show
me the monuments, and every thing else remarkable.
I remember seeing one of a venerable figure, which
my father said had been a judge.   The figure was
kneeling, as if it were alive, before a sort of desk,
with a book, I suppose the Bible, lying on it.   I
somehow fancied the figure had a sort of life in it, it
seemed so natural, or that the dead judge, that it
was done for, said his prayers at it still.   This was
a silly notion : but I was very young, and had passed
my little life in a remote place, where I had never
seen any thing, nor knew any thing . and the awe
which I felt at first being in a church took from me
all power but that of wondering.   I did not reason
about any thing : I was too young.   Now I understand why monuments are put up for the dead, and
why the figures which are put upon them are de-

scribed as doing the actions which they did in their lifetimes, and that they are a sort of pictures set up for our instruction. But all was new and surprising to me on that day,—the long windows with little panes, the pillars, the pews made of oak, the little hassocks for the people to kneel on, the form of the pulpit, with the sounding-board over it, gracefully carved in flower-work. To you, who have lived all your lives in populous places, and have been taken to church from the earliest time you can remember, my admiration of these things must appear strangely ignorant; but I was a lonely young creature, that had been brought up in remote places, where there was neither church nor church-going inhabitants. I have since lived in great towns, and seen the ways of churches and of worship; and I am old enough now to distinguish between what is essential in religion, and what is merely formal or ornamental.

When my father had done pointing out to me the things most worthy of notice about the church, the service was almost ready to begin: the parishioners had most of them entered, and taken their seats, and we were shown into a pew, where my mother was already seated. Soon after the clergyman entered, and the organ began to play what is called the Voluntary. I had never seen so many people assembled before. At first I thought that all eyes were upon me, and that because I was a stranger. I was terribly ashamed and confused at first: but my mother helped me to find out the places in the Prayer Book; and being busy about that, took off some of my painful apprehensions. I was no stranger to the order of the service, having often read in the Prayer Book at home; but, my thoughts

x 2

being confused, it puzzled me a little to find out the
responses and other things which I thought I knew
so well; but I went through it tolerably well. One
thing which has often troubled me since is, that I
am afraid I was too full of myself, and of thinking
how happy I was, and what a privilege it was for one
that was so young to join in the service with so
many grown people; so that I did not attend enough
to the instruction which I might have received. I
remember I foolishly applied every thing that was
said to myself, so as it could mean nobody but myself, I was so full of my own thoughts. All that
assembly of people seemed to me as if they were
come together only to show me the way of a church.
Not but that I received some very affecting impressions from some things which I heard that day: but
the standing-up and the sitting-down of the people, the
organ, the singing,—the way of all these things took
up more of my attention than was proper; or I
thought it did. I believe I behaved better, and was
more serious, when I went a second time and a third
time: for now we went, as a regular thing, every
Sunday; and continued to do so, till, by a still further
change for the better in my father's circumstances,
we removed to London. Oh it was a happy day
for me, my first going to St. Mary's Church before
that day, I used to feel like a little outcast in the
wilderness; like one that did not belong to the world
of Christian people. I have never felt like a little
outcast since. But I never can hear the sweet noise
of bells, that I don't think of the angels singing, and
what poor but pretty thoughts I had of angels in my
uninstructed solitude.

ARABELLA HARDY;

OR, THE SEA VOYAGE.

I was born in the East Indies. I lost my father and
mother young. At the age of five, my relations
thought it proper that I should be sent to England
for my education. I was to be intrusted to the care
of a young woman who had a character for great
humanity and discretion; but just as I had taken
leave of my friends, and we were about to take our
passage, the young woman suddenly fell sick, and
could not go on board. In this unpleasant emergency
no one knew how to act. The ship was at the very
point of sailing, and it was the last which was to sail
for the season. At length the captain, who was
known to my friends, prevailed upon my relation,
who had come with us to see us embark, to leave the
young woman on shore, and to let me embark separately. There was no possibility of getting any other
female attendant for me in the short time allotted for
our preparation; and the opportunity of going by
that ship was thought too valuable to be lost. No
other ladies happened to be going; and so I was
consigned to the care of the captain and his crew,—
rough and unaccustomed attendants for a young
creature, delicately brought up as I had been : but
indeed they did their best to make me not feel the
difference. The unpolished sailors were my nursery-

maids and my waiting-women. Every thing was
done by the captain and the men to accommodate me
and make me easy. I had a little room made out of
the cabin, which was to be considered as my room,
and nobody might enter into it. The first mate had
a great character for bravery and all sailor-like accomplishments; but with all this he had a gentleness
of manners, and a pale, feminine cast of face, from
ill health and a weakly constitution, which subjected
him to some ridicule from the officers, and caused
him to be named Betsy. He did not much like the
appellation; but he submitted to it the better, saying
that those who gave him a woman's name well knew
that he had a man's heart, and that, in the face of
danger, he would go as far as any man. To this
young man, whose real name was Charles Atkinson,
by a lucky thought of the captain, the care of me was
especially intrusted. Betsy was proud of his charge;
and, to do him justice, acquitted himself with great
diligence and adroitness through the whole of the
voyage. From the beginning I had somehow looked
upon Betsy as a woman, hearing him so spoken of;
and this reconciled me in some measure to the want
of a maid, which I had been used to. But I was a
manageable girl at all times, and gave nobody much
trouble.

I have not knowledge enough to give an account
of my voyage, or to remember the names of the seas
we passed through, or the lands which we touched
upon, in our course. The chief thing I can remember (for I do not recollect the events of the voyage in
any order) was Atkinson taking me upon deck to see
the great whales playing about in the sea. There
was one great whale came bounding up out of the

sea, and then he would dive into it again, and then he would come up at a distance where nobody expected him ; and another whale was following after him. Atkinson said they were at play, and that the lesser whale loved that bigger whale, and kept it company all through the wide seas : but I thought it strange play, and a frightful kind of love , for I every minute expected they would come up to our ship and toss it. But Atkinson said a whale was a gentle creature, and it was a sort of sea elephant : and that the most powerful creatures in nature are always the least hurtful. And he told me how men went out to take these whales, and stuck long pointed darts into them , and how the sea was discoloured with the blood of these poor whales for many miles' distance: and I admired the courage of the men ; but I was sorry for the inoffensive whale. Many other pretty sights he used to show me, when he was not on watch, or doing some duty for the ship. No one was more attentive to his duty than he : but at such times as he had leisure he would show me all pretty sea sights,—the dolphins and porpoises that came before a storm ; and all the colours which the sea changed to,—how sometimes it was a deep blue, and then a deep green, and sometimes it would seem all on fire. All these various appearances he would show me, and attempt to explain the reason of them to me as well as my young capacity would admit of. There was a lion and a tiger on board, going to England as a present to the king ; and it was a great diversion to Atkinson and me, after I had got rid of my first terrors, to see the ways of these beasts in their dens, and how venturous the sailors were in putting their hands through the grates, and patting

their rough coats.   Some of the men had monkeys,
which ran loose about; and the sport was for the
men to lose them, and find them again.   The monkeys would run up the shrouds, and pass from rope
to rope, with ten times greater alacrity than the most
experienced sailor could follow them : and sometimes
they would hide themselves in the most unthought-of
places ; and when they were found they would grin,
and make mouths, as if they had sense.   Atkinson
described to me the ways of these little animals in
their native woods ; for he had seen them.   Oh how
many ways he thought of to amuse me in that long
voyage !

Sometimes he would describe to me the odd shapes
and varieties of fishes that were in the sea, and tell
me tales of the sea-monsters that lay hid at the bottom, and were seldom seen by men, and what a
glorious sight it would be if our eyes could be sharpened to behold all the inhabitants of the sea at
once, swimming in the great deeps, as plain as we
see the gold and silver fish in a bowl of glass.   With
such notions he enlarged my infant capacity to take
in many things.

When in foul weather I have been terrified at the
motion of the vessel as it rocked backwards and for-
wards, he would still my fears, and tell me that I
used to be rocked so once in a cradle, and that the
sea was God's bed and the ship our cradle, and we
were as safe in that greater motion as when we felt
that lesser one in our little wooden sleeping-places.
When the wind was up, and sang through the sails,
and disturbed me with its violent clamours, he would
call it music, and bid me hark to the sea-organ ; and
with that name he quieted my tender apprehensions.

When I have looked around with a mournful face at
seeing all *men* about me, he would enter into my
thoughts, and tell me pretty stories of his mother and
his sisters, and a female cousin that he loved better
than his sisters, whom he called Jenny; and say
that when we got to England I should go and see
them; and how fond Jenny would be of his little
daughter, as he called me. And with these images
of women and females which he raised in my fancy,
he quieted me for a while. One time, and never but
once, he told me that Jenny had promised to be his
wife, if ever he came to England; but that he had
his doubts whether he should live to get home, for he
was very sickly. This made me cry bitterly.

That I dwell so long upon the attention of this
Atkinson, is only because his death, which happened
just before we got to England, affected me so much,
that he alone of all the ship's crew has engrossed my
mind ever since . though, indeed, the captain and all
were singularly kind to me, and strove to make up
for my uneasy and unnatural situation. The boat-
swain would pipe for my diversion, and the sailor-boy
would climb the dangerous mast for my sport. The
rough foremast-man would never willingly appear before me till he had combed his long black hair smooth
and sleek, not to terrify me. The officers got up a
sort of play for my amusement; and Atkinson, or as
they called him, Betsy, acted the heroine of the
piece. All ways that could be contrived were thought
upon to reconcile me to my lot. I was the universal
favourite; I do not know how deservedly; but I suppose it was because I was alone, and there was no
female in the ship besides me. Had I come over
with female relations or attendants, I should have

excited no particular curiosity: I should have required no uncommon attentions. I was one little woman among a crew of men; and I believe the homage which I have read that men universally pay to women was in this case directed to me, in the absence of all other womankind. I do not know how that might be; but I was a little princess among them, and I was not six years old.

I remember, the first drawback which happened to my comfort was Atkinson's not appearing the whole of one day. The captain tried to reconcile me to it by saying that Mr. Atkinson was confined to his cabin; that he was not quite well, but a day or two would restore him. I begged to be taken in to see him; but this was not granted. A day, and then another, came, and another, and no Atkinson was visible; and I saw apparent solicitude on the faces of all the officers, who nevertheless strove to put on their best countenances before me, and to be more than usually kind to me. At length, by the desire of Atkinson himself, as I have since learned, I was permitted to go into his cabin, and see him. He was sitting up, apparently in a state of great exhaustion; but his face lighted up when he saw me; and he kissed me, and told me that he was going a great voyage, far longer than that which we had passed together, and he should never come back. And though I was so young, I understood well enough that he meant this of his death; and I cried sadly: but he comforted me, and told me that I must be his little executrix, and perform his last will, and bear his last words to his mother and his sisters, and to his cousin Jenny, whom I should see in a short time; and he gave me his blessing, as a father would bless his child; and he sent a last kiss by me to all his female relations; and he made me promise that I would go and see them when I got to England. And soon after this he died; but I was in another part of the ship when he died: and I was not told it till we got to shore, which was a few days after; but they kept telling me that he was better and better, and that I should soon see him, but that it disturbed him to talk with any one. Oh what a grief it was when I learned that I had lost an old shipmate, that had made an irksome situation so bearable by his kind assiduities! and to think that he was gone, and that I could never repay him for his kindness!

When I had been a year and a half in England, the captain, who had made another voyage to India and back, thinking that time had alleviated a little the sorrow of Atkinson's relations, prevailed upon my friends, who had the care of me in England, to let him introduce me to Atkinson's mother and sisters. Jenny was no more. She had died in the interval, and I never saw her. Grief for his death had brought on a consumption, of which she lingered about a twelvemonth, and then expired. But in the mother and the sisters of this excellent young man I have found the most valuable friends I possess on this side the great ocean. They received me from the captain as the little *protégée* of Atkinson: and from them I have learned passages of his former life; and this in particular,—that the illness of which he died was brought on by a wound, of which he never quite recovered, which he got in a desperate attempt, when he was quite a boy, to defend his captain against a superior force of the enemy which had boarded him, and which, by his premature valour inspiriting the men, they finally succeeded in repulsing. This was that Atkinson, who, from his pale and feminine appearance, was called Betsy : this was he whose womanly care of me got him the name of a woman ; who, with more than female attention, condescended to play the handmaid to a little unaccompanied orphan, that fortune had cast upon the care of a rough sea-captain and his rougher crew.

THE
ADVENTURES OF ULYSSES.

[FROM CHAPMAN'S HOMER.]

———

PREFACE.

——

THIS work is designed as a supplement to the "Adventures of Telemachus." It treats of the conduct and sufferings of Ulysses, the father
of Telemachus. The picture which it exhibits is that of a brave man
struggling with adversity; by a wise use of events, and with an inimitable presence of mind under difficulties, forcing out a way for himself
through the severest trials to which human life can be exposed; with
enemies, natural and preternatural, surrounding him on all sides The
agents in this tale, besides men and women, are giants, enchanters,
sirens,—things which denote external force or internal temptations;
the twofold danger which a wise fortitude must expect to encounter in
its course through this world. The fictions contained in it will be
found to comprehend some of the most admired inventions of Grecian
mythology.

The groundwork of the story is as old as the "Odyssey;" but the
moral and the colouring are comparatively modern. By avoiding the
prolixity which marks the speeches and the descriptions in Homer, I
have gained a rapidity to the narration, which I hope will make it
more attractive, and give it more the air of a romance, to young
readers; though I am sensible, that, by the curtailment, I have sacri-
ficed in many places the manners to the passion, the subordinate cha-
racteristics to the essential interest of the story. The attempt is not to
be considered as seeking a comparison with any of the direct translations of the "Odyssey," either in prose or verse; though if I were to

state the obligations which I have had to one obsolete version,* I should run the hazard of depriving myself of the very slender degree of reputation which I could hope to acquire from a trifle like the present undertaking.

CHAPTER I.

The Cicons.—The Fruit of the Lotos-tree —Polyphemus and the Cyclops. — The Kingdom of the Winds, and God Æolus's Fatal Present.— The Læstrygonian Man-eaters.

This history tells of the wanderings of Ulysses and his followers in their return from Troy, after the destruction of that famous city of Asia by the Grecians. He was inflamed with a desire of seeing again, after a ten-years' absence, his wife and native country Ithaca. He was king of a barren spot, and a poor country in comparison of the fruitful plains of Asia, which he was leaving, or the wealthy kingdoms which he touched upon in his return ; yet, wherever he came, he could never see a soil which appeared in his eyes half so sweet or desirable as his country earth. This made him refuse the offers of the goddess Calypso to stay with her, and partake of her immortality in the delightful island ; and this gave him strength to break from the enchantments of Circe, the daughter of the Sun.

From Troy, ill winds cast Ulysses and his fleet upon the coast of the Cicons, a people hostile to the Grecians. Landing his forces, he laid siege to their chief city, Ismarus, which he took, and with it much spoil, and slew many people. But success proved

---

* The translation of Homer, by Chapman, in the reign of James I.

fatal to him ; for his soldiers, elated with the spoil, and the good store of provisions which they found in that place, fell to eating and drinking, forgetful of their safety, till the Cicons, who inhabited the coast, had time to assemble their friends and allies from the interior ; who, mustering in prodigious force, set upon the Grecians while they negligently revelled and feasted, and slew many of them, and recovered the spoil. They, dispirited and thinned in their numbers, with difficulty made their retreat good to the ships.

Thence they set sail, sad at heart, yet something cheered, that, with such fearful odds against them, they had not all been utterly destroyed. A dreadful tempest ensued, which for two nights and two days tossed them about; but the third day the weather cleared, and they had hopes of a favourable gale to carry them to Ithaca ; but as they doubled the Cape of Malea, suddenly a north wind arising drove them back as far as Cythera. After that, for the space of nine days, contrary winds continued to drive them in an opposite direction to the point to which they were bound: and the tenth day they put in at a shore where a race of men dwell that are sustained by the fruit of the lotos-tree   Here Ulysses sent some of his men to land for fresh water, who were met by certain of the inhabitants, that gave them some of their country food to eat, not with any ill intention towards them, though in the event it proved pernicious; for having eaten of this fruit, so pleasant it proved to their appetite, that they in a minute quite forgot all thoughts of home or of their countrymen, or of ever returning back to the ships to give an account of what sort of inhabitants dwelt there, but they would needs stay and live there among them, and eat of that precious food for ever; and when Ulysses sent other of his men to look for them, and to bring them back by force, they strove and wept, and would not leave their food for heaven itself, so much the pleasure of that enchanting fruit had bewitched them.   But Ulysses caused them to be bound hand and foot, and cast under the hatches ; and set sail with all possible speed from that baneful coast, lest others after them might taste the lotos, which had such strange qualities to make men forget their native country and the thoughts of home.

Coasting on all that night by unknown and out-of-the-way shores, they came by daybreak to the land where the Cyclops dwell ; a sort of giant shepherds, that neither sow nor plough, but the earth untilled produces for them rich wheat and barley and grapes : yet they have neither bread nor wine, nor know the arts of cultivation, nor care to know them; for they live each man to himself, without laws or government, or any thing like a state or kingdom ; but their dwellings are in caves, on the steep heads of mountains, every man's household governed by his own caprice, or not governed at all, their wives and children as lawless as themselves ; none caring for others, but each doing as he or she thinks good. Ships or boats they have none, nor artificers to make them , no trade or commerce, or wish to visit other shores : yet they have convenient places for harbours and for shipping. Here Ulysses, with a chosen party of twelve followers, landed, to explore what sort of men dwelt there, — whether hospitable and friendly to strangers, or altogether wild and savage ; for, as yet, no dwellers appeared in sight.

The first sign of habitation which they came to was a giant's cave, rudely fashioned, but of a size which betokened the vast proportions of its owner; the pillars which supported it being the bodies of huge oaks or pines, in the natural state of the tree; and all about showed more marks of strength than skill in whoever built it. Ulysses, entering it, admired the savage contrivances and artless structure of the place, and longed to see the tenant of so outlandish a mansion; but well conjecturing that gifts would have more avail in extracting courtesy, than strength would succeed in forcing it, from such a one as he expected to find the inhabitant, he resolved to flatter his hospitality with a present of Greek wine, of which he had store in twelve great vessels,—so strong, that no one ever drank it without an infusion of twenty parts of water to one of wine, yet the fragrance of it was even then so delicious, that it would have vexed a man who smelled it to abstain from tasting it, but whoever tasted it, it was able to raise his courage to the height of heroic deeds. Taking with them a goat-skin flagon full of this precious liquor, they ventured into the recesses of the cave. Here they pleased themselves a whole day with beholding the giant's kitchen, where the flesh of sheep and goats lay strewed; his dairy, where goat milk stood ranged in troughs and pails; his pens, where he kept his live animals; but those he had driven forth to pasture with him when he went out in the morning. While they were feasting their eyes with a sight of these curiosities, their ears were suddenly deafened with a noise like the falling of a house. It was the owner of the cave, who had been abroad all day, feeding his flock, as his custom was, in the mountains, and now drove them home in the evening from pasture. He threw down a pile of firewood, which he had been gathering against supper time, before the mouth of the cave, which occasioned the crash they heard. The Grecians hid themselves in the remote parts of the cave at sight of the uncouth monster. It was Polyphemus, the largest and savagest of the Cyclops, who boasted himself to be the son of Neptune. He looked more like a mountain crag than a man; and to his brutal body he had a brutish mind answerable. He drove his flock, all that gave milk, to the interior of the cave, but left the rams and the he goats without. Then, taking up a stone so massy that twenty oxen could not have drawn it, he placed it at the mouth of the cave to defend the entrance, and sat him down to milk his ewes and his goats; which done, he lastly kindled a fire, and throwing his great eye round the cave, (for the Cyclops have no more than one eye, and that placed in the midst of their forehead,) by the glimmering light he discerned some of Ulysses's men.

"Ho, guests! what are you?—merchants or wandering thieves?" he bellowed out in a voice which took from them all power of reply, it was so astounding.

Only Ulysses summoned resolution to answer, that they came neither for plunder nor traffic, but were Grecians, who had lost their way, returning from Troy; which famous city, under the conduct of Agamemnon, the renowned son of Atreus, they had sacked, and laid level with the ground. Yet now they prostrated themselves humbly before his feet, whom they acknowledged to be mightier than they, and besought him that he would bestow the rites of hospitality upon them; for that Jove was the avenger of wrongs done to strangers, and would fiercely resent any injury which they might suffer.

"Fool!" said the Cyclop, "to come so far to preach to me the fear of the gods. We Cyclops care not for your Jove, whom you fable to be nursed by a goat, nor any of your blessed ones. We are stronger than they, and dare bid open battle to Jove himself, though you and all your fellows of the earth join with him!" And he bade them tell him where their ship was in which they came, and whether they had any companions. But Ulysses, with a wise caution, made answer, that they had no ship or companions, but were unfortunate men, whom the sea, splitting their ship in pieces, had dashed upon his coast, and they alone had escaped. He replied nothing, but, griping two of the nearest of them as if they had been no more than children, he dashed their brains out against the earth, and (shocking to relate!) tore in pieces their limbs, and devoured them, yet warm and trembling, making a lion's meal of them, lapping the blood. for the Cyclops are *man-eaters*, and esteem human flesh to be a delicacy far above goat's or kid's; though, by reason of their abhorred customs, few men approach their coast, except some stragglers, or now and then a shipwrecked mariner. At a sight so horrid, Ulysses and his men were like distracted people. He, when he had made an end of his wicked supper, drained a draught of goat's milk down his prodigious throat, and lay down and slept among his goats. Then Ulysses drew his sword, and half resolved to thrust it with all his might in at the bosom of the sleeping monster: but wiser thoughts restrained him, else they had there without help all perished; for none but Polyphemus himself could have removed that mass of stone which he had placed to guard the entrance. So they were constrained to abide all that night in fear.

When day came the Cyclop awoke, and, kindling a fire, made his breakfast of two other of his unfortunate prisoners; then milked his goats, as he was accustomed; and pushing aside the vast stone, and shutting it again, when he had done, upon the prisoners, with as much ease as a man opens and shuts a quiver's lid, he let out his flock, and drove them before him with whistlings (as sharp as winds in storms) to the mountains.

Then Ulysses, of whose strength or cunning the Cyclop seems to have had as little heed as of an infant's, being left alone with the remnant of his men which the Cyclop had not devoured, gave manifest proof how far manly wisdom excels brutish force. He chose a stake from among the wood which the Cyclop had piled up for firing, in length and thickness like a mast, which he sharpened, and hardened in the fire; and selected four men, and instructed them what they should do with this stake, and made them perfect in their parts.

When the evening was come, the Cyclop drove home his sheep, and as fortune directed it, either of purpose, or that his memory was overruled by the gods to his hurt, (as in the issue it proved,) he drove the males of his flock, contrary to his custom, along with the dams into the pens. Then shutting to the stone of the cave, he fell to his horrible supper. When he had despatched two more of the Grecians, Ulysses waxed bold with the contemplation of his project, and took a bowl of Greek wine, and merrily dared the Cyclop to drink.

" Cyclop," he said, " take a bowl of wine from the hand of your guest : it may serve to digest the man's flesh that you have eaten, and show what drink our ship held before it went down. All I ask in recompense, if you find it good, is to be dismissed in a whole skin. Truly you must look to have few visitors, if you observe this new custom of eating your guests."

The brute took and drank, and vehemently enjoyed the taste of wine, which was new to him, and swilled again at the flagon, and entreated for more : and prayed Ulysses to tell him his name, that he might bestow a gift upon the man who had given him such brave liquor. The Cyclops, he said, had grapes, but this rich juice, he swore, was simply divine. Again Ulysses plied him with the wine, and the fool drank it as fast as he poured it out, and again he asked the name of his benefactor, which Ulysses, cunningly dissembling, said, " My name is Noman : my kindred and friends in my own country call me Noman."—" Then," said the Cyclop, " this is the kindness I will show thee, Noman : I will eat thee last of all thy friends." He had scarce expressed his savage kindness when the fumes of the strong wine overcame him, and he reeled down upon the floor, and sank into a dead sleep.

Ulysses watched his time while the monster lay insensible ; and, heartening up his men, they placed the sharp end of the stake in the fire till it was heated red-hot ; and some god gave them a courage beyond that which they were used to have, and the four men with difficulty bored the sharp end of the huge stake, which they had heated red-hot, right into the eye of the drunken cannibal, and Ulysses helped to thrust it in with all his might still further and further, with effort, as men bore with an auger, till the scalded blood gushed out, and the eyeball smoked, and the strings of the eye cracked as the burning rafter broke in it, and the eye hissed as hot iron hisses when it is plunged into water.

He, waking, roared with the pain, so loud that all the cavern broke into claps like thunder. They fled, and dispersed into corners. He plucked the burning stake from his eye, and hurled the wood madly about the cave. Then he cried out with a mighty voice for his brethren the Cyclops, that dwelt hard by in caverns upon hills. They, hearing the terrible shout, came flocking from all parts to inquire what ailed Poly-phemus, and what cause he had for making such horrid clamours in the night-time to break their sleeps, if his fright proceeded from any mortal; if strength or craft had given him his death-blow. He made answer from within, that Noman had hurt him, Noman had killed him, Noman was with him in the cave. They replied, " If no man has hurt thee, and no man is with thee, then thou art alone ; and the evil which afflicts thee is from the hand of Heaven, which none can resist or help." So they left him, and went their way, thinking that some disease troubled him. He, blind, and ready to split with the anguish of the pain, went groaning up and down in the dark to find the doorway, which when he found, he removed the stone, and sat in the threshold, feel-ing if he could lay hold on any man going out with the sheep, which (the day now breaking) were begin-ning to issue forth to their accustomed pastures. But Ulysses, whose first artifice in giving himself that ambiguous name had succeeded so well with the Cyclop, was not of a wit so gross to be caught by that palpable device ; but, casting about in his mind all the ways which he could contrive for escape, (no less than all their lives depending on the success,) at last he thought of this expedient : he made knots of the osier twigs upon which the Cyclop commonly slept, with which he tied the fattest and fleeciest of the rams together, three in a rank , and under the belly of the middle ram he tied a man, and himself last; wrapping himself fast with both his hands in the rich wool of one, the fairest of the flock.

And now the sheep began to issue forth very fast . the males went first ; the females, unmilked, stood by, bleating, and requiring the hand of their shepherd in vain to milk them, their full bags sore with being unemptied, but he much sorer with the loss of sight. Still, as the males passed, he felt the backs of those fleecy fools, never dreaming that they carried his enemies under their bellies. So they passed on till the last ram came loaded with his wool and Ulysses together. He stopped that ram, and felt him, and had his hand once in the hair of Ulysses, yet knew it not ; and he chid the ram for being last, and spoke to it as if it understood him, and asked it whether it did not wish that its master had his eye again, which that abominable Noman with his execrable rout had put out, when they had got him down with wine ; and he willed the ram to tell him whereabouts in the cave his enemy lurked, that he might dash his brains, and strew them about, to ease his heart of that tormenting revenge which rankled in it. After a deal of such foolish talk to the beast, he let it go.

When Ulysses found himself free, he let go his
hold, and assisted in disengaging his friends. The
rams which had befriended them they carried off
with them to the ships, where their companions,
with tears in their eyes, received them as men
escaped from death. They plied their oars, and set
their sails; and when they were got as far off from
shore as a voice could reach, Ulysses cried out to the
Cyclop: "Cyclop, thou shouldst not have so much
abused thy monstrous strength as to devour thy
guests. Jove, by my hand, sends thee requital to pay
thy savage inhumanity." The Cyclop heard, and
came forth enraged; and in his anger he plucked a
fragment of a rock, and threw it with blind fury at the
ships. It narrowly escaped lighting upon the bark
in which Ulysses sat; but with the fall it raised so
fierce an ebb as bore back the ship till it almost
touched the shore. "Cyclop," said Ulysses, "if
any ask thee who imposed on thee that unsightly
blemish in thine eye, say it was Ulysses, son of
Laertes: the King of Ithaca am I called, the waster
of cities." Then they crowded sail, and beat the old
sea, and forth they went with a forward gale,—sad
for fore past losses, yet glad to have escaped at any
rate,—till they came to the isle where Æolus reigned,
who is god of the winds.

Here Ulysses and his men were courteously received
by the monarch, who showed him his twelve children
which have rule over the twelve winds. A month
they stayed and feasted with him, and at the end of
the month he dismissed them with many presents,
and gave to Ulysses, at parting, an ox's hide, in
which were enclosed *all the winds:* only he left
abroad the western wind, to play upon their sails,

and waft them gently home to Ithaca. This bag, bound in a glittering silver band so close that no breath could escape, Ulysses hung up at the mast His companions did not know its contents, but guessed that the monarch had given to him some treasures of gold or silver.

Nine days they sailed smoothly, favoured by the western wind; and by the tenth they approached so nigh as to discern lights kindled on the shores of their country earth when, by ill fortune, Ulysses, overcome with fatigue of watching the helm, fell asleep. The mariners seized the opportunity, and one of them said to the rest, " A fine time has this leader of ours : wherever he goes, he is sure of presents, when we come away empty-handed. And see what King Æolus has given him !—store, no doubt of gold and silver." A word was enough to those covetous wretches, who, quick as thought, untied the bag; and, instead of gold, out rushed with mighty noise *all the winds*. Ulysses with the noise awoke, and saw their mistake, but too late; for the ship was driving with all the winds back far from Ithaca, far as to the Island of Æolus, from which they had parted ; in one hour measuring back what in nine days they had scarcely tracked, and in sight of home too ! Up he flew amazed, and, raving, doubted whether he should not fling himself into the sea for grief of his bitter disappointment. At last he hid himself under the hatches for shame. And scarce could he be prevailed upon, when he was told he had arrived again in the harbour of King Æolus, to go himself or send to that monarch for a second succour; so much the disgrace of having misused his royal bounty (though it was the crime of his followers, and not his own) weighed upon him; and when at last he went, and took a herald with him, and came where the god sat on his throne, feasting with his children, he would not thrust in among them at their meat, but set himself down, like one unworthy, in the threshold.

Indignation seized Æolus to behold him in that manner returned; and he said, " Ulysses, what has brought you back? Are you so soon tired of your country? or did not our present please you? We thought we had given you a kingly passport." Ulysses made answer: " My men have done this ill mischief to me: they did it while I slept."— " Wretch:" said Æolus, "avaunt, and quit our shores! it fits not us to convoy men whom the gods hate, and will have perish."

Forth they sailed, but with far different hopes than when they left the same harbour the first time with all the winds confined, only the west wind suffered to play upon their sails to waft them in gentle murmurs to Ithaca. They were now the sport of every gale that blew, and despaired of ever seeing home more. Now those covetous mariners were cured of their surfeit for gold, and would not have touched it if it had laid in untold heaps before them.

Six days and nights they drove along; and on the seventh day they put into Lamos, a port of the Læstrygonians. So spacious this harbour was, that it held with ease all their fleet, which rode at anchor, safe from any storms. all but the ship in which Ulysses was embarked. He, as if prophetic of the mischance which followed, kept still without the harbour, making fast his bark to a rock at the land's point, which he climbed with purpose to survey the country. He saw a city with smoke ascending from the roofs, but neither ploughs going, nor oxen yoked, nor any sign of agricultural works. Making choice of two men, he sent them to the city to explore what sort of inhabitants dwelt there. His messengers had not gone far before they met a damsel, of stature surpassing human, who was coming to draw water from a spring. They asked her who dwelt in that land. She made no reply, but led them in silence to her father's palace. He was a monarch, and named Antiphas He and all his people were giants. When they entered the palace, a woman, the mother of the damsel, but far taller than she, rushed abroad, and called for Antiphas. He came, and, snatching up one of the two men, made as if he would devour him. The other fled. Antiphas raised a mighty shout, and instantly, this way and that, multitudes of gigantic people issued out at the gates, and making for the harbour, tore up huge pieces of the rocks, and flung them at the ships which lay there,—all which they utterly overwhelmed and sank, and the unfortunate bodies of men which floated, and which the sea did not devour, these cannibals thrust through with harpoons, like fishes, and bore them off to their dire feast. Ulysses, with his single bark that had never entered the harbour, escaped; that bark which was now the only vessel left of all the gallant navy that had set sail with him from Troy He pushed off from the shore, cheering the sad remnant of his men, whom horror at the sight of their countrymen's fate had almost turned to marble.

CHAPTER II.

The House of Circe.—Men changed into Beasts.—The Voyage
to Hell —The Banquet of the Dead.

On went the single ship till it came to the Island of
Ææa, where Circe, the dreadful daughter of the
Sun, dwelt.   She was deeply skilled in magic, a
haughty beauty, and had hair like the Sun.   The Sun
was her parent, and begot her and her brother Æætes
(such another as herself) upon Perse, daughter to
Oceanus.

Here a dispute arose among Ulysses's men, which
of them should go ashore, and explore the country ;
for there was a necessity that some should go to procure water and provisions, their stock of both being
nigh spent : but their hearts failed them when they
called to mind the shocking fate of their fellows
whom the Læstrygonians had eaten, and those which
the foul Cyclop Polyphemus had crushed between
his jaws ; which moved them so tenderly in the recollection, that they wept.   But tears never yet supplied any man's wants this Ulysses knew full well ;
and dividing his men (all that were left) into two
companies, at the head of one of which was himself, and at the head of the other Eurylochus, a man
of tried courage, he cast lots which of them should
go up into the country ; and the lot fell upon Eurylochus and his company, two and twenty in number,
who took their leave, with tears, of Ulysses and his
men that stayed, whose eyes wore the same wet badges
of weak humanity . for they surely thought never to
see these their companions again, but that, on every

coast where they should come, they should find nothing but savages and cannibals.

Eurylochus and his party proceeded up the country, till in a dale they descried the house of Circe, built of bright stone, by the road's side. Before her gate lay many beasts,—as wolves, lions, leopards,—which, by her art, of wild she had rendered tame. These arose when they saw strangers, and ramped upon their hinder paws, and fawned upon Eurylochus and his men, who dreaded the effects of such monstrous kindness; and, staying at the gate, they heard the enchantress within, sitting at her loom, singing such strains as suspended all mortal faculties, while she wove a web, subtile and glorious, and of texture inimitable on earth, as all the housewiferies of the deities are. Strains so ravishingly sweet provoked even the sagest and prudentist heads among the party to knock and call at the gate The shining gate the enchantress opened, and bade them come in and feast. They unwise followed, all but Eurylochus, who stayed without the gate, suspicious that some train was laid for them. Being entered, she placed them in chairs of state, and set before them meal and honey and Smyrna wine, but mixed with baneful drugs of powerful enchantment. When they had eaten of these, and drunk of her cup, she touched them with her charming rod, and straight they were transformed into swine,—having the bodies of swine, the bristles and snout and grunting noise of that animal; only they still retained the minds of men, which made them the more to lament their brutish transformation. Having changed them, she shut them up in her sty with many more whom her wicked sorceries had formerly changed, and gave them

swine's food — mast and acorns and chestnuts—
to eat.

Eurylochus, who beheld nothing of these sad
changes from where he was stationed without the
gate, only, instead of his companions that entered,
(who he thought had all vanished by witchcraft,)
beheld a herd of swine, hurried back to the ship to
give an account of what he had seen; but so
frightened and perplexed, that he could give no distinct report of any thing: only he remembered a
palace, and a woman singing at her work, and gates
guarded by lions. But his companions, he said, were
all vanished.

Then Ulysses—suspecting some foul witchcraft—
snatched his sword and his bow, and commanded
Eurylochus instantly to lead him to the place; but
Eurylochus fell down, and, embracing his knees,
besought him, by the name of a man whom the
gods had in their protection, not to expose his
safety, and the safety of them all, to certain destruction.

" Do thou then stay, Eurylochus," answered
Ulysses; eat thou and drink in the ship in safety,
while I go alone upon this adventure: necessity,
from whose law is no appeal, compels me."

So saying, he quitted the ship, and went on shore,
accompanied by none: none had the hardihood to
offer to partake that perilous adventure with him, so
much they dreaded the enchantments of the witch.
Singly he pursued his journey till he came to the
shining gates which stood before her mansion, but
when he essayed to put his foot over her threshold
he was suddenly stopped by the apparition of a young
man bearing a golden rod in his hand, who was the

god Mercury. He held Ulysses by the wrist, to stay his entrance; and "Whither wouldest thou go," he said, "O thou most erring of the sons of men? Knowest thou not that this is the house of great Circe, where she keeps thy friends in a loathsome sty, changed from the fair forms of men into the detestable and ugly shapes of swine? Art thou prepared to share their fate, from which nothing can ransom thee?" But neither his words, nor his coming from heaven, could stop the daring foot of Ulysses, whom compassion for the misfortune of his friends had rendered careless of danger. which when the god perceived, he had pity to see valour so misplaced, and gave him the flower of the herb *moly*, which is sovereign against enchantments. The moly is a small unsightly root, its virtues but little known, and in low estimation; the dull shepherd treads on it every day with his clouted shoes: but it bears a small white flower, which is medicinal against charms, blights, mildews, and damps. "Take this in thy hand," said Mercury, "and with it boldly enter her gates: when she shall strike thee with her rod, thinking to change thee, as she has changed thy friends, boldly rush in upon her with thy sword, and extort from her the dreadful oath of the gods, that she will use no enchantments against thee, then force her to restore thy abused companions.' He gave Ulysses the little white flower; and, instructing him how to use it, vanished.

When the god had departed, Ulysses with loud knockings beat at the gate of the palace. The shining gates were opened as before, and great Circe with hospitable cheer invited in her guest. She placed him on a throne with more distinction than she had used to his fellows; she mingled wine in a costly bowl, and he drank of it, mixed with those poisonous drugs. When he had drunk, she struck him with her charming rod, and "To your sty!" she cried. "Out swine! mingle with your companions!" But those powerful words were not proof against the preservative which Mercury had given to Ulysses: he remained unchanged, and, as the god had directed him, boldly charged the witch with his sword, as if he meant to take her life, which when she saw, and perceived that her charms were weak against the antidote which Ulysses bore about him, she cried out, and bent her knees beneath his sword, embracing his, and said, "Who or what manner of man art thou? Never drank any man before thee of this cup but he repented it in some brute's form. Thy shape remains unaltered as thy mind. Thou canst be none other than Ulysses, renowned above all the world for wisdom, whom the Fates have long since decreed that I must love. This haughty bosom bends to thee. O Ithacan! a goddess woos thee to her bed."

"O Circe!" he replied, "how canst thou treat of love or marriage with one whose friends thou hast turned into beasts? and now offerest him thy hand in wedlock, only that thou mightest have him in thy power, to live the life of a beast with thee,—naked, effeminate, subject to thy will, perhaps to be advanced in time to the honour of a place in thy sty. What pleasure canst thou promise which may tempt the soul of a reasonable man,—thy meats, spiced with poison; or thy wines drugged with death? Thou must swear to me, that thou wilt never attempt against me the treasons which thou hast practised upon my friends." The enchantress, won by the terror of his threats, or by the violence of that new love which she felt kindling in her veins for him, swore by Styx, the great oath of the gods, that she meditated no injury to him. Then Ulysses made show of gentler treatment, which gave her hopes of inspiring him with a passion equal to that which she felt. She called her handmaids, four that served her in chief,—who were daughters to her silver fountains, to her sacred rivers, and to her conse- crated woods,—to deck her apartments, to spread rich carpets, and set out her silver tables with dishes of the purest gold, and meat as precious as that which the gods eat, to entertain her guest. One brought water to wash his feet ; and one brought wine to chase away, with a refreshing sweetness, the sorrows that had come of late so thick upon him, and hurt his noble mind. They strewed perfumes on his head . and after he had bathed in a bath of the choicest aromatics, they brought him rich and costly apparel to put on. Then he was conducted to a throne of massy silver; and a regale, fit for Jove when he banquets, was placed before him. But the feast which Ulysses desired was to see his friends (the partners of his voyage) once more in the shapes of men ; and the food which could give him nourish- ment must be taken in at his eyes. Because he missed this sight, he sat melancholy and thought- ful, and would taste of none of the rich delicacies placed before him; which when Circe noted, she easily divined the cause of his sadness, and leaving the seat in which she sat throned, went to her sty, and let abroad his men, who came in like swine, and filled the ample hall, where Ulysses sat,

with gruntings.   Hardly had he time to let his sad
eye run over their altered forms and brutal metamorphosis, when, with an ointment which she
smeared over them, suddenly their bristles fell off,
and they started up in their own shapes, men as
before.   They knew their leader again, and clung
about him with joy of their late restoration, and
some shame for their late change ; and wept so loud,
blubbering out their joy in broken accents, that the
palace was filled with a sound of pleasing mourning ;
and the witch herself, great Circe, was not unmoved
at the sight.   To make her atonement complete, she
sent for the remnant of Ulysses's men who stayed
behind at the ship, giving up their great commander
for lost ; who, when they came, and saw him again
alive, circled with their fellows, no expression can tell
what joy they felt ; they even cried out with rapture ;
and, to have seen their frantic expressions of mirth,
a man might have supposed they were just in sight
of their country earth, the cliffs of rocky Ithaca.
Only Eurylochus would hardly be persuaded to enter
that palace of wonders ; for he remembered with a
kind of horror how his companions had vanished
from his sight.

Then great Circe spake, and gave order that there
should be no more sadness among them, nor remembering of past sufferings , for as yet they fared
like men that are exiles from their country; and if
a gleam of mirth shot among them, it was suddenly
quenched with the thought of their helpless and home-
less condition.   Her kind persuasions wrought upon
Ulysses and the rest, that they spent twelve months in
all manner of delight with her in her palace , for
Circe was a powerful magician, and could command the

moon from her sphere, or unroot the solid oak from its place to make it dance for their diversion : and by the help of her illusions she could vary the taste of pleasures, and contrive delights, recreations, and jolly pastimes,—to " fetch the day about from sun to sun, and rock the tedious year as in a delightful dream."

At length Ulysses awoke from the trance of the faculties into which her charms had thrown him ; and the thought of home returned with tenfold vigour to goad and sting him,—that home where he had left his virtuous wife Penelope and his young son Telemachus. One day, when Circe had been lavish of her caresses, and was in her kindest humour, he moved to her subtly, and as it were afar off, the question of his home-return ; to which she answered firmly : " O Ulysses, it is not in my power to detain one whom the gods have destined to further trials. But leaving me, before you pursue your journey home, you must visit the house of Ades, or Death, to consult the shade of Tiresias, the Theban prophet ; to whom alone, of all the dead, Proserpine, Queen of Hell, has committed the secret of future events : it is he that must inform you whether you shall ever see again your wife and country."—"O Circe," he cried, " that is impossible. Who shall steer my course to Pluto's kingdom ? Never ship had strength to make that voyage."—" Seek no guide," she replied ; " but raise you your mast, and hoist your white sails, and sit in your ship in peace : the north wind shall waft you through the seas till you shall cross the expanse of the ocean, and come to where grow the poplar groves and willows pale of Proserpine, — where Pyri-

phlegethon and Cocytus and Acheron mingle their
waves. Cocytus is an arm of Styx, the forgetful
river. Here dig a pit, and make it a cubit broad and
a cubit long; and pour in milk and honey and wine,
and the blood of a ram, and the blood of a black
ewe ; and turn away thy face while thou pourest in,
and the dead shall come flocking to taste the milk
and the blood : but suffer none to approach thy offering till thou hast inquired of Tiresias all which thou
wishest to know."

He did as great Circe had appointed. He raised
his mast, and hoisted his white sails, and sat in his
ship in peace. The north wind wafted him through
the seas till he crossed the ocean, and came to the
sacred woods of Proserpine. He stood at the confluence of the three floods, and digged a pit, as she
had given directions, and poured in his offering,—
the blood of a ram and the blood of a black ewe,
milk and honey and wine ; and the dead came to
his banquet,—aged men and women and youths,
and children who died in infancy. But none of
them would he suffer to approach and dip their
thin lips in the offering till Tiresias was served,—
not though his own mother was among the number,
whom now for the first time he knew to be dead ;
for he had left her living when he went to Troy;
and she had died since his departure, and the tidings
never reached him. Though it irked his soul to use
constraint upon her, yet, in compliance with the injunction of great Circe, he forced her to retire along
with the other ghosts. Then Tiresias, who bore a
golden sceptre, came and lapped of the offering ;
and immediately he knew Ulysses, and began to pro-
phesy. *He denounced woe to Ulysses,—woe, woe, and*

many sufferings, through the anger of Neptune for the putting-out of the eye of the sea-god's son. Yet there was safety after suffering, if they could abstain from slaughtering the oxen of the Sun after they landed in the Triangular Island. For Ulysses, the gods had destined him from a king to become a beggar, and to perish by his own guests, unless he slew those who knew him not.

This prophecy, ambiguously delivered, was all that Tiresias was empowered to unfold, or else there was no longer place for him; for now the souls of the other dead came flocking in such numbers, tumultuously demanding the blood, that freezing horror seized the limbs of the living Ulysses, to see so many, and all dead, and he the only one alive in that region Now his mother came and lapped the blood, without restraint from her son: and now she knew him to be her son, and inquired of him why he had come alive to their comfortless habitations; and she said, that affliction for Ulysses's long absence had preyed upon her spirits, and brought her to the grave.

Ulysses's soul melted at her moving narration, and forgetting the state of the dead, and that the airy texture of disembodied spirits does not admit of the embraces of flesh and blood, he threw his arms about her to clasp her: the poor ghost melted from his embrace, and, looking mournfully upon him, vanished away.

Then saw he other females,—Tyro, who, when she lived, was the paramour of Neptune, and by him had Pelias and Neleus; Antiope, who bore two like sons to Jove,—Amphion and Zethus, founders of Thebes; Alcmena, the mother of Hercules, with her fair daughter, afterwards her daugter-in-law, Megara. There also Ulysses saw Jocasta, the unfortunate mother and wife of Œdipus; who, ignorant of kin, wedded with her son, and when she had discovered the unnatural alliance, for shame and grief hanged herself. He continued to drag a wretched life above the earth, haunted by the dreadful Furies. There was Leda, the wife of Tyndarus, the mother of the beautiful Helen, and of the two brave brothers, Castor and Pollux, who obtained this grace from Jove,—that, being dead, they should enjoy life alternately, living in pleasant places under the earth; for Pollux had prayed that his brother Castor, who was subject to death, as the son of Tyndarus, should partake of his own immortality, which he derived from an immortal sire. This the Fates denied: therefore Pollux was permitted to divide his immortality with his brother Castor, dying and living alternately. There was Iphimedeia, who bore two sons to Neptune that were giants,—Otus and Ephialtes: Earth in her prodigality never nourished bodies to such portentous size and beauty as these two children were of, except Orion. At nine years old they had imaginations of climbing to Heaven to see what the gods were doing: they thought to make stairs of mountains, and were for piling Ossa upon Olympus, and setting Pelion upon that; and had perhaps performed it, if they had lived till they were striplings; but they were cut off by death in the infancy of their ambitious project. Phædra was there, and Procris and Ariadne, mournful for Theseus's desertion; and Mæra and Clymene and Eryphile, who preferred gold before wedlock faith.

But now came a mournful ghost, that late was

L   D

Agamemnon, son of Atreus, the mighty leader of all the host of Greece and their confederate kings that warred against Troy. He came with the rest to sip a little of the blood at that uncomfortable banquet. Ulysses was moved with compassion to see him among them, and asked him what untimely fate had brought him there; if storms had overwhelmed him coming from Troy, or if he had perished in some mutiny by his own soldiers at a division of the prey.

"By none of these," he replied, "did I come to my death, but slain at a banquet to which I was invited by Ægisthus after my return home. He conspiring with my adulterous wife, they laid a scheme for my destruction, training me forth to a banquet as an ox goes to the slaughter: and, there surrounding me, they slew me with all my friends about me.

"Clytemnestra, my wicked wife, forgetting the vows which she swore to me in wedlock. would not lend a hand to close my eyes in death. But nothing is so heaped with impieties as such a woman, who would kill her spouse that married her a maid. When I brought her home to my house a bride, I hoped in my heart that she would be loving to me and to my children. Now her black treacheries have cast a foul aspersion on her whole sex. Blest husbands will have their loving wives in suspicion for her bad deeds."

"Alas!" said Ulysses, "there seems to be a fatality in your royal house of Atreus, and that they are hated of Jove for their wives. For Helen's sake, your brother Menelaus's wife, what multitudes fell in the wars of Troy!"

Agamemnon replied, "For this cause, be not thou more kind than wise to any woman. Let not thy words express to her at any time all that is in thy mind: keep still some secrets to thyself. But thou by any bloody contrivances of thy wife never need'st fear to fall. Exceeding wise she is, and to her wisdom she has a goodness as eminent; Icarius's daughter, Penelope the chaste: we left her a young bride when we parted from our wives to go to the wars, her first child suckling at her breast,—the young Telemachus, whom you shall see grown up to manhood on your return: and he shall greet his father with befitting welcomes. My Orestes, my dear son, I shall never see again. His mother has deprived his father of the sight of him, and perhaps will slay him as she slew his sire. It is now no world to trust a woman in. But what says fame? Is my son yet alive? lives he in Orchomen, or in Pylus? or is he resident in Sparta, in his uncle's court? As yet, I see, divine Orestes is not here with me."

To this Ulysses replied, that he had received no certain tidings where Orestes abode: only some uncertain rumours, which he could not report for truth.

While they held this sad conference, with kind tears striving to render unkind fortunes more palatable, the soul of the great Achilles joined them. "What desperate adventure has brought Ulysses to these regions?" said Achilles: "to see the end of dead men, and their foolish shades?"

Ulysses answered him, that he had come to consult Tiresias respecting his voyage home. "But thou, O son of Thetis!" said he, "why dost thou disparage the state of the dead? Seeing that, as

alive, thou didst surpass all men in glory, thou must
needs retain thy pre-eminence here below · so great
Achilles triumphs over death."

But Achilles made reply, that he had much rather
be a peasant-slave upon earth than reign over all
the dead,—so much did the inactivity and slothful
condition of that state displease his unquenchable
and restless spirit. Only he inquired of Ulysses if
his father Peleus were living, and how his son Neoptolemus conducted himself.

Of Peleus, Ulysses could tell him nothing; but of
Neoptolemus he thus bore witness. "From Scyros I
convoyed your son by sea to the Greeks; where I
can speak of him; for I knew him. He was chief in
council and in the field. When any question was
proposed, so quick was his conceit in the forward
apprehension of any case, that he ever spoke first,
and was heard with more attention than the older
heads. Only myself and aged Nestor could compare
with him in giving advice. In battle I cannot speak
his praise, unless I could count all that fell by his
sword. I will only mention one instance of his manhood. When we sat hidden in the belly of the wooden
horse, in the ambush which deceived the Trojans to
their destruction, I, who had the management of
that stratagem, still shifted my place from side to
side to note the behaviour of our men In some I
marked their hearts trembling, through all the pains
which they took to appear valiant; and, in others,
tears, that, in spite of manly courage, would gush
forth. And to say truth, it was an adventure of high
enterprise, and as perilous a stake as was ever
played in war's game. But in him I could not observe the least sign of weakness; no tears nor

tremblings, but his hand still on his good sword, and ever urging me to set open the machine, and let us out before the time was come for doing it : and when we sallied out, he was still first in that fierce destruction and bloody midnight desolation of King Priam's city."

This made the soul of Achilles to tread a swifter pace, with high-raised feet, as he vanished away, for the joy which he took in his son being applauded by Ulysses.

A sad shade stalked by, which Ulysses knew to be the ghost of Ajax, his opponent, when living, in that famous dispute about the right of succeeding to the arms of the deceased Achilles. They being adjudged by the Greeks to Ulysses, as the prize of wisdom above bodily strength, the noble Ajax in despite went mad, and slew himself. The sight of his rival, turned to a shade by his dispute, so subdued the passion of emulation in Ulysses, that, for his sake, he wished that judgment in that controversy had been given against himself, rather than so illustrious a chief should have perished for the desire of those arms which his prowess (second only to Achilles in fight) so eminently had deserved. "Ajax," he cried, "all the Greeks mourn for thee as much as they lamented for Achilles. Let not thy wrath burn for ever, great son of Telamon. Ulysses seeks peace with thee, and will make any atonement to thee that can appease thy hurt spirit." But the shade stalked on, and would not exchange a word with Ulysses, though he prayed it with many tears and many earnest entreaties. "He might have spoken to me," said Ulysses, "since I spoke to him; but I see the resentments of the dead are eternal."

Then Ulysses saw a throne, on which was placed a judge distributing sentence. He that sat on the throne was Minos, and he was dealing out just judgments to the dead. He it is that assigns them their place in bliss or woe.

Then came by a thundering ghost,—the large-limbed Orion, the mighty hunter, who was hunting there the ghosts of the beasts which he had slaughtered in desert hills upon the earth. for the dead delight in the occupations which pleased them in the time of their living upon the earth.

There was Tityus, suffering eternal pains because he had sought to violate the honour of Latona as she passed from Pytho into Panopeus. Two vultures sat perpetually preying upon his liver with their crooked beaks; which, as fast as they devoured, is for ever renewed: nor can he fray them away with his great hands.

There was Tantalus, plagued for his great sins, standing up to his chin in water, which he can never taste; but still, as he bows his head, thinking to quench his burning thirst, instead of water he licks up unsavoury dust. All fruits pleasant to the sight, and of delicious flavour, hang in ripe clusters about his head, seeming as though they offered themselves to be plucked by him; but when he reachès out his hand, some wind carries them far out of his sight into the clouds: so he is starved in the midst of plenty by the righteous doom of Jove, in memory of that inhuman banquet at which the sun turned pale, when the unnatural father served up the limbs of his little son in a dish, as meat for his divine guests.

There was Sisyphus, that sees no end to his labours. His punishment is, to be for ever rolling up a vast stone to the top of a mountain; which, when it gets to the top, falls down with a crushing weight, and all his work is to be begun again. He was bathed all over in sweat, that reeked out a smoke which covered his head like a mist. His crime had been the revealing of state secrets.

There Ulysses saw Hercules: not that Hercules who enjoys immortal life in heaven among the gods, and is married to Hebe. or youth; but his shadow, which remains below. About him the dead flocked as thick as bats, hovering around, and cuffing at his head: he stands with his dreadful bow, ever in the act to shoot.

There also might Ulysses have seen and spoken with the shades of Theseus and Pirithous and the old heroes; but he had conversed enough with horrors: therefore, covering his face with his hands that he might see no more spectres, he resumed his seat in his ship, and pushed off. The bark moved of itself, without the help of any oar, and soon brought him out of the regions of death into the cheerful quarters of the living, and to the Island of Ææa, whence he had set forth.

CHAPTER III.

THE SONG OF THE SIRENS.—SCYLLA AND CHARYBDIS.—THE OXEN OF THE SUN.—THE JUDGMENT.—THE CREW KILLED BY LIGHTNING.

" UNHAPPY man, who at thy birth wast appointed twice to die! Others shall die once; but thou, besides that death that remains for thee, common to all

ℓ   ） men, hast in thy lifetime visited the shades of death. Thee Scylla, thee Charybdis, expect. Thee the deathful Sirens lie in wait for, that taint the minds of those who ever listen to them with their sweet singing. Whosoever shall but hear the call of any Siren, he will so despise both wife and children, through their sorceries, that the stream of his affection never again shall set homewards; nor shall he take joy in wife or children thereafter, or they in him."

With these prophetic greetings great Circe met Ulysses on his return. He besought her to instruct him in the nature of the Sirens, and by what method their baneful allurements were to be resisted.

"They are sisters three," she replied, "that sit in a mead (by which your ship must needs pass) circled with dead men's bones. These are the bones of men whom they have slain, after with fawning invitements they have enticed them into their fen. Yet such is the celestial harmony of their voices accompanying the persuasive magic of their words, that, knowing this, you shall not be able to withstand their entice- ments. Therefore, when you are to sail by them, you shall stop the ears of your companions with wax, that they may hear no note of that dangerous music; but for yourself, that you may hear, and yet live, give them strict command to bind you hand and foot to the mast, and in no case to set you free till you are out of the danger of the temptation, though you should entreat it, and implore it ever so much, but to bind you rather the more for your requesting to be loosed. So shall you escape that snare."

Ulysses then prayed her that she would inform him what Scylla and Charybdis were, which she had taught him by name to fear. She replied, " Sailing from Ææa to Trinacria, you must pass at an equal distance between two fatal rocks. Incline never so little either to the one side or the other, and your ship must meet with certain destruction. No vessel ever yet tried that pass without being lost but the 'Argo,' which owed her safety to the sacred freight she bore,—the fleece of the golden-backed ram, which could not perish. The biggest of these rocks which you shall come to, Scylla hath in charge. There, in a deep whirlpool at the foot of the rock, the abhorred monster shrouds her face; who if she were to show her full form, no eye of man or god could endure the sight : thence she stretches out all her six long necks, peering and diving to suck up fish, dolphins, dog-fish, and whales, whole ships and their men,—whatever comes within her raging gulf. The other rock is lesser, and of less ominous aspect; but there dreadful Charybdis sits, supping the black deeps. Thrice a day she drinks her pits dry, and thrice a day again she belches them all up : but, when she is drinking, come not nigh; for, being once caught, the force of Neptune cannot redeem you from her swallow. Better trust to Scylla, for she will but have for her six necks six men : Charybdis, in her insatiate draught, will ask all."

Then Ulysses inquired, in case he should escape Charybdis, whether he might not assail that other monster with his sword : to which she replied, that he must not think that he had an enemy subject to death or wounds to contend with; for Scylla could never die. Therefore his best safety was in flight, and to invoke none of the gods but Cratis, who is Scylla's mother, and might perhaps forbid her daughter to devour them. For his conduct after he arrived at Trinacria, she referred him to the admonitions which had been given him by Tiresias.

Ulysses having communicated her instructions, as far as related to the Sirens, to his companions, who had not been present at that interview,—but concealing from them the rest, as he had done the terrible predictions of Tiresias, that they might not be deterred by fear from pursuing their voyage,—the time for departure being come, they set their sails, and took a final leave of great Circe; who by her art calmed the heavens, and gave them smooth seas, and a right fore-wind (the seaman's friend) to bear them on their way to Ithaca.

They had not sailed past a hundred leagues, before the breeze which Circe had lent them suddenly stopped. It was stricken dead. All the sea lay in prostrate slumber. Not a gasp of air could be felt. The ship stood still. Ulysses guessed that the island of the Sirens was not far off, and that they had charmed the air so with their devilish singing. Therefore he made him cakes of wax, as Circe had instructed him, and stopped the ears of his men with them: then, causing himself to be bound hand and foot, he commanded the rowers to ply their oars, and row as fast as speed could carry them past that fatal shore. They soon came within sight of the Sirens, who sang in Ulysses's hearing,—

> "Come here, thou, worthy of a world of praise,
> That dost so high the Grecian glory raise,—
> Ulysses! Stay thy ship, and that song hear
> That none pass'd ever, but it bent his ear,
> But left him ravish'd, and instructed more
> By us than any ever heard before.
> For we know all things,—whatsoever were
> In wide Troy labour'd, whatsoever there

The Grecians and the Trojans both sustain'd
By those high issues that the gods ordain'd :
And whatsoever all the earth can show,
To inform a knowledge of desert, we know "

These were the words; but the celestial harmony
of the voices which sang them no tongue can describe : it took the ear of Ulysses with ravishment.
He would have broken his bonds to rush after them ;
and threatened, wept, sued, entreated, commanded,
crying out with tears and passionate imprecations,
conjuring his men by all the ties of perils past which
they had endured in common, by fellowship and love,
and the authority which he retained among them, to
let him loose ; but at no rate would they obey him.
And still the Sirens sang.   Ulysses made signs, motions, gestures, promising mountains of gold if they
would set him free ; but their oars only moved faster.
And still the Sirens sang. And still, the more he
adjured them to set him free, the faster with cords
and ropes they bound him ; till they were quite out
of hearing of the Sirens' notes, whose effect great
Circe had so truly predicted. And well she might
speak of them ; for often she had joined her own enchanting voice to theirs, while she has sat in the
flowery meads, mingled with the Sirens and the
Water Nymphs, gathering their potent herbs and
drugs of magic quality. Their singing altogether
has made the gods stoop, and " heaven drowsy with
the harmony."

Escaped that peril, they had not sailed yet a
hundred leagues further, when they heard a roar afar
off, which Ulysses knew to be the barking of
Scylla's dogs, which surround her waist, and bark
incessantly. Coming nearer, they beheld a smoke

ascend, with a horrid murmur, which arose from that other whirlpool, to which they made nigher approaches than to Scylla. Through the furious eddy which is in that place, the ship stood still as a stone ; for there was no man to lend his hand to an oar : the dismal roar of Scylla's dogs at a distance, and the nearer clamours of Charybdis, where every thing made an echo, quite taking from them the power of exertion. Ulysses went up and down, encouraging his men, one by one, giving them good words ; telling them that they were in greater perils when they were blocked up in the Cyclop's cave : yet Heaven assisting his counsels, he had delivered them out of that extremity ;—that he could not believe but they remembered it ; and wished them to give the same trust to the same care which he had now for their welfare ;—that they must exert all the strength and wit which they had, and try if Jove would not grant them an escape, even out of this peril. In particular he cheered up the pilot who sat at the helm, and told him that he must show more firmness than other men, as he had more trust committed to him ; and had the sole management, by his skill, of the vessel in which all their safeties were embarked ;—that a rock lay hid within those boiling whirlpools which he saw, on the outside of which he must steer, if he would avoid his own destruction, and the destruction of them all

They heard him, and like men took to the oars, but little knew what opposite danger, in shunning that rock, they must be thrown upon ; for Ulysses had concealed from them the wounds, never to be healed, which Scylla was to open : their terror would else have robbed them all of all care to steer, or move

an oar, and have made them hide under the hatches,
for fear of seeing her, where he and they must have
died an idle death. But, even then, he forgot the
precautions which Circe had given him to prevent
harm to his person ; who had willed him not to arm,
or show himself once to Scylla ; but disdaining not to
venture life for his brave companions, he could not
contain, but armed in all points, and taking a lance
in either hand, he went up to the fore-deck, and looked
when Scylla would appear.

She did not show herself as yet; and still the
vessel steered closer by her rock, as it sought to shun
that other more dreaded : for they saw how horribly
Charybdis's black throat threw into her all the whirl-
ing deep, which she disgorged again ; that all about
her boiled like a kettle, and the rock roared with
troubled waters ; which when she supped in again,
all the bottom turned up, and disclosed far under
shore the swart sands naked, whose whole stern
sight frayed the startled blood from their faces, and
made Ulysses turn his to view the wonder of whirlpools. Which when Scylla saw from out her black
den, she darted out her six long necks, and swooped
up as many of his friends ; whose cries Ulysses
heard, and saw them too late, with their heels turned
up, and their hands thrown to him for succour, who
had been their help in all extremities, but could not
deliver them now ; and he heard them shriek out as
she tore them ; and, to the last, they continued to
throw their hands out to him for sweet life. In all
his sufferings he never had beheld a sight so full of
miseries.

Escaped from Scylla and Charybdis, but with a
diminished crew, Ulysses and the sad remains of his

followers reached the Trinacrian shore. Here, landing, he beheld oxen grazing, of such surpassing size
and beauty, that, both from them and from the shape
of the island, (having three promontories jutting into
the sea,) he judged rightly that he was come to the
Triangular Island, and the oxen of the Sun, of which
Tiresias had forewarned him.

So great was his terror, lest through his own fault,
or that of his men, any violence or profanation should
be offered to the holy oxen, that even then, tired as
they were with the perils and fatigues of the day
past, and unable to stir an oar or use any exertion,
and though night was fast coming on, he would have
had them re-embark immediately, and make the best
of their way from that dangerous station : but his
men, with one voice, resolutely opposed it ; and even
the too-cautious Eurylochus himself withstood the
proposal ; so much did the temptation of a little
ease and refreshment (ease tenfold sweet after such
labours) prevail over the sagest counsels, and the apprehension of certain evil outweigh the prospect of
contingent danger. They expostulated, that the
nerves of Ulysses seemed to be made of steel, and
his limbs not liable to lassitude like other men's ;
that waking or sleeping seemed indifferent to him ;
but that they were men, not gods, and felt the common appetites for food and sleep : that in the night-
time all the winds most destructive to ships are
generated, that black night still required to be served
with meat and sleep, and quiet havens and ease ;
that the best sacrifice to the sea was in the morning.
With such sailor-like sayings and mutinous arguments, which the majority have always ready to
justify disobedience to their betters, they forced

Ulysses to comply with their requisition, and, against
his will, to take up his night-quarters on shore. But
he first exacted from them an oath, that they would
neither maim nor kill any of the cattle which they
saw grazing, but content themselves with such food
as Circe had stowed their vessel with when they
parted fiom Æææa. This they, man by man, severally promised, imprecating the heaviest curses on
whoever should break it; and, mooring their bark
within a creek, they went to supper, contenting themselves that night with such food as Circe had given
them, not without many sad thoughts of their friends
whom Scylla had devoured, the grief of which kept
them, great part of the night, waking.

In the morning Ulysses urged them again to a
religious observance of the oath that they had sworn;
not in any case to attempt the blood of those fair
herds which they saw grazing, but to content themselves with the ship's food; for the god who owned
those cattle sees and hears all.

They faithfully obeyed, and remained in that good
mind for a month; during which they were confined
to that station by contrary winds, till all the wine
and the bread were gone which they had brought
with them. When their victuals were gone, necessity compelled them to stray in quest of whatever fish or fowl they could snare, which that coast
did not yield in any great abundance. Then Ulysses
prayed to all the gods that dwelt in bountiful heaven,
that they would be pleased to yield them some means
to stay their hunger, without having recourse to profane and forbidden violations: but the ears of heaven
seemed to be shut, or some god incensed plotted
his ruin; for at mid-day, when he should chiefly

have been vigilant and watchful to prevent mischief,
a deep sleep fell upon the eyes of Ulysses, during
which he lay totally insensible of all that passed in
the world, and what his friends or what his enemies
might do for his welfare or destruction   Then Eurylochus took his advantage.   He was the man of most
authority with them after Ulysses.   He represented
to them all the misery of their condition . how that
every death is hateful and grievous to mortality ; but
that, of all deaths, famine is attended with the most
painful, loathsome, and humiliating circumstances ;
that the subsistence which they could hope to draw from
fowling or fishing was too precarious to be depended
upon ; that there did not seem to be any chance of
the winds changing to favour their escape , but that
they must inevitably stay there and perish, if they let
an irrational superstition deter them from the means
which Nature offered to their hands ; that Ulysses
might be deceived in his belief that these oxen had
any sacred qualities above other oxen : and even
admitting that they were the property of the god of
the Sun, as he said they were, the Sun did neither
eat nor drink ; and the gods were best served, not by
a scrupulous conscience, but by a thankful heart,
which took freely what they as freely offered. With
these and such-like persuasions he prevailed on his
half-famished and half-mutinous companions to begin
the impious violation of their oath by the slaughter
of seven of the fairest of these oxen which were
grazing. Part they roasted and ate, and part they
offered in sacrifice to the gods ; particularly to Apollo,
god of the Sun, vowing to build a temple to his godhead when they should arrive at Ithaca, and deck it
with magnificent and numerous gifts. Vain men,

l   D

and superstition worse than that which they so lately
derided, to imagine that prospective penitence can
excuse a present violation of duty, and that the pure
natures of the heavenly powers will admit of com-
promise or dispensation for sin!

But to their feast they fell; dividing the roasted
portions of the flesh, savoury and pleasant meat to
them, but a sad sight to the eyes and a savour of
death in the nostrils of the waking Ulysses, who
just woke in time to witness, but not soon enough to
prevent, their rash and sacrilegious banquet. He had
scarce time to ask what great mischief was this
which they had done unto him, when, behold, a pro-
digy! The ox-hides which they had stripped began
to creep as if they had life; and the roasted flesh
bellowed, as the ox used to do when he was living.
The hair of Ulysses stood up an end with affright at
these omens; but his companions, like men whom
the gods had infatuated to their destruction, persisted
in their horrible banquet.

The Sun, from his burning chariot, saw how
Ulysses's men had slain his oxen; and he cried to his
father Jove: "Revenge me upon these impious men,
who have slain my oxen, which it did me good to
look upon when I walked my heavenly round. In all
my daily course I never saw such bright and beautiful creatures as those my oxen were." The father
promised that ample retribution should be taken
of those accursed men; which was fulfilled shortly
after, when they took their leaves of the fatal
island.

Six days they feasted, in spite of the signs of
heaven; and on the seventh, the wind changing,
they set their sails, and left the island: and their

hearts were cheerful with the banquets they had
held, all but the heart of Ulysses, which sank
within him, as with wet eyes he beheld his friends,
and gave them for lost, as men devoted to divine
vengeance: which soon overtook them; for they
had not gone many leagues before a dreadful tempest
arose which burst their cables. Down came their
mast, crushing the skull of the pilot in its fall: off
he fell from the stern into the water; and the bark,
wanting his management, drove along at the wind's
mercy. Thunders roared, and terrible lightnings of
Jove came down: first a bolt struck Eurylochus, then
another, and then another, till all the crew were
killed, and their bodies swam about like sea-mews;
and the ship was split in pieces. Only Ulysses survived; and he had no hope of safety but in tying
himself to the mast, where he sat riding upon the
waves, like one that in no extremity would yield to
fortune. Nine days was he floating about with all
the motions of the sea, with no other support than
the slender mast under him, till the tenth night cast
him, all spent and weary with toil, upon the friendly
shores of the Island Ogygia.

CHAPTER IV.

The Island of Calypso —Immortality Refused.

HENCEFORTH the adventures of the single Ulysses
must be pursued. Of all those faithful partakers of
his toil, who with him left Asia, laden with the spoils
of Troy, now not one remains, but all a prey to the
remorseless waves, and food for some great fish;

their gallant navy reduced to one ship, and that
finally swallowed up and lost.   Where now are all
their anxious thoughts of home ?—that perseverance
with which they went through the severest sufferings
and the hardest labours to which poor seafarers were
ever exposed, that their toils at last might be crowned
with the sight of their native shores and wives at
Ithaca ?   Ulysses is now in the Isle Ogygia, called
the Delightful Island.   The poor shipwrecked chief,
the slave of all the elements, is once again raised by
the caprice of fortune into a shadow of prosperity.
He that was cast naked upon the shore, bereft of all
his companions, has now a goddess to attend upon
him ; and his companions are the nymphs which
never die.   Who has not heard of Calypso,—her
grove crowned with alders and poplars ; her grotto,
against which the luxuriant vine laid forth his purple
grapes ; her ever-new delights, crystal fountains,
running brooks, meadows flowering with sweet balm-
gentle and with violet,—blue violets, which, like
veins, enamelled the smooth breasts of each fragrant
mead ?   It were useless to describe over again what
has been so well told already, or to relate those
soft arts of courtship which the goddess used to
detain Ulysses, — the same in kind which she
afterwards practised upon his less wary son, whom
Minerva, in the shape of Mentor, hardly preserved
from her snares, when they came to the Delightful Island together in search of the scarce departed
Ulysses.

A memorable example of married love, and a
worthy instance how dear to every good man his
country is, was exhibited by Ulysses.   If Circe loved
him sincerely, Calypso loves him with tenfold more

warmth and passion. She can deny him nothing but his departure. She offers him every thing, even to a participation of her immortality · if he will stay and share in her pleasures, he shall never die. But death with glory has greater charms for a mind heroic than a life that shall never die, with shame; and when he pledged his vows to his Penelope he reserved no stipulation that he would forsake her whenever a goddess should think him worthy of her bed, but they had sworn to live and grow old together . and he would not survive her if he could; nor meanly share in immortality itself, from which she was excluded.

These thoughts kept him pensive and melancholy in the midst of pleasure. His heart was on the seas, making voyages to Ithaca. Twelve months had worn away, when Minerva from heaven saw her favourite , how he sat pining on the sea-shores, (his daily custom,) wishing for a ship to carry him home. She (who is Wisdom herself) was indignant that so wise and brave a man as Ulysses should be held in effeminate bondage by an unworthy goddess; and, at her request, her father Jove ordered Mercury to go down to the earth to command Calypso to dismiss her guest. The divine messenger tied fast to his feet his winged shoes, which bear him over land and seas; and took in his hand his golden rod, the ensign of his authority. Then, wheeling in many an airy round, he stayed not till he alighted on the firm top of the Mountain Pieria : thence he fetched a second circuit over the seas, kissing the waves in his flight with his feet, as light as any sea-mew fishing dips her wings, till he touched the Isle Ogygia, and soared up from the blue sea to the grotto of the goddess, to whom his errand was ordained.

His message struck a horror, checked by love, through all the faculties of Calypso. She replied to it, incensed : " You gods are insatiate, past all that live, in all things which you affect; which makes you so envious and grudging. It afflicts you to the heart when any goddess seeks the love of a mortal man in marriage, though you yourselves without scruple link yourselves to women of the earth. So it fared with you when the delicious-fingered Morning shared Orion's bed: you could never satisfy your hate and your jealousy till you had incensed the chastity-loving dame, Diana, *who leads the precise life*, to come upon him by stealth in Ortygia, and pierce him through with her arrows. And when rich-haired Ceres gave the reins to her affections, and took Iasion (well worthy) to her arms, the secret was not so cunningly kept but Jove had soon notice of it; and the poor mortal paid for his felicity with death, struck through with lightnings. And now you envy me the possession of a wretched man, whom tempests have cast upon my shores, making him lawfully mine; whose ship Jove rent in pieces with his hot thunderbolts, killing all his friends. Him I have preserved, loved, nourished; made him mine by protection; my creature,—by every tie of gratitnde, mine; have vowed to make him deathless like myself: him you will take from me. But I know your power, and that it is vain for me to resist. Tell your king that I obey his mandates."

With an ill grace, Calypso promised to fulfil the commands of Jove; and, Mercury departing, she went to find Ulysses, where he sat outside the grotto, not knowing of the heavenly message, drowned in discontent, not seeing any human probability of his ever returning home.

She said to him, " Unhappy man, no longer afflict
yourself with pining after your country, but build
you a ship, with which you may return home, since
it is the will of the gods ; who doubtless, as they are
greater in power than I, are greater in skill, and best
can tell what is fittest for man. But I call the gods and
my inward conscience to witness that I had no thought
but what stood with thy safety, nor would have done or
counselled any thing against thy good. I persuaded
thee to nothing which I should not have followed myself in thy extremity ; for my mind is innocent and
simple. Oh if thou knewest what dreadful sufferings
thou must yet endure, before ever thou reachest thy
native land, thou wouldest not esteem so haidly of a
goddess's offer to share her immortality with thee ;
nor, for a few years' enjoyment of a perishing Penelope, refuse an imperishable and never-dying life with
Calypso."

He replied, " Ever-honoured, great Calypso, let it
not displease thee, that I, a mortal man, desire to
see and converse again with a wife that is mortal :
human objects are best fitted to human infirmities.
I well know how far in wisdom, in feature, in
stature, proportion, beauty, in all the gifts of the
mind, thou exceedest my Penelope : she is mortal,
and subject to decay, thou immortal, ever growing,
yet never old : yet in her sight all my desires ter-
minate : all my wishes, in the sight of her, and of my
country earth. If any god, envious of my return,
shall lay his dreadful hand upon me as I pass
the seas, I submit ; for the same powers have
given me a mind not to sink under oppression.
In wars and waves, my sufferings have not been
small."

She heard his pleaded reasons, and of force she must assent : so to her nymphs she gave in charge from her sacred woods to cut down timber, to make Ulysses a ship. They obeyed, though in a work unsuitable to their soft fingers ; yet to obedience no sacrifice is hard : and Ulysses busily bestirred himself, labouring far more hard than they, as was fitting, till twenty tall trees, driest and fittest for timber, were felled. Then, like a skilful shipwright, he fell to joining the planks ; using the plane, the axe, and the auger, with such expedition, that in four days' time a ship was made, complete with all her decks, hatches, side-boards, yards. Calypso added linen for the sails and tackling ; and when she was finished she was a goodly vessel for a man to sail in, alone or in company, over the wide seas. By the fifth morning she was launched ; and Ulysses, furnished with store of provisions, rich garments, and gold and silver, given him by Calypso, took a last leave of her and of her nymphs, and of the Isle Ogygia which had so befriended him.

CHAPTER V.

The Tempest.—The Sea Bird's Gift.—The Escape by Swimming.— The Sleep in the Woods.

At the stern of his solitary ship Ulysses sat, and steered right artfully. No sleep could seize his eyelids. He beheld the Pleiads, the Bear, which is by some called the Wain, that moves round about Orion, and keeps still above the ocean ; and the slow-setting sign Bootes, which some name the Wagoner.

Seventeen days he held his course; and on the eighteenth, the coast of Phæacia was in sight. The figure of the land, as seen from the sea, was pretty and circular, and looked something like a shield.

Neptune, returning from visiting his favourite Æthiopians, from the mountains of the Solymi descried Ulysses ploughing the waves, his domain. The sight of the man he so much hated for Polyphemus's sake, his son, whose eye Ulysses had put out, set the god's heart on fire, and snatching into his hand his horrid sea sceptre, the trident of his power, he smote the air and the sea, and conjured up all his black storms, calling down night from the cope of heaven, and taking the earth into the sea, as it seemed, with clouds, through the darkness and indistinctness which prevailed; the billows rolling up before the fury of all the winds, that contended together in their mighty sport.

Then the knees of Ulysses bent with fear, and then all his spirit was spent; and he wished he had been among the number of his countrymen who fell before Troy, and had their funerals celebrated by all the Greeks, rather than to perish thus, where no man could mourn him or know him.

As he thought these melancholy thoughts, a huge wave took him, and washed him overboard, ship and all upset amidst the billows, he struggling afar off, clinging to her stern broken off, which he yet held; her mast cracking in two with the fury of that gust of mixed winds that struck it; sails and sail-yards fell into the deep, and he himself was long drowned under water, nor could get his head above, wave so met with wave, as if they strove which should depress him most ; and the gorgeous garments given him by Calypso clung about him, and hindered his swimming. Yet neither for this, nor for the over-throw of his ship, nor his own perilous condition, would he give up his drenched vessel ; but, wrestling with Neptune, got at length hold of her again, and then sat in her hull, insulting over death, which he had escaped, and the salt waves, which he gave the seas again to give to other men. His ship, striving to live, floated at random, cuffed from wave to wave, hurled to and fro by all the winds : now Boreas tossed it to Notus, Notus pased it to Eurus, and Eurus to the West Wind, who kept up the horrid tennis.

Them in their mad sport Ino Leucothea beheld,— Ino Leucothea, now a sea-goddess, but once a mortal, and the daughter of Cadmus. She with pity beheld Ulysses the mark of their fierce contention ; and, rising from the waves, alighted on the ship, in shape like to the sea-bird which is called a cormorant ; and in her beak she held a wonderful girdle made of sea-weeds, which grow at the bottom of the ocean, which she dropped at his feet ; and the bird spake to Ulysses, and counselled him not to trust any more to that fatal vessel against which God Neptune had levelled his furious wrath, nor to those ill-befriending garments which Calypso had given him, but to quit both it and them, and trust for his safety to swimming. " And here," said the seeming bird, " take this girdle, and tie about your middle, which has virtue to protect the wearer at sea, and you shall safely reach the shore ; but when you have landed, cast it far from you back into the sea." He did as the sea-bird instructed him : he stripped himself naked, and, fastening the wondrous girdle about his middle, cast himself into the seas to swim. The bird dived past his sight into the fathomless abyss of the ocean.

Two days and two nights he spent in struggling with the waves, though sore buffeted, and almost spent, never giving up himself for lost; such confidence he had in that charm which he wore about his middle, and in the words of that divine bird. But the third morning the winds grew calm, and all the heavens were clear. Then he saw himself nigh land, which he knew to be the coast of the Phæacians, a people good to strangers, and abounding in ships. by whose favour he doubted not that he should soon obtain a passage to his own country. And such joy he conceived in his heart as good sons have, that esteem their father's life dear, when long sickness has held him down to his bed and wasted his body, and they see at length health return to the old man, with restored strength and spirits, in reward of their many prayers to the gods for his safety: so precious was the prospect of home return to Ulysses, that he might restore health to his country, (his better parent,) that had long languished as full of distempers in his absence. And then for his own safety's sake he had joy to see the shores, the woods, so nigh and within his grasp as they seemed, and he laboured with all the might of hands and feet to reach with swimming that nigh-seeming land.

But when he approached near, a horrid sound of a huge sea beating against rocks informed him that here was no place for landing, nor any harbour for man's resort· but, through the weeds and the foam which the sea belched up against the land, he could dimly discover the rugged shore all bristled with flints, and all that part of the coast one impending rock, that seemed impossible to climb; and the water all about so deep, that not a sand was there for any tired foot to rest upon; and every moment he feared lest some wave more cruel than the rest should crush him against a cliff, rendering worse than vain all his landing: and, should he swim to seek a more commodious haven further on, he was fearful, lest, weak and spent as he was, the winds would force him back a long way off into the main, where the terrible god Neptune, for wrath that he had so nearly escaped his power, having gotten him again into his domain, would send out some great whale (of which those seas breed a horrid number) to swallow him up alive; with such malignity he still pursued him.

While these thoughts distracted him with diversity of dangers, one bigger wave drove against a sharp rock his naked body, which it gashed and tore, and wanted little of breaking all his bones, so rude was the shock. But, in this extremity, she prompted him that never failed him at need. Minerva (who is Wisdom itself) put it into his thoughts no longer to keep swimming off and on, as one dallying with danger, but boldly to force the shore that threatened him, and to hug the rock that had torn him so rudely; which with both hands he clasped, wrestling with extremity, till the rage of that billow which had driven him upon it was passed · but then again the rock drove back that wave so furiously, that it reft him of his hold, sucking him with it in its return; and the sharp rock, his cruel friend, to which he clinged for succour, rent the flesh so sore from his hands in parting, that he fell off, and could sustain no longer. Quite under water he fell ; and, past the help of fate, there had the hapless Ulysses lost all portion that he had in this life, if Minerva had not prompted his wisdom in that peril to essay another course, and to explore some other shelter, ceasing to attempt that landing-place.

She guided his wearied and nigh-exhausted limbs to the mouth of the fair river Callicoe, which, not far from thence, disbursed its watery tribute to the ocean. Here the shores were easy and accessible, and the rocks (which rather adorned than defended its banks) so smooth, that they seemed polished of purpose to invite the landing of our sea-wanderer, and to atone for the uncourteous treatment which those less hospitable cliffs had afforded him. And the god of the river, as if in pity, stayed his current, and smoothed his waters, to make his landing more easy : for sacred to the ever-living deities of the fresh waters, be they mountain stream, river, or lake, is the cry of erring mortals that seek their aid : by reason, that, being inland bred, they partake more of the gentle humanities of our nature than those marine deities whom Neptune trains up in tempests in the unpitying recesses of his salt abyss.

So, by the favour of the river's god, Ulysses crept to land, half drowned. Both his knees faltering, his strong hands falling down through weakness from the excessive toils he had endured, his cheeks and nostrils flowing with froth of the sea brine, much of which he had swallowed in that conflict, voice and breath spent, down he sank as in death. Dead weary he was. It seemed that the sea had soaked through his heart, and the pains he felt in all his veins were little less than those which one feels that

has endured the torture of the rack. But when his
spirits came a little to themselves, and his recollection by degrees began to return, he rose up, and un-
loosing from his waist the girdle or charm which
that divine bird had given him, and remembering the
charge which he had received with it, he flung it far
from him into the river. Back it swam with the
course of the ebbing stream till it reached the sea,
where the fair hands of Ino Leucothea received it, to
keep it as a pledge of safety to any future shipwrecked mariner, that, like Ulysses, should wander
in those perilous waves.

Then he kissed the humble earth in token of safety;
and on he went by the side of that pleasant river, till
he came where a thicker shade of rushes that grew
on its banks seemed to point out the place where he
might rest his sea-wearied limbs. And here a fresh
perplexity divided his mind,—whether he should pass
the night, which was coming on, in that place,
where, though he feared no other enemies, the damps
and frosts of the chill sea-air in that exposed situation might be death to him in his weak state; or
whether he had better climb the next hill, and pierce
the depth of some shady wood, in which he might
find a warm and sheltered though insecure repose,
subject to the approach of any wild beast that roamed
that way. Best did this last course appear to him,
though with some danger, as that which was more
honourable, and savoured more of strife and self-
exertion, than to perish without a struggle, the pas-
sive victim of cold and the elements.

So he bent his course to the nearest woods ; where,
entering in, he found a thicket, mostly of wild
olives and such low trees, yet growing so intertwined

and knit together, that the moist wind had not leave
to play through their branches, nor the sun's scorching beams to pierce their recesses, nor any shower to
beat through, they grew so thick, and, as it were,
folded each in the other. Here, creeping in, he
made his bed of the leaves which were beginning to
fall, of which was such abundance, that two or three
men might have spread them ample coverings, such
as might shield them from the winter's rage, though
the air breathed steel, and blew as it would burst.
Here, creeping in, he heaped up store of leaves all
about him, as a man would billets upon a winter fire,
and lay down in the midst. Rich seed of virtue
lying hid in poor leaves! Here Minerva soon gave
him sound sleep; and here all his long toils past
seemed to be concluded, and shut up within the little
sphere of his refreshed and closed eyelids.

CHAPTER VI.

THE PRINCESS NAUSICAA. — THE WASHING. — THE GAME WITH THE
BALL. — THE COURT OF PHÆACIA AND KING ALCINOUS.

MEANTIME Minerva, designing an interview between
the king's daughter of that country and Ulysses when
he should awake, went by night to the palace of the
King Alcinous, and stood at the bed side of the
Princess Nausicaa in the shape of one of her favourite attendants, and thus addressed the sleeping
princess :—

"Nausicaa, why do you lie sleeping here, and
never bestow a thought upon your bridal ornaments,
of which you have many and beautiful, laid up in

2 B 2

your wardrobe against the day of your marriage,
which cannot be far distant; when you shall have
need of all, not only to deck your own person, but to
give away in presents to the virgins, that, honouring
you, shall attend you to the temple? Your reputation stands much upon the timely care of these
things: these things are they which fill father and
reverend mother with delight. Let us arise betimes
to wash your fair vestments of linen and silks in the
river, and request your sire to lend you mules and a
coach; for your wardrobe is heavy, and the place
where we must wash is distant; and, besides, it fits
not a great princess like you to go so far on foot."

So saying, she went away, and Nausicaa awoke
full of pleasing thoughts of her marriage, which the
dream had told her was not far distant; and as soon
as it was dawn she arose and dressed herself, and
went to find her parent.

The queen, her mother, was already up, and seated
among her maids, spinning at her wheel, as the
fashion was in those primitive times, when great
ladies did not disdain housewifery; and the king,
her father, was preparing to go abroad at that early
hour to counsel with his grave senate.

"My father," she said, "will you not order mules
and a coach to be got ready, that I may go and wash,
I and my maids, at the cisterns that stand without
the city?"

"What washing does my daughter speak of?"
said Alcinous.

"Mine and my brothers' garments," she replied,
"that have contracted soil by this time with lying by
so long in the wardrobe. Five sons have you, that
are my brothers: two of them are married, and three

are bachelors. These last it concerns to have their garments neat and unsoiled : it may advance their fortunes in marriage. And who but me, their sister, should have a care of these things ? You yourself, my father, have need of the whitest apparel, when you go, as now, to the council."

She used this plea, modestly dissembling her care of her own nuptials to her father; who was not displeased at this instance of his daughter's discretion : for a seasonable care about marriage may be permitted to a young maiden, provided it be accompanied with modesty, and dutiful submission to her parents in the choice of her future husband. And there was no fear of Nausicaa's choosing wrongly or improperly ; for she was as wise as she was beautiful, and the best in all Phæacia were suitors to her for her love. So Alcinous readily gave consent that she should go, ordering mules and a coach to be prepared. And Nausicaa brought from her chamber all her vestments, and laid them up in the coach ; and her mother placed bread and wine in the coach, and oil in a golden cruse, to soften the bright skins of Nausicaa and her maids when they came out of the river.

Nausicaa, making her maids get up into the coach with her, lashed the mules, till they brought her to the cisterns which stood a little on the outside of the town, and were supplied with water from the river Callicoe.

There her attendants unyoked the mules, took out the clothes, and steeped them in the cisterns, washing them in several waters, and afterwards treading them clean with their feet ; venturing wagers who should have done soonest and cleanest, and using many pretty pastimes to beguile their labours as young maids use, while the princess looked on. When they had laid their clothes to dry, they fell to playing again ; and Nausicaa joined them in a game with the ball, which is used in that country; which is performed by tossing the ball from hand to hand with great expedition, she who begins the pastime singing a song. It chanced that the princess, whose turn it became to toss the ball, sent it so far from its mark, that it fell beyond into one of the cisterns of the river ; at which the whole company, in merry consternation, set up a shriek so loud that it waked the sleeping Ulysses, who was taking his rest, after his long toils, in the woods, not far distant from the place where these young maids had come to wash.

At the sound of female voices Ulysses crept forth from his retirement, making himself a covering with boughs and leaves as well as he could to shroud his nakedness. The sudden appearance of his weather-beaten and almost naked form so frighted the maidens, that they scudded away into the woods and all about to hide themselves: only Minerva, (who had brought about this interview, to admirable purposes, by seemingly accidental means,) put courage into the breast of Nausicaa, and she stayed where she was, and resolved to know what manner of man he was, and what was the occasion of his strange coming to them.

He, not venturing (for delicacy) to approach and clasp her knees, as suppliants should, but standing far off, addressed this speech to the young princess :—

" Before I presume rudely to press my petitions, I

should first ask whether I am addressing a mortal woman, or one of the goddesses. If a goddess, you seem to me to be likest to Diana, the chaste huntress, the daughter of Jove. Like hers are your lineaments, your stature, your features, and air divine."

She making answer that she was no goddess, but a mortal maid, he continued :—

" If a woman, thrice blessed are both the authors of your birth ; thrice blessed are your brothers, who even to rapture must have joy in your perfections, to see you grown so like a young tree, and so graceful. But most blessed of all that breathe is he that has the gift to engage your young neck in the yoke of marriage. I never saw that man that was worthy of you. I never saw man or woman that at all parts equalled you. Lately at Delos (where I touched) I saw a young palm which grew beside Apollo's temple , it exceeded all the trees which ever I beheld for straightness and beauty : I can compare you only to that. A stupor past admiration strikes me, joined with fear, which keeps me back from approaching you to embrace your knees. Nor is it strange ; for one of freshest and firmest spirit would falter, approaching near to so bright an object but I am one whom a cruel habit of calamity has prepared to receive strong impressions Twenty days the unrelenting seas have tossed me up and down, coming from Ogygia ; and at length cast me shipwrecked last night upon your coast. I have seen no man or woman since I landed but yourself. All that I crave is clothes, which you may spare me ; and to be shown the way to some neighbouring town. The gods, who have care of strangers, will requite you for these courtesies."

She, admiring to hear such complimentary words proceed out of the mouth of one whose outside looked so rough and unpromising, made answer: " Stranger, I discern neither sloth nor folly in you; and yet I see that you are poor and wretched: from which I gather that neither wisdom nor industry can secure felicity: only Jove bestows it upon whomsoever he pleases. He, perhaps, has reduced you to this plight. However, since your wanderings have brought you so near to our city, it lies in our duty to supply your wants. Clothes, and what else a human hand should give to one so suppliant, and so tamed with calamity, you shall not want. We will show you our city, and tell you the name of our people. This is the land of the Phæacians, of which my father, Alcinous, is king."

Then calling her attendants, who had dispersed on the first sight of Ulysses, she rebuked them for their fear, and said, " This man is no Cyclop, nor monster of sea or land, that you should fear him; but he seems manly, staid, and discreet, and though decayed in his outward appearance, yet he has the mind's riches, wit and fortitude, in abundance. Show him the cisterns where he may wash him from the sea-weeds and foam that hang about him, and let him have garments that fit him out of those which we have brought with us to the cisterns.

Ulysses retiring a little out of sight, cleansed him in the cisterns from the soil and impurities with which the rocks and waves had covered all his body; and, clothing himself with befitting raiment which the princess's attendants had given him, he presented himself in more worthy shape to Nausicaa. She admired to see what a comely personage he was, now he was dressed in all parts : she thought him some king or hero, and secretly wished that the gods would be pleased to give her such a husband.

Then causing her attendants to yoke her mules, and lay up the vestments, which the sun's heat had sufficiently dried, in the coach, she ascended with her maids, and drove off to the palace : bidding Ulysses, as she departed, keep an eye upon the coach, and to follow it on foot at some distance ; which she did, because, if she had suffered him to have ridden in the coach with her, it might have subjected her to some misconstructions of the common people, who are always ready to vilify and censure their betters, and to suspect that charity is not always pure charity, but that love or some sinister intention lies hid under its disguise. So discreet and attentive to appearance in all her actions was this admirable princess.

Ulysses, as he entered the city, wondered to see its magnificence ; its markets, buildings, temples ; its walls and rampires ; its trade, and resort of men ; its harbours for shipping, which is the strength of the Phæacian state. But when he approached the palace, and beheld its riches, the proportion of its architecture, its avenues, gardens, statues, fountains, he stood wrapt in admiration, and almost forgot his own condition in surveying the flourishing estate of others . but, recollecting himself, he passed on boldly into the inner apartment, where the king and queen were sitting at dinner with their peers ; Nausicaa having prepared them for his approach.

To them humbly kneeling, he made it his request, that since fortune had cast him naked upon their shores, they would take him into their protection, and grant him a conveyance by one of the ships, of which their great Phæacian state had such good store, to carry him to his own country. Having delivered his request, to grace it with more humility, he went and sat himself down upon the hearth among the ashes, as the custom was in those days when any would make a petition to the throne.

He seemed a petitioner of so great state, and of so superior a deportment, that Alcinous himself arose to do him honour, and, causing him to leave that abject station which he had assumed, placed him next to his throne upon a chair of state; and thus he spake to his peers:—

"Lords and councillors of Phæacia, ye see this man, who he is we know not, that is come to us in the guise of a petitioner. He seems no mean one: but, whoever he is, it is fit, since the gods have cast him upon our protection, that we grant him the rights of hospitality while he stays with us , and, at his departure, a ship well manned, to convey so worthy a personage as he seems to be, in a manner suitable to his rank, to his own country."

This counsel the peers with one consent approved; and wine and meat being set before Ulysses, he ate and drank, and gave the gods thanks who had stirred up the royal bounty of Alcinous to aid him in that extremity. But not as yet did he reveal to the king and queen who he was, or whence he had come: only in brief terms he related his being cast upon their shores, his sleep in the woods, and his meeting with the Princess Nausicaa; whose generosity, mingled with discretion, filled her parents with delight, as Ulysses in eloquent phrases adorned and commended her virtues. But Alcinous, humanely considering that in consequence of the troubles which his guest had undergone he required rest, as well as refreshment by food, dismissed him early in the evening to his chamber, where, in a magnificent apartment, Ulysses found a smoother bed, but not a sounder repose, than he had enjoyed the night before, sleeping upon leaves which he had scraped together in his necessity.

CHAPTER VII.

The Songs of Demodocus.—The Convoy Home.—The Mariners Transformed to Stone.—The Young Shepherd.

WHEN it was daylight Alcinous caused it to be proclaimed by the heralds about the town, that there was come to the palace a stranger, shipwrecked on their coast, that in mien and person resembled a god ; and he invited all the chief people of the city to come and do honour to the stranger.

The palace was quickly filled with guests, old and young ; for whose cheer, and to grace Ulysses more, Alcinous made a kingly feast, with banquetings and music. Then Ulysses being seated at a table next the king and queen, in all men's view, after they had feasted, Alcinous ordered Demodocus, the court-singer, to be called to sing some song of the deeds of heroes, to charm the ear of his guest. Demodocus came, and reached his harp, where it hung between two pillars of silver ; and then the blind singer, to whom, in recompence of his lost sight, the Muses had given an inward discernment, a soul and a voice to excite the hearts of men and gods to delight, began in grave and solemn strains to sing the glories of men highliest famed. He chose a poem, whose subject was, The stern Strife stirred up between Ulysses and great Achilles, as, at a banquet sacred to the gods, in dreadful language they expressed their difference; while Agamemnon sat rejoiced in soul to hear those Grecians jar: for the oracle in Pytho had told him, that the period of their wars in Troy should then be, when the kings of Greece, anxious to arrive at the wished conclusion, should fall to strife, and contend which must end the war, force or stratagem.

This brave contention he expressed so to the life, in the very words which they both used in the quarrel, as brought tears into the eyes of Ulysses at the remembrance of past passages of his life; and he held his large purple weed before his face to conceal it. Then, craving a cup of wine, he poured it out in secret libation to the gods, who had put it into the mind of Demodocus unknowingly to do him so much honour. But when the moving poet began to tell of other occurrences where Ulysses had been present, the memory of his brave followers who had been with him in all difficulties, now swallowed up and lost in the ocean, and of those kings that had fought with him at Troy, some of whom were dead, some exiles like himself, forced itself so strongly upon his mind, that, forgetful where he was, he sobbed outright with passion; which yet he restrained, but not so cunningly but Alcinous perceived it, and, without taking notice of it to Ulysses, privately gave signs that Demodocus should cease from his singing.

Next followed dancing in the Phæacian fashion,

when they would show respect to their guests,
which was succeeded by trials of skill, games of
strength, running, racing, hurling of the quoit, mock
fights, hurling of the javelin, shooting with the bow;
in some of which Ulysses, modestly challenging his
entertainers, performed such feats of strength and
prowess as gave the admiring Phæacians fresh
reason to imagine that he was either some god, or
hero of the race of the gods.

These solemn shows and pageants, in honour of
his guest, King Alcinous continued for the space of
many days, as if he could never be weary of showing
courtesies to so worthy a stranger. In all this time
he never asked him his name, nor sought to know
more of him than he of his own accord disclosed:
till on a day as they were seated feasting, after the
feast was ended, Demodocus being called, as was
the custom, to sing some grave matter, sang how
Ulysses, on that night when Troy was fired, made
dreadful proof of his valour, maintaining singly a
combat against the whole household of Deiphobus;
to which the divine expresser gave both act and
passion, and breathed such a fire into Ulysses's deeds,
that it inspired old death with life in the lively expressing of slaughters, and rendered life so sweet
and passionate in the hearers, that all who heard felt
it fleet from them in the narration: which made
Ulysses even pity his own slaughterous deeds, and
feel touches of remorse, to see how song can revive
a dead man from the grave, yet no way can it defend
a living man from death: and in imagination he
underwent some part of death's horrors, and felt in
his living body a taste of those dying pangs which
he had dealt to others, that, with the strong conceit,

tears (the true interpreters of unutterable emotion) stood in his eyes.

Which King Alcinous noting, and that this was now the second time that he had perceived him to be moved at the mention of events touching the Trojan wars, he took occasion to ask whether his guest had lost any friend or kinsman at Troy, that Demodocus's singing had brought into his mind. Then Ulysses, drying the tears with his cloak, and observing that the eyes of all the company were upon him, desirous to give them satisfaction in what he could, and thinking this a fit time to reveal his true name and destination, spake as follows.—

"The courtesies which ye all have shown me, and in particular yourself and princely daughter, O King Alcinous! demand from me that I should no longer keep you in ignorance of what or who I am; for to reserve any secret from you, who have with such openness of friendship embraced my love, would argue either a pusillanimous or an ungrateful mind in me. Know, then, that I am that *Ulysses*, of whom I perceive ye have heard something; who heretofore have filled the world with the renown of my policies. I am he, by whose counsels, if Fame is to be believed at all, more than by the united valour of all the Grecians, Troy fell. I am that unhappy man whom the heavens and angry gods have conspired to keep an exile on the seas, wandering to seek my home, which still flies from me. The land which I am in quest of is Ithaca, in whose ports some ship belonging to your navigation-famed Phæacian state may haply at some time have found a refuge from tempests. If ever you have experienced such kindness, requite it now, by granting to me, who am the king of that land, a passport to that land."

Admiration seized all the court of Alcinous to behold in their presence one of the number of those heroes who fought at Troy; whose divine story had been made known to them by songs and poems, but of the truth they had little known, or rather they had hitherto accounted those heroic exploits as fictions and exaggerations of poets: but, having seen and made proof of the real Ulysses, they began to take those supposed inventions to be real verities, and the tale of Troy to be as true as it was delightful.

Then King Alcinous made answer: "Thrice fortunate ought we to esteem our lot in having seen and conversed with a man of whom report hath spoken so loudly, but, as it seems, nothing beyond the truth Though we could desire no felicity greater than to have you always among us, renowned Ulysses, yet, your desire having been expressed so often and so deeply to return home, we can deny you nothing, though to our own loss. Our kingdom of Phæacia, as you know, is chiefly rich in shipping. In all parts of the world, where there are navigable seas, or ships can pass, our vessels will be found. You cannot name a coast to which they do not resort. Every rock and every quicksand is known to them, that lurks in the vast deep. They pass a bird in flight; and with such unerring certainty they make to their destination, that some have said that they have no need of pilot or rudder, but that they move instinctively, self-directed, and know the minds of their voyagers. Thus much, that you may not fear to trust yourself in one of our Phæacian ships. To-morrow, if you please, you shall launch forth. To-

day spend with us in feasting, who never can do
enough when the gods send such visitors."

Ulysses acknowledged King Alcinous's bounty;
and, while these two royal personages stood inter-
changing courteous expressions, the heart of the
Princess Nausicaa was overcome. She had been
gazing attentively upon her father's guest, as he
delivered his speech : but when he came to that
part where he declared himself to be Ulysses, she
blessed herself, and her fortune, that in relieving a
poor shipwrecked mariner, as he seemed no better,
she had conferred a kindness on so divine a hero as
he proved ; and, scarce waiting till her father had
done speaking, with a cheerful countenance she addressed Ulysses, bidding him to be cheerful, and
when he returned home, as by her father's means
she trusted he would shortly, sometimes to remember
to whom he owed his life, and who met him in the
woods by the river Callicoe.

" Fair flower of Phæacia," he replied, " so may all
the gods bless me with the strife of joys in that
desired day, whenever I shall see it, as I shall always
acknowledge to be indebted to your fair hand for the
gift of life which I enjoy, and all the blessings which
shall follow upon my home-return. The gods give
thee, Nausicaa, a princely husband ; and from you two
spring blessings to this state." So prayed Ulysses,
his heart overflowing with admiration and grateful
recollections of King Alcinous's daughter.

Then, at the king's request, he gave them a brief
relation of all the adventures that had befallen him
since he launched forth from Troy : during which the
Princess Nausicaa took great delight (as ladies are
commonly taken with these kind of travellers' stories)

to hear of the monster Polyphemus, of the men that devour each other in Læstrygonia, of the enchantress Circe, of Scylla, and the rest; to which she listened with a breathless attention, letting fall a shower of tears from her fair eyes, every now and then, when Ulysses told of some more than usual distressful passage in his travels: and all the rest of his auditors, if they had before entertained a high respect for their guest, now felt their veneration increased tenfold, when they learned from his own mouth what perils, what sufferance, what endurance, of evils beyond man's strength to support, this much-sustaining, almost heavenly man, by the greatness of his mind and by his invincible courage, had struggled through.

The night was far spent before Ulysses had ended his narrative: and with wishful glances he cast his eyes towards the eastern parts, which the sun had begun to flecker with his first red; for, on the morrow, Alcinous had promised that a bark should be in readiness to convoy him to Ithaca.

In the morning a vessel well manned and appointed was waiting for him; into which the king and queen heaped presents of gold and silver, massy plate, apparel, armour, and whatsoever things of cost or rarity they judged would be most acceptable to their guest: and, the sails being set, Ulysses, embarking with expressions of regret, took his leave of his royal entertainers, of the fair Princess, (who had been his first friend,) and of the peers of Phæacia; who, crowding down to the beach to have the last sight of their illustrious visitant, beheld the gallant ship with all her canvas spread, bounding and curvetting over the waves like a horse proud of his rider, or as if she knew that in her capacious womb's rich freightage she bore Ulysses.

He whose life past had been a series of disquiets, in seas among rude waves, in battles amongst ruder foes, now slept securely, forgetting all; his eyelids bound in such deep sleep as only yielded to death: and, when they reached the nearest Ithacan port by the next morning, he was still asleep. The mariners, not willing to awake him, landed him softly, and laid him in a cave at the foot of an olive tree, which made a shady recess in that narrow harbour, the haunt of almost none but the sea-nymphs, which are called Naiads: few ships before this Phæacian vessel having put into that haven, by reason of the difficulty and narrowness of the entrance. Here leaving him asleep, and disposing in safe places near him the presents with which King Alcinous had dismissed him, they departed for Phæacia, where these wretched mariners never again set foot: but just as they arrived, and thought to salute their country earth,— in sight of their city's turrets, and in open view of their friends, who from the harbour with shouts greeted their return,—their vessel and all the mariners which were in her were turned to stone, and stood transformed and fixed in sight of the whole Phæacian city; where it yet stands, by Neptune's vindictive wrath, who resented thus highly the contempt which those Phæacians had shown in convoying home a man whom the god had destined to destruction. Whence it comes to pass, that the Phæacians at this day will at no price be induced to lend their ships to strangers, or to become the carriers for other nations, so highly do they still dread the displeasure of their sea-god, while they see that terrible monument ever in sight.

When Ulysses awoke, (which was not till some time after the mariners had departed,) he did not at first know his country again ; either that long absence had made it strange, or that Minerva (which was more likely) had cast a cloud about his eyes, that he should have greater pleasure hereafter in discovering his mistake : but like a man suddenly awaking in some desert isle, to which his sea-mates have transported him in his sleep, he looked around, and discerning no known objects, he cast his hands to heaven for pity, and complained on those ruthless men who had beguiled him with a promise of conveying him home to his country, and perfidiously left him to perish in an unknown land. But then the rich presents of gold and silver given him by Alcinous, which he saw carefully laid up in secure places near him, staggered him ; which seemed not like the act of wrongful or unjust men, such as turn pirates for gain, or land helpless passengers in remote coasts to possess themselves of their goods.

While he remained in this suspense, there came up to him a young shepherd, clad in the finer sort of apparel, such as kings' sons wore in those days when princes did not disdain to tend sheep ; who, accosting him, was saluted again by Ulysses, who asked him what country that was on which he had been just landed, and whether it were part of a continent or an island. The young shepherd made show of wonder to hear any one ask the name of that land , as country people are apt to esteem those for mainly ignorant and barbarous who do not know the names of places which are familiar to *them*, though perhaps they who ask have had no opportunities of knowing, and may have come from far countries.

" I had thought," said he, " that all people knew
our land. It is rocky and barren, to be sure ; but well
enough : it feeds a goat or an ox well ; it is not
wanting either in wine or in wheat ; it has good
springs of water, some fair rivers, and wood enough,
as you may see. It is called Ithaca."

Ulysses was joyed enough to find himself in his
own country : but so prudently he carried his joy,
that, dissembling his true name and quality, he pretended to the shepherd that he was only some
foreigner who by stress of weather had put into that
port ; and framed on the sudden a story to make it
plausible how he had come from Crete in a ship of
Phæacia. when the young shepherd, laughing, and
taking Ulysses's hand in both his, said to him, " He
must be cunning, I find, who thinks to overreach you.
What ! cannot you quit your wiles and your subtleties,
now that you are in a state of security ? must the
first word with which you salute your native earth
be an untruth ? and think you that you are unknown ?"

Ulysses looked again ; and he saw not a shepherd,
but a beautiful woman, whom he immediately knew
to be the goddess Minerva, that in the wars of
Troy had frequently vouchsafed her sight to him ;
and had been with him since in perils, saving him
unseen.

" Let not my ignorance offend thee, great Minerva,"
he cried, " or move thy displeasure, that in that
shape I knew thee not ; since the skill of discerning
deities is not attainable by wit or study, but hard
to be hit by the wisest of mortals. To know thee
truly through all thy changes, is only given to those
whom thou art pleased to grace. To all men thou

takest all likenesses. All men in their wits think that they know thee, and that they have thee. Thou art Wisdom itself. But a semblance of thee, which is false wisdom, often is taken for thee; so thy counterfeit view appears to many, but thy true presence to few : those are they, which, loving thee above all, are inspired with light from thee to know thee. But this I surely know, that, all the time the sons of Greece waged war against Troy, I was sundry times graced with thy appearance; but, since, I have never been able to set eyes upon thee till now, but have wandered at my own discretion, to myself a blind guide, erring up and down the world, wanting thee."

Then Minerva cleared his eyes, and he knew the ground on which he stood to be Ithaca, and that cave to be the same which the people of Ithaca had in former times made sacred to the sea-nymphs, and where he himself had done sacrifices to them a thousand times ; and full in his view stood Mount Nerytus, with all his woods . so that now he knew for a certainty that he was arrived in his own country; and, with the delight which he felt, he could not forbear stooping down and kissing the soil.

CHAPTER VIII.

The change from a King to a Beggar.—Eumeus and the Herdsmen.—Telemachus.

Not long did Minerva suffer him to indulge vain transports : but, briefly recounting to him the events which had taken place in Ithaca during his absence,

l   )

she showed him that his way to his wife and throne did not lie so open, but that, before he were reinstated in the secure possession of them, he must encounter many difficulties. His palace, wanting its king, was become the resort of insolent and imperious men, the chief nobility of Ithaca and of the neighbouring isles, who, in the confidence of Ulysses being dead, came as suitors to Penelope. The queen (it was true) continued single, but was little better than a state-prisoner in the power of these men, who, under a pretence of waiting her decision, occupied the king's house, rather as owners than guests, lording and domineering at their pleasure, profaning the palace, and wasting the royal substance, with their feasts and mad riots. Moreover, the goddess told him, how, fearing the attempts of these lawless men upon the person of his young son Telemachus, she herself had put it into the heart of the Prince to go and seek his father in far countries; how, in the shape of Mentor, she had borne him company in his long search, which though failing, as she meant it should fail, in its first object, had yet had this effect,—that through hardships he had learned endurance; through experience he had gathered wisdom; and, wherever his footsteps had been, he had left such memorials of his worth, as the fame of Ulysses's son was already blown throughout the world;—that it was now many days since Telemachus had arrived in the island, to the great joy of the queen, his mother, who had thought him dead, by reason of his long absence, and had begun to mourn for him with a grief equal to that which she endured for Ulysses; the goddess herself having so ordered the course of his adventures, that the time of his return should correspond

with the return of Ulysses, that they might together
concert measures how to repress the power and insolence of those wicked suitors. This the goddess
told him; but of the particulars of his son's adventures, of his having been detained in the Delightful
Island, which his father had so lately left, of Calypso
and her nymphs, and the many strange occurrences
which may be read with profit and delight in the
history of the prince's adventures, she forbore to tell
him as yet, as judging that he would hear them with
greater pleasure from the lips of his son, when he
should have him in an hour of stillness and safety,
when their work should be done, and none of their
enemies left alive to trouble them.

Then they sat down, the goddess and Ulysses, at
the foot of a wild olive tree, consulting how they
might with safety bring about his restoration. And
when Ulysses revolved in his mind how that his
enemies were a multitude, and he single, he began to
despond; and he said, " I shall die an ill death, like
Agamemnon: in the threshold of my own house I
shall perish, like that unfortunate monarch, slain by
some one of my wife's suitors." But then, again,
calling to mind his ancient courage, he secretly
wished that Minerva would but breathe such a spirit
into his bosom as she inflamed him with in the hour
of Troy's destruction, that he might encounter with
three hundred of those impudent suitors at once, and
strew the pavements of his beautiful palace with their
bloods and brains.

And Minerva knew his thoughts: and she said,
" I will be strongly with thee, if thou fail not to do
thy part. And for a sign between us that I will perform my promise, and for a token on thy part of

obedience, I must change thee, that thy person may not be known of men."

Then Ulysses bowed his head to receive the divine impression; and Minerva, by her great power, changed his person so that it might not be known. She changed him to appearance into a very old man, yet such a one as by his limbs and gait seemed to have been some considerable person in his time, and to retain yet some remains of his once prodigious strength. Also, instead of those rich robes in which King Alcinous had clothed him, she threw over his limbs such old and tattered rags as wandering beggars usually wear. A staff supported his steps, and a scrip hung to his back, such as travelling mendicants use to hold the scraps which are given to them at rich men's doors. So from a king he became a beggar, as wise Tiresias had predicted to him in the Shades.

To complete his humiliation, and to prove his obedience by suffering, she next directed him in this beggarly attire to go and present himself to his old herdsman, Eumæus, who had the care of his swine and his cattle, and had been a faithful steward to him all the time of his absence. Then, strictly charging Ulysses that he should reveal himself to no man but to his own son, whom she would send to him when she saw occasion, the goddess went her way.

The transformed Ulysses bent his course to the cottage of the herdsman; and, entering in at the front court, the dogs, of which Eumæus kept many fierce ones for the protection of the cattle, flew with open mouths upon him, as those ignoble animals have oftentimes an antipathy to the sight of any thing like a beggar; and would have rent him in pieces with their teeth, if Ulysses had not had the prudence to let fall his staff, which had chiefly provoked their fury, and sat himself down in a careless fashion upon the ground. But, for all that, some serious hurt had certainly been done to him, so raging the dogs were, had not the herdsman, whom the barking of the dogs had fetched out of the house, with shouting and with throwing of stones repressed them.

He said, when he saw Ulysses, " Old father, how near you were to being torn in pieces by these rude dogs ! I should never have forgiven myself, if, through neglect of mine, any hurt had happened to you. But Heaven has given me so many cares to my portion, that I might well be excused for not attending to every thing ; while here I lie grieving and mourning for the absence of that majesty which once ruled here, and am forced to fatten his swine and his cattle for food to evil men, who hate him, and who wish his death ; when he perhaps strays up and down the world, and has not wherewith to appease hunger, if indeed he yet lives, (which is a question,) and enjoys the cheerful light of the sun." This he said, little thinking that he of whom he spoke now stood before him, and that in that uncouth disguise and beggarly obscurity was present the hidden majesty of Ulysses.

Then he had his guest into the house, and set meat and drink before him ; and Ulysses said, " May Jove and all the other gods requite you for the kind speeches and hospitable usage which you have shown me !"

Eumæus made answer, " My poor guest, if one in

much worse plight than yourself had arrived here, it were a shame to such scanty means as I have, if I had let him depart without entertaining him to the best of my ability. Poor men, and such as have no houses of their own, are by Jove himself recommended to our care. But the cheer which we that are servants to other men have to bestow is but sorry at most; yet freely and lovingly I give it you. Indeed, there once ruled here a man, whose return the gods have set their faces against, who, if he had been suffered to reign in peace and grow old among us, would have been kind to me and mine. But he is gone; and, for his sake, would to God that the whole posterity of Helen might perish with her, since in her quarrel so many worthies have perished! But such as your fare is, eat it, and be welcome; such lean beasts as are food for poor herdsmen. The fattest go to feed the voracious stomachs of the queen's suitors. Shame on their unworthiness! There is no day in which two or three of the noblest of the herd are not slain to support their feasts and their surfeits."

Ulysses gave good ear to his words; and, as he ate his meat, he even tore it and rent it with his teeth, for mere vexation that his fat cattle should be slain to glut the appetites of those godless suitors. And he said, "What chief or what ruler is this that thou commendest so highly, and sayest that he perished at Troy? I am but a stranger in these parts. It may be I have heard of some such in my long travels."

Eumæus answered, "Old father, never any one, of all the strangers that have come to our coast with news of Ulysses being alive, could gain credit with

the queen or her son yet. These travellers, to get
raiment or a meal, will not stick to invent any lie.
Truth is not the commodity they deal in. Never did
the queen get any thing of them but lies. She re-
ceives all that come, graciously; hears their stories,
inquires all she can; but all ends in tears and dis-
satisfaction. But in God's name, old father, if you
have got a tale, make the most on't; it may gain
you a cloak or a coat from somebody to keep you
warm: but, for him who is the subject of it, dogs
and vultures long since have torn him limb from
limb, or some great fish at sea has devoured him, or
he lieth with no better monument upon his bones
than the sea sand. But for me past all the race of
men were tears created; for I never shall find so
kind a royal master more: not if my father or my
mother could come again and visit me from the
tomb, would my eyes be so blessed as they should
be with the sight of him again, coming as from the
dead. In his last rest my soul shall love him. He
is not here, nor do I name him as a flatterer, but
because I am thankful for his love and care which he
had to me, a poor man; and if I knew surely that
he were past all shores that the sun shines upon, I
would invoke him as a deified thing."

For this saying of Eumæus the waters stood in
Ulysses's eyes; and he said, " My friend, to say and
to affirm positively that he cannot be alive is to give
too much license to incredulity. For, not to speak
at random, but with as much solemnity as an oath
comes to, I say to you, that Ulysses shall return;
and whenever that day shall be, then shall you give
to me a cloak and a coat; but till then I will not
receive so much as a thread of a garment, but rather

go naked : for no less than the gates of hell do I hate that man whom poverty can force to tell an untruth, Be Jove, then, witness to my words, that this very year, nay, ere this month be fully ended, your eyes shall behold Ulysses dealing vengeance in his own palace upon the wrongers of his wife and his son."

To give the better credence to his words, he amused Eumæus with a forged story of his life ; feigning of himself that he was a Cretan born, and one that went with Idomeneus to the wars of Troy. Also he said that he knew Ulysses, and related various passages which he alleged to have happened betwixt Ulysses and himself, which were either true in the main as having really happened between Ulysses and some other person, or were so like to truth, as corresponding with the known character and actions of Ulysses, that Eumæus's incredulity was not a little shaken. Among other things, he asserted that he had lately been entertained in the court of Thesprotia, where the king's son of the country had told him that Ulysses had been there but just before him, and was gone upon a voyage to the oracle of Jove in Dodona, whence he should shortly return, and a ship would be ready by the bounty of the Thesprotians to convoy him straight to Ithaca. "And, in token that what I tell you is true," said Ulysses, "if your king come not within the period which I have named, you shall have leave to give your servants commandment to take my old carcass, and throw it headlong from some steep rock into the sea, that poor men, taking example by me, may fear to lie." But Eumæus made answer, that that would be small satisfaction or pleasure to him.

So, while they sat discoursing in this manner,

supper was served in and the servants of the herdsman, who had been out all day in the fields, came in
to supper, and took their seats at the fire; for the
night was bitter and frosty. After supper, Ulysses,
who had well eaten and drunken, and was refreshed
with the herdsman's good cheer, was resolved to try
whether his host's hospitality would extend to the
lending him a good warm mantle or rug to cover him
in the night season; and, framing an artful tale for
the purpose, in a merry mood, filling a cup of Greek
wine, he thus began :—

"I will tell you a story of your king Ulysses and
myself. If there is ever a time when a man may
have leave to tell his own stories, it is when he has
drunken a little too much. Strong liquor driveth the
fool, and moves even the heart of the wise,—moves
and impels him to sing and to dance, and break forth
in pleasant laughters, and perchance to prefer a
speech too, which were better kept in. When the
heart is open, the tongue will be stirring. But you
shall hear. We led our powers to ambush once
under the walls of Troy."

The herdsmen crowded about him, eager to hear
any thing which related to their king Ulysses and
the wars of Troy; and thus he went on :—

"I remember Ulysses and Menelaus had the direction of that enterprise, and they were pleased to join
me with them in the command. I was at that time
in some repute among men; though Fortune has
played me a trick since, as you may perceive. But
I was somebody in those times, and could do something. Be that as it may, a bitter freezing night it
was,—such a night as this: the air cut like steel,
and the sleet gathered on our shields like crystal.

There were some twenty of us, that lay close couched
down among the reeds and bulrushes that grew in
the moat that goes round the city. The rest of us
made tolerable shift; for every man had been careful
to bring with him a good cloak or mantle to wrap
over his armour and keep himself warm: but I, as it
chanced, had left my cloak behind me, as not expecting that the night would prove so cool; or rather, I
believe, because I had at that time a brave suit of
new armour on, which, being a soldier, and having
some of the soldier's vice about me,—*vanity*,—I was
not willing should be hidden under a cloak. But I
paid for my indiscretion with my sufferings; for with
the inclement night, and the wet of the ditch in
which we lay, I was wellnigh frozen to death: and,
when I could endure no longer, I jogged Ulysses,
who was next to me, and had a nimble ear, and made
known my case to him, assuring him that I must
inevitably perish. He answered, in a low whisper,
'Hush! lest any Greek should hear you, and take
notice of your softness.' Not a word more he said,
but showed as if he had no pity for the plight I was
in. But he was as considerate as he was brave; and
even then, as he lay with his head reposing upon his
hand, he was meditating how to relieve me, without
exposing my weakness to the soldiers. At last, raising up his head, he made as if he had been asleep,
and said, 'Friends, I have been warned in a dream
to send to the fleet to King Agamemnon for a supply,
to recruit our numbers; for we are not sufficient for
this enterprise:' and, they believing him, one Thoas
was despatched on that errand, who departing, for
more speed, as Ulysses had foreseen, left his upper
garment behind him, a good warm mantle, to which

I succeeded, and, by the help of it, got through the
night with credit. This shift Ulysses made for one
in need, and would to Heaven that I had now that
strength in my limbs which made me in those days
to be accounted fit to be a leader under Ulysses! I
should not then want the loan of a cloak or a mantle
to wrap about me, and shield my old limbs from the
night air."

The tale pleased the herdsmen; and Eumæus,
who more than all the rest was gratified to hear tales
of Ulysses, true or false, said, that for his story he
deserved a mantle and a night's lodging, which he
should have; and he spread for him a bed of goat
and sheep skins by the fire : and the seeming beggar,
who was indeed the true Ulysses, lay down and
slept under that poor roof, in that abject disguise to
which the will of Minerva had subjected him.

When morning was come, Ulysses made offer to
depart, as if he were not willing to burthen his host's
hospitality any longer, but said that he would go and
try the humanity of the town's folk, if any there
would bestow upon him a bit of bread or a cup of
drink. Perhaps the queen's suitors (he said) out of
their full feasts would bestow a scrap on him : for he
could wait at table, if need were, and play the nimble
serving-man; he could fetch wood (he said) or build
a fire, prepare roast meat or boiled, mix the wine
with water, or do any of those offices which recommended poor men like him to services in great men's
houses.

"Alas! poor guest," said Eumæus, "you know
not what you speak. What should so poor and old
a man as you do at the suitors' tables ? Their light
minds are not given to such grave servitors. They

must have youths, richly tricked out in flowing vests,
with curled hair, like so many of Jove's cup bearers,
to fill out the wine to them as they sit at table, and
to shift their trenchers. Their gorged insolence
would but despise and make a mock at thy age.
Stay here. Perhaps the queen or Telemachus,
hearing of thy arrival, may send to thee of their
bounty."

As he spake these words, the steps of one crossing the front court were heard, and a noise of the
dogs fawning and leaping about as for joy: by which
token Eumæus guessed that it was the prince, who,
hearing of a traveller being arrived at Eumæus's cottage that brought tidings of his father, was come to
search the truth; and Eumæus said, "It is the tread
of Telemachus, the son of King Ulysses." Before
he could well speak the words the prince was at the
door; whom Ulysses rising to receive, Telemachus
would not suffer that so aged a man as he appeared
should rise to do respect to him; but he courteously
and reverently took him by the hand, and inclined
his head to him, as if he had surely known that it
was his father indeed : but Ulysses covered his eyes
with his hands, that he might not show the waters
which stood in them. And Telemachus said, "Is
this the man who can tell us tidings of the king, my
father ?"

"He brags himself to be a Cretan born," said
Eumæus, "and that he has been a soldier and a
traveller; but whether he speak the truth or not, he
alone can tell. But, whatsoever he has been, what
he is now is apparent. Such as he appears, I give
him to you; do what you will with him : his boast at
present is that he is at the very best a supplicant."

"Be he what he may," said Telemachus, "I accept him at your hands. But where I should bestow him I know not, seeing that, in the palace, his age would not exempt him from the scorn and contempt which my mother's suitors in their light minds would be sure to fling upon him : a mercy if he escaped without blows ; for they are a company of evil men, whose profession is wrongs and violence."

Ulysses answered, " Since it is free for any man to speak in presence of your greatness, I must say that my heart puts on a wolfish inclination to tear and to devour, hearing your speech, that these suitors should with such injustice rage, where you should have the rule solely. What should the cause be ? Do you wilfully give way to their ill manners ? Or has your government been such as has procured ill-will towards you from your people ? Or do you mistrust your kinsfolk and friends in such sort, as, without trial, to decline their aid ? A man's kindred are they that he might trust to when extremities run high."

Telemachus replied, " The kindred of Ulysses are few. I have no brothers to assist me in the strife ; but the suitors are powerful in kindred and friends. The house of old Arcesius has had this fate from the heavens, that from old it still has been supplied with single heirs. To Arcesius, Laertes only was born, from Laertes descended only Ulysses ; from Ulysses, I alone have sprung, whom he left so young, that from me never comfort arose to him. But the end of all rests in the hands of the gods."

Then, Eumæus departing to see to some necessary business of his herds, Minerva took a woman's shape, and stood in the entry of the door, and was seen to

Ulysses : but by his son she was not seen ; for the presences of the gods are invisible save to those to whom they will to reveal themselves. Nevertheless, the dogs which were about the door saw the goddess, and durst not bark, but went crouching and licking of the dust for fear. And, giving signs to Ulysses that the time was now come in which he should make himself known to his son, by her great power she changed back his shape. into the same which it was before she transformed him ; and Telemachus, who saw the change, but nothing of the manner by which it was effected, only he saw the appearance of a king in the vigour of his age where but just now he had seen a worn and decrepit beggar, was struck with fear, and said, " Some god has done this house this houour ;" and he turned away his eyes, and would have worshipped. But his father permitted not, but said, " Look better at me. I am no deity : why put you upon me the reputation of godhead ? I am no more but thy father: I am even he. I am that Ulysses, by reason of whose absence thy youth has been exposed to such wrongs from injurious men." Then kissed he his son, nor could any longer refrain those tears which he had held under such mighty restraint before, though they would ever be forcing themselves out in spite of him ; but now, as if their sluices had burst, they came out like rivers, pouring upon the warm cheeks of his son. Nor yet by all these violent arguments could Telemachus be persuaded to believe that it was his father, but he said some deity had taken that shape to mock him ; for he affirmed, that it was not in the power of any man, who is sustained by mortal food, to change his shape so in a moment from age to youth: " for, but now," said he, "you were all wrinkles, and were old : and now you look as the gods are pictured."

His father replied, "Admire, but fear not, and know me to be at all parts substantially thy father, who in the inner powers of his mind, and the unseen workings of a father's love to thee, answers to his outward shape and pretence. There shall no more Ulysseses come here. I am he, that after twenty years' absence, and suffering a world of ill, have recovered at last the sight of my country earth. It was the will of Minerva that I should be changed as you saw me. She put me thus together : she puts together or takes to pieces whom she pleases. It is the law of her free power to do it,—sometimes to show her favourites under a cloud, and poor, and again to restore to them their ornaments. The gods raise and throw down men with ease."

Then Telemachus could hold out no longer : but he gave way now to a full belief and persuasion of that which for joy at first he could not credit,—that it was indeed his true and very father that stood before him ; and they embraced, and mingled their tears.

Then said Ulysses, "Tell me who these suitors are, what are their numbers, and how stands the queen thy mother affected by them ?"

"She bears them still in expectation," said Telemachus, "which she never means to fulfil, that she will accept the hand of some one of them in second nuptials . for she fears to displease them by an absolute refusal So from day to day she lingers them on with hope, which they are content to bear the deferring of, while they have entertainment at free cost in our palace.

2 D 2

Then said Ulysses, " Reckon up their numbers, that we may know their strength and ours, if we, having none but ourselves, may hope to prevail against them."

" O father!" he replied, " I have ofttimes heard of your fame for wisdom, and of the great strength of your arm; but the venturous mind which your speeches now indicate moves me even to amazement: for in no wise can it consist with wisdom or a sound mind, that two should try their strengths against a host. Nor five, or ten, or twice ten strong, are these suitors, but many more by much: from Dulichium came there fifty and two, they and their servants; twice twelve crossed the seas hither from Samos; from Zacynthus, twice ten; of our native Ithacans, men of chief note, are twelve who aspire to the bed and crown of Penelope; and all these under one strong roof,—a fearful odds against two! My father, there is need of caution, lest the cup which your great mind so thirsts to taste of vengeance prove bitter to yourself in the drinking; and therefore it were well that we should bethink us of some one who might assist us in this undertaking."

" Thinkest thou," said his father, "if we had Minerva and the king of skies to be our friends, would their sufficiencies make strong our part? Or must we look out for some further aid yet?"

" They you speak of are above the clouds," said Telemachus, " and are sound aids indeed, as powers that not only exceed human, but bear the chiefest sway among the gods themselves."

Then Ulysses gave directions to his son to go and mingle with the suitors, and in no wise to impart his secret to any,—not even to the queen, his mother;

but to hold himself in readiness, and to have his weapons and his good armour in preparation. And he charged him, that when he himself should come to the palace, as he meant to follow shortly after, and present himself in his beggar's likeness to the suitors, that whatever he should see which might grieve his heart, with what foul usage and contumelious language soever the suitors should receive his father, coming in that shape, though they should strike and drag him by the heels along the floors, that he should not stir nor make offer to oppose them, further than by mild words to expostulate with them, until Minerva from heaven should give the sign which should be the prelude to their destruction. And Telemachus, promising to obey his instructions, departed; and the shape of Ulysses fell to what it had been before, and he became to all outward appearance a beggar, in base and beggarly attire.

CHAPTER IX.

THE QUEEN'S SUITORS.—THE BATTLE OF THE BEGGARS.—THE ARMOUR TAKEN DOWN —THE MEETING WITH PENELOPE.

FROM the house of Eumæus the seeming beggar took his way, leaning on his staff, till he reached the palace; entering in at the hall where the suitors sat at meat. They, in the pride of their feasting, began to break their jests in mirthful manner when they saw one looking so poor and so aged approach. He, who expected no better entertainment, was nothing moved at their behaviour; but, as became the character which he had assumed, in a suppliant posture crept by turns to every suitor, and held out his hands for some charity, with such a natural and beggar-resembling grace, that he might seem to have practised begging all his life; yet there was a sort of dignity in his most abject stoopings, that whoever had seen him would have said, " If it had pleased Heaven that this poor man had been born a king, he would gracefully have filled a throne." And some pitied him, and some gave him alms, as their present humours inclined them; but the greater part reviled him, and bade him begone, as one that spoiled their feast: for the presence of misery has this power with it,—that, while it stays, it can dash and overturn the mirth even of those who feel no pity, or wish to relieve it; Nature bearing this witness of herself in the hearts of the most obdurate.

Now, Telemachus sat at meat with the suitors, and knew that it was the king, his father, who in that shape begged an alms; and when his father came and presented himself before him in turn, as he had done to the suitors one by one, he gave him of his own meat which he had in his dish, and his own cup to drink; and the suitors were past measure offended to see a pitiful beggar, as they esteemed him, to be so choicely regarded by the prince.

Then Antinous, who was a great lord, and of chief note among the suitors, said, " Prince Telemachus does ill to encourage these wandering beggars, who go from place to place, affirming that they have been some considerable persons in their time; filling the ears of such as hearken to them with lies, and pressing with their bold feet into kings' palaces.

This is some saucy vagabond, some travelling Egyptian."

" I see," said Ulysses, " that a poor man should get but little at your board ; scarce should he get salt from your hands, if he brought his own meat."

Lord Antinous, indignant to be answered with such sharpness by a supposed beggar, snatched up a stool, with which he smote Ulysses where the neck and shoulders join. This usage moved not Ulysses ; but in his great heart he meditated deep evils to come upon them all, which for a time must be kept close , and he went and sat himself down in the doorway to eat of that which was given him ; and he said, " For life or possessions a man will fight ; but for his belly this man smites. If a poor man has any god to take his part, my Lord Antinous shall not live to be the queen's husband."

Then Antinous raged highly, and threatened to drag him by the heels, and to rend his rags about his ears, if he spoke another word.

But the other suitors did in no wise approve of the harsh language, nor of the blow which Antinous had dealt ; and some of them said, " Who knows but one of the deities goes about, hid under that poor disguise ? for in the likeness of poor pilgrims the gods have many times descended to try the dispositions of men, whether they be humane or impious." While these things passed, Telemachus sat and observed all, but held his peace, remembering the instructions of his father. But secretly he waited for the sign which Minerva was to send from heaven.

That day, there followed Ulysses to the Court one of the common sort of beggars, Irus by name,—one

that had received alms before-time of the suitors,
and was their ordinary sport, when they were inclined
(as that day) to give way to mirth, to see him eat
and drink; for he had the appetite of six men, and
was of huge stature and proportions of body, yet
had in him no spirit nor courage of a man. This
man thinking to curry favour with the suitors, and
recommend himself especially to such a great lord as
Antinous was, began to revile and scorn Ulysses,
putting foul language upon him, and fairly challenging him to fight with the fist. But Ulysses, deeming
his railings to be nothing more than jealousy, and
that envious disposition which beggars commonly
manifest to brothers in their trade, mildly besought
him not to trouble him, but to enjoy that portion
which the liberality of their entertainers gave him, as
he did, quietly; seeing that, of their bounty, there
was sufficient for all.

But Irus, thinking that this forbearance in Ulysses
was nothing more than a sign of fear, so much the
more highly stormed and bellowed, and provoked
him to fight: and by this time the quarrel had
attracted the notice of the suitors, who with loud
laughters and shouting egged on the dispute; and
Lord Antinous swore by all the gods it should be a
battle, and that in that hall the strife should be
determined. To this the rest of the suitors, with
violent clamours, acceded; and a circle was made
for the combatants, and a fat goat was proposed as
the victor's prize, as at the Olympic or the Pythian
games. Then Ulysses, seeing no remedy, or being
not unwilling that the suitors should behold some
proof of that strength which ere long in their own
persons they were to taste of, stripped himself, and

prepared for the combat. But first he demanded
that he should have fair play shown him ; that none
in that assembly should aid his opponent, or take
part against him . for, being an old man, they might
easily crush him with their strengths. And Telemachus passed his word that no foul play should be
shown him, but that each party should be left to their
own unassisted strengths ; and to this he made
Antinous and the rest of the suitors swear

But when Ulysses had laid aside his garments,
and was bare to the waist, all the beholders admired
at the goodly sight of his large shoulders being of
such exquisite shape and whiteness, and at his
great and brawny bosom, and the youthful strength
which seemed to remain in a man thought so old ;
and they said, "What limbs and what sinews he
has !" and coward fear seized on the mind of
that great vast beggar, and he dropped his threats
and his big words, and would have fled : but Lord
Antinous stayed him, and threatened him, that if
he declined the combat he would put him in a ship,
and land him on the shores where King Echetus
reigned,—the roughest tyrant which at that time the
world contained, and who had that antipathy to rascal
beggars such as he, that, when any landed on his
coast, he would crop their ears and noses, and give
them to the dogs to tear. So Irus, in whom fear of
King Echetus prevailed above the fear of Ulysses,
addressed himself to the fight. But Ulysses, provoked to be engaged in so odious a strife with a
fellow of his base conditions, and loathing longer to
be made a spectacle to entertain the eyes of his foes,
with one blow, which he struck him beneath the ear,
so shattered the teeth and jaw-bone of this soon-

baffled coward, that he laid him sprawling in the
dust, with small stomach or ability to renew the
contest. Then, raising him on his feet, he led him
bleeding and sputtering to the door, and put his staff
into his hand, and bade him go use his command
upon dogs and swine, but not presume himself
to be lord of the guests another time, nor of the
beggary!

The suitors applauded in their vain minds the
issue of the contest, and rioted in mirth at the
expense of poor Irus, who they vowed should be
forthwith embarked, and sent to King Echetus; and
they bestowed thanks on Ulysses for ridding the
Court of that unsavoury morsel, as they called him:
but in their inward souls they would not have cared
if Irus had been victor, and Ulysses had taken the
foil, but it was mirth to them to see the beggars
fight. In such pastimes and light entertainments the
day wore away.

When evening was come, the suitors betook themselves to music and dancing; and Ulysses leaned
his back against a pillar from which certain lamps
hung which gave light to the dancers, and he made
show of watching the dancers; but very different
thoughts were in his head. And, as he stood near
the lamps, the light fell upon his head, which was
thin of hair, and bald, as an old man's. And Eurymachus, a suitor, taking occasion from some words
which were spoken before, scoffed, and said, " Now
I know for a certainty that some god lurks under the
poor and beggarly appearance of this man; for as he
stands by the lamps, his sleek head throws beams
around it, like as it were a glory." And another
said, " He passes his time, too, not much unlike the

gods ; lazily living exempt from labour, taking offerings of men."—" I warrant," said Eurymachus again, " he could not raise a fence or dig a ditch for his livelihood, if a man would hire him to work in a garden."

" I wish," said Ulysses, " that you who speak this, and myself, were to be tried at any task work: that I had a good crooked scythe put in my hand, that was sharp and strong, and you such another, where the grass grew longest, to be up by daybreak, mowing the meadows till the sun went down, not tasting of food till we had finished : or that we were set to plough four acres in one day of good glebe land, to see whose furrows were evenest and cleanest ; or that we might have one wrestling-bout together ; or that in our right hands a good steel-headed lance were placed, to try whose blows fell heaviest and thickest upon the adversary's head-piece. I would cause you such work, as you should have small reason to reproach me with being slack at work. But you would do well to spare me this reproach, and to save your strength till the owner of this house shall return,—till the day when Ulysses shall return ; when, returning, he shall enter upon his birthright."

This was a galling speech to the suitors, to whom Ulysses's return was indeed the thing which they most dreaded , and a sudden fear fell upon their souls, as if they were sensible of the real presence of that man who did indeed stand amongst them, but not in that form as they might know him : and Eurymachus, incensed, snatched a massy cup which stood on a table near, and hurled it at the head of the supposed beggar, and but narrowly missed the hitting of him; and all the suitors rose, as at once, to thrust him out of the hall, which they said his beggarly presence and his rude speeches had profaned. But Telemachus cried to them to forbear, and not to presume to lay hands upon a wretched man to whom he had promised protection. He asked if they were mad, to mix such abhorred uproar with his feasts. He bade them take their food and their wine; to sit up or to go to bed at their free pleasures, so long as he should give license to that freedom but why should they abuse his banquet, or let the words which a poor beggar spake have power to move their spleens so fiercely?

They bit their lips, and frowned for anger, to be checked so by a youth: nevertheless, from that time they had the grace to abstain, either for shame, or that Minerva had infused into them a terror of Ulysses's son.

So that day's feast was concluded without bloodshed; and the suitors, tired with their sports, departed severally each man to his apartment. Only Ulysses and Telemachus remained. And now Telemachus, by his father's direction, went and brought down into the hall armour and lances from the armoury; for Ulysses said, "On the morrow we shall have need of them." And moreover he said, "If any one shall ask why you have taken them down, say it is to clean them, and scour them from the rust which they have gathered since the owner of this house went for Troy." And, as Telemachus stood by the armour, the lights were all gone out, and it was pitch dark, and the armour gave out glistering beams as of fire; and he said to his father, "The pillars of the house are on fire." And his

father said, " It is the gods who sit above the stars,
and have power to make the night as light as the
day;" and he took it for a good omen. And
Telemachus fell to cleaning and sharpening of the
lances.

Now, Ulysses had not seen his wife Penelope in
all the time since his return; for the queen did not
care to mingle with the suitors at their banquets, but,
as became one that had been Ulysses's wife, kept
much in private, spinning, and doing her excellent
housewiferies among her maids in the remote apartments of the palace. Only upon solemn days she
would come down and show herself to the suitors.
And Ulysses was filled with a longing desire to see
his wife again, whom for twenty years he had not
beheld; and he softly stole through the known
passages of his beautiful house, till he came where
the maids were lighting the queen through a stately
gallery that led to the chamber where she slept.
And when the maids saw Ulysses they said, " It is
the beggar who came to the Court to-day, about whom
all that uproar was stirred up in the hall : what does
he here ?" But Penelope gave commandment that
he should be brought before her; for she said, " It
may be that he has travelled, and has heard something concerning Ulysses."

Then was Ulysses right glad to hear himself named
by his queen ; to find himself in no wise forgotten,
nor her great love towards him decayed in all that
time that he had been away. And he stood before
his queen, and she knew him not to be Ulysses,
but supposed that he had been some poor traveller.
And she asked him of what country he was.

He told her (as he had before told to Eumæus) that

he was a Cretan born, and, however poor and cast
down he now seemed, no less a man than brother to
Idomeneus, who was grandson to King Minos; and,
though he now wanted bread, he had once had it in
his power to feast Ulysses. Then he feigned how
Ulysses, sailing for Troy, was forced by stress of
weather to put his fleet in at a port of Crete, where
for twelve days he was his guest, and entertained by
him with all befitting guest-rites; and he described
the very garments which Ulysses had on, by which
Penelope knew he had seen her lord.

In this manner Ulysses told his wife many tales
of himself, at most but painting, but painting so near
to the life, that the feeling of that which she took in
at her ears became so strong, that the kindly tears
ran down her fair cheeks while she thought upon
her lord, dead as she thought him, and heavily
mourned the loss of him whom she missed, whom
she could not find, though in very deed he stood so
near her.

Ulysses was moved to see her weep: but he kept
his own eyes as dry as iron or horn in their lids;
putting a bridle upon his strong passion, that it
should not issue to sight.

Then told he how he had lately been at the Court
of Thresprotia, and what he had learned concerning
Ulysses there, in order as he had delivered to
Eumæus: and Penelope was wont to believe that
there might be a possibility of Ulysses being alive;
and she said, "I dreamed a dream this morn n .
Methought I had twenty household fowl which did
eat wheat steeped in water from my hand; and there
came suddenly from the clouds a crook-beaked hawk,
who soused on them, and killed them all, trussing their

necks ; then took his flight back up to the clouds. And,
in my dream, methought that I wept and made great
moan for my fowls, and for the destruction which the
hawk had made ; and my maids came about me to
comfort me. And in the height of my griefs the
hawk came back , and, lighting upon the beam of my
chamber, he said to me in a man's voice, which
sounded strangely, even in my dream, to hear a hawk
to speak: ' Be of good cheer,' he said, ' O daughter
of Icarius ; for this is no dream which thou hast
seen, but that which shall happen to thee indeed.
Those household fowl which thou lamentest so without reason are the suitors who devour thy substance,
even as thou sawest the fowl eat from thy hand ; and
the hawk is thy husband, who is coming to give
death to the suitors.' And I awoke, and went to see
to my fowls, if they were alive, whom I found eating
wheat from their troughs, all well and safe as before
my dream."

Then said Ulysses, " This dream can endure no
other interpretation than that which the hawk gave
to it, who is your lord, and who is coming quickly to
effect all that his words told you."

" Your words," she said, " my old guest, are so
sweet, that, would you sit and please me with your
speech, my ears would never let my eyes close their
spheres for very joy of your discourse : but none that
is merely mortal can live without the death of sleep,
so the gods who are without death themselves have
ordained it, to keep the memory of our mortality in
our minds, while we experience, that, as much as we
live, we die every day; in which consideration I will
ascend my bed, which I have nightly watered with
my tears since he that was the joy of it departed for

that bad city:" she so speaking, because she could not bring her lips to name the name of Troy, so much hated. So for that night they parted,—Penelope to her bed, and Ulysses to his son, and to the armour and the lances in the hall, where they sat up all night cleaning and watching by the armour.

CHAPTER X.

THE MADNESS FROM ABOVE. — THE BOW OF ULYSSES.—THE SLAUGHTER.—THF CONCLUSION.

WHEN daylight appeared a tumultuous concourse of the suitors again filled the hall; and some wondered, and some inquired, what meant that glittering store of armour and lances which lay on heaps by the entry of the door: and to all that asked, Telemachus made reply, that he had caused them to be taken down to cleanse them of the rust and of the stain which they had contracted by laying so long unused, even ever since his father went for Troy; and with that answer their minds were easily satisfied. So to their feasting and vain rioting again they fell. Ulysses, by Telemachus's order, had a seat and a mess assigned him in the doorway; and he had his eye ever on the lances. And it moved gall in some of the great ones there present to have their feast still dulled with the society of that wretched beggar, as they deemed him; and they reviled and spurned at him with their feet. Only there was one Philætius, who had something of a better nature than the rest, that spake kindly to him, and had his age in respect.

He, coming up to Ulysses, took him by the hand
with a kind of fear, as if touched exceedingly with
imagination of his great worth, and said thus to him :
" Hail, father stranger ! My brows have sweat to
see the injuries which you have received ; and my
eyes have broken forth in tears when I have only
thought, that, such being oftentimes the lot of
worthiest men, to this plight Ulysses may be reduced,
and that he now may wander from place to place as
you do : for such, who are compelled by need to
range here and there, and have no firm home to fix
their feet upon, God keeps them in this earth, as
under water ; so are they kept down and depressed.
And a dark thread is sometimes spun in the fates of
kings."

At this bare likening of the beggar to Ulysses,
Minerva from heaven made the suitors for foolish joy
to go mad, and roused them to such a laughter as
would never stop : they laughed without power of
ceasing ; their eyes stood full of tears for violent
joys. But fears and horrible misgivings succeeded ;
and one among them stood up and prophesied "Ah,
wretches !" he said, " what madness from heaven
has seized you, that you can laugh ? See you not
that your meat drops blood ? A night, like the night
of death, wraps you about, you shriek without knowing it ; your eyes thrust forth tears : the fixed walls,
and the beam that bears the whole house up, fall
blood ; ghosts choke up the entry ; full is the hall
with apparitions of murdered men ; under your feet
is hell ; the sun falls from heaven, and it is midnight
at noon." But, like men whom the gods had infatuated to their destruction, they mocked at his fears ;
and Eurymachus said, " This man is surely mad :

conduct him forth into the market-place ; set him in
the light; for he dreams that 'tis night within the
house."

But Theoclymenus, (for that was the prophet's
name,) whom Minerva had graced with a prophetic
spirit, that he, foreseeing, might avoid the destruction which awaited them, answered, and said, "Eurymachus, I will not require a guide of thee : for I have
eyes and ears, the use of both my feet, and a sane
mind within me; and with these I will go forth of
the doors, because I know the imminent evils which
await all you that stay, by reason of this poor guest,
who is a favourite with all the gods." So saying,
he turned his back upon those inhospitable men,
and went away home, and never returned to the
palace.

These words which he spoke were not unheard by
Telemachus, who kept still his eye upon his father,
expecting fervently when he would give the sign
which was to precede the slaughter of the suitors.

They, dreaming of no such thing, fell sweetly to
their dinner, as joying in the great store of banquet
which was heaped in full tables about them ; but
there reigned not a bitterer banquet planet in all
heaven than that which hung over them this day, by
secret destination of Minerva.

There was a bow which Ulysses left when he went
for Troy. It had lain by since that time, out of use,
and unstrung; for no man had strength to draw that
bow save Ulysses. So it had remained as a monument of the great strength of its master. This bow,
with the quiver of arrows belonging thereto, Telemachus had brought down from the armoury on the
last night, along with the lances : and now Minerva,

intending to do Ulysses an honour, put it into the
mind of Telemachus to propose to the suitors to try
who was strongest to draw that bow; and he promised, that, to the man who should be able to draw
that bow, his mother should be given in marriage,—
Ulysses's wife the prize to him who should bend the
bow of Ulysses.

There was great strife and emulation stirred up
among the suitors at those words of the Prince Telemachus. And to grace her son's words, and to
confirm the promise which he had made, Penelope
came and showed herself that day to the suitors;
and Minerva made her that she appeared never so
comely in their sight as on that day: and they were
inflamed with the beholding of so much beauty proposed as the price of so great manhood; and they
cried out, that if all those heroes who sailed to
Colchis for the rich purchase of the golden-fleeced
ram had seen earth's richer prize, Penelope, they
would not have made their voyage, but would have
vowed their valours and their lives to her; for she
was at all parts faultless.

And she said, "The gods have taken my beauty
from me since my lord went for Troy." But Telemachus willed his mother to depart, and not be present at that contest; for he said, " It may be, some
rougher strife shall chance of this than may be expedient for a woman to witness." And she retired,
she and her maids, and left the hall.

Then the bow was brought into the midst, and a
mark was set up by Prince Telemachus; and Lord
Antinous, as the chief among the suitors, had the
first offer; and he took the bow, and, fitting an arrow
to the string, he strove to bend it. But not with all

his might and main could he once draw together the
ends of that tough bow; and when he found how
vain a thing it was to endeavour to draw Ulysses's
bow, he desisted, blushing for shame and for mere
anger. Then Eurymachus adventured, but with no
better success . but as it had torn the hands of Antinous, so did the bow tear and strain his hands, and
marred his delicate fingers , yet could he not once
stir the string. Then called he to the attendants to
bring fat and unctuous matter ; which melting at the
fire, he dipped the bow therein, thinking to supple it,
and make it more pliable : but not with all the helps
of art could he succeed in making it to move. After
him Liodes and Amphinomus and Polybus and
Eurynomus and Polyctorides essayed their strength ;
but not any one of them, or of the rest of those
aspiring suitors, had any better luck : yet not the
meanest of them there but thought himself well
worthy of Ulysses's wife ; though, to shoot with
Ulysses's bow, the completest champion among them
was by proof found too feeble.

Then Ulysses prayed that he might have leave to
try : and immediately a clamour was raised among
the suitors, because of his petition ; and they scorned
and swelled with rage at his presumption, and that a
beggar should seek to contend in a game of such
noble mastery. But Telemachus ordered that the
bow should be given him, and that he should have
leave to try, since they had failed ; " for," he said,
" the bow is mine, to give or to withhold :" and none
durst gainsay the prince.

Then Ulysses gave a sign to his son, and he commanded the doors of the hall to be made fast : and all
wondered at his words, but none could divine the

cause. And Ulysses took the bow into his hands;
and before he essayed to bend it he surveyed it at
all parts, to see whether, by long lying by, it had contracted any stiffness which hindered the drawing:
and, as he was busied in the curious surveying of his
bow, some of the suitors mocked him, and said,
" Past doubt, this man is a right cunning archer, and
knows his craft well. See how he turns it over and
over, and looks into it, as if he could see through
the wood!" And others said, "We wish some one
would tell out gold into our laps but for so long a
time as he shall be in drawing of that string." But
when he had spent some little time in making proof
of the bow, and had found it to be in good plight,
like as an harper in tuning his harp draws out a
string, with such ease or much more did Ulysses
draw to the head the string of his own tough bow;
and, in letting it go, it twanged with such a shrill
noise as a swallow makes when it sings through the
air: which so much amazed the suitors, that their
colours came and went, and the skies gave out a
noise of thunder, which at heart cheered Ulysses ·
for he knew that now his long labours, by the disposal
of the Fates, drew to an end. Then fitted he an
arrow to the bow; and, drawing it to the head, he
sent it right to the mark which the prince had set up.
Which done, he said to Telemachus, " You have got
no disgrace yet by your guest , for I have struck the
mark I shot at, and gave myself no such trouble in
teasing the bow with fat and fire as these men did,
but have made proof that my strength is not impaired,
nor my age so weak and contemptible as these were
pleased to think it. But come : the day going down
calls us to supper; after which succeed poem and

harp, and all delights which used to crown princely banquetings."

So saying, he beckoned to his son, who straight girt his sword to his side, and took one of the lances (of which there lay great store from the armoury) in his hand, and, armed at all points, advanced towards his father.

The upper rags which Ulysses wore fell from his shoulder, and his own kingly likeness returned ; when he rushed to the great hall door with bow and quiver full of shafts, which down at his feet he poured, and in bitter words presignified his deadly intent to the suitors. " Thus far," he said, " this contest has been decided harmless : now for us there rests another mark, harder to hit, but which my hands shall essay notwithstanding, if Phœbus, god of archers, be pleased to give me the mastery " With that he let fly a deadly arrow at Antinous, which pierced him in the throat, as he was in the act of lifting a cup of wine to his mouth. Amazement seized the suitors as their great champion fell dead; and they raged highly against Ulysses, and said that it should prove the dearest shaft which he ever let fly; for he had slain a man whose like breathed not in any part of the kingdom : and they flew to their arms, and would have seized the lances ; but Minerva struck them with dimness of sight, and they went erring up and down the hall, not knowing where to find them. Yet so infatuated were they by the displeasure of Heaven, that they did not see the imminent peril which impended over them , but every man believed that this accident had happened beside the intention of the doer. Fools ! to think by shutting their eyes to evade destiny, or that any other cup remained for them but that which their great Antinous had tasted!

Then Ulysses revealed himself to all in that presence, and that he was the man whom they held to be dead at Troy, whose palace they had usurped, whose wife in his life time they had sought in impious marriage, and that for this reason destruction was come upon them. And he dealt his deadly arrows among them, and there was no avoiding him, nor escaping from his horrid person, and Telemachus by his side plied them thick with those murderous lances from which there was no retreat, till fear itself made them valiant, and danger gave them eyes to understand the peril. Then they which had swords drew them, and some with shields that could find them, and some with tables and benches, snatched up in haste, rose in a mass to overwhelm and crush those two: yet they singly bestirred themselves like men. and defended themselves against that great host, and through tables, shields, and all, right through, the arrows of Ulysses clove, and the irresistible lances of Telemachus; and many lay dead, and all had wounds. And Minerva, in the likeness of a bird, sate upon the beam which went across the hall, clapping her wings with a fearful noise: and sometimes the great bird would fly among them, cuffing at the swords and at the lances, and up and down the hall would go, beating her wings, and troubling every thing, that it was frightful to behold; and it frayed the blood from the cheeks of those heaven-hated suitors. But to Ulysses and his son she appeared in her own divine similitude, with her snake-fringed shield, a goddess armed, fighting their battles. Nor did that dreadful pair desist till they had laid all their foes at their feet. At their feet they lay in shoals : like fishes when the fishermen break up their nets, so they lay gasping and sprawling at the feet of Ulysses and his son. And Ulysses remembered the prediction of Tiresias, which said that he was to perish by his own guests, unless he slew those who knew him not.

Then certain of the queen's household went up, and told Penelope what had happened ; and how her lord Ulysses was come home, and had slain the suitors. But she gave no heed to their words, but thought that some frenzy possessed them, or that they mocked her ; for it is the property of such extremes of sorrow as she had felt not to believe when any great joy cometh. And she rated and chid them exceedingly for troubling her. But they the more persisted in their asseverations of the truth of what they affirmed ; and some of them had seen the slaughtered bodies of the suitors dragged forth of the hall. And they said, "That poor guest, whom you talked with last night, was Ulysses" Then she was more fully persuaded that they mocked her ; and she wept. But they said, "This thing is true which we have told. We sat within, in an inner room in the palace, and the doors of the hall were shut on us : but we heard the cries and the groans of the men that were killed, but saw nothing, till at length your son called us to come in ; and, entering, we saw Ulysses standing in the midst of the slaughtered." But she, persisting in her unbelief, said that it was some god which had deceived them to think it was the person of Ulysses.

By this time Telemachus and his father had cleansed their hands from the slaughter, and were

come to where the queen was talking with those of
her household; and when she saw Ulysses she
stood motionless, and had no power to speak,—
sudden surprise and joy and fear and many passions
so strove within her   Sometimes she was clear that
it was her husband that she saw, and sometimes the
alteration which twenty years had made in his
person (yet that was not much) perplexed her, that
she knew not what to think, and for joy she could not
believe, and yet for joy she would not but believe;
and, above all, that sudden change from a beggar
to a king troubled her, and wrought uneasy
scruples in her mind. But Telemachus, seeing her
strangeness, blamed her, and called her an ungentle
and tyrannous mother, and that she showed a too
great curiousness of modesty to abstain from embracing his father, and to have doubts of his person,
when, to all present, it was evident that he was the
very real and true Ulysses.

Then she mistrusted no longer, but ran and fell
upon Ulysses's neck, and said, " Let not my husband
be angry that I held off so long with strange delays:
it is the gods, who, severing us for so long time,
have caused this unseemly distance in me. If
Menelaus's wife had used half my caution she would
never have taken so freely to a stranger's bed;
and she might have spared us all these plagues
which have come upon us through her shameless
deed."

These words, with which Penelope excused herself,
wrought more affection in Ulysses than if. upon a
first sight, she had given up herself implicitly to his
embraces; and he wept for joy to possess a wife so
discreet, so answering to his own staid mind, that

had a depth of wit proportioned to his own, and one
that held chaste virtue at so high a price. And he
thought the possession of such a one cheaply purchased with the loss of all Circe's delights, and
Calypso's immortality of joys; and his long labours
and his severe sufferings past seemed as nothing,
now they were crowned with the enjoyment of his
virtuous and true wife, Penelope. And as sad men
at sea, whose ship has gone to pieces nigh shore,
swimming for their lives, all drenched in foam and
brine, crawl up to some poor patch of land, which
they take possession of with as great a joy as if they
had the world given them in fee,—with such delight
did this chaste wife cling to her lord restored, till
the dark night fast coming on reminded her of that
more intimate and happy union, when in her long-
widowed bed she should once again clasp a living
Ulysses.

So, from that time, the land had rest from the
suitors. And the happy Ithacans, with songs and
solemn sacrifices of praise to the gods, celebrated
the return of Ulysses, for he that had been so long
absent was returned to wreak the evil upon the heads
of the doers · in the place where they had done
the evil, there wreaked he his vengeance upon
them.

CUPID'S REVENGE.[1]

LEONTIUS, Duke of Lycia, who in times past had
borne the character of a wise and just governor, and
was endeared to all ranks of his subjects, in his latter
days fell into a sort of dotage, which manifested
itself in an extravagant fondness for his daughter
Hidaspes. This young maiden, with the Prince
Leucippus, her brother, were the only remembrances
left to him of a deceased and beloved consort. For
her, nothing was thought too precious. Existence
was of no value to him but as it afforded opportunities
of gratifying her wishes. To be instrumental in relieving her from the least little pain or grief, he
would have lavished his treasures to the giving away
of the one-half of his dukedom

All this deference on the part of the parent had yet
no power upon the mind of the daughter to move her
at any time to solicit any unbecoming suit, or to disturb the even tenor of her thoughts. The humility
and dutifulness of her carriage seemed to keep pace
with his apparent willingness to release her from the
obligations of either. She might have satisfied her
wildest humours and caprices ; but, in truth, no such

---

[1] This story was originally published in "Harper's Magazine." It
was printed from the author's manuscript, which the publishers purchased of Lamb's friend, Thomas Allsop By the kind permission of
the Messrs Harper, "Cupid's Revenge" appears in this volume. —
EDITOR OF ELIANA

troublesome guests found harbour in the bosom of the quiet and unaspiring maiden.

Thus far the prudence of the princess served to counteract any ill effects which this ungovernable partiality in a parent was calculated to produce in a less virtuous nature than Hidaspes's : and this foible of the duke's, so long as no evil resulted from it, was passed over by the courtiers as a piece of harmless frenzy.

But upon a solemn day,—a sad one, as it proved for Lycia,—when the returning anniversary of the princess's birth was kept with extraordinary rejoicings, the infatuated father set no bounds to his folly, but would have his subjects to do homage to her for that day, as to their natural sovereign ; as if he, indeed, had been dead, and she, to the exclusion of the male succession, was become the rightful ruler of Lycia. He saluted her by the style of Duchess , and with a terrible oath, in the presence of his nobles, he confirmed to her the grant of all things whatsoever that she should demand on that day, and for the six next following ; and if she should ask any thing, the execution of which must be deferred until after his death, he pronounced a dreadful curse upon his son and successor if he failed to see to the performance of it.

Thus encouraged, the princess stepped forth with a modest boldness ; and, as if assured of no denial, spake as follows.

But, before we acquaint you with the purport of her speech, we must premise, that in the land of Lycia, which was at that time pagan, above all their other gods the inhabitants did in an especial manner adore the deity who was supposed to have influence

in the disposing of people's affections in *love*. Him,
by the name of God Cupid, they feigned to be a
beautiful boy, and *winged*, as indeed, between young
persons, these frantic passions are usually least
under constraint ; while the wings might signify the
haste with which these ill-judged attachments are
commonly dissolved, and do indeed go away as
lightly as they come, flying away in an instant to
light upon some newer fancy. They painted him
blindfolded, because these silly affections of lovers
make them blind to the defects of the beloved object,
which every one is quick-sighted enough to discover
but themselves, or because love is for the most part
led blindly, rather than directed by the open eye of
the judgment, in the hasty choice of a mate. Yet,
with that inconsistency of attributes with which the
heathen people commonly over-complimented their
deities, this blind love, this Cupid, they figured with
a bow and arrows ; and, being sightless, they yet
feigned him to be a notable archer and an unerring
marksman. No heart was supposed to be proof
against the point of his inevitable dart. By such in-
credible fictions did these poor pagans make a shift
to excuse their vanities, and to give a sanction to
their irregular affections, under the notion that love
was irresistible ; whereas, in a well-regulated mind,
these amorous conceits either find no place at all, or,
having gained a footing, are easily stifled in the
beginning by a wise and manly resolution.

This frenzy in the people had long been a source
of disquiet to the discreet princess ; and many were
the conferences she had held with the virtuous
prince, her brother, as to the best mode of taking off
the minds of the Lycians from this vain superstition.

An occasion, furnished by the blind grant of the old
duke, their father, seemed now to present itself.

The courtiers then, being assembled to hear the
demand which the princess should make, began to
conjecture, each one according to the bent of his
own disposition, what the thing would be that she
should ask for.   One said, " Now surely she will ask
to have the disposal of the revenues of some wealthy
province, to lay them out—as was the manner of
Eastern princesses—in costly dresses and jewels
becoming a lady of so great expectancies."   Another
thought that she would seek an extension of power,
as women naturally love rule and dominion.   But
the most part were in hope that she was about to beg
the hand of some neighbour prince in marriage, who,
by the wealth and contiguity of his dominions, might
add strength and safety to the realm of Lycia.   But
in none of these things was the expectation of these
crafty and worldly-minded courtiers gratified; for
Hidaspes, first making lowly obeisance to her father,
and thanking him on bended knees for so great grace
conferred upon her,—according to a plan precon-
certed with Leucippus,—made suit as follows :—

" Your loving care of me, O princely father, by
which in my tenderest age you made up to me for
the loss of a mother at those years when I was
scarcely able to comprehend the misfortune, and
your bounties to me ever since, have left me nothing
to ask for myself, as wanting and desiring nothing.
But, for the people whom you govern, I beg and desire a boon.   It is known to all nations, that the men
of Lycia are noted for a vain and fruitless superstition,—the more hateful as it bears a show of true
religion, but is indeed nothing more than a self-

pleasing and bold wantonness. Many ages before this, when every man had taken to himself a trade, as hating idleness far worse than death, some one that gave himself to sloth and wine, finding himself by his neighbours rebuked for his unprofitable life, framed to himself a god, whom he pretended to obey in his dishonesty; and, for a name, he called him Cupid. This god of merely man's creating—as the nature of man is ever credulous of any vice which takes part with his dissolute conditions — quickly found followers enough. They multiplied in every age, especially among your Lycians, who to this day remain adorers of this drowsy deity, who certainly was first invented in drink, as sloth and luxury are commonly the first movers in these idle love-passions. This *winged boy*—for so they fancy him—has his sacrifices, his loose images set up in the land, through all the villages; nay, your own sacred palace is not exempt from them, to the scandal of sound devotion, and dishonour of the true deities, which are only they who give good gifts to man,—as Ceres, who gives us corn; the planter of the olive, Pallas; Neptune, who directs the track of ships over the great ocean, and binds distant lands together in friendly commerce; the inventor of medicine and music, Apollo; and the cloud-compelling Thunderer of Olympus. whereas the gifts of this idle deity—if indeed he have a being at all out of the brain of his frantic worshippers—usually prove destructive and pernicious. My suit, then, is, that this unseemly idol throughout the land be plucked down, and cast into the fire; and that the adoring of the same may be prohibited on pain of death to any of your subjects henceforth found so offending."

Leontius, startled at this unexpected demand from the princess, with tears besought her to ask some wiser thing, and not to bring down upon herself and him the indignation of so great a god.

"There is no such god as you dream of," said then Leucippus boldly, who had hitherto forborne to second the petition of the princess; "but a vain opinion of him has filled the land with love and wantonness. Every young man and maiden, that feel the least desire to one another, dare in no case to suppress it; for they think it to be Cupid's motion, and that he is a god!"

Thus pressed by the solicitations of both his children, and fearing the oath which he had taken, in an evil hour the misgiving father consented; and a proclamation was sent throughout all the provinces for the putting-down of the idol, and suppression of the established Cupid-worship.

Notable, you may be sure, was the stir made in all places among the priests, and among the artificers in gold, in silver, or in marble, who made a gainful trade, either in serving at the altar, or in the manufacture of the images no longer to be tolerated. The cry was clamorous as that at Ephesus when a kindred idol was in danger; for "great had been Cupid of the Lycians." Nevertheless, the power of the duke, backed by the power of his more popular children, prevailed; and the destruction of every vestige of the old religion was but as the work of one day throughout the country.

And now, as the pagan chronicles of Lycia inform us, the displeasure of Cupid went out,—the displeasure of a great god,—flying through all the dukedom, and sowing evils. But, upon the first movers of the profanation, his angry hand lay heaviest ; and there was imposed upon them a strange misery, that all might know that Cupid's revenge was mighty. With his arrows hotter than plagues, or than his own anger, did he fiercely right himself; nor could the prayers of a few concealed worshippers, nor the smoke arising from an altar here and there which had escaped the general overthrow, avert his wrath, or make him to cease from vengeance, until he had made of the once flourishing country of Lycia a most wretched land. He sent no famines, he let loose no cruel wild beasts among them,—inflictions with one or other of which the rest of the Olympian deities are fabled to have visited the nations under their displeasure,—but took a nearer course of his own ; and his invisible arrows went to the *moral heart* of Lycia, infecting and filling court and country with desires of unlawful marriages, unheard-of and monstrous affections, prodigious and misbecoming unions.

The symptoms were first visible in the changed bosom of Hidaspes This exemplary maiden,—whose cold modesty, almost to a failing, had discouraged the addresses of so many princely suitors that had sought her hand in marriage,—by the venom of this inward pestilence, came on a sudden to cast eyes of affection on a mean and deformed creature, Zoilus by name, who was a dwarf, and lived about the palace, the common jest of the courtiers. In her besotted eyes he was grown a goodly gentleman : and to her maidens, when any of them reproached him with the defect of his shape in her hearing, she would reply, that " to them, indeed, he might appear defective, and unlike a man, as, indeed, no man was like unto him; for in form and complexion he was beyond painting. He is like," she said, "to nothing that we have seen; yet he doth resemble Apollo, as I have fancied him, when, rising in the east, he bestirs himself, and shakes daylight from his hair." And, overcome with a passion which was heavier than she could bear, she confessed herself a wretched creature, and implored forgiveness of God Cupid, whom she had provoked; and, if possible, that he would grant it to her that she might enjoy her love. Nay, she would court this piece of deformity to his face; and when the wretch, supposing it to be done in mockery, has said that he could wish himself more ill-shaped than he was, so it would contribute to make her grace merry, she would reply, "Oh think not that I jest; unless it be a jest not to esteem my life in comparison with thine; to hang a thousand kisses in an hour upon those lips; unless it be a jest to vow that I am willing to become your wife, and to take obedience upon me." And by his "own white hand," taking it in hers,—so strong was the delusion,—she besought him to swear to marry her.

The term had not yet expired of the seven days within which the doting duke had sworn to fulfil her will, when, in pursuance of this frenzy, she presented herself before her father, leading in the dwarf by the hand, and, in the face of all the courtiers, solemnly demanding his hand in marriage. And, when the apish creature made show of blushing at the unmerited honour, she, to comfort him, bade him not to be ashamed; for, "in her eyes, he was worth a kingdom."

And now, too late, did the fond father repent him of his dotage. But when by no importunity he could prevail upon her to desist from her suit, for his oath's sake he must needs consent to the marriage. But the ceremony was no sooner, to the derision of all present, performed, than with the just feelings of an outraged parent, he commanded the head of the presumptuous bridegroom to be stricken off, and committed the distracted princess close prisoner to her chamber, where, after many deadly swoonings, with intermingled outcries upon the cruelty of her father, she, in no long time after, died; making ineffectual appeals, to the last, to the mercy of the offended Power,—the Power that had laid its heavy hand upon her, to the bereavement of her good judgment first, and finally to the extinction of a life that might have proved a blessing to Lycia.

Leontius had scarcely time to be sensible of her danger before a fresh cause for mourning overtook him. His son Leucippus, who had hitherto been a pattern of strict life and modesty, was stricken with a second arrow from the deity, offended for his overturned altars, in which the prince had been a chief instrument. The god caused his heart to fall away, and his crazed fancy to be smitten with the excelling beauty of a wicked widow, by name Bacha. This woman, in the first days of her mourning for her husband, by her dissembling tears and affected coyness had drawn Leucippus so cunningly into her snares, that, before she would grant him a return of love, she extorted from the easy-hearted prince a contract of marriage, to be fulfilled in the event of his father's death. This guilty intercourse, which they covered with the name of marriage, was not carried with such secrecy but that a rumour of it ran about the palace, and by some officious courtier was

2 F 2

l   )

brought to the ears of the old duke; who, to satisfy
himself of the truth, came hastily to the house of
Bacha, where he found his son courting. Taking
the prince to task roundly, he sternly asked who that
creature was that had bewitched him out of his
honour thus. Then Bacha, pretending ignorance of
the duke's person, haughtily demanded of Leucippus
what saucy old man that was, that without leave had
burst into the house of an afflicted widow to hinder
her paying her tears (as she pretended) to the dead.
Then the duke declaring himself, and threatening her
for having corrupted his son, giving her the reproach-
ful terms of witch and sorceress, Leucippus mildly
answered, that he " did her wrong." The bad
woman, imagining that the prince for very fear
would not betray their secret, now conceived a project of monstrous wickedness; which was no less
than to ensnare the father with the same arts which
had subdued the son, that she might no longer be a
concealed wife, nor a princess only under cover, but,
by a union with the old man, become at once the
true and acknowledged Duchess of Lycia. In a posture of humility she confessed her ignorance of the
duke's quality; but, now she knew it, she besought
his pardon for her wild speeches, which proceeded,
she said, from a distempered head, which the loss of
a dear husband had affected. He might command
her life, she told him, which was now of small value
to her. The tears which had accompanied her
words, and her mourning weeds, (which, for a blind
to the world, she had not yet cast off,) heightening
her beauty, gave a credence to her protestations of
her innocence. But the duke continuing to assail
her with reproaches, with a matchless confidence,

assuming the air of injured virtue, in a somewhat
lofty tone she replied, that though he were her
sovereign, to whom in any lawful cause she was
bound to submit, yet, if he sought to take away her
honour, she stood up to defy him. *That*, she said,
was a jewel dearer than any he could give her, which,
so long as she should keep, she should esteem herself richer than all the princes of the earth that were
without it. If the prince, his son, knew any thing to
her dishonour, let him tell it. And here she chal-
lenged Leucippus before his father to speak the
worst of her. If he would, however, sacrifice a
woman's character to please an unjust humour of the
duke's, she saw no remedy, she said, now *he* was dead
(meaning her late husband) that with his life would
have defended her reputation.

Thus appealed to, Leucippus, who had stood awhile
astonished at her confident falsehoods, though ignorant of the full drift of them, considering that not
the reputation only, but probably the life, of a woman
whom he had so loved, and who had made such
sacrifices to him of love and beauty, depended upon
his absolute concealment of their contract, framed
his mouth to a compassionate untruth, and with
solemn asseverations confirmed to his father her assurances of her innocence. He denied not that with
rich gifts he had assailed her virtue, but had found
her relentless to his solicitations; that neither gold
nor greatness had any power over her. Nay, so far he
went on to give force to the protestations of this artful woman, that he confessed to having offered marriage to her, which she, who scorned to listen to any
second wedlock, had rejected.

All this while Leucippus secretly prayed to

l   *)*

Heaven to forgive him while he uttered these bold
untruths; since it was for the prevention of a greater
mischief only, and had no malice in it.

But, warned by the sad sequel which ensued, be
thou careful, young reader, how in any case you tell
a lie. Lie not, if any man but ask you "How you
do," or "What o'clock it is." Be sure you make no
false excuse to screen a friend that is most dear to
you. Never let the most well-intended falsehood
escape your lips; for Heaven, which is entirely
Truth, will make the seed which you have sown of
untruth to yield miseries a thousand-fold upon yours,
as it did upon the head of the ill-fated and mistaken
Leucippus.

Leontius, finding the assurances of Bacha so con-
fidently seconded by his son, could no longer withhold his belief; and, only forbidding their meeting
for the future, took a courteous leave of the lady,
presenting her at the same time with a 'valuable
ring, in recompense, as he said, of the injustice
which he had done her in his false surmises of her
guiltiness. In truth, the surpassing beauty of the
lady, with her appearing modesty, had made no less
impression on the heart of the fond old duke than
it had awakened in the bosom of his more pardon-
able son. His first design was to make her his mistress; to the better accomplishment of which,
Leucippus was dismissed from the Court, under the
pretext of some honourable employment abroad.
In his absence, Leontius spared no offers to induce
her to comply with his purpose. Continually he
solicited her with rich offers, with messages, and by
personal visits. It was a ridiculous sight, if it were
not rather a sad one, to behold this second and worse

dotage, which by Cupid's wrath had fallen upon this fantastical *old new lover*. All his occupation now was in dressing and pranking himself up in youthful attire to please the eyes of his new mistress. His mornings were employed in the devising of trim fashions, in the company of tailors, embroiderers, and feather-dressers So infatuated was he with these vanities, that, when a servant came and told him that his daughter was dead,—even she whom he had but lately so highly prized,—the words seemed spoken to a deaf person. He either could not or would not understand them ; but, like one senseless, fell to babbling about the shape of a new hose and doublet. His crutch, the faithful prop of long aged years, was discarded ; and he resumed the youthful fashion of a sword by his side, when his years wanted strength to draw it. In this condition of folly, it was no difficult task for the widow, by affected pretences of honour, and arts of amorous denial, to draw in this doting duke to that which she had all along aimed at,—the offer of his crown in marriage. She was now Duchess of Lycia ! In her new elevation the mask was quickly thrown aside, and the impious Bacha appeared in her true qualities. She had never loved the duke, her husband ; but had used him as the instrument of her greatness. Taking advantage of his amorous folly, which seemed to gain growth the nearer he approached to his grave, she took upon her the whole rule of Lycia . placing and displacing, at her will, all the great officers of state , and filling the Court with creatures of her own, the agents of her guilty pleasures, she removed from the duke's person the oldest and trustiest of his dependents.

Leucippus, who at this juncture was returned from his foreign mission, was met at once with the news of his sister's death and the strange wedlock of the old duke. To the memory of Hidaspes he gave some tears; but these were swiftly swallowed up in his horror and detestation of the conduct of Bacha. In his first fury he resolved upon a full disclosure of all that had passed between him and his wicked step-mother. Again, he thought, by killing Bacha, to rid the world of a monster. But tenderness for his father recalled him to milder counsels. The fatal secret, nevertheless, sat upon him like lead, while he was determined to confide it to no other. It took his sleep away, and his desire of food; and if a thought of mirth at any time crossed him, the dreadful truth would recur to check it, as if a messenger should have come to whisper to him of some friend's death. With difficulty he was brought to wish their high-nesses faint joy of their marriage; and at the first sight of Bacha, a friend was fain to hold his wrist hard to prevent him from fainting. In an interview, which after, at her request, he had with her alone, the bad woman shamed not to take up the subject lightly; to treat as a trifle the marriage vow that had passed beween them, and, seeing him sad and silent, to threaten him with the displeasure of the duke, his father, if by words or looks he gave any suspicion to the world of their dangerous secret. " What had happened," she said, "was by no fault of hers. People would have thought her mad if she had re-fused the duke's offer. She had used no arts to entrap his father. It was Leucippus's own resolute denial of any such thing as a contract having passed between them which had led to the proposal."

ℓ   D

The prince, unable to extenuate his share of blame in the calamity, humbly besought her, that " since, by his own great fault, things had been brought to their present pass, she would only live honest for the future, and not abuse the credulous age of the old duke, as he well knew she had the power to do. For himself, seeing that life was no longer desirable to him, if his death was judged by her to be indispensable to her security, she was welcome to lay what trains she pleased to compass it, so long as she would only suffer his father to go to his grave in peace, since *he* had never wronged her.

This temperate appeal was lost upon the heart of Bacha, who from that moment was secretly bent upon effecting the destruction of Leucippus. Her project was, by feeding the ears of the duke with exaggerated praises of his son, to awaken a jealousy in the old man, that she secretly preferred Leucippus. Next, by wilfully insinuating the great popularity of the prince (which was no more indeed than the truth) among the Lycians, to instil subtle fears into the duke that his son had laid plots for circumventing his life and throne. By these arts she was working upon the weak mind of the duke almost to distraction, when, at a meeting concocted by herself between the prince and his father, the latter taking Leucippus soundly to task for these alleged treasons, the prince replied only by humbly drawing his sword, with the intention of laying it at his father's feet; and begging him, since he suspected him, to sheathe it in his own bosom, for of his life he had been long weary. Bacha entered at this crisis, and, ere Leucippus could finish his submission, with loud outcries alarmed the courtiers, who, rushing into the

presence, found the prince with sword in hand indeed, but with far other intentions than this bad
woman imputed to him, plainly accusing him of
having drawn it upon his father! Leucippus was
quickly disarmed ; and the old duke, trembling
between fear and age, committed him to close prison,
from which, by Bacha's aims, he never should have
come out alive but for the interference of the common
people, who, loving their prince, and equally detest-
ing Bacha, in a simultaneous mutiny arose, and
rescued him from the hands of the officers.

The Court was now no longer a place of living for
Leucippus ; and hastily thanking his countrymen for
his deliverance, which in his heart he rather depre-
cated than welcomed, as one that wished for death,
he took leave of all court hopes, and, abandoning the
palace, betook himself to a life of penitence in
solitudes.

Not so secretly did he select his place of penance,
in a cave among lonely woods and fastnesses, but
that his retreat was traced by Bacha ; who, baffled
in her purpose, raging like some she-wolf, despatched
an emissary of her own to destroy him privately.

There was residing at the Court of Lycia, at this
time, a young maiden, the daughter of Bacha by
her first husband, who had hitherto been brought up
in the obscurity of a poor country abode with an
uncle ; but whom Bacha now publicly owned, and
had prevailed upon the easy duke to adopt as successor to the throne in wrong of the true heir, his
suspected son Leucippus.

This young creature, Urania by name, was as artless and harmless as her mother was crafty and
wicked. To the unnatural Bacha she had been an

object of neglect and aversion ; and for the project of supplanting Leucippus only had she fetched her out of retirement. The bringing-up of Urania had been among country hinds and lasses: to tend her flocks or superintend her neat dairy had been the extent of her breeding. From her calling she had contracted a pretty rusticity of dialect, which, among the fine folks of the Court, passed for simplicity and folly. She was the unfittest instrument for an ambitious design that could be chosen : for her manners in a palace had a tinge still of her old occupation ; and to her mind the lowly shepherdess's life was best.

Simplicity is oft a match for prudence : and Urania was not so simple but she understood that she had been sent for to Court only in the prince's wrong , and in her heart she was determined to defeat any designs that might be contriving against her brother-in-law. The melancholy bearing of Leucippus had touched her with pity. This wrought in her a kind of love, which, for its object, had no further end than the well-being of the beloved. She looked for no return of it, nor did the possibility of such a blessing in the remotest way occur to her,—so vast a distance she had imaged between her lowly bringing-up and the courtly breeding and graces of Leucippus. Hers was no raging flame, such as had burned destructive in the bosom of poor Hidaspes. Either the vindictive god in mercy had spared this young maiden, or the wrath of the confounding *Cupid* was restrained by a higher Power from discharging the most malignant of his arrows against the peace of so much innocence. Of the extent of her mother's malice she was too guileless to have entertained conjecture ; but from hints and whispers, and, above all, from that tender watchfulness with which a true affection like Urania's tends the safety of its object,—fearing even where no cause for fear subsists,—she gathered that some danger was impending over the prince, and with simple heroism resolved to countermine the treason.

It chanced upon a day that Leucippus had been indulging his sad meditations in forests far from human converse, when he was struck with the appearance of a human being, so unusual in that solitude. There stood before him a seeming *youth*, of delicate appearance, clad in coarse and peasantly attire. "I am come," he said, "to seek out the prince, and to be his poor boy and servant, if he will let me."—"Alas! poor youth,'' replied Leucippus, "why do you follow me, who am as poor as you are?"—"In good faith," was the pretty answer, "I shall be well and rich enough if you will but love me." And, saying so, he wept. The prince, admiring this strange attachment in a boy, was moved with compassion, and seeing him exhausted, as if with long travel and hunger, invited him to his poor habitation, setting such refreshments before him as that barren spot afforded. But by no entreaties could he be prevailed upon to take any sustenance; and all that day, and for the two following, he seemed supported only by some gentle flame of love that was within him. He fed only upon the sweet looks and courteous entertainment which he received from Leucippus. Seemingly, he wished to die under the loving eyes of his master. "I cannot eat," he prettily said, "but I shall eat to-morrow."—"You will be dead by that time," replied Leucippus. "I shall be well

then," said he, " since you will not love me." Then
the prince asked him why he sighed so. "To think,"
was the innocent reply, " that such a fine man as
you should die, and no gay lady love him."—" But
you will love me," said Leucippus. "Yes, sure,"
said he, " till I die: and when I am in heaven I
shall wish for you " " This is a love," thought the
other, " that I never yet heard tell of. But come, thou
art sleepy, child: go in, and I will sit with thee."
Then, from some words which the poor youth dropped,
Leucippus, suspecting that his wits were beginning
to ramble, said, " What portends this ? "—" I am
not sleepy," said the youth; " but you are sad. I
would that I could do any thing to make you merry!
Shall I sing ? " But soon, as if recovering strength,
" There is one approaching ! " he wildly cried out.
" Master, look to yourself ! "

His words were true: for now entered, with provided weapon, the wicked emissary of Bacha, that
we told of; and, directing a mortal thrust at the
prince, the supposed boy, with a last effort, interpos-
ing his weak body, received it in his bosom, thanking
the heavens in death that he had saved " so good a
master."

Leucippus, having slain the villain, was at leisure
to discover, in the features of his poor servant, the
countenance of his devoted sister-in-law! Through
solitary and dangerous ways she had sought him in
that disguise; and, finding him, seems to have
resolved upon a voluntary death by fasting,—partly
that she might die in the presence of her beloved,
and partly that she might make known to him in
death the love which she wanted boldness to disclose
to him while living, but chiefly because she knew,

that by her demise, all obstacles would be removed that stood between her prince and his succession to the throne of Lycia.

Leucippus had hardly time to comprehend the strength of love in his Urania, when a trampling of horses resounded through his solitude. It was a party of Lycian horsemen, that had come to seek him, dragging the detested Bacha in their train, who was now to receive the full penalty of her misdeeds. Amidst her frantic fury upon the missing of her daughter, the old duke had suddenly died, not without suspicion of her having administered poison to him. Her punishment was submitted to Leucippus, who was now, with joyful acclaims, saluted as the rightful Duke of Lycia. He, as no way moved with his great wrongs, but considering her simply as the parent of Urania, saluting her only by the title of " Wicked Mother," bade her to live. " That reverend title," he said, and pointed to the bleeding remains of her child, "must be her pardon. He would use no extremity against her, but leave her to Heaven." The hardened mother, not at all relenting at the sad spectacle that lay before her, but making show of dutiful submission to the young duke, and with bended knees approaching him, suddenly with a dagger inflicted a mortal stab upon him ; and, with a second stroke stabbing herself, ended both their wretched lives.

Now was the tragedy of Cupid's wrath awfully completed ; and, the race of Leontius failing in the deaths of both his children, the chronicle relates, that under their new duke, Ismenus, the offence to the angry Power was expiated ; his statues and altars were, with more magnificence than ever, re-edified; and he ceased thenceforth from plaguing the land.

Thus far the pagan historians relate erring. But from this vain idol story a not unprofitable moral may be gathered against the abuse of the natural but dangerous *passion of love*. In the story of Hidaspes, we see the preposterous linking of beauty with deformity; of princely expectancies with mean and low conditions, in the case of the prince, her brother; and of decrepit age with youth, in the ill end of their doting father, Leontius By their examples we are warned to decline all *unequal and ill-assorted unions*.

THE
DEFEAT OF TIME;
OR, A
TALE OF THE FAIRIES.[1]

TITANIA and her moonlight Elves were assembled
under the canopy of a huge oak, that served to shelter
them from the moon's radiance, which, being now at
her full noon, shot forth intolerable rays—intolerable,
I mean, to the subtil texture of their little shadowy
bodies—but dispensing an agreeable coolness to us
grosser mortals. An air of discomfort sate upon the
Queen, and upon her Courtiers Their tiny frisk-
ings and gambols were forgot ; and even Robin Goodfellow, for the first time in his little airy life, looked
grave ; for the Queen had had melancholy forebod-
ings of late, founded upon an ancient Prophecy, laid
up in the records of Fairy Land, that the date of
Fairy existence would be *then* extinct, when men
should cease to believe in them. And she knew how
that the race of the Nymphs, which were her pre-
decessors, and had been the Guardians of the sacred
floods, and of the silver fountains, and of the consecrated hills and woods, had utterly disappeared
before the chilling touch of man's incredulity ; and

---

[1] From Hone's *Table Book.*

she sighed bitterly at the approaching fate of herself
and of her subjects, which was dependent upon so
fickle a lease as the capricious and ever-mutable faith
of man. When, as if to realize her fears, a melancholy shape came gliding in, and *that* was—TIME,
who with his intolerable scythe mows down kings
and kingdoms : at whose dread approach the fays
huddled together, as a flock of timorous sheep, and
the most courageous among them crept into acorn
cups, not enduring the sight of that ancientest of
monarchs. Titania's first impulse was to wish the
presence of her false lord, King Oberon, who was
far away, in the pursuit of a strange beauty, a fay
of Indian land—that with his good lance and sword,
like a faithful knight and husband, he might defend
her against Time. But she soon checked that
thought as vain, for what could the prowess of
the mighty Oberon himself, albeit the stoutest
champion in Fairy Land, have availed against so
huge a giant, whose bald top touched the skies !
So in the mildest tone she besought the Spectre,
that in his mercy he would overlook, and pass by,
her small subjects, as too diminutive and powerless
to add any worthy trophy to his renown. And she
besought him to employ his resistless strength
against the ambitious children of men, and to lay
waste their aspiring works, to tumble down their
towers and turrets, and the babels of their pride, fit
objects of his devouring scythe, but to spare her and
her harmless race, who had no existence beyond a
dream ; frail objects of a creed ; that lived but in the
faith of the believer. And with her little arms, as
well as she could, she grasped the stern knees of
Time, and waxing speechless with fear, she beckoned

to her chief attendants, and maids of honour, to
come forth from their hiding-places, and to plead the
Plea of the Fairies. And one of those small delicate
creatures came forth at her bidding, clad all in white
like a chorister, and in a low melodious tone, not
louder than the hum of a pretty bee—when it seems
to be demurring whether it shall settle upon this
sweet flower or that, before it settles—set forth her
humble petition. "We Fairies," she said, "are the
most inoffensive race that live, and least deserving
to perish. It is we that have the care of all sweet
melodies, that no discords may offend the Sun, who
is the great soul of music. We rouse the lark at
morn ; and the pretty echoes, which respond to all
the twittering quire, are of our making. Wherefore,
great King of Years, as ever you have loved the
music which is raining from a morning cloud, sent
from the messenger of day, the lark, as he mounts
to Heaven's gate, beyond the ken of mortals ; or if
ever you have listened with a charmed ear to the
night bird, that

> In the flowery Spring,
> Amidst the leaves set, makes the thickets ring
> Of her sour sorrows, sweeten'd with her song

spare our tender tribes ; and we will muffle up the
sheep-bell for thee, that thy pleasure take no interruption, whenever thou shall listen unto Philomel."

And Time answered, that " he had heard that song
too long ; and he was even wearied with that ancient
strain, that recorded the wrongs of Tereus. But if
she would know in what music Time delighted, it
was, when sleep and darkness lay upon crowded
cities, to hark to the midnight chime, which is tolling
from a hundred clocks, like the last knell over the

soul of a dead world, or to the crush of the fall of some age-worn edifice, which is as the voice of himself when he disparteth kingdoms."

A second female Fay took up the Plea, and said, " We be the handmaids of the Spring, and tend upon the birth of all sweet buds ; and the pastoral cowslips are our friends, and the pansies ; and the violets, like nuns ; and the quaking hare-bell is in our wardship ; and the Hyacinth, once a fair youth, and dear to Phœbus."

Then Time made answer, in his wrath striking the harmless ground with his hurtful scythe, that " they must not think that he was one that cared for flowers, except to see them wither, and to take her beauty from the rose."

And a third Fairy took up the Plea, and said, " We are kindly things ; and it is we that sit at evening, and shake rich odours from sweet bowers upon discoursing lovers, that seem to each other to be their own sighs ; and we keep off the bat, and the owl, from their privacy, and the ill-boding whistler ; and we flit in sweet dreams across the brains of infancy, and conjure up a smile upon its soft lips to beguile the careful mother, while its little soul is fled for a brief minute or two to sport with our youngest fairies."

Then Saturn (which is Time) made answer, that " They should not think that he delighted in tender babes, that had devoured his own, till foolish Rhea cheated him with a stone, which he swallowed, thinking it to be the infant Jupiter." And thereat in token he disclosed to view his enormous tooth, in which appeared monstrous dents, left by that unnatural meal ; and his great throat, that seemed capable of devouring up the earth and all its inhabitants at one meal. "And for lovers," he continued, "my delight is, with a hurrying hand to snatch them away from their love-meetings by stealth at nights, and to ravish away hours from them like minutes whilst they are together, and in absence to stand like a motionless statue, or their leaden planet of mishap, (whence I had my name,) till I make their minutes seem ages."

Next stood up a male Fairy, clad all in green, like a forester, or one of Robin Hood's mates, and doffing his tiny cap, said: "We are small foresters, that live in woods, training the young boughs in graceful intricacies, with blue snatches of the sky between; we frame all shady roofs and arches rude; and sometimes, when we are plying our tender hatches, men say, that the tapping woodpecker is nigh: and it is we that scoop the hollow cell of the squirrel; and carve quaint letters upon the rinds of trees, which in sylvan solitudes sweetly recall to the mind of the heat-oppressed swain, ere he lies down to slumber, the name of his fair one, dainty Aminta, gentle Rosalind, or chastest Laura, as it may happen."

Saturn, nothing moved with this courteous address, bade him begone, or "if he would be a woodman, to go forth, and fell oak for the fairies' coffins, which would forthwith be wanting. For himself, he took no delight in haunting the woods, till their golden plumage (the yellow leaves) were beginning to fall, and leave the brown black limbs bare, like Nature in her skeleton dress."

Then stood up one of those gentle Fairies, that are good to man, and blushed red as any rose, while he told a modest story of one of his own good deeds.

" It chanced upon a time," he said, "that while we were looking cowslips in the meads, while yet the dew was hanging on the buds, like beads, we found a babe left in its swathing clothes—a little sorrowful deserted thing ; begot of love, but begetting no love in others ; guiltless of shame, but doomed to shame for its parents' offence in bringing it by indirect courses into the world. It was pity to see the abandoned little orphan left to the world's care by an unnatural mother, how the cold dew kept wetting its childish coats ; and its little hair, how it was bedabbled, that was like gossamer. Its pouting mouth, unknowing how to speak, lay half opened like a rose-lipt shell, and its cheek was softer than any peach, upon which the tears, for very roundness, could not long dwell, but fell off, in clearness like pearls, some on the grass, and some on his little hand, and some haply wandered to the little dimpled well under his mouth, which Love himself seemed to have planned out, but less for tears than for smilings. Pity it was, too, to see how the burning sun scorched its helpless limbs, for it lay without shade, or shelter, or mother's breast, for foul weather or fair. • So having compassion on its sad plight, my fellows and I turned ourselves into grasshoppers, and swarmed about the babe, making such shrill cries, as that pretty little chirping creature makes in its mirth, till with our noise we attracted the attention of a passing rustic, a tender-hearted hind, who wondering at our small but loud concert, strayed aside curiously, and found the babe, where it lay on the remote grass, and taking it up, lapt it in his russet coat, and bore it to his cottage, where his wife kindly nurtured it, till it grew up a goodly personage. How this babe prospered

l)

afterwards, let proud London tell. This was that
famous Sir Thomas Gresham, who was the chiefest
of her merchants . the richest, the wisest. Witness
his many goodly vessels on the Thames, freighted
with costly merchandise : jewels from Ind, and pearls
for courtly dames, and silks of Samarcand. And
witness, more than all, that stately Bourse (or Exchange) which he caused to be built, a mart for merchants from East and West, whose graceful summit
still bears, in token of the Fairies' favours, his chosen
crest, the Grasshopper. And, like the grasshopper,
may it please you, great King, to suffer us also to
live, partakers of the green earth !''

The Fairy had scarce ended his Plea, when a shrill
cry, not unlike the grasshopper's, was heard. Poor
Puck—or Robin Goodfellow, as he is sometimes
called—had recovered a little from his first fright, and
in one of his mad freaks had perched upon the beard
of old Time, which was flowing, ample, and majestic,
and was amusing himself with plucking at a hair, which
was indeed so massy, that it seemed to him that he
was removing some huge beam of timber rather than
a hair; which Time by some ill chance perceiving,
snatched up the Impish Mischief with his great hand,
and asked "What it was ?"

" Alas !" quoth Puck, "a little random elf am I,
born in one of Nature's sports, a very weed, created
for the simple, sweet enjoyment of myself, but for no
other purpose, worth, or need, that ever I could learn.
'Tis I that bob the angler's idle cork, till the patient
man is ready to breathe a curse. I steal the morsel
from the gossip's fork, or stop the sneezing chanter
in mid Psalm ; and when an infant has been born
with hard or homely features, mothers say that I

changed the child at nurse ; but to fulfil any graver
purpose I have not wit enough, and hardly the will.
I am a pinch of lively dust to frisk upon the wind ; a
tear would make a puddle of me ; and so I tickle myself with the lightest straw, and shun all griefs
that might make me stagnant.   This is my small
philosophy."

Then Time, dropping him on the ground, as a
thing too inconsiderable for his vengeance, grasped
fast his mighty scythe ; and now, not Puck alone,
but the whole State of Fairies had gone to inevitable wreck and destruction, had not a timely apparition interposed, at whose boldness Time was
astounded, for he came not with the habit or the
forces of a deity, who alone might cope with Time,
but as a simple mortal, clad as you might see a
forester, that hunts after wild coneys by the cold
moonshine ; or a stalker of stray deer, stealthy and
bold.   But by the golden lustre in his eye, and the
passionate wanness in his cheek, and by the fair and
ample space of his forehead, which seemed a palace
framed for the habitation of all glorious thoughts, he
knew that this was his great rival, who had power
given him to rescue whatsoever victims Time should
clutch, and to cause them to live for ever in his immortal verse.   And muttering the name of Shake-
peare, Time spread his roc-like wings, and fled the
controlling presence.   And the liberated Court of the
Fairies, with Titania at their head, flocked around the
gentle ghost, giving him thanks, nodding to him, and
doing him courtesies, who had crowned them henceforth with a permanent existence, to live in the minds
of men, while verse shall have power to charm, or
Midsummer moons shall brighten.

         *   *   *   *   *

ι   Ɒ

What particular endearments passed between the
Fairies and their Poet, passes my pencil to delineate ;
but if you are curious to be informed, I must refer
you, gentle reader, to the " Plea of the Fairies," a
most agreeable poem, lately put forth by my friend,
Thomas Hood : of the first half of which the above
is nothing but a meagre and a harsh prose-abstract.
Farewell.

ELIA.

*The words of Mercury are harsh after the songs of
Apollo.*

CHARLES LAMB.

A Memoir.

BY

BARRY CORNWALL.

ι   Ɗ

PREFACE.

In my seventy-seventh year, I have been invited to place on record my recollections of Charles Lamb.

I am, I believe, nearly the only man now surviving who knew much of the excellent "Elia." Assuredly I knew him more intimately than any other existing person, during the last seventeen or eighteen years of his life.

In this predicament, and because I am proud to associate my name with his, I shall endeavour to recall former times, and to bring my old friend before the eyes of a new generation.

I request the "courteous reader" to accept, for what they are worth, these desultory labours of a lover of letters; and I hope that the advocate for modern times will try to admit into the circle of his sympathy my recollections of a fine Genius departed.

No harm—possibly some benefit—will accrue to any one who may consent to extend his acquaintance to one of the rarest and most delicate of the Humorists of England.

B. W. Procter.

May, 1866.

l   D

CHARLES LAMB.

CHAPTER I.

Introduction—Biography, Few Events—One Predominant—His Devotion to it—Tendency to Literature—First Studies—Influence of Antique Dwellings—Early Friends—Humour—Qualities of Mind—Sympathy for Neglected Objects—A Nonconformist—Predilections—Character—Taste—Style.

THE biography of Charles Lamb lies within a narrow compass. It comprehends only few events. His birth and parentage, and domestic sorrows; his acquaintance with remarkable men; his thoughts and habits; and his migrations from one home to another; constitute the sum and substance of his almost uneventful history. It is a history with one event, predominant.

For this reason, and because I, in common with many others, hold a book needlessly large to be a great evil, it is my intention to confine the present memoir within moderate limits. My aim is not to write the " Life and Times " of Charles Lamb. Indeed, Lamb had no influence on his own times. He had little or nothing in common with his generation, which was almost a stranger to him. There was no reciprocity between them. His contemplations were retrospective. He was, when living, the centre of a

small social circle : and I shall therefore deal incident-
ally with some of its members. In other respects, this
memoir will contain only what I recollect and what I
have learned from authentic sources, of my old friend.

The fact that distinguished Charles Lamb from
other men was his entire devotion to one grand and
tender purpose. There is, probably, a romance involved in every life. In his life it exceeded that of
others. In gravity, in acuteness, in his noble battle
with a great calamity, it was beyond the rest.
Neither pleasure nor toil ever distracted him from his
holy purpose. Everything was made subservient to
it. He had an insane sister, who, in a moment of
uncontrollable madness, had unconsciously destroyed
her own mother ; and to protect and save this sister
—a gentlewoman, who had watched like a mother
over his own infancy—the whole length of his life
was devoted. What he endured, through the space
of nearly forty years, from the incessant fear and frequent recurrence of his sister's insanity, can now
only be conjectured. In this constant and uncomplaining endurance, and in his steady adherence to a
great principle of conduct, his life was heroic.

We read of men giving up all their days to a single
object: to religion, to vengeance, to some over-
powering selfish wish ; of daring acts done to avert
death or disgrace, or some oppressing misfortune.
We read mythical tales of friendship ; but we do not
recollect any instance in which a great object has
been so unremittingly carried out throughout a
whole life, in defiance of a thousand difficulties, and
of numberless temptations, straining the good resolution to its utmost, except in the case of our poor
clerk of the India House.

This was, substantially, his life. His actions, thoughts, and sufferings were all concentred on this one important end. It was what he had to do; it was in his reach; and he did it, therefore, manfully, religiously. He did not waste his mind on too many things; for whatever too much expands the mind weakens it; nor on vague or multitudinous thoughts and speculations, nor on dreams or things distant or unattainable. However interesting, they did not absorb him, body and soul, like the safety and welfare of his sister.

Subject to this primary unflinching purpose, the tendency of Lamb's mind pointed strongly towards literature. He did not seek literature, however; and he gained from it nothing except his fame. He worked laboriously at the India House from boyhood to manhood: for many years without repining, although he must have been conscious of an intellect qualified to shine in other ways than in entering up a trader's books. None of those coveted offices, which bring money and comfort in their train, ever reached Charles Lamb. He was never under that bounteous shower which Government leaders and persons of influence direct towards the heads of their adherents. No Dives ever selected him for his golden bounty. No potent critic ever shouldered him up the hill of fame. In the absence of these old-fashioned helps, he was content that his own unassisted efforts should gain for him a certificate of capability to the world. and that the choice reputation which he thus earned should, with his own qualities, bring round him the unenvying love of a host of friends.

Lamb had always been a studious boy and a great reader; and after passing through Christ's Hospital and the South Sea House, and being for some years in the India House, this instinctive passion of his mind (for literature) broke out. In this he was without doubt influenced by the example and counsel of Samuel Taylor Coleridge, his school-fellow and friend, for whom he entertained a high and most tender respect. The first books which he loved to read were volumes of poetry, and essays on serious and religious themes. The works of the old poets, the history of Quakers, the biography of Wesley, the controversial papers of Priestly, and other books on devout subjects, sank into his mind. From reading he speedily rose to writing; from being a reader he became an author. His first writings were entirely serious. These were verses, or letters, wherein religious thoughts and secular criticisms took their places in turn; or they were grave dramas, which exhibit and lead to the contemplation of character: and which nourish those moods out of which humour ultimately arises.

So much has been already published, that it is needless to encumber this short narrative with any minute enumeration of the qualities which constitute his station in literature; but I shall, as a part of my task, venture to refer to some of those which distinguish him from other writers.

Lamb's very curious and peculiar humour showed itself early. It was perhaps born of the solitude in which his childhood passed away; perhaps cherished by the seeds of madness that were in him,—that were in his sister,—that were in the ancestry from which he sprung. Without doubt, it caught colour from the scenes in the midst of which he grew up. Born in the Temple; educated in Christ's Hospital; and

passed onwards to the South Sea House; his first
visions were necessarily of antiquity. The grave old
buildings tenanted by lawyers and their clerks, were
replaced by "the old and awful cloisters" of the
School of Edward, and these in turn gave way to the
palace of the famous Bubble, now desolate, with its
unpeopled Committee Rooms, its pictures of Go-
vernors of Queen Anne's time, "its dusty maps of
Mexico, dim as dreams, and soundings of the Bay of
Panama." These things, if they impressed his mind
imperfectly at first, in time formed themselves into
the shape of truths, and assumed significance and
importance; as words and things, glanced over
hastily in childhood, grow and ripen, and enrich the
understanding in after days.

Lamb's earliest friends and confidants (with one
exception) were singularly void of wit and the love of
jesting. His sister was grave; his father gradually
sinking into dotage; Coleridge was immersed in
religious subtleties and poetic dreams; and Charles
Lloyd, sad and logical and analytical, was the anti-
thesis of all that is lively and humorous. But
thoughts and images stole in from other quarters;
and Lamb's mind was essentially quick and productive. Nothing lay barren in it, and much of what
was planted there, grew and spread and became
beautiful. He himself has sown the seeds of
humour in many English hearts. His own humour
is essentially English. It is addressed to his own
countrymen; to the men "whose limbs were made
in England:" not to foreign intellects, nor perhaps
to the universal mind. Humour, which is the humour
of a man, (of the writer himself or of his creations,)
must frequently remain, in its fragrant blossoming

state, in the land of its birth. Like some of the
most delicate wines and flowers, it will not bear
travel.

Apart from his humour and other excellences,
Charles Lamb combined qualities such as are seldom
united in one person; which indeed seem not easily
reconcileable with each other: namely, much prudence,
with much generosity: great tenderness of heart,
with a firm will. To these was superadded that racy
humour which has served to distinguish him from
other men. There is no other writer that I know of,
in whom tenderness and good sense and humour are
so intimately and happily blended; no one whose
view of men and things is so invariably generous
and true, and independent. These qualities made
their way slowly and fairly. They were not taken up
as a matter of favour or fancy, and then abandoned
They struggled through many years of neglect, and
some of contumely, before they took their stand
triumphantly, and as things not to be ignored by
any one.

Lamb pitied all objects which had been neglected
or despised. Nevertheless the lens through which
he viewed the objects of his pity,—beggars, and
chimney-sweepers, and convicts,—was always clear:
it served him even when their short-comings were to
be contemplated. For he never paltered with truth.
He had no weak sensibilities, few tears for imaginary
griefs. But his heart opened wide to real distress.
He never applauded the fault; but he pitied the
offender. He had a word of compassion for the
sheep-stealer, who was arrested and lost his ill-
acquired sheep, " his first, last, and only hope of a
mutton pie;" and vented his feelings in that sonnet

(rejected by the magazines) which he has called
" The Gypsey's Malison." Although he was willing
to acknowledge merit when it was successful, he
preferred it, perhaps, when it was not clothed with
prosperity.

By education and habit, he was an Unitarian.
Indeed, he was a true Nonconformist in all things.
He was not a dissenter by imitation, nor from any
deep principle or obstinate heresy ; nor was he made
servile and obedient by formal logic alone. His
reasoning always rose and streamed through the
heart. He liked a friend for none of the ordinary
reasons ; because he was famous, or clever, or
powerful, or popular. He at once took issue with
the previous verdicts, and examined the matter in
his own way. If a man was unfortunate he gave
him money. If he was calumniated, he accorded
him sympathy. He gave freely ; not to merit but to
want.

He pursued his own fancies ; his own predilections. He did not neglect his own instinct, (which is
always true,) and aim at things foreign to his nature.
He did not cling to any superior intellect, nor cherish
any inferior humorist or wit.

Perhaps no one ever thought more independently.
He had great enjoyment in the talk of able men, so
that it did not savour of form or pretension. He
liked the strenuous talk of Hazlitt, who never descended to fine words. He liked the unaffected quiet
conversation of Manning, the vivacious excursive
talk of Leigh Hunt. He heard with wondering admiration the monologues of Coleridge. Perhaps he
liked the simplest talk the best ; expressions of pity
or sympathy, or affection for others, from young

2 H 2

people, who thought and said little or nothing about themselves.

He had no craving for popularity, nor even for fame. I do not recollect any passage in his writings, nor any expression in his talk, which runs counter to my opinion. In this respect he seems to have differed from Milton, (who desired fame, like " Blind Thamyris and blind Mæonides,") and to have rather resembled Shakespeare, who was indifferent to fame or assured of it, but perhaps he resembled no one.

Lamb had not many personal antipathies, but he had a strong aversion to pretence and false repute. In particular, he resented the adulation of the epitaph-mongers who endeavoured to place Garrick, the actor, on a level with Shakespeare. Of that greatest of all poets he has said such things as I imagine Shakespeare himself would have liked to hear. He has also uttered brave word in behalf of Shakespeare's cotemporary dramatists : partly because they deserved them ; partly because they were unjustly forgotten. The sentence of oblivion, passed by ignorant ages on the reputation of these fine authors, he has annulled, and forced the world to confess that the preceding judges were incompetent to entertain the case.

I cannot imagine the mind of Charles Lamb, even in early boyhood, to have been weak or childish. In his first letters you see that he was a thinker. He is for a time made sombre by unhappy reflections. He is a reader of thoughtful books. The witticisms which he coined for sixpence each (for the *Morning Chronicle*) had, no doubt, less of metallic lustre than those which he afterwards meditated, and which were highly estimated. *Effodiuntur opes.* His jests

were never the mere overflowings of the animal
spirits ; but were exercises of the mind. He brought
the wisdom of old times and old writers to bear upon
the taste and intellect of his day. What was in a
manner foreign to his age, he naturalized and
cherished. And he did this with judgment and great
delicacy. His books never unhinge or weaken the
mind : but bring before it tender and beautiful
thoughts, which charm and nourish it, as only good
books can. No one was ever worse from reading
Charles Lamb's writings; but many have become
wiser and better. Sometimes, as he hints, "he
affected that dangerous figure, irony ;" and he would
sometimes interrupt grave discussion, when he
thought it too grave, with some light jest, which
nevertheless was " not quite irrelevant." Long
talkers, as he confesses, " hated him ;" and assuredly
he hated long talkers.

In his countenance you might sometimes read—
what may be occasionally read on almost all fore-
heads—the letters and lines of old, unforgotten
calamity. Yet there was at the bottom of his nature
a buoyant self-sustaining strength : for although he
encountered frequent seasons of mental distress,
his heart recovered itself in the interval, and rose
and sounded, like music played to a happy tune.
Upon fit occasion, his lips could shut in a firm
fashion ; but the gentle smile that played about his
face showed that he was always ready to relent. His
quick eye never had any sullenness : his mouth,
tender and tremulous, showed that there would be
nothing cruel or inflexible in his nature.

On referring to his letters, it must be confessed
that in literature Lamb's taste, like that of all others,

was at first imperfect. For taste is a portion of our
judgment, and must depend a good deal on our
experience, and on our opportunities of comparing
the claims of different pretenders. Lamb's affections
swayed him at all times. He sympathized deeply
with Cowper and his melancholy history; and at
first estimated his verse perhaps beyond its strict
value. He was intimate with Southey, and anticipated that he would rival Milton. Then his taste
was at all times peculiar. He seldom worshipped
the Idol which the multitude had set up. I was
never able to prevail on him to admit that " Paradise
Lost " was greater than " Paradise Regained;" I
believe, indeed, he liked the last the best. He would
not discuss the Poetry of Lord Byron or Shelley. with
a view of being convinced of their beauties. Apart
from a few points like these, his opinions must be
allowed to be sound ; almost always; if not as to
the style of the author, then as to the quality of his
book or passage which he chose to select. And his
own style was always good, from the beginning, in
verse as well as in prose His first sonnets are unaffected, well sustained, and well written.

I do not know much of the opinion of others , but
to my thinking the style of Charles Lamb, in his
" Elia," and in the letters written by him in the later
(the last twenty) years of his life, is full of grace ; not
antiquated, but having a touch of antiquity. It is
self-possessed, choice, delicate, penetrating, his words
running into the innermost sense of things. It is
not, indeed, adapted to the meanest capacity, but is
racy, and chaste, after his fashion. Perhaps it is
sometimes scriptural : at all events it is always
earnest and sincere. He was painfully in earnest,

in his advocacy of Hazlitt and Hunt, and in his pleadings for·Hogarth and the old dramatists. Even in his humour, his fictitious (as well as his real) personages have a character of reality about them which gives them their standard value They all ring like true coin. In conversation he loved to discuss persons or books, and seldom ventured upon the stormy sea of politics; his intimates lying on the two opposite shores, Liberal and Tory. Yet, when occasion moved him, he did not refuse to express his liberal opinions There was little or nothing cloudy or vague about him; he required that there should be known ground even in fiction. He rejected the poems of Shelley, (many of them so consummately beautiful,) because they were too exclusively ideal. Their efflorescence, he thought, was not natural. He preferred Southey's " Don Roderick " to his " Curse of Kehama ;" of which latter the poem he says " I don't feel that firm footing in it " that I do in " Roderick." My imagination goes sinking and floundering in the vast spaces of unopened systems and faiths. I am put out of the palé of my old sympathies."

Charles Lamb has much respect for some of the modern authors. In particular, he admired (to the full extent of his capacity for liking) Coleridge, and Wordsworth, and Burns. But with these exceptions his affections rested mainly on writers who had lived before him; on *some* of them; for there were "things in books' clothing," from which he turned away loathing. He was not a worshipper of the customs and manners of old times, so much as of the tangible objects that old times have bequeathed to us , the volumes tinged with decay, the buildings (the Temple, Christ's Hospital, &c.) coloured and enriched by the hand of age. Apart from these, he clung to the time present; for if he hated anything in the extreme degree, he hated change. He clung to life, although life had bestowed upon him no magnificent gifts, none, indeed, beyond books, and friends, (a "ragged regiment,") and an affectionate contented mind. He had, he confesses, "an intolerable disinclination to dying;" which beset him especially in the winter months. "I am not content to pass away like a weaver's shuttle. Any alteration in this earth of mine discomposes me. My household gods plant a terrible fixed foot, and are not rooted up without blood." He seems never to have looked into the Future. His eyes were on the present or (oftener) on the past. It was always thus from his boyhood. His first readings were principally Beaumont and Fletcher, Massinger, Isaac Walton, &c. "I gather myself up" (he writes) "unto the old things." He has indeed extracted the beauty and innermost value of Antiquity, whenever he has pressed it into his service.

CHAPTER II.

BIRTH AND PARENTAGE—CHRIST'S HOSPITAL—SOUTH SEA HOUSE AND INDIA HOUSE—CONDITION OF FAMILY—DEATH OF MOTHER—MARY IN ASYLUM—JOHN LAMB—CHARLES'S MEANS OF LIVING—HIS HOME —HIS DESPONDENCY—ALICE W.—BROTHER AND SISTER.

ON the South side of Fleet Street, near to where it adjoins Temple Bar, lies the Inner Temple. It extends southwards to the Thames, and contains long ranges of melancholy buildings, in which lawyers (those reputed birds of prey) and their followers congregate. It is a district very memorable. About seven hundred years ago, it was the abiding place of the Knights Templars; who erected there a church, which still uplifts its round tower, (its sole relic,) for the wonder of modern times. Fifty years since, I remember, you entered the precinct through a lowering archway that opened into a gloomy passage, Inner Temple lane. On the east side rose the church; and on the west was a dark line of chambers, since pulled down and rebuilt, and now called Johnson's Buildings. At some distance westward was an open court, in which was a sun dial: and, in the midst, a solitary fountain, that sent its silvery voice into the air above, the murmur of which, descending, seemed to render the place more lonely. Midway, between the Inner Temple Lane and the Thames was, and I believe still is, a range of substantial chambers, (overlooking the gardens and the busy river,) called Crown Office Row. In one of these chambers, on the 18th day of February, 1775, Charles Lamb was born.

He was the son of John and Elizabeth Lamb; and he and his brother John and his sister Mary (both of whom were considerably older than himself) were the only children of their parents. John was twelve years, and Mary (properly Mary Anne) was ten years older than Charles. Their father held the post of clerk to Mr. Samuel Salt, a barrister, one of the benchers of the Inner Temple; a mild, amiable man, very indolent, very shy, and, as I imagine, not much known in what is called "the profession." Lamb sprang, paternally, from a humble stock, which had its root in the county of Lincoln. At one time of his life his father appears to have dwelt at Stamford. In his

imaginary ascent from plain Charles Lamb to Pope
Innocent, one of the gradations is Lord Stamford.
His mother's family came from Hertfordshire, where
his grandmother was a housekeeper in the Plumer
family, and where several of his cousins long resided.
He did not attempt to trace his ancestry (of which
he wisely made no secret) beyond two or three generations. In an agreeable sonnet, entitled "The
Family Name," he speaks of his sire's sire, but no
further; "We trace our stream no higher." Then
he runs into some pleasant conjectures as to his possible progenitors, of whom he knew nothing.

"Perhaps some shepherd on Lincolnian plains,"

he says, first received the name; perhaps some martial lord, returned from "holy Salem;" and then he
concludes with a resolve,

"No deed of mine shall shame thee, gentle Name,"

which he kept religiously throughout his life.

When Charles was between seven and eight years
of age, he became a scholar in Christ's Hospital; a
presentation having been given to his father, for the
son's benefit. He entered that celebrated School on
the 9th of October, 1782, and remained there until
the 23rd November, 1789, being then between fourteen and fifteen years old. The records of his boyhood are very scanty. He was always a grave,
inquisitive boy. Once, when walking with his sister
through some churchyard, he inquired anxiously,
"where do the naughty people lie?" the unqualified
panegyrics which he encountered on the tombstones
doubtless suggesting the inquiry. Mr. Samuel Le
Grice (his schoolfellow) states that he was an amiable, gentle youth, very sensible, and keenly observ-

ing, that "his complexion was clear brown, his countenance mild, his eyes differing in colour, and that he had a slow and peculiar walk " He adds that he was never mentioned without the addition of his Christian name, Charles, implying a general feeling of kindness towards him. His delicate frame and difficulty of utterance, it is said, unfitted him for joining in any boisterous sports. After he left Christ's Hospital, he returned home, where he had access to the large miscellaneous library of Mr. Salt. He and his sister were (to use his own words) "tumbled into a spacious closet of good old English reading, and browsed at will on that fair and wholesome pasturage." This, however, could not have lasted long, for it was the destiny of Charles Lamb to be compelled to labour almost from his boyhood. He was able to read Greek, and had acquired great facility in Latin composition, when he left the Hospital ; but unconquerable impediment in his speech deprived him of an " exhibition " in the school and, as a consequence, of the benefit of a College education.

The state of Christ's Hospital, at the time when Lamb was a scholar there, may be ascertained with tolerable correctness from his two essays, entitled " Recollections of Christ's Hospital " and " Christ's Hospital five and thirty years ago." These papers when read together show the different (favourable and unfavourable) points of this great establishment. They leave no doubt as to its extensive utility. Although, strictly speaking, it was a charitable home for the sustenance and education of boys, slenderly provided, or unprovided, with the means of learning, they were neither lifted up beyond their own family nor depressed by mean habits, such as an ordinary

charity school is supposed to generate. They floated
onwards towards manhood in a wholesome middle
region, between a too rare ether and the dense and
abject atmosphere of pauperism. The Hospital boy
(as Lamb says) never felt himself to be a charity boy.
The antiquity and regality of the foundation to which
he belonged, and the mode or style of his education,
sublimated him beyond the heights of the labouring
classes. From the " Christ's Hospital five and thirty
years ago," it would appear that the comforts enjoyed
by Lamb himself exceeded those of his schoolfellows;
owing to his friends supplying him with extra delicacies. There is no doubt that great tyranny was
then exercised by the older boys (the monitors) over
the younger ones ; that the scholars had anything
but choice and ample rations ; and that hunger (" the
eldest, strongest of the passions ") was not a tyrant
unknown throughout this large Institution.

Lamb remained at Christ's Hospital for seven
years ; but on the half-holidays (two in every week)
he used to go to his parents' home, in the Temple,
and when there would muse on the terrace or by the
lonely fountain, or contemplate the dial, or pore over
the books in Mr. Salt's library; until those antiquely-
coloured thoughts rose up in his mind, which in after
years he presented to the world.

Amongst the advantages which Charles derived
from his stay at Christ's Hospital, was one which,
although accidental, was destined to have great effect
on his subsequent life. It happened that he reckoned,
amongst his school-fellows, one who afterwards
achieved a very extensive reputation, namely, Samuel
Taylor Coleridge. This youth was his elder by two
years ; and his example influenced Lamb materially

on many occasions, and ultimately led him into literature. Coleridge's projects, at the outset of life,
were vacillating. In this respect Lamb was no fol-
lower of his schoolfellow: his own career being steady
and unswerving, from his entrance into the India
House until the day of his freedom from service,
between thirty and forty years. His literary tastes,
indeed, took independently almost the same tone as
those of his friend, and their religious views (for
Coleridge in his early years became an Unitarian)
were the same When Coleridge left Christ's Hospital he went to the University—to Jesus College,
Cambridge, but came back occasionally to London,
where the intimacy between him and Lamb was
cemented. Their meetings at the smoky little public-
house in the neighbourhood of Smithfield—the "Salutation and Cat;" consecrated by pipes and tobacco,
(Orinoco) by egg-hot and Welch rabbits, and metaphysics and poetry; are exultingly referred to in
Lamb's letters. Lamb entertained for Coleridge's
genius the greatest respect, until death dissolved
their friendship. In his earliest verses (so dear to a
young poet) he used to submit his thoughts to Coleridge's amendments or critical suggestions: and on
one occasion was obliged to cry out " Spare my ewe
lambs, they are the reflected images of my own feelings."

It was at a very tender age that Charles Lamb
entered the "work-a-day" world. His elder brother,
John, had at that time a clerkship in the South Sea
House, and Charles passed a short time there under
his brother's care or control, and must thus have
gained some knowledge of figures. The precise nature of his occupation in this deserted place, however,

(where some forms of business were kept up, "though
the soul be long since fled," and where the directors
met mainly "to declare a dead dividend,") is not
stated in the charming paper of "The South Sea
House." Charles remained in this office only until
the 5th April, 1792, when he obtained an appointment
(through the influence, I believe, of Mr Salt) as clerk
in the Accountant's Office of the East India Company.
He was then seventeen years of age.

About three years after Charles became a clerk in
the India House, his family appear to have moved
from Crown Office Row, into poor lodgings at No. 7,
Little Queen Street, Holborn. His father at that
time had a small pension from Mr. Salt, whose service he had left, being almost fatuous ; his mother
was ill and bedridden ; and his sister Mary was tired
out, by needlework all day, and by taking care of her
mother throughout the night. "Of all the people in
the world " (Charles says) " she was most thoroughly
devoid of all selfishness." There was also, as a
member of the family, an old aunt, who had a trifling
annuity for her life, which she poured into the common fund. John Lamb (Charles's elder brother) lived
elsewhere ; having occasional intercourse only with
his kindred. He continued, however, to visit them
whilst he preserved his "comfortable" clerkship in
the South Sea House.

It was under this state of things that they all drifted
down to the terrible year, 1796. It was a year dark
with horror. There was an hereditary taint of insanity in the family, which caused even Charles to be
placed, for a short time, in Hoxton Lunatic Asylum.
" The six weeks that finished last year and began
this (1796), your very humble servant spent very

agreeably in a madhouse at Hoxton." These are his words when writing to Coleridge. Mary Lamb had previously been repeatedly attacked by the same dreadful disorder; and this now broke out afresh in a sudden burst of acute madness. She had been moody and ill for some little time previously, and the illness came to a crisis on the 23rd of September, 1796. On that day, just before dinner, Mary seized a "case knife" which was lying on the table; pursued a little girl (her apprentice) round the room; hurled about the dinner forks; and, finally, in a fit of uncontrollable frenzy, stabbed her mother to the heart. Charles was at hand, only in time to snatch the knife out of her grasp, before further hurt could be done. He found his father wounded in the forehead by one of the forks, and his aunt lying insensible and apparently dying, on the floor of the room.

This happened on a Thursday; and on the following day an inquest was held on the mother's body, and a verdict of Mary's lunacy was immediately found by the jury The Lambs had a few friends. Mr. Norris—the friend of Charles's father and of his own childhood—"was very kind to us;" and Sam Le Grice, "then in town" (Charles writes) "was a brother to me, and gave up every hour of his time in constant attendance on my father."

After the fatal deed, Mary Lamb was deeply afflicted. Her act was in the first instance totally unknown to her. Afterwards, when her consciousness returned and she was informed of it, she suffered great grief. And subsequently, when she became "calm and serene," and saw the misfortune in a clearer light, this was "far, very far from an indecent or forgetful serenity," as her brother says. She had no defiant air ; no affectation, nor too extravagant a display of sorrow. She saw her act, as she saw other things, by the light of her own clear and gentle good sense. She was sad; but the deed was past recall. and at the time of its commission had been utterly beyond either her control or knowledge.

After the inquest, Mary Lamb was placed in a lunatic asylum ; where, after a short time, she recovered her serenity. A rapid recovery after violent madness is not an unusual mark of the disease , it being in cases of quiet, inveterate insanity, that the return to sound mind (if it ever recur) is more gradual and slow. The recovery, however, was only temporary in her case. She was throughout her life subject to frequent recurrences of the same disease. At one time her brother Charles writes, " Poor Mary's disorder so frequently recurring has made us a sort of marked people." At another time he says, " I consider her as perpetually on the brink of madness." And so, indeed, she continued during the remainder of her life ; and she lived to the age of eighty-two years.

Charles was now left alone in the world. His father was imbecile . his sister insane ; and his brother afforded no substantial assistance or comfort. He was scarcely out of boyhood when he learned that the world has its dangerous places and barren deserts ; and that he had to struggle for his living, without help. He found that he had to take upon himself all the cares of a parent or protector (to his sister) even before he had studied the duties of a man.

Sudden as death came down the necessary knowledge : how to live, and how to live well. The terrible event that had fallen upon him and his, instead of casting him down, and paralyzing his powers, braced and strung his sinews into preternatural firmness. It is the character of a feeble mind to lie prostrate before the first adversary. In his case it lifted him out of that momentary despair which always follows a great calamity. It was like extreme cold to the system, which often overthrows the weak and timid, but gives additional strength and power of endurance to the brave and the strong. " My aunt was lying apparently dying," (writes Lamb) " my father with a wound in his poor forehead, and my mother a murdered corpse, in the next room. I felt that I had something else to do than to regret. *I had the whole weight of the family upon me:* for my brother—little disposed at any time to take care of old age and infirmity—has now, with his bad leg, exemption from such duties; and I am now left alone."

In about a month after his mother's death (3rd October) Charles writes, " My poor, dear, dearest sister, the unhappy and unconscious instrument of the Almighty's judgment on our house, is restored to her senses; to a dreadful sense of what has passed; awful to her mind, but tempered with a religious resignation. She knows how to distinguish between a deed committed in a fit of frenzy and the terrible guilt of a mother's murder." In another place he says, " She bears her situation as one who has no right to complain." He himself visits her and upholds her, and rejoices in her continued reason. For her use he borrows books, (" for reading was her daily bread,") and gives up his time and all his thoughts to her comfort.

Thus, in their quiet grief, making no show, yet suffering more than could be shown by clamorous

sobs or frantic words, the two—brother and sister—
enter upon the bleak world together   " Her love," as
Mr. Wordsworth states in the epitaph on Charles
Lamb, " was as the love of mothers " towards her
brother.   It may be said that his love for her was
the deep life-long love of the tenderest son.   In one
letter, he writes, " It was not a family where I could
take Mary with me ; and I am afraid that there is
something of dishonesty in any pleasures I take without her."   Many years afterwards, (in 1834, the very
year in which he died,) he writes to Miss Fryer,
" It is no new thing for me to be left with my sister.
When she is not violent, *her rambling chat is better
to me than the sense and sanity of the world* "   Surely
there is great depth of pathos in these unaffected
words : in the love that has outlasted all the troubles
of life, and is thus tenderly expressed, almost at his
last hour.

John Lamb, the elder brother of Charles, held a
clerkship, with some considerable salary, in the South
Sea House.   I do not retain an agreeable impression
of him.   If not rude, he was sometimes, indeed
generally, abrupt and unprepossessing in manner.
He was assuredly deficient in that courtesy which
usually springs from a mind at friendship with the
world.   Nevertheless, without much reasoning power
(apparently) he had much cleverness of character ;
except when he had to purchase paintings, at which
times his judgment was often at fault.   One of his
sayings is mentioned in the (Elia) essay of " My
Relations."   He seems to have been, on one occasion, contemplating a group of Eton boys at play,
when he observed, " What a pity it is to think that
these fine ingenuous lads will some day be changed

into frivolous members of Parliament." Like some
persons who, although case-hardened at home, over-
flow with sympathy towards distant objects, he cared
less for the feelings of his neighbour close at hand
than for the eel out of water or the oyster disturbed
in his shell.

John Lamb was the favourite of his mother, as the
deformed child is frequently the dearest. " She
would always love my brother above Mary," Charles
writes in 1796, " although he was not worth one
tenth of the affection which Mary had a right to
claim. Poor Mary ! my mother never understood
her right." In another place, (after he had been un-
burthening his heart to Coleridge,) he writes cautiously, " *Since* this has happened " [the death of
his mother] " he has been very kind and brotherly :
but I fear for his mind. He has taken his ease in
the world, and is not fit to struggle with difficulties.
Thank God, I can unconnect myself with him, and
shall manage my father's moneys myself, if I take
charge of Daddy, which poor John has not hinted a
wish at any future time to share with me." Mary
herself, when she was recovering, said that, " she
knew she must go to Bethlehem for life ; that one of
her brothers would have it so ; the other would not
wish it, but would be obliged to go with the
stream."

At this time, reckoning up their several means of
living, Charles Lamb and his father had together an
income of £170 or £180 ; out of which, he says,
" we can spare £50 or £60 at least for Mary whilst
she stays in an asylum. If I and my father and an
old maid-servant can't live, and live comfortably, on
£130 or £120 a year, we ought to burn by slow fires.

I almost would, so that Mary might not go into an
hospital." She was then recovering her health ;
had become serene and cheerful ; and Charles was
passionately desirous that, after a short residence in
the lunatic establishment wherein she then was, she
should return home : " But the surviving members of
her family," (these are Sir Thomas Talfourd's words,)
" especially John, who enjoyed a fair income from the
South Sea House, opposed her discharge." Charles,
however, ultimately succeeded in his pious desire,
upon entering into a solemn undertaking to take care
of his sister thereafter. He provided a lodging for
her at Hackney, and spent all his Sundays and holidays with her. I never heard of John Lamb having
contributed anything, in money or otherwise, towards
the support of his deranged sister, or to assist his
young struggling brother. Soon after this time,
Charles took his sister Mary to live with himself
entirely. Whenever the approach of one of her fits
of insanity, was announced, by some irritability or
change of manner, he would take her, under his arm,
to Hoxton Asylum. It was very afflicting to encounter the young brother and his sister walking together (weeping together) on this painful errand ;
Mary herself, although sad, very conscious of the
necessity for temporary separation from her only
friend. They used to carry a strait jacket with
them.

In the latter days of his father's life, Charles must
have had an uncomfortable home. " I go home at
night overwearied, quite faint, and then to cards with
my father : who will not let me enjoy a meal in peace.
After repeated games at cribbage " (he is writing to
Coleridge,) " I have got my father's leave to write ;

with difficulty got it : for when I expostulated about playing any more, he replied, ' If you won't play with me, you might as well not come home at all.' The argument was unanswerable, and I set to afresh." Soon after this, the father, who at last had become entirely imbecile, died ; and the pension which he had received from Mr. Salt, the old bencher, ceased. The aunt, who had been taken for a short time to the house of a rich relation, but had been sent back, also died in the following month. " My poor old aunt," (Charles writes,) " who was the kindest creature to me when I was at school, and used to bring me good things ; when I, schoolboy like, used to be ashamed to see her come, and open her apron, and bring out her basin with some nice thing which she had saved for me—the good old creature is now lying on her death-bed. She says, poor thing, she is glad she has come home to die with me. I was always her favourite." Thus Charles was left to his own poor resources (scarcely, if at all, exceeding £100 a year) ; and these remained very small for some considerable time. His writings were not calculated to attract immediate popularity, and the increase of his salary at the India House was slow. Even in 1809 (November), almost fifteen years later, the addition of twenty pounds a year, which comes to him on the resignation of a clerk in the India House, is very important, and is the subject of a joyful remark by his sister Mary.

The impression made, in the first instance, on Charles Lamb, by the terrible death of his mother, cannot be explained in any condensed manner. His mind, short of insanity, seems to have been utterly upset. He had been fond of poetry to excess almost all his leisure hours seemed to have been devoted to the books of poets and religious writers; to the composition of poetry; and to criticising various writers in verse. But afterwards, in his distress, he requests Coleridge to " mention nothing of poetry. I have destroyed every vestige of past vanities of that kind. Never send me a book, I charge you. I am wedded" (he adds) " to the fortunes of my sister and my poor old father." At another time he writes, " On the dreadful day I preserved a tranquillity, not of despair." Some persons coming into the " house of misery," and persuading him to take food, he says, " in an agony of emotion, I found my way mechanically into the adjoining room, and fell on my knees by the side of her coffin, asking forgiveness of Heaven, and sometimes of her, for forgetting her so soon." A few days later, he says to his friend, " You are the only correspondent, and, I might add, the only friend I have in the world. I go nowhere and see no acquaintance." At this time, he gave away all Coleridge's letters; burned all his own poetry; all the numerous poetical extracts he had made; and the little journal of " My foolish passion, which I had long time kept." Subsequently, when he becomes better, he writes again to his friend, " Correspondence with you has roused me a little from my lethargy, and made me conscious of my existence.'

Charles was now entirely alone with his sister. She was the only object between him and God: and out of this misery and desolation sprang that wonderful love between brother and sister, which has no parallel in history. Neither would allow any stranger to partake of the close affection that seemed to be

solely the other's right. Doubts have existed whether
Charles Lamb ever gave up for the sake of Mary the
one real attachment of his youth. It has been considered somewhat probable that Alice W. was an
imaginary being; some Celia or Campaspe or Linda-
mira; that she was in effect one of those visions
which float over us when we escape from childhood.
But it may have been a real love, driven deeper into
the heart, and torn out for another love, more holy
and as pure : for he was capable of a grand sacrifice.
No one will perhaps ever ascertain the truth precisely. It must remain undiscovered—magnified by
the mist of uncertainty—like those Hesperian Gardens
which inspired the verses of poets, but are still surrounded by fable. For my own part, I am persuaded
that the attachment was real. He says that his
sister would often "lend an ear to his desponding
love-sick lay." After he himself had been in a
lunatic asylum, he writes to Coleridge, that his "head
ran upon him, in his madness, as much almost as on
another person, *who was the more immediate cause of
my frenzy*" Later in the year he burned the "little
journal of his foolish passion;" and when writing
to his friend on the subject of his love sonnets, he
says, "it is a passion of which I retain nothing."
It is clear, I think, that it was love for a real person,
however transient it may have been. But the fact,
whether true or false, is inexpressibly unimportant.
It could not add to his stature . it could not diminish
it. His whole life is acted . and in it are numerous
other things which substantially raise and honour
him. The ashes (if ashes there were) are cold. His
struggles and pains, and hopes and visions are over.
All lie, diffused, intermingled in that vast Space

which has No Name; like the winds and light of
yesterday, which came and gave pleasure for a
moment, and now have changed and left us, for
ever.

In contrast with this apocryphal attachment,
stands out his deep and unalterable love for his
sister Mary. " God love her," he says; " may we
two never love each other less." They never did.
Their affection continued throughout life, without
interruption; without a cloud, except such as rose
from the fluctuations of her health. It is said that
a woman rises or falls with the arm on which she
leans. In this case, Mary Lamb at all times had a
safe support, an arm that never shook nor wavered,
but kept its elevation, faithful and firm throughout
life.

It is difficult to explain fully the great love of
Charles for his sister, except in his own words.
Whenever her name occurs in the correspondence,
the tone is always the same, always tender, without abatement, without change. " I am a fool " (he
writes) " bereft of her co-operation. I am used to
look up to her, in the least and biggest perplexities.
To say all that I find her, would be more than I
think anybody could possibly understand. She is
older, wiser, and better than I am; and all my
wretched imperfections I cover to myself, by resolutely thinking on her goodness. She would share
life and death with me." This (to anticipate) was
written in 1805, when she was suffering from one of
her attacks of illness. After she became better, he
became better also, and opened his heart to the
pleasures and objects around him. It was open at
all times to want and sickness and wretchedness;

and generally to the friendly voices and homely
realities that rose up and surrounded him in his
daily walk through life.

During all his years he was encircled by groups of
loving friends. There were no others habitually
round him. It is reported of some person that he
had not merit enough to create a foe. In Lamb's
case, I suppose, he did not possess that peculiar
merit: for he lived and died without an enemy.

CHAPTER III.

JEM WHITE—COLERIDGE—LAMB'S INSPIRATION—EARLY LETTERS—
POEM PUBLISHED—CHARLES LLOYD—LIKING FOR BURNS, &C.—
QUAKERISM—ROBERT SOUTHEY—SOUTHEY AND COLERIDGE—ANTI-
JACOBIN—ROSAMOND GRAY—GEORGE DYER—MANNING—MARY'S
ILLNESSES—MIGRATIONS—HESTER SAVORY.

AFTER the pain arising from the deaths of his parents
had somewhat subsided, and his sorrow, exhausting
itself in the usual manner, had given way to calm,
the story of Lamb becomes mainly an account of
his intercourse with society. He was surrounded,
during his somewhat monotonous career, by affectionate and admiring friends, who helped to bring
out his rare qualities,—who stimulated his genius,
and who are in fact interwoven with his own history. One of the earliest of these was his schoolfellow James (familiarly Jem) White. This youth,
who at the beginning of this period was his most
frequent companion, had great cleverness and abundant animal spirits, under the influence of which he
had produced a small volume, entitled, " Original

Letters of Sir John Falstaff and his Friends." These
letters were ingenious imitations of the style and
tone of thought of the celebrated Shakesperean
knight and his familiars. Beyond this merit they
are perhaps not sufficiently full of that enduring
matter which is intended for posterity. Nevertheless,
they contain some good and a few excellent things.
The letter of Davy (Justic Shallow's servant) giving
an account to his master of the death of poor Abram
Slender, is very touching. Slender dies from mere
love of sweet Ann Page ; " Master Abram is dead ;
gone your worship. A' sang his soul and body quite
away. A' turned like the latter end of a lover's
lute." White's book was published in 1796 ; and
one of the early copies was sold at the Roxburgh
sale for five guineas. Is it possible that the imitations could have been mistaken for originals ? Afterwards, the little book could be picked up for eighteen-
pence ; even for sixpence. It was always a great
favourite with Lamb. He reviewed it, after White's
death, in the *Examiner*. Lamb's friendship and
sympathy in taste with White, induced him to
attach greater value to this book than it was perhaps
strictly entitled to ; he even passes some commenda-
tion on the frontispiece ; which is undoubtedly a
very poor specimen of art. It is remarkable how
Lamb, who was able to enter so completely into
Hogarth's sterling humour, could ever have placed
any value upon this counterfeit coin.

But Lamb had a great regard for Jem White.
They had been boys together, schoolfellows in
Christ's Hospital, and these very early friendships
seldom undergo any severe critical tests. At all
events, Lamb thought highly of White's book, which

he used often to purchase and give away to his friends, in justification of his own taste and to extend the fame of the author. The copy which he gave me I have still. White, it seems, after leaving Christ's Hospital as a scholar, took some office there; but eventually left it, and became an agent for newspapers. In one of the Elia essays, "The praise of Chimney Sweepers," Lamb has set forth some of the merits of his old friend. Undoubtedly Jem White must have been a thoroughly kind-hearted man, since he could give a dinner every year, on St. Bartholomew's day, to the little chimney-sweepers of London; waiting on them, and cheering them up with his jokes and lively talk; creating at least one happy day annually in each of their poor lives. At the date of the essay (May, 1822) he had died. In Lamb's words, "James White is extinct; and with him the suppers have long ceased. He carried away with him half the fun of the world when he died— of my world at least. His old clients look for him among the pens; and, missing him, reproach the altered feast of St. Bartholomew, and the glory of Smithfield departed for ever.

The great friend and mentor, however, of Charles Lamb's youth, was (as has frequently been asserted) Samuel Taylor Coleridge, who was a philosopher, and who was considered, almost universally, to be the greater genius of the two. It may be so; and there is little doubt that, in mere capacity, in the power of accumulating and disbursing ideas; and in the extent and variety of his knowledge, he exceeded Lamb and also most of his other cotemporaries; but the mind of Lamb was quite as original, and more compact. The two friends were very dissimilar, the one wandering amongst lofty ill-defined objects; whilst the other "clung to the realities of life." It is fortunately not necessary to enter into any comparative estimate of these two remarkable persons. Each had his positive qualities and peculiarities, by which he was distinguishable from other men; and by these he may therefore be separately and more safely judged.

In his mature age (when I knew him) Coleridge had a full round face, a fine broad forehead, rather thick lips, and strange dreamy eyes; which were often lighted up by eagerness, but wanted concentration, and were adapted apparently for musing or speculation, rather than for precise, or rapid judgment. Yet he was very shrewd as well as eloquent; was (slightly) addicted to jesting; and would talk "at sight" upon any subject with extreme fluency and much knowledge. "His white hair," in Lamb's words, "shrouded a capacious brain." Coleridge had browsed and expatiated over all the rich regions of literature, at home and abroad. In youth, his studies had, in the first instance, been mainly in theology, he having selected the "Church" for his profession. Although he was educated in the creed and rites of the Church of England, he became for a time an Unitarian preacher, and scattered his eloquent words over many human audiences. He was fond of questions of logic, and of explaining his systems and opinions by means of diagrams; but his projects were seldom consummated; and his talk (sometimes) and his prose writing (often) were tedious and diffuse. His "Christabel," from which he derived much of his fame, remained, after a lapse of more than thirty years, incomplete at his death. He gained much reputation from the " Ancient Mariner," (which is perhaps his best poem,) but his translation of Schiller's " Wallenstein " is the only achievement that shows him capable of a great prolonged effort. Lamb used to boast that he supplied one line to his friend in the fourth scene of that tragedy, where the description of the Pagan deities occurs. In speaking of Saturn, he is figured as " an old man melancholy." " That was *my* line," Lamb would say, exultingly. I forget how it was originally written, except that it had not the extra (or eleventh) syllable, which it now possesses.

There is some beautiful writing in this fourth scene, which may be read after Mr. Wordsworth's equally beautiful reference to the Olympian gods and goddesses, in the fourth book of the " Excursion," entitled, " Despondency Corrected." The last explains more completely than the other the attributes of the deities specially named

The most elaborate (perhaps impartial) sketches of Coleridge—his great talents, combined with his great weaknesses—may be found in Hazlitt's Essays, " The Spirit of the Age " and " My First Acquaintance with Poets ;" and in the eighth chapter of Mr. Carlyle's " Life of John Sterling."

In Lamb's letters it is easy to perceive that the writer soon became aware of the foibles of his friend. " Cultivate simplicity, Coleridge," is his admonition as early as 1796. In another place his remark is, " You have been straining your faculties to bring together things infinitely distant and unlike." Again " I grieve from my very soul to observe you in your plans of life veering about from this hope to the other and settling nowhere." Robert Southey, whose prose

style was the perfection of neatness, and who was
intimate with Coleridge throughout his life, laments
that it is "extraordinary that he should write in so
rambling and inconclusive a manner;" his mind,
which was undoubtedly very pliable and subtle,
"turning and winding, till you get weary of following his mazy movements."

Charles Lamb, however, always sincerely admired
and loved his old schoolfellow, and grieved deeply
when he died.   The recollection of this event, which
happened many years afterwards, (in 1834,) never left
Lamb until his own death : he used perpetually to
exclaim, "Coleridge is dead, Coleridge is dead," in
a low, musing, meditative voice   These exclamations (addressed to no one) were, as Lamb was a
most unaffected man, assuredly involuntary, and
showed that he could not get rid of the melancholy
truth.   At this distance of time, many persons
(judging by what he has left behind him) wonder at
the extent of admiration which possessed some of
Coleridge's cotemporaries : Charles Lamb accorded
to his genius something scarcely short of absolute
worship :   Robert Southey considered his capacity
as exceeding that of almost all other writers ; and
Leigh Hunt, speaking of Coleridge's personal appearance, says " he had a mighty intellect put upon
a sensual body."   Persons who were intimate with
both have suggested that even Wordsworth was indebted to him for some of his philosophy.   As late as
1818 Lamb, when dedicating his works to him, says
that Coleridge " first kindled in him if not the power
the love of poetry and beauty and kindness."   He
must be judged, however, by what he has actually *done*.

I am not here as the valuer of Coleridge's merits.

I have no pretensions and no desire to assume so delicate an office His dreams and intentions were undoubtedly good, and, had he been able to carry them out for the benefit of the world, would have entitled himself to the name of a great poet, a great genius. His readiness to discuss *all* subjects, and his ability to talk on most of them with ease, were marvellous. But he was always infirm of purpose, and never did justice to his own capacity. Amongst other men of talent who have sung Coleridge's praises should be named Hazlitt, who knew him in 1798, and has enshrined him in the first of his charming papers, entitled " Winterslow Essays." Hazlitt admits his feebleness of purpose ; but speaks of his genius, shining upon his own (then) dumb inarticulate nature, as the sun " upon the puddles of the road." Coleridge at that time was an Unitarian minister, and had come to preach, instead of the minister for the time being, at Shrewsbury. Hazlitt rose before daylight (it was in January) and walked from Wem to Shrewsbury, a distance of ten miles, to hear the " celebrated " man, who combined the inspirations of poet and preacher in one person, enlighten a Shropshire congregation. " Never, the longest day I have to live " (says he,) " shall I have such another walk as this cold, raw, comfortless one, in the winter of 1798. When I got there [to the Chapel] the organ was playing the 100th Psalm, and when it was done, Mr. Coleridge rose and gave out his text,—' And he went up into the mountain to pray, HIMSELF ALONE.' The preacher then launched into his subject, like an eagle dallying with the wind," &c. Coleridge was at that time only five and twenty years of age , yet he seems even then to have

l   *D*

been able to decide on many writers in logic and rhetoric, philosophy and poetry. Of course, he was
familiar with the works of his friend Wordsworth ; of
whom he cleverly observed, in reply to the depre-
ciating opinion of Mackintosh, " He strides on so far
before you, that he dwindles in the distance."[1]

It would be very interesting, were it practicable, to
trace with certainty the sources that supplied Charles
Lamb's inspiration. But this must always be impossible. For inspiration, in all cases, proceeds from
many sources, although there may be one influence
predominating.   It is clear that a great Tragedy
mainly determined his conduct through life, and
operated therefore materially on his thoughts as well
as actions. The terrible death of his mother concentrated and strengthened his mind, and prevented
its dissipation into trifling and ignoble thoughts.
The regularity of the India House labour upheld him.
The extent and character of his acquaintance also
helped to determine the quality of the things which
he produced. Had he seen less, his mind might
have become warped and rigid, as from want of
space. Had he seen too much, his thoughts might
have been split and exhausted upon too many points,
—and would thus have been so perplexed and ha-
rassed, that the value of his productions now known
and current through all classes might scarcely have
exceeded a negative quantity. Then, in his companions he must be accounted fortunate. Coleridge
helped to unloose his mind from too precise notions :

---

[1] The most convincing evidence of Coleridge's powers is to be found
in his Table Talk. It appears from it that he was ready to discuss
(almost) any subject ; and that he was capable of talking ably upon
most, and cleverly upon all.

Southey gave it consistency and correctness : Manning expanded his vision : Hazlitt gave him daring : perhaps even poor George Dyer, like some unrecognised virtue, may have kept alive and nourished the pity and tenderness which were originally sown within him. We must leave the difficulty as we must leave the great problems of Nature, unexplained : and be content with what is self-evident before us. We know, at all events, that he had an open heart, and that the heart is a fountain which never fails.

The earliest productions of Lamb which have come down to us, namely, verses, and criticism, and letters, . are all in a grave and thoughtful tone. The letters, at first, are on melancholy subjects, but afterwards stray into criticism or into details of his readings, or account of his predilections for books and authors. At one or two and twenty he had read and formed an opinion on Shakespeare, on Beaumont and Fletcher, on Massinger, Milton, Cowley. Izaac Walton, Burns, Collins, and others ; some of these, be it observed, lying much out of the ordinary course of a young man's reading. 'He was also acquainted with the writings of Priestley and Wesley, and Jonathan Edwards ; for the first of whom he entertained the deepest respect.

Lamb's verses were always good, steady, and firm, and void of those magniloquent commonplaces which so clearly betray the immature writer. They were at no time misty or inconsequent ; but contained proof that he had reasoned out his idea. From the age of twenty-one to the age of fifty-nine, when he died. he hated fine words and flourishes of rhetoric. His imagination (not very lofty, perhaps) is to be discovered less in his verse than in his prose humour, than in his letters and essays. In these it was never trivial; but was always knit together by good sense, or softened by tenderness. Real humour seldom makes its appearance in the first literary ventures of young writers. Accordingly, symptoms of humour (which, nevertheless, were not long delayed) are not to be discovered in Charles Lamb's first letters or poems; the latter, when prepared for publication in 1796, being especially grave. They are entitled " Poems by Charles Lamb, of the India House," and are inscribed to " Mary Ann Lamb, the author's best friend and sister." After some procrastination, the book containing them was published in 1797, conjointly with other verses by Coleridge and Charles Lloyd. " We came into our first battle," (Charles says in his dedication to Coleridge, in 1818,) " under cover of the greater Ajax." In this volume, Lloyd's verses took precedence of Lamb's, at Coleridge's suggestion. This suggestion, the reason of which is not very obvious, was very readily acceded to; Lamb having a sincere regard for Lloyd, who (with a fine reasoning mind) was subject to that sad mental disease which was common to both their families. Lamb has addressed some verses to Lloyd at this date, which indicate the great respect he felt towards his friend's intellect :

> " I'll think less meanly of myself,
> That Lloyd will sometimes think of me."

This joint volume was published without much success. In the same year Lamb and his sister paid a visit to Coleridge, then living at Stowey, in Somersetshire; after which Coleridge, for what purpose does not very clearly appear, migrated to Germany. This happened in the year 1798.

Charles Lloyd, one of the triumvirate of 1797, was the son of a banker at Birmingham. He was educated as a Quaker, but seceded from that body, and afterwards became "perplexed in mind," and very desponding. He often took up his residence in London, but did not mingle much with society. An extreme melancholy darkened his latter days, and, as I believe, he died insane. He published various poems, and translated, from the Italian into English blank verse, the tragedies of Alfieri. His poems are distinguished rather by a remarkable power of intellectual analysis than by the delicacy or fervour of the verse.

The last time I saw Charles Lloyd was in company with Hazlitt. We heard that he had taken lodgings at a working brazier's shop in Fetter Lane, and we visited him there and found him in bed, much depressed, but very willing to discuss certain problems with Hazlitt, who carried on the greater part of the conversation. We understood that he had selected these noisy apartments, in order that they might distract his mind from the fears and melancholy thoughts which at that time distressed him.

It was soon after the publication of the joint volume that Charles chronicles the different tastes of himself and his friend. "Burns," he says, "is the god of my idolatry, as Bowles of yours." Posterity has universally joined in the preference of Lamb. Burns, indeed, was always one of his greatest favourites. He admired and sometimes quoted a line or two from the last stanza of the "Lament for James, Earl of Glencairn," "The bridegroom may forget his bride," &c., and I have more than once heard him repeat, in a fond tender voice, when the subject of poets or

2 K 2

poetry came under discussion, the following beautiful lines from the Epistle to Simpson of Ochiltree :

> " The Muse, nae poet ever fand her,
> Till by himsel he learn'd to wander,
> Adown some trotting burn's meander
> An' no think't lang."

These he would press upon the attention of any one present, (chaunting them aloud,) and would bring down the volume of Burns, and open it, in order that the page might be impressed upon the hearer's memory. Sometimes—in a way scarcely discernible— he would kiss the volume : as he would also a book by Chapman or Sir Philip Sidney, or any other which he particularly valued. I have seen him read out a passage from the Holy Dying and the Urn Burial, and express in the same way his devotion and gratitude.

Lamb had been brought up an Unitarian, but he appears to have been occasionally fluctuating in a matter as to which boys are not apt to entertain very rigid opinions. At one time he longed to be with superior thinkers. " I am always longing to be with men more excellent than myself," are his words. At another time he writes, " I have had thoughts of turning Quaker, lately." A visit, however, to one of the Quaker meetings in 1797, decides him against such conversion · " This cured me of Quakerism. I love it in the books of Penn and Woolmar; but I detest the vanity of man, thinking he speaks by the Spirit." A similar story is told of Coleridge. Mr. Justice Coleridge's statement is, " He told us a humorous story of his enthusiastic fondness for Quakers, when at Cambridge, and his attending one of their meetings, which had entirely cured him."

In 1797 Charles Lamb (who had been introduced to Southey by Coleridge two years previously) accompanied Lloyd to a little village near Christchurch in Hampshire, where Southey was at that time reading. This little holiday (of a fortnight) seems to have converted the acquaintanceship between Southey and Lamb into something like intimacy. He then paid another visit (which he had long meditated) to Coleridge, who was residing at Stowey. It must have been shortly after this first visit, (for Lamb went again to Stowey, and met Wordsworth there in 1801,) that Coleridge undertook the office of minister to an Unitarian congregation at Shrewsbury, and preached there, as detailed by Hazlitt in the manner already set forth. In 1798 he took his departure for Germany, and this led to a familiar correspondence between Lamb and Southey. The opening of Lamb's humour may probably be referred to this friendship with a congenial humorist, and one like himself, taking a strong interest in worldly matters. Coleridge, between whom and Lamb there was not much similarity of feeling, beyond their common love for poetry and religious writings, was absent, and Lamb was enticed by the kindred spirit of Southey into the accessible regions of humour. These two friends never arrived at that close friendship which had been forming between Coleridge and Lamb ever since their school-days at Christ's Hospital. But they interchanged ideas on poetical and humorous topics, and did not perplex themselves with anything speculative or transcendental. The first letter to Southey, which has been preserved, (July, 1798,) announces that Lamb is ready to enter into any jocose contest. It includes a list of queries to be defended by Coleridge at Leipsic or

Gottingen; the first of which was " Whether God loves a lying angel better than a true man ?" Some of these queries, in all probability, had relation to Coleridge's own infirmities: at all events, they were sent over to him in reply to the benediction which he had thought proper to bequeath to Charles on leaving England " Poor Lamb, if he wants *any knowledge* he may apply to *me*." I must believe that this message was jocose, otherwise it would have been insolent in the extreme degree. Coleridge's answers to the queries above adverted to are not known; I believe that the proffered knowledge was not afforded so readily as it was demanded.—It has been surmised that there was some interruption of the good feeling between Coleridge and Lamb about this period of their lives; but I cannot discern this in the letters that occurred between the two schoolfellows. The message of Coleridge, and the questions in reply, occur in 1798; and in May, 1800, there is a letter from Lamb to Coleridge, and subsequently two others, in the same year, all couched in the old customary, friendly tone. In addition to this, Charles Lamb, many years afterwards, said that there had been an uninterrupted friendship of fifty years between them. In one letter of Lamb's, indeed, (17th March, 1800,) it appears that his early notions of Coleridge being a "very good man" had been traversed by some doubts; but these " foolish impressions" were shortlived, and did not apparently form any check to the continuance of their lifelong friendship.

It is clear that Lamb's judgment was at this time becoming independent. In one of his letters to Coleridge, when comparing his friend's merits with those of Southey, he says, " Southey has no pretensions to

vie with you in the sublime of poetry, but he tells a
plain story better." Even to Southey he is equally
candid. Writing to him on the subject of a volume
of poems which he had lately published, he remarks,
"The Rose is the only insipid poem in the volume ;
it has neither thorns nor sweetness."

In 1798 or 1799, Lamb contributed to the Annual
Anthology, (which Mr. Cottle, a bookseller of Bristol,
published,) jointly with Coleridge and Southey. In 1800
he was introduced by Coleridge, to Godwin. It is clear
that Charles's intimacy with Coleridge and Southey,
and Lloyd, was not productive of unmitigated pleasure. For the " Antijacobin " made its appearance
about this time, and denounced them all in a manner
which in the present day would itself be denounced
as infamous. Some of these gentlemen, (Lamb's
friends,) in common with many others, argued at
first favourably of the actors in the great French
Revolution, and this had excited much displeasure
in the Tory ranks. Accordingly they were represented as being guilty of blasphemy and slander, and
as being adorers of a certain French revolutionist,
named Lepaux ; of whom Lamb at all events was
entirely ignorant. They were, moreover, the subject
of a caricature by Gilray, in which Lamb and Lloyd
were portrayed as toad and frog. I cannot think
with Sir T. Talfourd, that all these libels were ex-
cusable, on the ground of the " sportive wit " of the
offending parties. Lamb's writings had no reference
whatever to political subjects . they were, on the
contrary, as the first writings of a young man generally are, serious,—even religious. Referring to
Coleridge, it is stated that he " was dishonoured at
Cambridge for preaching Deism, and that he had

l   )

since left his native country, and left his poor children fatherless, and his wife destitute :" *ex his disce
his friends Lamb and Southey*.   A scurrilous libel of
this stamp would now be rejected by all persons of
good feeling or good character.   It would be spurned
by a decent publication, or if published would be consigned to the justice of a jury.

The little story of Rosamond Gray was wrought
out of the artist's brain in the year 1798, stimulated,
as Lamb confesses, by the old ballad of "An old
woman clothed in gray," which he had been reading.
It is defective as a regular tale.   It wants circumstance and probability, and is slenderly provided with
character.   There is moreover no construction in the
narrative, and little or no progress in the events.
Yet it is very daintily told.   The mind of the author
wells out in the purest streams.   Having to deal with
one foul incident, the tale is nevertheless without
speck or blemish.   A virgin nymph, born of a lily,
could not have unfolded her thoughts more delicately.
And, in spite of its improbability, Rosamond Gray is
very pathetic.   It touches the sensitive points in
young hearts; and it was by no means without success; the author's first success.   It sold much better
than his poems, and added "a few pounds" to his
slender income.

George Dyer, once a pupil in Christ's Hospital,
possessing a good reputation as a classical scholar,
and who had preceded Lamb in the school, about
this time came into the circle of his familiars.   Dyer
was one of the simplest and most inoffensive men in
the world; in his heart there existed nothing but
what was altogether pure and unsophisticated.   He
seemed never to have outgrown the innocence of

childhood ; or rather he appeared to be without those germs or first principles of evil which sometimes begin to show themselves even in childhood itself. He was not only without any of the dark passions himself, but he would not perceive them in others. He looked only on the sunshine. Hazlitt, speaking of him in his " Conversation of Authors," says, " He lives amongst the old authors, if he does not enter much into their spirit. He handles the covers, and turns over the pages, and is familiar with the names and dates. He is busy and self-involved. He hangs like a film and cobweb upon letters, or is like the dust upon the outside of knowledge, which should not too rudely be brushed aside. He follows learning as its shadow, but as such he is respectable. He browses on the husks and leaves of books." And Lamb says, " The Gods, by denying him the very faculty of discrimination, have effectually cut off every seed of envy in his bosom."

Dyer was very thin and short in person, and was extremely near-sighted ; and his motions were often (apparently) spasmodic. His means of living were very scanty, he subsisted mainly by supervising the press, being employed for that purpose by booksellers when they were printing Greek or Latin books. He dwelt in Clifford's Inn, " like a dove in an asp's nest," as Charles Lamb wittily says ; and he might often have been seen with a classical volume in his hand, and another in his pocket, walking slowly along Fleet Street or its neighbourhood, unconscious of gazers ; cogitating over some sentence, the correctness of which it was his duty to determine. You might meet him murmuring to himself in a low voice, and apparently tasting the flavour of the words.

Dyer's knowledge of the drama (which formed part
of the subject of his first publication) may be guessed,
by his having read Shakespeare, " an irregular genius," and having dipped into Rowe and Otway; but
never having heard of any other writers in that class.
In absence of mind, he probably exceeded every other
living man. Lamb has set forth one instance (which
I know to be a fact) of Dyer's forgetfulness, in his
" Oxford in the Vacation ;" and to this various others
might be added, such as his emptying his snuff-box
into the teapot when he was preparing breakfast for
a hungry friend, &c. But it is scarcely worth while
to chronicle minutely the harmless foibles of this inoffensive old man. If I had to write his epitaph I
should say that he was neither much respected nor at
all hated ; too good to dislike, too inactive to excite
great affection ; and that he was as simple as the
daisy, which we think we admire, and daily tread
under foot.

In 1799 Charles Lamb visited Cambridge, and
there, through the introduction of Lloyd, made the
important acquaintance of Mr. Thomas Manning,
then a mathematical tutor in the university. This
soon grew into a close intimacy. Charles readily perceived the intellectual value of Manning ; and seems
to have eagerly sought his friendship, which, he says,
(December, 1799,) will render the prospect of the
approaching century very pleasant. " That century
must needs commence auspiciously for me " (he
adds) " that brings with it Manning's friendship as
an earnest of its after gifts." At first sight it appears
strange that there should be formed a close friendship
between a youth, a beginner or student in poetry (no
more) and a professor of science at one of our great

seats of learning. But these men had, I suppose, an
intuitive perception of each other's excellences. And
there sometimes lie behind the outer projections of
character a thousand concealed shades which readily
intermingle with those of other people. There were
amongst Lamb's tender thoughts, and Manning's
mathematical tendencies, certain neutral qualities
which assimilated with each other, and which
eventually served to cement that union between them
which continued unshaken during the lives of both.
Lamb's correspondence assumed more character, and
showed more critical quality, after the intimacy with
Manning began. His acquaintance with Southey, in
the first instance, had the effect of increasing the
activity of his mind. Previously to that time, his
letters had consisted chiefly of witticisms, (clever,
indeed, but not of surpassing quality,) religious
thoughts, reminiscences, &c., for the most part un-
adorned and simple. Afterwards, especially after the
Manning era. they exhibit far greater weight of
meaning, more fecundity, original thoughts, and
brilliant allusions; as if the imagination had begun
to awaken and enrich the understanding. Manning's
solid, scientific mind had, without doubt, the effect of
arousing the sleeping vigour of Lamb's intellect,

A long correspondence took place between them.
At first Lamb sent Manning his opinions only;
"opinion is a species of property that I am always
desirous of sharing with my friends." Then he com-
municates the fact that George Dyer, "that good-
natured poet, is now more than nine months gone
with twin volumes of odes." Afterwards he tells him
that he is reading Burnet's history of his own times;
"full of scandal, as all true history is." On Man-

ning quitting England for China, (1806,) the letters
become less frequent ; they continue, however, during
his absence ; one of them, surpassing the Elia essay,
to " Distant Correspondents," is very remarkable ;
and when the Chinese traveller returned to London,
he was very often a guest at Lamb's residence. I
have repeatedly met him there. His countenance
was that of an intelligent, steady, almost serious
man. His journey to the celestial empire had not
been unfruitful of good ; his talk at all times being
full of curious information, including much anecdote, and some (not common) speculations on men
and things. When he returned, he brought with him
a native of China, whom he took one evening to a
ball in London ; where the foreigner from Shanghai, or
Pekin, inquired with much *naïveté* as to the amount
of money which his host had given to the dancers for
their evening's performance, and was persuaded with
difficulty that their exertions were entirely gratui-
tous. Manning had a curious habit of bringing with
him (in his waistcoat pocket) some pods of the red
pepper, whenever he expected to partake of a meal.
His original intention (as I understood) when he set
out for China, was to frame and publish a Chinese
and English dictionary ; yet—although he brought
over much material for the purpose—his purpose was
never carried into effect. Lamb had great love and
admiration for him. In a letter to Coleridge, in after
years (1826), he says, " I am glad you esteem Manning ; though you see but his husk or shrine. He
discloses not, save to select worshippers ; and will
leave the world without any one hardly but me knowing how stupendous a creature he is."

During these years Lamb's correspondence with

Coleridge, Wordsworth, Walter Wilson, and Manning (principally with Manning) goes on. It is sometimes critical, sometime jocose. He discusses the merits of various authors, and more than once expresses his extreme distate for didactic writing. Now, he says, it is too directly instructive. Then he complains that the knowledge, insignificant and vapid as it is, must come in the *shape* of knowledge. He could not obtain at Newberry's shop any of the old "classics of the Nursery," he says; whilst "Mrs. Barbauld's and Mrs. Trimmer's nonsense lay in piles about."—His own domestic affairs struggle on as usual; at one time calm and pleasant: at another time troubled and uncomfortable; owing to the frequent recurrence of his sister's malady. In general he bore these changes with fortitude; I do not observe more than one occasion on which (being then himself ill) his firmness seemed altogether to give way. In 1798, indeed, he had said, "I consider her perpetually on the brink of madness." But in May, 1800, his old servant Hetty having died, and Mary, (sooner than usual) falling ill again, Charles was obliged to remove her to an asylum; and was left in the house alone with Hetty's dead body. "My heart is quite sick," (he cries,) "and I don't know where to look for relief. My head is very bad. I almost wish that Mary were dead." This was the one solitary cry of anguish that he uttered, during his long years of anxiety and suffering. At all other times he bowed his head in silence, uncomplaining.

Charles Lamb, with his sister, left Little Queen Street, on or before 1800; in which year he seems to have migrated, first to Chapel Street, Pentonville; next to Southampton Buildings, Chancery Lane: and finally to No. 16, Mitre Court Buildings, in the Temple, " a pistol shot off Baron Masere's ; " and here he resided for about nine years.

It was during his stay at Pentonville that he " fell in love," with a young Quaker, called Hester Savory As (he confesses) " I have never spoken to her during my life," it may be safely concluded that the attachment was essentially Platonic. This was the young girl who inspired those verses, now so widely known and admired. I remember them as being the first lines which I ever saw of Charles Lamb's writing. I remember and admire them still ; for their natural unaffected style ; no pretence, no straining for images and fancies, flying too high above the subject ; but dealing with thoughts that were near his affections, in a fit and natural manner. The conclusion of the poem, composed and sent after her death (in February, 1803) to Manning, who was then in Paris, is very sad and tender :—

" My sprightly neighbour, gone before
    To that unknown and silent shore,
    Shall we not meet, as heretofore,
        Some summer morning ?

" When from thy cheerful eyes a ray
    Hath struck a bliss upon the day,
    A bliss that will not go away.
        A sweet forewarning."

CHAPTER IV.

(MIGRATIONS)—"JOHN WOODVIL"—BLACKESMOOR—WORDSWORTH—
RICKMAN—GODWIN—VISIT TO THE LAKES—MORNING POST—
HAZLITT—NELSON—ODE TO TOBACCO—DRAMATIC SPECIMENS, &C.
—INNER TEMPLE LANE—REFLECTOR—HOGARTH AND SIR J. REY-
NOLDS—LEIGH HUNT—LAMB, HAZLITT, AND HUNT—RUSSELL STREET
AND THEATRICAL FRIENDS

IT is not always easy to fix Charles Lamb's doings
(writings or migrations) to any precise date. The
year may generally be ascertained; but the day or
month is often a matter of surmise only. Even the
dates of the letters are often derived from the post-
marks, or are sometimes conjectured from circumstances.[1] Occasionally the labours of a drama or
of lyric poems traverse several years, and are not to
be referred to any one definite period. Thus "John
Woodvil" (his tragedy) was begun in 1799, printed
in 1800, and submitted to Mr. Kemble (then manager

---

[1] As Lamb's changes of residence were frequent, it may be convenient to chronicle them in order, in this place, although the precise
date of his moving from one to another, can scarcely be specified
in a single instance. 1775, Charles Lamb, born in Crown Office Row,
Temple. 1795, lives at No, 7, Little Queen Street, Holborn. 1800,
(early,) lives at No 45, Chapel Street, Pentonville. Same year, lives
in Sonthampton Buildings, Chancery Lane. Same year, removes to
No. 16, Mitre Court Buildings, Temple. 1809, removes to No 4,
Inner Temple Lane. 1817, removes to Russell Street, Covent Garden.
1823, removes to Colebrook Row, Islington. 1826, removes to Enfield
1829, removes into lodgings in Enfield. 1830, lodges in Southampton
Buildings. 1833, lives at Mrs. Walden's, in Church Street, Edmon
ton; where he dies on the 27th December, 1834.

L

of Drury Lane Theatre) in the Christmas of that
year , but was not published until 1801.

After this tragedy had been in Mr. Kemble's hands
for about a year, Lamb naturally became urgent to
hear his decision upon it.   Upon appyling for this,
he found that his play was—lost !   This was at once
acknowledged, and a "courteous request made for
another copy, if I had one by me."   Luckily, another
copy existed.   The "first runnings" of a genius
were not, therefore, altogether lost, by having been
cast, without a care, into the dusty limbo of the theatre.
The other copy was at once supplied, and the play
very speedily rejected.   It was afterwards facetiously
brought forward in one of the early numbers of the
Edinburgh Review, and there noticed as a rude specimen of the earliest age of the drama, "older than
Æschylus !"   Lamb met these accidents of fortune
manfully, and did not abstain from exercising his
own Shandean humour thereon.   It must be confessed that "John Woodvil" is not a tragedy likely
to bring much success to a playhouse.   It is such a
drama as a young poet, full of love for the Eliza-
bethan writers, and without any knowledge of the
requisitions of the stage, would be likely to produce.
There is no plot ; little probability in the story ;
which itself is not very scientifically developed.
There are some pretty lines, especially some which
have often been the subject of quotation ; but there
is not much merit in the characters of the drama,
with the exception of the heroine, who is a heroine
of the " purest water."   Lamb's friend, Southey, in
writing to a correspondent pronounces the following
opinion.   " Lamb is printing his play, which will
please you by the exquisite beauty of its poetry,

and provoke you by the exquisite silliness of its story."

In October, 1799, Lamb went to see the remains of the old house (Gilston) in Hertfordshire, where his grandmother once lived, and the " old church where the bones of my honoured granddame lie." This visit was, in later years, recorded in the charming paper entitled " Blackesmoor in H———shire." He found that the house where he had spent his pleasant holidays, when a little boy, had been demolished ; it was, in fact, taken down for the purpose of reconstruction ; but out of the ruins he conjures up pleasant ghosts, whom he restores and brings before a younger generation. There are few of his papers in which the past years of his life are more delightfully revived. The house had been " reduced to an antiquity." But we go with him to the grass plat, where he used to read Cowley , to the tapestried bedrooms where the mythological people of Ovid used to stand forth, half alive ; even to " that haunted bedroom in which old Sarah Battle died," and into which he " used to creep in a passion of fear." These things are all touched with a delicate pen ; mixed and incorporated with tender reflections ; for " The solitude of childhood " (as he says) " is not so much the mother of thought as the feeder of love." With him it was both.

Lamb became acquainted with Wordsworth when he visited Coleridge, in the summer of 1800. At that time his old schoolfellow lived at Stowey, and the greater poet was his neighbour. It is not satisfactorily shown in what manner the poetry of Wordsworth first attracted the notice of Charles Lamb, nor its first effect upon him. Perhaps the verse of Coleridge was not a bad stepping-stone to that elevation which enabled Charles to look into the interior of Wordsworth's mind   The two poets were not unlike in some respects ; although Coleridge seldom (except perhaps in the " Ancient Mariner") ventured into the plain downright phraseology of the other.   It is very soon apparent, however, that Lamb was able to admit Wordsworth's great merits.   In August, 1800, (just after the completion of his visit to Stowey,) he writes, " I would pay five and forty thousand carriages," (parcel fares,) " to read Wordsworth's tragedy.   Pray give me an order on Longman for the ' Lyrical Ballads.' "   And in October, 1800, the two authors must have been on familiar terms with each other; for in a letter addressed by Lamb to Wordsworth, " Dear Wordsworth," it appears that the latter had requested him to advance money for the purchase of books, to a considerable amount.   This was at a time when Lamb was " not plethorically abounding in cash." The books required an outlay of eight pounds, and Lamb had not the sum then in his possession.   " It is a scurvy thing" (he writes) " to cry give me the money first ; and I am the first of the Lambs that has done this for many centuries."   Shortly afterwards Lamb sent his play to Wordsworth, who (this was previous to 30th January, 1861,) appears to have invited Charles to visit him in Cumberland.   Our humorist did not accept this invitation, being doubtful whether he could "afford so desperate a journey," "and being" (he says) " not at all romance-bit about Nature ;" the earth and sea and sky being, " when all is said, but a house to live in."

It is not part of my task to adjust the claims of the various writers of verse in this country to their stations in the Temple of Fame.   If Keats was by nature the most essentially a poet in the present century, there is little doubt that Wordsworth has left his impress more broadly and more permanently than any other of our later writers upon the literature of England.   There are barren, unpeopled wastes in the " Excursion," and in some of the longer poems ; but when his Genius stirs, we find ourselves in rich places which have no parallel in any book since the death of Milton.   When his lyrical ballads first appeared, they encountered much opposition and some contempt. Readers had not for many years been accustomed to drink the waters of Helicon pure and undefiled ; and Wordsworth (a prophet of the true faith) had to gird up his loins, march into the desert, and prepare for battle.   He has, indeed, at last achieved a conquest , but a long course of time, although sure of eventual success, elapsed before he could boast of victory. The battle has been perilous.   When the " Excursion" was published (in 1814) Lamb wrote a review of it for " The Quarterly Review."   Whatever might have been the actual fitness of this performance, it seems to have been hacked to pieces ; more than a third of the substance cut away; the warm expressions converted into cold ones ; and (in Lamb's phrase) " the eyes pulled out and the bleeding sockets left." This mangling (or amendment, as I suppose it was considered) was the work of the late Mr. Gifford. Charles had a great admiration for Wordsworth.   It was short of prostration, however.   He states that the style of " Peter Bell " does not satisfy him : but " ' Hartleap Well ' is the tale for me," are his words in 1819.

I have a vivid recollection of Wordsworth, who was a very grave man, with strong features and a deep

L   D

voice.   I met him first at the chambers (they were in
the Temple) of Mr. Henry Crabb Robinson, one of
the most amiable of men.   I was a young versifier,
and Wordsworth was just emerging out of a cloud of
ignorant contumely into the sunrise of his fame.   He
was fond (perhaps too fond) of reciting his own poetry
before friends and strangers.   I was not attracted by
his manner. which was almost too solemn, but I was
deeply impressed by some of the weighty notes in his
voice, when he was delivering out his oracles.   I
forget whether it was " Dion " or the beautiful poem
of " Laodamia " that he read ; but I remembered the
reading long afterwards, as one recollects the roll of
the spent thunder.

I   met Wordsworth occasionally afterwards, at
Charles Lamb's, at Mr. Rogers's, and elsewhere, and
once he did me the honour to call upon me.   I remember that he had a very gentle aspect when he
looked at my children.   He took the hand of my dear
daughter (who died lately) in his hand, and spoke
some words to her, the recollection of which, perhaps, helped, with other things, to incline her to
poetry.   Hazlitt says that Wordsworth's face, notwithstanding his constitutional gravity, sometimes
revealed indications of dry humour.   And once, at a
morning visit, I heard him give an account of his
having breakfasted in company with Coleridge, and
allowed him to expatiate to the extent of his lungs.
" How could you permit him to go on and weary himself?" said Rogers ; " why, you are to meet him at
dinner this evening."   " Yes," replied Wordsworth ;
" I know that very well ; but we like to take the *sting*
out of him beforehand."

About a year after Lamb's first knowledge of Man-

L   *D*

ning, his small stock of friends was enlarged by the
acquisition of Mr. John Rickman, one of the clerks of
the House of Commons. "He is a most pleasant
hand" (writes Lamb), "a fine rattling fellow, who
has gone through life laughing at solemn apes; himself hugely literate, from matter of fact, to Xenophon
and Plato : he can talk Greek with Porson, and nonsense with me." "He understands you" (he adds)
"the first time. You never need speak twice to him.
Fullest of matter, with least verbosity." A year or
two afterwards, when Rickman went to Ireland, Lamb
wrote to Manning .—" I have lost by his going what
seems to me I never can recover,—*a finished man.* I
almost dare pronounce you never saw his equal His
memory will come to me as the brazen serpent to the
Israelites." Robert Southey also, when writing to
his brother, (in 1804,) says :—" Coleridge and Rickman, with William Taylor, make my Trinity of living
greatness." A voluminous correspondence took place
between Southey and Rickman, ranging from 1800 to
1839, in the course of which a variety of important
subjects—namely, History, Antiquities, Political Economy, Poor Law, and general Politics, were delibe-
rately argued between them. From this it appears
that Southey, whose reading was very extensive, must
have had great trust in the knowledge and judgment
of Rickman.

Lamb s acquaintance with Godwin, Holcroft, and
Clarkson, was formed about this time. Godwin had
been introduced to Lamb by Coleridge, in 1800. The
first interview is made memorable by Godwin's opening question · "And pray, Mr Lamb, are you toad
or frog?" This inquiry, having reference to Gilray's
offensive caricature, did not afford promise of a very

cheerful intimacy. Lamb, however, who accorded
great respect to Godwin's intellect, did not resent it;
but received his approaches favourably, and, indeed,
entertained him at breakfast the next morning. The
acquaintance afterwards expanded into familiarity:
but I never observed the appearance of any warm
friendship between them. Godwin's precision and extreme coldness of manner (perhaps of disposition)
prevented this, and Lamb was able, through all his
admiration of the other's power, to discern those
points in his character, which were obnoxious to his
own. Some years previously, Charles had entertained much dislike to the philosopher's opinions,
and referred to him as "that Godwin," and afterwards, when eulogising the quick and fine intellect
of Rickman, he says, "He does not want explanation, translations, limitations, as Godwin does, when
you make an assertion." When Godwin published
his "Essay on Sepulchres," wherein he professed to
erect a wooden slab and a white cross, to be *perpetually* renewed to the end of time, ("to survive the
fall of empires," as Miss Lamb says,) in order to
distinguish the site of every great man's grave,
Lamb speaks of the project in these terms: "Godwin has written a pretty absurd book about Sepulchres. He was affronted, because I told him that it
was better than Hervey, but not so good as Sir
Thomas Browne." Sufficient intimacy, however,
had arisen between them to induce Lamb to write a
facetious epilogue to Godwin's tragedy of Antonio;
or, the Soldier's Return." This came out in 1800,
and was very speedily damned; although Lamb said
that "it had one fine line:" which indeed he repeated
occasionally. Godwin bore this failure, it must be

admitted, without being depressed by it, although he was a very poor man, and although he was "£500 *ideal* money out of pocket by the failure."

In 1802, Lamb visited Coleridge, who was then living near Keswick, in Cumberland. For the first time in his life, he beheld lakes and mountains; and the effect upon him was startling and unexpected. It was much like the impression made by the first sight of the Alps upon Leigh Hunt, who had theretofore always maintained that those merely great heaps of earth ought to have no effect upon a properly constituted mind; but he freely confesses afterwards, that he had been mistaken. Lamb had been more than once invited to visit the romantic Lake country. He had no desire to inspect the Ural chain, where the malachite is hidden, nor the silver regions of Potosi, but he was all at once affected by a desire of "visiting remote regions." It was a sudden irritability, which could only be quieted by travel. Charles and his sister therefore went, without giving any notice to Coleridge, who, however, received them very kindly, and gave up all his time in order to show them the wonders of the neighbourhood. The visitors arrived there in a "gorgeous sunset," (the only one that Lamb saw during his stay in the country,) and thought that they had got "into fairy land." "We entered Coleridge's study," (he writes to Manning, shortly afterwards,) "just in the dusk, when the mountains were all dark. Such an impression I never received from objects of sight, nor do I suppose I ever can again. Glorious creatures, Skiddaw, &c. I shall never forget how ye lay about that night, like an entrenchment, gone to bed, as it seemed, for the night."

They went to Coleridge's House, in which " he had a large antique, ill-shaped room, with an old organ, never played upon, an Eolian harp, and shelves of scattered folios," and remained there three weeks, visiting Wordsworth's Cottage, he himself being absent, and meeting the Clarksons (" good, hospitable people "). They tarried there one night, and met Lloyd. They clambered up to the top of Skiddaw, " and went to Grassmere, Ambleside, Ullswater, and over the middle of Helvellyn." Coleridge then dwelt upon a small hill by the side of Keswick, quite " enveloped on all sides by a net of mountains." On his return to London, Lamb wrote to his late host, saying, " I feel I shall remember your mountains to the last day of my life. They haunt me perpetually. I am like a man who has been falling in love unknown to himself, which he finds out when he leaves the lady." He soon subsided, however, into his old natural metropolitan happiness.

Wordsworth was not in the Lake country when Lamb visited Coleridge, but after his return the great poet visited Charles in London, passed some time there; and then departed for Yorkshire, where he went in order to be married.

At this time Lamb contributed (generally facetiæ) to various newspapers, now forgotten. One of them, it was said jocosely, had " two and twenty readers; including the printer, the pressmen, and the devil." But he was still very poor, so poor that Coleridge offered to supply him with prose translations from the German, in order that he might versify them for the " Morning Post," and thus obtain a little money. In one of his letters Lamb says : " If I got or could but get £50 a year only, in addition to what I have, I should live in affluence."

About the time that he is writing this, he is recommending Chapman's "Homer" to Coleridge; is refusing to admit Coleridge's *bonâ fide* debt to himself of £15; is composing Latin letters; and in other respects deporting himself like a "gentleman who lives at home at ease;" not like a poor clerk, obliged to husband his small means, and to deny himself the cheap luxury of books that he had long coveted. "Do you remember," (his sister says to him, in the Essay on "Old China,") "the brown suit that grew so threadbare, all because of that folio of Beaumont and Fletcher that you dragged home late at night from Barker's, in Covent Garden;" "when you set off near ten o'clock, on Saturday night, from Islington, fearing you should be too late; and when you lugged it home, wishing it was twice as cumbersome," &c.

These realities of poverty, very imperfectly covered over by words of fiction, are very touching. It is deeply interesting, that Essay, where the rare enjoyments of a poor scholar are brought into contrast and relief with the indifference that grows upon him when his increased income enables him to acquire any objects he pleases Those things are no longer distinguished as "enjoyments" which are not purchased by a sacrifice. "A purchase is but a purchase now. Formerly it used to be a triumph. A thing was worth buying, when we felt the money that we paid for it."

(1804) The intimacy of that extraordinary man, William Hazlitt, was the great gain of Lamb at this period of his life. If Lamb's youngest and tenderest

reverence was given to Coleridge, Hazlitt's intellect must also have commanded his later permanent respect. Without the imagination and extreme
facility of Coleridge, he had almost as much subtlety
and far more stedfastness of mind. Perhaps this
stedfastness remained sometimes until it took the
colour of obstinacy; but, as in the case of his constancy to the first Napoleon, it was obstinacy riveted
and made firm by some concurring respect. I do
not know that Hazlitt had the more affectionate
nature of the two; but assuredly he was less tossed
about and his sight less obscured by floating fancies
and vast changing projects (*muscæ volitantes*) than
the other. To the one is ascribed fierce and envious
passions : coarse thoughts and habits—(he has indeed been crowned by defamation;) whilst to Coleridge has been awarded reputation and glory, and
praise from a thousand tongues. To secure justice
we must wait for unbiassed posterity.

I meet, at present, with few persons who recollect
much of Hazlitt. Some profess to have heard
nothing of him, except his prejudices and violence;
but his prejudices were few, and his violence, (if
violence he had,) was of very rare occurrence. He
was extremely patient, indeed, although earnest when
discussing points in politics, respecting which he held
very strong and decided opinions. But he circulated
his thoughts on many other subjects, whereon he
ought not to have excited offence or opposition. He
wrote (and he wrote well) upon many things lying
far beyond the limits of politics. To use his own
words, "I have at least glanced over a number of
subjects; painting, poetry, prose, plays, politics, par-
liamentary speakers, metaphysical lore, books, men,

and things." This list, extensive as it is, does not specify very precisely all the subjects on which he wrote. His thoughts range over the literature of Elizabeth and James's times, and of the time of Charles II.; over a large portion of modern literature; over the distinguishing character of men, their peculiarities of mind and manners, over the wonders of poetry, the subtleties of metaphysics, and the luminous regions of art. In painting, his criticisms (it is prettily said, by Leigh Hunt) cast a light upon the subject, like the glory reflected " from a painted window." I myself have, in my library, eighteen volumes of Hazlitt's works, and I do not possess all that he published. Besides being an original thinker, Hazlitt excelled in conversation. He was, moreover, a very temperate liver: yet his enemies proclaimed to the world that he was wanting even in sobriety. During the thirteen years that I knew him intimately, and (at certain seasons) saw him almost every day, I know that he drank nothing stronger than water; except tea, indeed, in which he indulged in the morning. Had he been as temperate in his political views as in his cups, he would have escaped the slander that pursued him through life.

The great intimacy between these two distinguished writers, Charles Lamb and William Hazlitt, (for they had known each other before,) seems to have commenced in a singular manner. They were one day at Godwin's, when " a fierce dispute was going on between Holcroft and Coleridge, as to which was best, ' Man as he was, or Man as he is to be.' 'Give me,' says Lamb, ' man as he is *not* to be.' " " This was the beginning " (Hazlitt says) " of a friendship which, I believe, still continues." Hazlitt married

in 1805, and his wife soon became familiar with Mary
Lamb.   Indeed, Charles and his sister more than
once visited the Hazlitts, who at that time lived at
Winterslow, near Salisbury Plain , and enjoyed their
visits greatly, walking from eight to twenty miles a
day, and seeing Wilton, Stonehenge, and the other
(to them unaccustomed) sights of the country "The
quiet, lazy, delicious month" passed there, is referred
to, in one of Miss Lamb's pleasant letters.   And the
acquaintance soon deepened into friendship.   Whatever goodwill was exhibited by Hazlitt (and there
was much) is repaid by Lamb in his letter to Southey,
published in the *London Magazine*, (October, 1823,)
wherein he places on record his pride and admiration
of his friend.   "So far from being ashamed of the
intimacy," (he says,) "it is my boast that I was
able, for so many years, to have preserved it entire ;
and I think I shall go to my grave without finding or
expecting to find such another companion."

Lamb's respect for men and things did not depend
on repute. His fondness for old books seldom (never,
perhaps, except in the single case of the Duchess of
Newcastle,) deluded him into a respect for old books
which were without merit.   He required that excellence should be combined with antiquity.   A great
name was generally to him simply a great name . no
more.   If it had lasted through centuries, indeed, as
in the case of Michael Angelo, then he admitted
that "a great name implied greatness."   He did not
think that greatness lay in the "thews and sinews,"
or in the bulk alone.   When Nelson was walking on
the quay at Yarmouth, the mob cried out in derision,
"What! make that little fellow a captain!"   Lamb
thought otherwise ; and in regret for the death of

that great seaman, he says, "I have followed him
ever since I saw him walking in Pall Mall, *looking
just as a hero should look* , " (*i. e.* simply). "He was
the only pretence of a great man we had." The
large stage blusterer and ostentatious drawcansir
were never, in Lamb's estimation, models for heroes.
In the case of the first Napoleon also, he writes :—
"He is a fine fellow, as my barber says ; and I should
not mind standing bareheaded at his table to do him
service in his fall." This was in August, 1815.

The famous "Ode to Tobacco" was written in
1805 ; and the pretty stories founded on the plays of
Shakespeare, were composed or translated about the
year 1806 ; Lamb taking the tragic, and his sister
the other share of the version. These tales were to
produce about £60 ; to them a sum which was most
important, for he and Mary at that time hailed the
addition of £20 to his salary, (on the retirement of
an elder clerk) as a grand addition to their comforts.

Charles was at this period (February, 1806) at
work upon a farce, to be called " Mr. H. ; " for which
he says, "if it has a 'good run,' I shall get £200,
and I hope £100 for the copyright." "Mr. H."
(which rested solely upon the absurdity of a name,
which after all was not irresistibly absurd) was
accepted at the theatre, but unfortunately it had *not*
'a good run.' It failed, not quite undeservedly perhaps, for (although it has since had some success in
America) there was not much probability of its
prosperity in London. It was acted once, (10th
December, 1806,) and was announced for repetition
on the following evening, but was withdrawn Lamb's
courage and good humour did not fail. He joked
about it to Wordsworth, said that he had many fears

l   ꝝ about it, and admitted that "John Bull required solider fare than a bare letter." As he says, in his letter to the poet, "a hundred hisses (hang the word, I write it like kisses) outweigh a thousand claps. The former come more directly from the heart. Well," (he adds) "it is withdrawn, and there's an end."

In 1807 were published "Specimens of Dramatic Poets cotemporary with Shakespeare," and these made Lamb known as a man conversant with our old English literature, and helped mainly to direct the taste of the public to those fine writers. The book brought repute (perhaps a little money) to him. Soon afterwards, he published "The Adventures of Ulysses," which was intended to be an introduction to the reading of "Telemachus," always a popular book. These "adventures" were derived from Chapman's "Translation of Homer," of which Lamb says, "Chapman is divine; and my abridgement has not, I hope, quite emptied him of his divinity."

In or about 1808, Miss Lamb's pretty little stories called "Mrs. Leicester's School" (to which Charles contributed three tales) were published; and soon afterwards a small book entitled "Poetry for Children," being a joint publication by brother and sister, came out. "It was done by me and Mary in the last six months" (January, 1809). It does not appear to what extent, if at all, it added to the poor clerk's means.

In the same year, (Miss Lamb writes in December, 1808,) Charles was invited by Tom Sheridan to write some scenes in a speaking Pantomime; the other parts of which (the eloquence not of words) had been already manufactured by Tom and his more

celebrated father, Richard Brinsley. Lamb and Tom
Sheridan had been, it seems, communicative over a
bottle of claret, when an agreement for the above
purpose was entered into between them. This was
subsequently carried into effect, and a drama was
composed. This drama, still extant in the British
Museum, in Lamb's own writing, appears to be a
species of comic opera, the scene of which is laid
in Gibraltar, but is without a name. I have not seen
it, but speak upon the report of others.

In 1809, Lamb moved once more into the Temple,
now to the top story of No. 4, Inner Temple Lane,
"where the household gods are slow to come, but
where I mean to live and die," (he says). From this
place) since pulled down and rebuilt) he writes to
Manning, who is in China : " Come, and bring any
of your friends the Mandarins with you. My best
room commands a court, in which there are trees
and a pump, the water of which is excellent cold—
with brandy ; and not very insipid without " He
sends Manning some of his little books, to give him
" some idea of European literature." It is in this
letter (January, 1810) that he speaks of Braham and
his singing, which I have elsewhere alluded to ; of
Kate with nine stars * * * * * * * * * (" though
she is but one "); of his book (for children) " on
titles of honour," exemplifying the eleven gradations,
by which Mr. C. Lamb rises in succession to be
Baron, Marquis, Duke, and Emperor Lamb, and
finally Pope Innocent, and other lively matters fit to
solace an English mathematician self-banished to
China.

In July, 1810, an abstinence from all spirituous
liquors took place Lamb says his sister has "taken

L   Ɒ

water like a hungry otter," whilst he "limps after her" for virtue's sake; but he is "full of cramps and rheumatism, and cold internally, so that fire don't warm him." It is scarcely necessary to state that the period of entire abstinence was very transient.

A quarterly magazine, called "The Reflector," was published in the autumn of 1810, and contained essays by Charles Lamb and several other writers. Amongst these are some of the best of Lamb's earlier writings—namely, the paper on Hogarth and that on the Tragedies of Shakespeare. It is singular that these two essays, which are as fine as anything of a similar nature in English criticism, should have been almost unnoticed (undiscovered, except by literary friends) until the year 1818, when Lamb's works were collected and published. The grand passage on "Lear" has caused the Essay on the Shakespeare Tragedies to be well known. Less known is the Essay on Hogarth, although it is more elaborate and critical; the labour being quite necessary in this case, as the pretensions of Hogarth to the grand style had been denounced by Sir Joshua Reynolds. In affluence of genius, in variety and exuberance of thought, there surely can exist little comparison between Reynolds and Hogarth. Reynolds was, indeed, the finest painter, especially the most superb colourist, of the English school. But Hogarth was the greatest inventor,—the greatest discoverer of character, in the English or any other school. As a painter of manners he is unapproached. In a kindred walk, he traversed all the passions from the lowest mirth to the profoundest melancholy, possessing the tragic element in the most eminent degree. And if grandeur can exist—

as I presume it can—in beings who have neither costume nor rank to set off their qualities, then some of
the characters of Hogarth in essential grandeur are
far beyond the conventional figures of many other
artists. Pain and joy and poverty and human daring
are not to be circumscribed by dress and fashion.
Their seat is deeper, (in the soul,) and is altogether
independent of such trivial accretions. In point of
expression, I never saw the face of the madman (in
the " Rake's Progress") exceeded in any picture,
ancient or modern. " It is a face " (Lamb says)
" that no one that has seen can easily forget." It is,
as he argues, human suffering stretched to its utmost
endurance. I cannot forbear directing the attention
of the reader to Lamb's bold and excellent defence of
Hogarth. He will like both painter and author, I
think, better than before. I have, indeed, been in
company where young men, professing to be painters,
spoke slightingly of Hogarth. To this I might have
replied that Hogarth did not paint for the applause
of tyros in art, but—for the world !

" The " Reflector" was edited by an old Christ's
Hospital boy, Mr. Leigh Hunt, who subsequently
became and during their joint lives remained one of
Lamb's most familiar friends. It was a quarterly
magazine, and received, of course, the contributions
of various writers ; amongst whom were Mr. Barnes,
(of the " Times,") Barron Field, Dr. Aiken, Mr.
Landseer, (the elder,) Charles Lamb, Octavius Gil-
christ, Mitchell, (the translator of Aristophanes,) and
Leigh Hunt himself. I do not observe Lamb's name
appended to any of the articles in the first volume ;
but the second comprises the Essays on Hogarth and
on Burial Societies, together with a paper on the

Custom of Hissing at the Theatres, under the signature of " Semel Damnatus." There is a good deal
of humour in this paper (which has not been republished, I believe). It professes to come from one of
a club of condemned authors ; no person being ad-
missible as a member until he had been unequivocally
damned.

I observe that in the letters, &c., of Lamb, which
were published in 1841, and copiously commented on
by Sir Thomas N. Talfourd, (the editor,) there is not
much beyond a bare mention of Leigh Hunt's name,
and no letter from Charles Lamb to Mr. Hunt is published. It is now too late to remedy this last defect;
my recent endeavours to obtain such letters having
resulted in disappointment : otherwise I should have
been very glad to record the extent of Lamb's liking
for a poor and able man whom I knew well for at
least forty years. I know that at one time Lamb
valued him, and that he always thought highly of his
intellect, as indeed he has testified in his famous re-
monstrance to Southey. And in Mr. Hunt's autobiography I find abundant evidence of his admiration
for Lamb, in a generous eulogy upon him.

Charles Lamb, William Hazlitt, and Leigh Hunt
formed a remarkable trio of men ; each of whom was
decidedly different from the others. Only one of
them (Hunt) cared much for praise. Hazlitt's sole
ambition was to sell his essays, which he rated
scarcely beyond their marketable value; and Lamb
saw enough of the manner in which praise and censure were at that time distributed, to place any high
value on immediate success. Of posterity neither of
them thought. Leigh Hunt, from temperament, was
more alive to pleasant influences (sunshine, freedom

for work, rural walks, complimentary words) than the others. Hazlitt cared little for these things ; a fierce argument or a well-contested game at rackets was more to his taste , whilst Lamb's pleasures (except perhaps from his pipe) lay amongst the books of the old English writers. His soul delighted in communion with ancient generations , more especially with men who had been unjustly forgotten Hazlitt's mind attached itself to abstract subjects ; Lamb's was more practical, and embraced men Hunt was somewhat indifferent to persons as well as to things, except in the cases of Shelley and Keats, and his own family ; yet he liked poetry and poetical subjects. Hazlitt (who was ordinarily very shy) was the best talker of the three. Lamb said the most pithy and brilliant things, Hunt displayed the most ingenuity. All three sympathized often with the same persons or the same books ; and this, no doubt, cemented the intimacy that existed between them for so many years. Moreover, each of them understood the others, and placed just value on their objections when any difference of opinion (not infrequent) arose between them. Without being debaters, they were accomplished talkers. They did not argue for the sake of conquest, but to strip off the mists and perplexities which sometimes obscure truth. These men —who lived long ago—had a great share of my regard. They were all slandered : chiefly by men who knew little of them, and nothing of their good qualities · or by men who saw them only through the mist of political or religious animosity. Perhaps it was partly for this reason that they came nearer to my heart

All the three men, Lamb, Hazlitt, and Hunt, were

2 M 2

l   D

throughout their lives Unitarians, as was also George
Dyer ; Coleridge was an Unitarian preacher in his
youth, having seceded from the Church of England ;
to which, however, he returned, and was in his latter
years a strenuous supporter of the National faith.
George Dyer once sent a pamphlet to convert Charles
to Unitarianism. "Dear blundering soul," (Lamb
said,) "why, I am as old a One Goddite as himself."
To Southey Lamb writes, "Being, as you know, not
quite a churchman, I felt a jealousy at the Church
taking to herself the whole deserts of Christianity."
His great, and indeed infinite reverence, nevertheless,
for Christ is shown in his own Christian virtues and
in constant expressions of reverence. In Hazlitt's
Paper of "Persons one would wish to have seen,"
Lamb is made to refer to Jesus Christ as he "who
once put on a semblance of mortality," and to say,
"If he were to come into the room, we should all fall
down and kiss the hem of his garment." I do not
venture to comment on these delicate matters, where
men like Hazlitt, and Lamb, and Coleridge (the
latter for a short time only) have entertained opinions
which differ from those of the generality of their
countrymen.

During these years, Mary Lamb's illnesses were
frequent, as usual. Her relapses were not dependent
on the seasons, they came in hot summer and with
the freezing winters. The only remedy seems to
have been extreme quiet, when any slight symptom
of uneasiness was apparent. Charles (poor fellow)
had to live, day and night, in the society of a person
who was—mad! If any exciting talk occurred he
had to dismiss his friend, with a whisper. If any
stupor or extraordinary silence was observed, then

he had to rouse her instantly. He has been seen to take the kettle from the fire and place it for a moment on her head-dress, in order to startle her into recollection. He lived in a state of constant anxiety;—and there was no help.

Not to neglect Charles Lamb's migrations, it should be noted that he moved his residence from Inner Temple Lane ("where he meant to live and die") into Russell Street, Covent Garden, in the latter part of the year 1817. When there, he became personally acquainted with several members of the theatrical profession; amongst others, with Munden and Miss Kelly, for both of whom he entertained the highest admiration. One of the (Elia) Essays is written to celebrate Munden's histrionic talent, and in his letters he speaks of " Fanny Kelly's divine plain face." The Barbara S. of the second (or last) series of essays is, in fact, Miss Kelly herself. All his friends knew that he was greatly attached to her. He also became acquainted with Miss Burrell— afterwards Mrs. Gould—but who, he says, " remained uncoined." Subsequently he was introduced to Liston and Elliston, each of whom received tokens of his liking. The first was the subject of an amusing fictitious biography. In Lamb's words it was "a lying life of Liston," uncontaminated by a particle of truth. Munden, he says, had faces innumerable ; Liston had only one; " but what a face !" he adds, admitting it to be beyond all vain description. Perhaps this subject of universal laughter and admiration never received such a compliment ; except from Hazlitt, who after commenting on Hogarth's excellences, his invention, his character, his satire, &c., concludes by saying, " I have never seen anything in the expression of comic humour equal to Hogarth's humour, except Liston's face."

In the course of time, official labour becomes tiresome, and the India House clerk grows splenetic. He complains sadly of his work. Even the incursions of his familiars annoy him ; although it annoys him more when they go away. In the midst of this trouble his works are collected and published ; and he emerges at once from the obscure shades of Leadenhall Street, into the full blaze of public notice. He wakes from dullness and discontent, and " finds himself famous."

CHAPTER V.

My Recollections—Russell Street—Personal Appearance—Manner—Tendency of Mind—Prejudices—Alleged Excesses—Mode of Life—Love of Smoking—His Lodgings—His Sister—Costume—Reading Aloud—Tastes and Opinions—London—Love of Books—Charity—Wednesday Parties—His Companions—Epitaph on them.

In the year 1817 or 1818 I first became personally acquainted with Charles Lamb. This was about the time of his removal from the Temple. It was in the course of the year 1818 that his works had been first collected and published. They came upon the world by surprise : scarcely any one, at that time, being aware that a fine genius and humorist existed, within the dull shades of London, whose quality very few of the critics had assayed, and none of them had commended. He was thus thrown (waif-like) amongst the great body of the people; was at once estimated, and soon rose into renown.

Persons who had been in the habit of traversing Covent Garden at that time, (seven-and-forty years ago,) might by extending their walk a few yards into Russell Street, have noted a small spare man, clothed in black, who went out every morning and returned every afternoon, as regularly as the hands of the clock moved toward certain hours. You could not mistake him. He was somewhat stiff in his manner, and almost clerical in dress; which indicated much wear. He had a long, melancholy face, with keen penetrating eyes; and he walked with a short, resolute step, City-wards. He looked no one in the face for more than a moment, yet contrived to see everything as he went on. No one who ever studied the human features could pass him by without recollecting his countenance : it was full of sensibility, and it came upon you like a new thought, which you could not help dwelling upon afterwards, it gave rise to meditation and did you good. This small, half-clerical man, was—Charles Lamb.

I had known him for a short time previously to 1818; having been introduced to him at Mr. Leigh Hunt's house, where I enjoyed his company once or twice over agreeable suppers; but I knew him slightly only, and did not see much of him until he and his sister went to occupy the lodgings in Russell Street, where he invited me to come and see him. They lived in the corner house adjoining Bow Street. This house belonged, at that time, to an ironmonger, (or brazier,) and was comfortable and clean,—and a little noisy. Charles Lamb was about forty years of age when I first saw him; and I knew him inti-

mately for the greater part of twenty years.   Small
and spare in person, and with small legs, ("immaterial
legs," Hood called them,) he had a dark complexion,
dark, curling hair, almost black, and a grave look,
lightening up occasionally, and capable of sudden
merriment.   His laugh was seldom excited by jokes
merely ludicrous; it was never spiteful; and his quiet
smile was sometimes inexpressibly sweet: perhaps
it had a touch of sadness in it.   His mouth was
well-shaped; his lip tremulous with expression; his
brown eyes were quick, restless, and glittering: and
he had a grand head, full of thought.   Leigh Hunt
said that "he had a head worthy of Aristotle."
Hazlitt calls it "a fine Titian head, full of dumb
eloquence."   I knew that, before he had attained the
age of twenty years, he had to make his way in the
world; and that his lines had not been cast in pleasant places.   I had heard, indeed, that his family
had at one time consisted of a father and mother and
an insane sister; all helpless and poor, and all
huddled together in a small lodging, scarcely large
enough to admit of their moving about without
restraint.   It is difficult to imagine a more dis-
heartening youth.   Nevertheless, out of this desert,
in which no hope was visible, he rose up eventually
a cheerful man, (cheerful when his days were not
clouded by his sister's illness,) a charming companion, full of pleasant and gentle fancies, and the
finest humorist of his age.

Although sometimes strange in manner, he was
thoroughly unaffected; in serious matters thoroughly
sincere.   He was, indeed, (as he confesses,) terribly
shy; diffident, not awkward in manner; with occasionally nervous twitching motions that betrayed this

infirmity. He dreaded the criticisms of servants far more than the observations of their masters. To undergo the scrutiny of the first, as he said to me, when we were going to breakfast with Mr. Rogers one morning, was "terrible." His speech was brief and pithy; not too often humorous; never sententious nor didactic. Although he sometimes talked whilst walking up and down the room, (at which time he seldom looked at the person with whom he was talking,) he very often spoke as if impelled by the necessity of speaking—suddenly, precipitately. If he could have spoken very easily he might possibly have uttered long sentences, expositions, or orations; such as some of his friends indulged in, to the utter confusion of their hearers.

But he knew the value of silence; and he knew that even truth may be damaged by too many words. When he did speak his words had a flavour in them beyond any that I have heard elsewhere. His conversation dwelt upon persons or things within his own recollection, or it opened, (with a startling doubt, or a question, or a piece of quaint humour,) the great circle of thought.

In temper he was quick, but easily appeased. He never affected that exemption from sensibility, which has sometimes been mistaken for philosophy; and has conferred reputation upon little men. In a word, he exhibited his emotions in a fine, simple, natural manner. Contrary to the usual habits of wits, no retort or reply by Lamb, however smart in character, ever gave pain. It is clear that ill-nature is not wit; and that there may be sparkling flowers which are not surrounded by thorns. Lamb's dissent was very intelligible, but never superfluously demonstrative:

often, indeed, expressed by his countenance only.
sometimes merely by silence.

He was more pleasant to some persons (more pleasant, I confess, to *me*) for the few faults or weaknesses that he had. He did not daunt us, nor throw
us to a distance, by his formidable virtues. We sympathized with him; and this sympathy, which is an
union between two similitudes, does not exist between perfect and imperfect natures. Like all of us,
he had a few prejudices: he did not like Frenchmen;
he shrunk from Scotchmen; (excepting, however,
Burns;) he disliked bankrupts; he hated close bar-
gainers. For the Jewish nation he entertained a
mysterious awe: the Jewesses he admired, with trembling; "Jael had those full, dark, inscrutable eyes,"
he says. Of Braham's triumphant singing he repeatedly spoke: there had been nothing like it in his
recollection: he considered him equal to Mrs. Sid-
dons. In his letters he characterises him as "a mixture of the Jew, the gentleman, and the angel." He
liked chimney-sweepers—the young ones—the "innocent blacknesses;" and with beggars he had a strong
sympathy. He always spoke tenderly of them, and
has written upon them an essay full of beauty. Do
not be frightened (he says) at the hard words, impos-
ture, &c. "Cast thy bread upon the waters: some
have unawares entertained angels."

Much injustice has been done to Lamb, by accusing him of excess in drinking. The truth is, that a
small quantity of any strong liquid (wine, &c.) disturbed his speech, which at best was but an eloquent
stammer. The distresses of his early life made him
ready to resort to any remedy which brought forgetfulness; and he himself, frail in body and excitable,

was very speedily affected. During all my intimacy
with him I never knew him drink immoderately; except once, when having been prevailed upon to abstain altogether from wine and spirits, he resented
the vow thus forced upon him, by imbibing an extraordinary quantity of the "spurious" liquid. When
he says, "The waters have gone over me," he speaks
in metaphor; not historically. He was never vanquished by water, and seldom by wine. His energy,
or mental power, was indeed subject to fluctuation;
no excessive merriment, perhaps, but much depression. "My waking life," he writes, "has much of
the confusion, the trouble, and obscure perplexity of
an ill dream. In the day time I stumble upon dark
mountains."

Lamb's mode of life was temperate · his dinner
consisting of meat, with vegetables and bread only.
"We have a sure hot joint on Sundays," he writes,
"and when had we better?" He appears to have
had a relish for game, roast pig, and brawn, &c.,
roast pig especially, when given to him; but his
poverty, first, and afterwards his economical habits,
prevented his indulging in such costly luxuries. He
was himself a small and delicate eater at all times;
and he entertained something like aversion towards
great feeders. During a long portion of his life his
means were much straitened. The reader may note
his want of money in several of his letters. Speaking
of a play, he says, "I am quite aground for a plan;
and *I must do something for money.*"

He was restless and fond of walking. I do not
think that he could ride on horseback; but he could
walk during all the day. He had, in that manner,
traversed the whole of London and its suburbs (espe-

cially the northern and north-eastern parts) frequently.
" I cannot sit and think," he said.   Tired with exercise, he went to bed early, except when friends supped
with him , and he always rose early, from necessity,
being obliged to attend at his office, in Leadenhall
Street, every day, from ten until four o'clock—sometimes later.   It was there that his familiar letters
were written.   On his return, after a humble meal,
he strolled (if it was summer) into the suburbs, or
traversed the streets where the old bookshops were
to be found.   He seldom or never gave dinners.
You were admitted at all times to his plain supper,
which was sufficiently good when any visitor came,
at other times it was spare. ˙ " We have *tried* to eat
suppers," Miss Lamb writes to Mrs. Hazlitt, " but
we left our appetites behind us ; and the dry loaf,
which offended you, now comes in at night unaccompanied."   You were sure of a welcome at his house ;
sure of easy unfettered talk.   After supper you might
smoke a pipe with your host, or gossip (upon any
subject) with him or his sensible sister.   Perhaps the
pipe was the only thing in which Lamb really exceeded.   He was fond of it from the very early years,
when he was accustomed to smoke " Orinooko " at
the " Salutation and Cat," with Coleridge, in 1796.
He attempted on several occasions to give it up, but
his struggles were overcome by counter influences.
" Tobacco," he says, " stood in its own light."   At
last, in 1805, he was able to conquer and abandon it,
—for a time.   His success, like desertion from a
friend, caused some remorse, and a great deal of
regret.   In writing to Coleridge, about his house,
which was " smoky," he inquires, " Have you cured
it ?   It is hard to cure anything of smoking."   Apart

from the mere pleasure of smoking, the narcotic soothed his nerves and controlled those perpetual apprehensions which his sister's frequent illnesses excited. Of Mary Lamb, Hazlitt has said (somewhere) that she was the most rational and wisest woman whom he had ever known .Lamb and his sister had an open party once a week, every Wednesday evening, when his friends generally went to visit him, without any special invitation. He invited you suddenly, not pressingly ; but with such heartiness that you at once agreed to come. There was usually a game at whist on these evenings, in which the stakes were very moderate, indeed, almost nominal.

When my thoughts turn backward, as they sometimes do, to these past days, I see my dear old friend again,—" in my mind's eye, Horatio ," with his outstretched hand, and his grave sweet smile of welcome. It was always in a room of moderate size, comfortably, but plainly furnished, that he lived. An old mahogany table was opened out in the middle of the room, round which, and near the walls, were old, high-backed chairs. (such as our grandfathers used,) and a long plain bookcase completely filled with old books. These were his " ragged veterans." In one of his letters he says, " My rooms are luxurious, one for prints and one for books , a summer and winter parlour." They, however, were not otherwise decorated. I do not remember ever to have seen a flower or an image in them. He had not been educated into expensive tastes. His extravagances were confined to books. These were all chosen by himself, all old, and all in " admired disorder ;" yet he could lay his hand on any volume in a moment. " You never saw," he writes, " a bookcase in more true har-

mony with the contents than what I have nailed up
in my room. Though new it has more aptitude for
growing old than you shall often see ; as one sometimes gets a friend in the middle of life who becomes
an old friend in a short time."

Here Charles Lamb sate, when at home, always
near the table. At the opposite side was his sister,
engaged in some domestic work, knitting or sewing,
or poring over a modern novel. " Bridget in some
things is behind her years " In fact, though she was
ten years older than her brother, she had more sympathy with modern books and with youthful fancies than
he had. She wore a neat cap, of the fashion of her
youth ; an old-fashioned dress. Her face was pale
and somewhat square, but very placid, with grey intelligent eyes. She was very mild in her manner to
strangers ; and to her brother gentle and tender always. She had often an upward look of peculiar
meaning, when directed towards him ; as though to
give him assurance that all was then well with her.
His affection for her was somewhat less on the surface; but always present. There was great gratitude
intermingled with it. " In the days of weakling infancy," he writes, " I was her tender charge, as I
have been her care in foolish manhood since." Then
he adds, pathetically, " I wish I could throw into a
heap the remainder of our joint existences, that we
might share them in equal division."

Lamb himself was always dressed in black. " I
take it," he says, " to be the proper costume of an
author." When this was once objected to, at a
wedding, he pleaded the raven's apology in the fable,
that " he had no other." His clothes were entirely
black; and he wore long black gaiters, up to the

knees. His head was bent a little forward, like one
who had been reading; and, if not standing or walking, he generally had in his hand an old book, a
pinch of snuff, or, later in the evening, a pipe. He
stammered a little, pleasantly, just enough to prevent
his making speeches : just enough to make you listen
eagerly for his words, always full of meaning, or
charged with a jest : or referring, (but this was rare,)
to some line or passage from one of the old Elizabe-
than writers, which was always ushered in with a
smile of tender reverence. When he read aloud it
was with a slight tone, which I used to think he had
caught from Coleridge ; Coleridge's recitation, however, rising to a chant Lamb's reading was not
generally in books of verse, but in the old lay
writers, whose tendency was towards religious
thoughts. He liked, however, religious verse : " I
can read," he writes to Bernard Barton, " the
homely old version of the Psalms in our prayer-
books, for an hour or two, without sense of weari-
ness." He avoided manuscripts as much as practicable : " all things read *raw* to me in manuscript."
Lamb wrote much, including many letters ; but his
hands were wanting in pliancy, (" inveterate clumsi-
ness " are his words,) and his handwriting was
therefore never good. It was neither text nor
running hand, and the letters did not indicate any
fluency ; it was not the handwriting of an old man
nor of a young man, yet it had a very peculiar
character ; stiff, resolute, distinct ; quite unlike all
others that I have seen, and easily distinguishable
amongst a thousand.

No one has described Lamb's manner or merits so
well as Hazlitt : " He always made the best pun and

the best remark in the course of the evening. His
serious conversation, like his serious writing, is his
best. No one ever stammered out such fine, piquant,
deep, eloquent things, in half a dozen sentences, as
he does. His jests scald like tears ; and he probes
a question with a play upon words. There was no
fuss or cant about him. He has furnished many a
text for Coleridge to preach upon." (*I. Plain Speaker.*)
Charles was frequently merry : but ever, at the back
of his merriment, there reposed a grave depth, in
which rich colours and tender lights were inlaid.
For his jests sprang from his sensibility . which was
as open to pleasure as to pain, This sensibility, if
it somewhat impaired his vigour, led him into curious
and delicate fancies, and taught him a liking for
things of the highest relish, which a mere robust
jester never tastes.

Large sounding words, unless embodying great
thoughts, (as in the case of Lear,) he did not treasure up or repeat. He was an admirer of what was
high and good, of what was delicate ; (especially ;)
but he delighted most to saunter along the humbler
regions, where kindness of heart and geniality of
humour made the way pleasant. His intellect was
very quick, piercing into the recondite meaning of
things in a moment. His own sentences were com-
pressed and full of meaning, his opinions independent and decisive, no qualifying or doubting. His
descriptions were not highly coloured ; but, as it were,
sharply cut, like a piece of marble, rather than like a
picture. He liked and encouraged friendly discussion ; but he hated contentious argument, which leads
to quarrel rather than to truth.

There was an utter want of parade in everything

l   *)*

he said and did, in everything about him and his
home. The only ornaments on his walls were a few
engravings in black frames: one after Leonardo da
Vinci, one after Titian; and four, I think, by
Hogarth, about whom he has written so well. Images
of quaint beauty, and all gentle, simple things (things
without pretension) pleased him to the fullest extent;
perhaps a little beyond their strict merit. I have
heard him express admiration for Leonardo da Vinci
that he did not accord to Raffaelle. Raffaelle was
too ostentatious of meaning; his merits were too
obvious,—too much thrust upon the understanding:
not retired nor involved, so as to need discovery or
solution   He preferred even Titian (whose meaning
is generally obvious enough) to Raffaelle; but Leonardo was above both. Without doubt, Lamb's
taste on several matters was peculiar; for instance,
there were a few obsolete words, such as *arride*,
agnize, *burgeon*, &c., which he fancied, and chose to
rescue from oblivion. Then he did not care for
music. I never heard a song in his house, nor any
conversation on the subject of melody or harmony.
" I have no ear," he says; yet the sentiment, apart
from the science of music, gave him great pleasure.
He reverenced the fine organ playing of Mr. Novello,
and admired the soaring singing of his daughter,—
" the tuneful daughter of a tuneful sire;" but he resented the misapplication of the theatres to sacred
music. He thought this a profanation of the good
old original secular purposes of a playhouse.

As a comprehension of all delights he loved
London; with its bustle and its living throngs of
men and women; its shops, its turns and windings;
the cries and noises of trade and life; beyond all

other things. He liked also old buildings and out of
the way places ; Colleges , solemn churchyards,
round which the murmuring thousands floated un-
heeding. In particular he was fond of visiting, in
his short vacations, the Universities of Oxford and
Cambridge. Although (he writes) " Mine have been
anything but studious hours," he professes to have
received great solace from those " repositories of
' mouldering ' learning." " What a place to be in is
an old library !" he exclaims, " where the souls of the
old writers seem reposing : as in some dormitory or
middle state." The odour of the " moth-scented "
coverings of the old books is " as fragrant as the
blooms of the tree of knowledge which grew in the
happy orchard." An ancient manor-house, that
Vanbrugh might have built, dwelt like a picture in
his memory. " Nothing fills a child's mind like an
old mansion," he says. Yet he could feel unaffectedly
the simplicity and beauty of a country life. The
heartiness of country people went to his heart direct,
and remained there for ever. The Fields and the
Gladmans, with their homely dwellings and hospitality, drew him to them like magnets. There was
nothing too fine or too lofty in these friends for his
tastes or his affection ; they did not " affront him
with their light." His fancy always stooped to
moralize : he hated the stilted attitudes and pretensions of poetasters and self-glorifying artists.—He
never spoke disparagingly of any person, nor over-
praised any one. When it was proposed to erect a
statue of Clarkson, during his life ; he objected to it :
" We should be modest," he says, " for a modest
man." He was himself eminently modest ; he never
put himself forward : he was always sought. He

had much to say on many subjects, and he was repeatedly pressed to say this, before he consented to
do so. He was almost teased into writing the Elia
Essays. These and all his other writings are brief
and to the point. He did not exhale in words. It
was said that Coleridge's talk was worth so many
guineas a sheet. Charles Lamb talked but sparingly.
He put forth only so much as had complete flavour.
I know that high pay and frequent importunity failed
to induce him to squander his strength in careless
essays : he waited until he could give them their full
share of meaning and humour.

When I speak of his extreme liking for London,
it must not be supposed that he was insensible to
great scenery. After his only visit to the Lake
country, and beholding Skiddaw, he writes back to
his host, " Oh ! its fine black head, and the bleak air
at the top of it, with a prospect of mountains all
about, making you giddy. It was a day that will
stand out like a mountain in my life ;" adding, however, " Fleet Street and the Strand are better places
to live in, for good and all. I could not *live* in Skiddaw. I could not spend there two or three years ;
but I must have a prospect of seeing Fleet Street at
the end of that time, or I should mope and pine
away." He loved even its smoke, and asserted that
it suited his vision. A short time previously he
had, in a touching letter to Wordsworth, (1801,)
enumerated the objects that he liked so much in
London. " These things," he writes, " work themselves into my mind : the rooms where I was born ;
a bookcase that has followed me about like a faithful dog, (only exceeding him in knowledge,) where-
ever I have moved , old chairs ; old tables ; squares

where I have sunned myself; my old school : these are my mistresses. Have I not enough, without your mountains ? I do not envy you . I should pity you, did I not know that the mind will make friends with anything."

Besides his native London, "the centre of busy interests," he had great liking for unpretending men, who would come and gossip with him in a friendly companionable way, or who liked to talk about old authors or old books. In his love of books he was very catholic. "Shaftesbury is not too genteel, nor Jonathan too low. But for books which are no books," such as "scientific treatises, and the histories of Hume, Smollett, and Gibbon," &c., he confesses that he becomes splenetic when he sees them perched up on shelves, "like false saints, who have usurped the true shrines" of the legitimate occupants. He loved old books and authors, indeed, beyond most other things. He used to say (with Shakespeare) "The Heavens themselves are old." He would rather have acquired an ancient forgotten volume than a modern one, at an equal price ; the very circumstance of its having been neglected and cast disdainfully into the refuse basket of a bookstall gave it value in his eyes. He bought it, and rejoiced in being able to remedy the injustice of fortune. He liked best those who had not thriven with posterity : his reverence for Margaret, Duchess of Newcastle, can only be explained in this way. It must not be forgotten that his pity or generosity towards neglected authors extended also to all whom the Goddess of Good Fortune had slighted. In this list were included all who had suffered in purse or in repute. He was ready to defend man or beast, whenever unjustly attacked. I remember that, at one of the monthly magazine dinners, when John Wilkes was too roughly handled, Lamb quoted the story (not generally known) of his replying, when the blackbirds are reported to have stolen all his cherries, " Poor birds, they are welcome." He said that those impulsive words showed the inner nature of the man more truly than all his political speeches. Lamb's charity extended to all things. I never heard him speak spitefully of any author. He thought that every one should have a clear stage unobstructed. His heart, young at all times, never grew hard or callous during life. There was always in it a tender spot, which Time was unable to touch. He gave away *greatly*, when the amount of his means are taken into consideration ; he gave away money,—even annuities, I believe, to old impoverished friends whose wants were known to him. I remember that once when we were sauntering together on Pentonville Hill, and he noticed great depression in me, which he attributed to want of money, he said, suddenly, in a stammering way, " My dear boy, I—I have a quantity of useless things. I have now—in my desk, a—a hundred pounds—that I don't—don't *know* what to do with. Take it." I was much touched : but I assured him that my depression did not arise from want of money. He was very home-loving ; he loved London as the best of places ; he loved his home as the dearest spot in London : it was the inmost heart of the sanctuary. Whilst at home he had no curiosity for what passed beyond his own territory. His eyes were never truant; no one ever saw him peeping out of the window, examining the crowds flowing by , no one ever surprised him gazing on vacancy. " I lose my-

self," he says, " in other men's minds. When I am
not walking I am reading ; I cannot sit and think;
books think for me." If it was not the time for his
pipe, it was always the time for an old play, or for a
talk with friends. In the midst of this society his
own mind grew green again and blossomed , or, as
he would have said, " burgeoned."

In the foregoing desultory account of Charles
Lamb I have, without doubt, set forth many things
that are frequently held as trivial. Nothing, however, seems to me unimportant which serves in any
way to illustrate a character. The floating straws,
it is said, show from what quarter the wind is blow-
ing. So the arching or knitting of the brow is
sometimes sufficient to indicate wonder or pride,
anger or contempt. On the stage, indeed, it is often
the sole means of expressing the fluctuation of
the passions. I myself have heard of a "Pooh!"
which interrupted a long intimacy, when the pander
was administering sweet words in too liberal a
measure.

As with Lamb so with his companions. Each was
notable for some individual mark or character. His
own words will best describe them :—"Not many
persons of science, and few professed *literati*, were
of his councils. They were for the most part persons
of an uncertain fortune. His intimados were, to
confess a truth, in the world's eye, a ragged regiment ;
he found them floating on the surface of society, and
the colour or something else in the weed pleased
him. The burrs stuck to him ; but they were good
and loving burrs, for all that."

None of Lamb's intimates were persons of title or
fashion, or of any political importance. They were

reading men, or authors, or old friends who had no name or pretensions. The only tie that held these last and Lamb together was a long standing mutual friendship; a sufficient link. None of them ever forsook him; they loved him, and in return he had a strong regard for them. His affections, indeed, were concentrated on few persons; not widened (weakened) by too general a philanthropy. When you went to Lamb's rooms on the Wednesday evenings, (his "At Home,") you generally found the card table spread out, Lamb himself one of the players. On the corner of the table was a snuff-box; and the game was enlivened by sundry brief ejaculations and pungent questions, which kept alive the wits of the party present. It was not "silent whist!" I do not remember whether, in common with Sarah Battle, Lamb had a weakness in favour of "Hearts." I suppose that it was at one of these meetings that he made that shrewd remark which has since escaped into notoriety: "Martin," (observed he,) "if dirt were trumps, what a hand you would hold." It is not known what influence Martin's trumps had on the rubber then in progress. —When the conversation became general, Lamb's part in it was very effective. His short clear sentences always produced effect. He never joined in talk unless he understood the subject; then, if the matter in question interested him, he was not slow in showing his earnestness. but I never heard him argue or talk for argument's sake. If he was indifferent to the question, he was silent.

The supper of cold meat, on these occasions, was always on the side table; not very formal, as may be imagined; and every one might rise, when it suited him, and cut a slice or take a glass of porter, with-

out reflecting on the abstinence of the rest of the
company. Lamb would, perhaps, call out and bid
the hungry guest help himself without ceremony.
We learn (from Hazlitt) that Martin Burney's eulogies
on books were sometimes intermingled with expressions of satisfaction with the veal pie which employed
him at the sideboard. After the game was won, (and
lost,) the ring of the cheerful glasses announced that
punch or brandy and water had become the order of
the night.

It was curious to observe the gradations in Lamb's
manner to his various guests ; although it was courteous to all. With Hazlitt he talked as though they
met the subject in discussion on equal terms ; with
Leigh Hunt he exchanged repartees ; to Wordsworth
he was almost respectful ; with Coleridge he was
sometimes jocose, sometimes deferring ; with Martin
Burney fraternally familiar ; with Manning affectionate ; with Godwin merely courteous ; or if friendly,
then in a minor degree. The man whom I found at
Lamb's house more frequently than any other person
was Martin Burney. He was now scarcely known ;
yet Lamb dedicated his prose works to him, in 1818,
and there described him as "no common judge of
books and men ; " and Southey, corresponding with
Rickman, when his "Joan of Arc" was being re-
printed, says, "The best omen I have heard of its
well-doing is that Martin Burney likes it." Lamb
was very much attached to Martin, who was a sincere
and able man, although with a very unprepossessing
physiognomy. His face was warped by paralysis,
which affected one eye and one side of his mouth.
He was plain and unaffected in manner, very diffident
and retiring : yet pronouncing his opinions, when

asked to do so, without apology or hesitation. He was a barrister; and travelled the western circuit at the same time as Sir Thomas Wilde (afterwards Lord Truro), whose briefs he used to read before the other considered them; marking out the principal facts and points for attention. Martin Burney had excellent taste in books; eschewed the showy and artificial, and looked into the sterling qualities of writing. He frequently accompanied Lamb in his visits to friends, and although very familiar with Charles, he always spoke of him, with respect, as *Mr.* Lamb. "He is on the top scale of my friend-ship ladder," Lamb says, "on which an angel or two is still climbing, and some, alas! descending." The last time I saw Burney was at the corner of a street in London, when he was overflowing on the subject of Raffaelle and Hogarth. After a great and prolonged struggle, he said, he had arrived at the conclusion that Raffaelle was the greater man of the two.

Notwithstanding Lamb's somewhat humble de-scription of his friends and familiars, some of them were men well known in literature. Amongst others, I met there Messrs. Coleridge, Manning, Hazlitt, Haydon, Wordsworth, Barron Field, Leigh Hunt, Clarkson, Sheridan Knowles, Talfourd, Kenny, God-win, the Burneys, Payne Collier, and others whose names I need not chronicle. I met there, also, on one or two occasions, Liston, and Miss Kelly, and, I believe, Rickman. Politics were rarely discussed amongst them. Anecdotes, characteristic, showing the strong and weak points of human nature, were frequent enough. But politics (especially party politics) were seldom admitted. Lamb disliked them as a theme for evening talk; he perhaps did not understand the subject scientifically. And when Hazlitt's impetuosity drove him, as it sometimes did, into fierce expressions on public affairs, these were usually received in silence; and the matter thus raised up for assent or controversy was allowed to drop.

Lamb's old associates are now dead. "They that lived so long," as he says, "and flourished so steadily, are all crumbled away." The beauty of these evenings was that every one was placed upon an easy level. No one out-topped the others. No one—not even Coleridge—was permitted to out-talk the rest. No one was allowed to hector the other, or to bring his own grievances too prominently forward; so as to disturb the harmony of the night. Every one had a right to speak, and to be heard; and no one was ever trodden or clamoured down, (as in some large assemblies,) until he had proved that he was not entitled to a hearing, or until he had abused his privilege. I never, in all my life, heard so much unpretending good sense talked, as at Charles Lamb's social parties. Often, a piece of sparkling humour was shot out that illuminated the whole evening. Sometimes there was a flight of high and earnest talk, that took one half way towards the stars.

It seems great matter for regret that the thoughts of men like Lamb's associates should have passed away altogether; for scarcely any of them, save Wordsworth and Coleridge, are now distinctly remembered; and it is, perhaps, not impossible to foretell the duration of *their* fame. All have answered their purpose, I suppose. Each has had his turn, and has given place to a younger thinker, as the father is replaced by the son. Thus Jeremy Taylor and Sir Thomas Browne, and Webster, and the old Dramatists, have travelled out of sight; and their thoughts are reproduced by modern writers; the originators of those thoughts often remaining unknown. Perhaps *One*, out of many thousand authors, survives into an immortality. The manner and the taste change. The armour and falchion of old give place to the new weapons of modern warfare, less weighty, but perhaps as trenchant. We praise the old authors, but we do not read them. The soul of Antiquity seems to survive only in its proverbs; which contain the very essence of wisdom.

CHAPTER VI.

LONDON MAGAZINE—CONTRIBUTORS—TRANSFER OF MAGAZINE— MONTHLY DINNERS AND VISITORS—COLEBROOK COTTAGE—LAMB'S WALKS—ESSAYS OF ELIA: THEIR EXCELLENCE AND CHARACTER— ENLARGED ACQUAINTANCE—VISIT TO PARIS—MISS ISOLA—QUARREL WITH SOUTHEY—LEAVES INDIA HOUSE—LEISURE—AMICUS REDIVIVUS —EDWARD IRVING.

THE "London Magazine" was established in January, 1820; the publishers being Messrs. Baldwin, Cradock, and Joy, and its editor being Mr. John Scott, who had formerly edited "The Champion" newspaper, and whose profession was exclusively that of a man of letters. At this distance of time, it is impossible to specify the authors of all the various papers which gave a tone to the Magazine; but as this publication forms, in fact, the great foundation of Lamb's fame, I think it well to enter somewhat minutely into its constitution and character.

Mr. John Scott was the writer of the several articles entitled " The living Authors;" of a good many of the earlier criticisms ; of some of the papers on politics ; and of some which may be termed " Controversial." The essays on Sir Walter Scott, Wordsworth, Godwin, and Lord Byron, are from his hand. He contributed also the critical papers, on the writings of Keats, Shelley, Leigh Hunt, and Hazlitt.

Mr. Hazlitt wrote all the articles which appear under the head " Drama;" the twelve essays entitled " Table Talk;" and the papers on Fonthill Abbey, and on the Angerstein pictures, and the Elgin marbles.

Mr. Charles Lamb's papers were the well-known Elia Essays, which first appeared in this Magazine. Mr. Elia (whose name he assumed) was, at one time, a clerk in the India House. He died, however, before the Essays were made public, and was ignorant of Lamb's intention to do honour to his name.

Mr. Thomas Carlyle was author of the " Life and Writings of Schiller," in the eighth, ninth, and tenth volumes of the Magazine. These papers, although very excellent, appear to be scarcely prophetic of the great fame which their author was afterwards destined, so justly, to achieve.

Mr. de Quincy's contributions were the " Confessions of an Opium Eater;" also various papers specified as being " by the Opium Eater;" the essay on Jean Paul Richter, and papers translated from the German, or dealing with German literature.

The Reverend Henry Francis Cary (the translator of Dante) wrote the Notices of the Early French Poets; the addition to Orford's " Royal and Noble

Authors;" and, I believe, the continuations of Johnson's "Lives of the Poets." Of these last, however,
I am not certain.

Mr. Allan Cunningham (the Scottish poet) was
author of the "Twelve Tales of Lyddal Cross;" of
the series of stories or papers styled "Traditional
Literature;" and of various other contributions in
poetry and prose.

Mr. John Poole contributed the "Beauties of the
living Dramatists;" being burlesque imitations of
modern writers for the stage; viz. Morton, Dibdin,
Reynolds, Moncrieff, &c.

Mr. John Hamilton Reynolds wrote, I believe, in
every number of the periodical, after it came into the
hands of Taylor and Hessey, who were his friends.
All the papers with the name of Henry Herbert affixed
were written by him; also the descriptive accounts of
the Coronation, Greenwich Hospital, The Cockpit
Royal, The Trial of Thurtell, &c.

Mr. Thomas Hood fleshed his maiden sword here;
and his first poems of length, "Lycus the Centaur"
and "The Two Peacocks of Bedfont" may be found
in the Magazine.

Mr. George Darley (author of "Thomas à Becket,"
&c) wrote the several papers entitled "Drama-
ticles;" some pieces of verse; and the Letters addressed to "The Dramatists of the Day."

Mr. Richard Ayton wrote "The Sea Roamers,"
the article on "Hunting," and such papers as are
distinguished by the signature "R.A."

Mr. Keats (the poet) and *Mr. James Montgomery*
contributed verses.

Sir John Bowring (I believe) translated into English verse the Spanish poetry, and wrote the several

papers which appear under the head of "Spanish Romances."

Mr. Henry Southern (editor of "The Retrospective Review") wrote the "Conversations of Lord Byron," and "The Fanariotes of Constantinople," in the tenth volume.

Mr. Walter Savage Landor was author of the Imaginary Conversation, between Southey and Porson, in volume eight.

Mr. Julius (Archdeacon) Hare reviewed the works of Landor in the tenth volume.

Mr. Elton contributed many translations from Greek and Latin authors : from the minor poems of Homer, from Catullus, Nonnus, Propertius, &c.

Messrs. Hartley Coleridge, John Clare, Cornelius Webb, Bernard Barton, and others sent poems; generally with the indicating name.

I myself was amongst the crowd of contributors ; and was author of various pieces, some in verse, and others in prose, now under the protection of that great Power which is called "Oblivion."

Finally the too celebrated *Thomas Griffiths Wainewright* contributed various fantasies, on Art and Arts; all or most of which may be recognised by his assumed name of Janus Weathercock.

To show the difficulty of specifying the authorship of all the articles contributed,—even Mr. Hessey (one of the proprietors) was unable to do so ; and, indeed, shortly before his death, applied to me for information on the subject.

By the aid of the gentlemen who contributed— each his quota—to the "London Magazine," it acquired much reputation, and a very considerable sale. During its career for five years, it had, for a

certain style of essay, no superior (scarcely an equal)
amongst the periodicals of the day. It was perhaps
not so widely popular as works directed to the multitude, instead of to the select few, might have been;
for thoughts and words addressed to the cultivated
intellect only must always reckon upon limited success. Yet the Magazine was successful, to an extent
that preserved its proprietors from loss; perhaps not
greatly beyond that point. Readers in those years
were insignificant in number, compared with readers
of the present time; when almost all men are able to
derive benefit from letters, and letters are placed
within every one's reach.

On the death of Mr. John Scott, the Magazine, in
July, 1821, passed into the hands of Messrs. Taylor
and Hessey; the former being the gentleman who
discovered the identity of Junius with Sir Philip
Francis; the latter being simply very courteous to all,
and highly respectable and intelligent.

John Scott was an able literary man. I do not remember much more of him than that he was a shrewd
and, I believe, a conscientious writer; that he had
great industry; was, generally, well read, and possessed a very fair amount of critical taste; that, like
other persons, he had some prejudices, and that he
was sometimes, moreover, a little hasty and irritable.
Yet he agreed well, as far as I know, with the regiment of mercenaries who marched under his flag.

When Taylor and Hessey assumed the management of the " London Magazine," they engaged no
editor. They were tolerably liberal paymasters: the
remuneration for each page of prose, (not very labori-
ous,) being, if the writer were a person of repute or
ability, one pound; and for each page of verse, two

pounds. Charles Lamb received (very fitly) for his brief and charming essays, two or three times the amount of the other writers. When they purchased the Magazine, the proprietors opened a house, in Waterloo Place, for the better circulation of the publication.

It was there that the contributors met once a month, over an excellent dinner, given by the firm ; and consulted and talked on literary matters together. These meetings were very social, all the guests coming with a determination to please and be pleased. I do not know that many important matters were arranged, for the welfare of the Magazine, at these dinners ; but the hearts of the contributors were opened, and with the expansion of the heart the intellect widened also. If there had been any shades of jealousy amongst them, they faded away before the light of the friendly carousal; if there was any envy, it died. All the fences and restraints of authorship were cast off, and the natural human being was disclosed.

Amongst others, Charles Lamb came to most of these dinners, always dressed in black; (his old snuff-coloured suit having been dismissed for years); always kind and genial ; conversational, not talkative, but quick in reply; eating little, and drinking moderately with the rest. Allan Cunningham, a stalwart man, was generally there ; very Scotch in aspect, but ready to do a good turn to any one. His talk was not too abundant, although he was a voluminous writer of prose. His songs, not unworthy of being compared with even those of Burns, are (as everybody knows) excellent. His face shone at these festivities. Reynolds came always. His good temper and vivacity were like condiments at the feast. There also came, once or twice, the Rev. H. F. Cary, the quiet gentleness of whose face almost interfered with its real intelligence. Yet he spoke well and with readiness, on any subject that he chose to discuss. He was very intimate with Lamb, who latterly often dined with him, and was always punctual: " By Cot's plessing we will not be absent at the grace" (he writes in 1834). Lamb's taste was very homely; he liked tripe and cow-heel, and once when he was suggesting a particular dish to his friend, he wrote " we were talking of roast shoulder of mutton and onion sauce ; but I scorn to prescribe hospitalities." Charles had great regard for Mr. Cary ; and in his last letter (written on his death-bed) he inquired for a book, which he was very uneasy about, and which he thought he had left at Mrs. Dyer's ; " It is Mr. Cary's book, (he says,) and I would not lose it for the world." Cary was entirely without vanity ; and he, who had traversed the ghastly regions of the Inferno, interchanged little courtesies on equal terms with workers who had never travelled beyond the pages of " The London Magazine " No one (it is said) who has performed anything great ever looks big upon it. Thomas Hood was there, almost silent, except when he shot out some irresistible pun, and disturbed the gravity of the company. Hood's labours were poetic, but his sports were passerine. It is remarkable that he, who was capable of jesting even on his own pre-judices and predilections, should not (like Catullus) have brought down the " Sparrow," and enclosed him in an ode. Lamb admired and was very familiar with him. " What a fertile genius he is," (Charles Lamb writes to Bernard Barton,) " and quiet withal." He then expatiates particularly on Hood's sketch of

"Very Deaf indeed!" wherein a footpad has stopped an old gentleman, but cannot make him understand what he wants, although the fellow is firing a pistol into his ear trumpet: "you'd like him very much," he adds. Although Lamb liked him very much, he was a little annoyed once by Hood writing a comical essay in imitation of (and so much like) one of his own, that people generally thought that Elia had awakened in an unruly mood.   Hazlitt attended once or twice; but he was a rather silent guest, rising into emphatic talk only when some political discussion (very rare) stimulated him. Mr. De Quincy appeared at only one of these dinners.   The expression of his face was intelligent, but cramped and somewhat peevish. He was self-involved, and did not add to the cheerfulness of the meeting. I have consulted this gentleman's three essays, of which Charles Lamb is professedly the subject; but I cannot derive from them anything illustrative of my friend Lamb's cha-racter. I have been mainly struck therein by De Quincy's attacks on Hazlitt; to whom the essays had no relation. I am aware that the two authors (Haz-litt and De Quincy) had a quarrel in 1823; Hazlitt having claimed certain theories or reasonings which the other had propounded as his own. In reply to Mr. De Quincy's claims to have had a familiar ac-quaintance with Charles Lamb, (in 1821 and 1823,) I have to observe that during these years (when I was almost continually with him) I never saw Mr. De Quincy at his house, and never heard Lamb speak of him or refer to his writings on any occasion. His visits to Lamb were surely very rare.

John Clare, a peasant from Northamptonshire, and a better poet than Bloomfield, was one of the visitors. He was thoroughly rustic ; dressed in conspicuously country fashion, and was as simple as a daisy. His delight at the wonders of London formed the staple of his talk. This was often stimulated into extravagance by the facetious fictions of Reynolds. Poor fellow, he died insane

About this time Lamb determined to leave London ; and in 1823 he moved into Colebrook Cottage, Islington, a small detached white house of six rooms. " The New River, rather elderly by this time," he says, " runs, if a moderate walking pace can be so termed, close to the foot of the house ; behind, is a spacious garden, &c., and the cheerful dining-room is studded all over and rough with old books : I feel like a great lord ; never having had a house before."

From this place (which a friend of his christened " petty Venice") he used often to walk into London, to breakfast or dine with an acquaintance. For walking was always grateful to him. When confined to his room in the India House, he counted it amongst his principal recreations, and even now, with the whole world of leisure before him, it ranked among his daily enjoyments. By himself, or with an acquaintance, and subsequently with Hood's dog Dash, (whose name should have been Rover,) he wandered over all the roads and by-paths of the adjoining country. He was a peripatetic, in every way, beyond the followers of Aristotle. Walking occupied his energies ; and when he returned home, he (like Sarah Battle) " unbent his mind over a book." " I cannot sit and think," is his phrase. If he now and then stopped for a minute at a rustic public house, tired with the excursive caprices of Dash—beguiled perhaps by the simple attractions of a village sign—I hold him ex-cusable for the glass of porter which sometimes in-vigorated him in his fatigue.

In the course of these walks he traversed all the green regions which lie on the north and north-east of the metropolis. In London he loved to frequent those streets where the old bookshops were, Wardour Street, Princes Street, Seven Dials : (where the shop has been long closed :) he loved also Gray's Inn, in the garden of which he met Dodd, just before his death ; "with his buffoon mask taken off,) and the Temple, into which you pass from the noise and crowd of Fleet Street,—into the quiet and "ample squares and green recesses," where the old Dial, "the garden god of Christian gardens," then told of Time, and where the still living fountain sends up its song into the listening air.

Of the Essays of " Elia,"[1] written originally for the "London Magazine," I feel it difficult to speak. They are the best amongst the good : his best. I see that they are genial, delicate, terse, full of thought and full of humour ; that they are delightfully personal ; and when he speaks of himself you cannot hear too much : that they are not imitations, but adoptions. We encounter his likings and fears, his fancies (his nature) in all. The words have an import never known before : the syllables have expanded their meaning, like opened flowers ; the goodness of others is heightened by his own tenderness ; and what is in nature hard and bad is qualified (qualified, not con-

---

[1] The first Essays of Elia were published by Taylor and Hessey under the title "Elia," in 1823. The second Essays were, together with the " Popular Fallacies," collected and published under the title of " The Last Essays of Elia," by Moxon in 1833.

cealed) by the tender light of pity, which always in-
termingles with his own vision. Gravity and laughter,
fact and fiction are heaped together, leavened in each
case by charity and toleration ; and all are marked by
a wise humanity. Lamb's humour, I imagine, often
reflected (sometimes, I hope, relieved) the load of
pain that always weighed on his own heart.

The first of the Essays ("The South Sea House")
appeared in the month of August, 1820: the last
("Captain Jackson") in November, 1824. Lamb's
literary prosperity during this period was at the
highest ; yet he was always loth to show himself too
much before the world. After the first series of essays
had been published (for they are divided into two
parts) he feigned that he was dead, and caused the
second series to be printed as by "a friend of the
late Elia." These were written somewhat reluctantly.
His words are, " To say the truth, it is time he
[Elia] were gone. The humour of the thing, if ever
there were much humour in it, was pretty well exhausted ; and a two-years-and-a-half existence has
been a tolerable duration for a phantom." It is thus
modestly that he speaks of essays which have delighted all cultivated readers.

I want a phrase to express the combination of
qualities which constitutes Lamb's excellence in
letters. In the absence of this, I must content myself with referring to some of the papers which live
most distinctly in my recollection. I will not transcribe any part of his eulogy on Hogarth ; nor of his
fine survey of " Lear," that grandest of all tragedies.
They are well known to students of books. I turn
for a moment to the Elia Essays only. In mere
variety of subject (extent in a small space) they sur-

pass almost all other essays. They are full of a witty
melancholy. Many of them may be termed autobio-
graphical, which trebles their interest with most
readers.

Let me recollect :—How he mourns over the ruins
of Blackesmoor (once his home on holidays) " reduced
to an antiquity." How he stalks, ghost-like, through
the desolate rooms of the South Sea House; or
treads the avenues of the Temple; (where the
benchers, " supposed to have been children once ")
are pacing the stony terraces. Then there is the
inimitable Sarah Battle, (unconquered even by
Chance,) arming herself for the war of whist , and
the young Africans, " preaching from their chimney-
pulpits lessons of patience to mankind." If your
appetite is keen, by all means visit Bobo, who invented roast pig: if gay, and disposed to saunter
through the pleasant lanes of Hertfordshire, go to
Mackery End, where the Gladmans and Brutons will
bid you welcome: if grave, let your eyes repose on
the face of dear old Bridget Elia, " in a season of distress the truest comforter." Should you wish to en-
large your humanity, place a few coins (maravedis)
in the palm of one of the beggars (" the blind Tobits ")
of London, and try to believe his tales, histories, or
fables, as though they were the veritable stories (told
by night) on the banks of the famous Tigris. Do not
despise the poorest of the poor—even the writer of
valentines ; " All valentines are not foolish," as you
may read in Elia's words ; and " All fools' day " may
cheer you, as the fool in " Lear " may make you wise
and tolerant.

I could go on for many pages—to the poor relations, and the old books, and the old actors ; to Dodd,

who " dying put on the weeds of Dominic;" and to
Mrs. Jordan and Dickey Suet; (both whom I well remember,) to Elliston, always on the stage; to Munden, with features ever changing; and to Liston with
only one face; " But what a face !" I forbear. I
pass also over Comberbatch (Coleridge), borrower of
books, and Captain Jackson, and Barbara S.; (Miss
Kelly;) and go to the rest of my little history.

The " Popular Fallacies," which in course of time
followed, and were eventually added to the second
series and re-published, are in manner essays also on
a small scale, brief, and dealing with abstract subjects
more than the " Elia " It may be interesting to know
that Lamb's two favourites were " That home is
home, though it is never so homely," and " That we
should rise with the lark." In the first of these he
enters into all the discomforts and terrible distrac-
tions of a poor man's home; in the second he des-
cants on the luxuries of bed, and the nutritious value
of dreams : " The busy part of mankind," he says,
" are content to swallow their sleep by wholesale : we
choose to linger in bed and digest our dreams." The
last " Fallacy " is remarkable for a sentence which
seems to refer to Alice W. :—" We were never much
in the world," he says; " disappointment early struck
a dark veil between us and its dazzling illusions ·"
he then concludes with " We once thought life to be
something, but it has unaccountably fallen from us
before its time. The sun has no purposes of ours to
light us to. Why should we get up ?"

It will be observed by the sagacious student of the
entire Essays, that however quaint or familiar, or
(rarely, however,) sprinkled with classical allusions,
they are never vulgar, nor commonplace, nor pe-

dantic. They are "natural with a self-pleasing quaintness." The phrases are not affected; but are derived from our ancestors, now gone to another country; they are brought back from the land of shadows and made denizens of England, in modern times. Lamb's studies were the lives and characters of men, his humours and tragic meditations were generally dug out of his own heart; there are in them earnestness, and pity, and generosity, and truth; and there is not a mean or base thought to be found throughout all.

In reading over these old essays, some of them affect me with a grave pleasure, amounting to pain. I seem to import into them the very feeling with which he wrote them; his looks and movements are transfigured, and communicated to me by the poor art of the printer. His voice, so sincere and earnest, rings in my ear again. He was no Feignwell: apart from his joke, never was a man so real, and free from pretence. No one as I believe will ever taste the flavour of certain writers as he has done. He was the last true lover of Antiquity. Although he admitted a few of the beauties of modern times, yet in his stronger love he soared backwards to old acclivities, and loved to rest there. His essays, like his sonnets, are (as I have said) reflections of his own feelings. And so, I think, should essays generally be. A history or sketch of science,—or a logical effort, may help the reader some way up the ladder of learning; but they do not link themselves with his affections. I myself prefer the affections to the sciences. The story of the heart is the deepest of all histories; and Shakespeare is profounder and longer lived than Maclaurin or Malthus or Ricardo.

Lamb's career throughout his later years was marked by an enlarged intercourse with society; (it had never been confined to persons of his own way of thinking;) by more frequent absences in the country and elsewhere; and by the reception of a somewhat wider body of acquaintance into his own house. He visited the Universities, in which he much delighted: he fraternised with many of the contributors to the "London Magazine." He received the letters and calls of his admirers; strangers and others. These were now much extended in number, by the publication of the "Essays of Elia." I was in the habit of seeing him very frequently at his home; I met him also at Mr. Cary's, at Leigh Hunt's, at Novello's, at Haydon's, once at Hazlitt's, and elsewhere. It must have been about this time that one of his visits (which always took place when the students were absent) was made to Oxford, where he met George Dyer, dreaming amongst the quadrangles, as he has described in his pleasant paper, called "Oxford in the Vacation." Lamb's letters to correspondents are perhaps not quite so frequent now, as formerly. He writes occasionally to his old friends; to Wordsworth and Southey and Coleridge; also to Manning, who is still in China, and to whom in December, 1815, he had sent one of his best and most characteristic letters, describing the (imaginary) death and decrepitude of his correspondent's friends in England: although he takes care (the next day) to tell him that his first was a "lying letter." Indeed that letter itself, humorous as it is, is so obviously manufactured in the fabulous district of hyperbole, that it requires no disavowal. Manning, however, returns to England not long afterwards, and

then the correspondence, if less humorous, is also
less built of improbabilities. He corresponds also
with Mr. Barron Field, who is relegated to the Judicial
Bench in New South Wales. Of him he inquires
about " The Land of Thieves :" he wants to know if
their poets be not plagiarists ; and suggests that half
the truth which his letters contain " will be converted
into lies " before they reach his correspondent.
Mr. Field is the gentleman to whom the pleasant
paper on " Distant Correspondents " is addressed.

In 1822 Charles Lamb and his sister travelled as
far as Paris ; neither of them understanding a word
of the French language. What tempted them to
undertake this expedition I never knew. Perhaps, as
he formerly said, when journeying to the Lakes, it was
merely a daring ambition to see " remote regions."
The French journey seems to have been almost barren
of good. He brought nothing back in his memory ;
and there is no account whatever of his adventures
there. It has been stated that Mary Lamb was
taken ill on the road, but I do not know this with
certainty. From a short letter to Barron Field, it
appears, indeed, that he thought Paris "a glorious
picturesque old city," to which London looked
" mean and new," although the former had " no
Saint Paul's or Westminster Abbey." " I and
sister," he writes, " are just returned from Paris.
We have eaten frogs !—It has been such a treat.
Nicest little delicate things, like Lilliputian rabbits."
But this is all. His Reminiscences, whatever they
were, do not enrich his correspondence. In conversation he used to tell how he had once intended
to ask the waiter for an egg, (œuf,) but called, in his
ignorance, for Eau de vie, and that the mistake pro-

duced so pleasant a result, that his inquiries afterwards for Eau de vie were very frequent.

In his travels to Cambridge, which began to be
frequent about this time, his gains were greater.
For there he first became acquainted with Miss
Emma Isola, for whom, as I can testify, he at all
times exhibited the greatest parental regard. When
he and Mary Lamb first knew her, she was a little
orphan girl, at school. They invited her to spend
her holidays with them : and she went accordingly :
the liking became mutual, and gradually deepened
into great affection   The visit once made and so
much relished, became habitual ; and Miss Isola's
holidays were afterwards regularly spent at the
Lambs' house. She used to take long walks with
Charles, when his sister was too old and infirm to
accompany him.   Ultimately she was looked upon
in the light of a child : and Charles Lamb when
speaking of her, (and he did this always tenderly,)
used invariably to call her "Our Emma." To show
how deep his regard was, he at one time was invited
to engage in some profitable engagement (1830)
whilst Miss Isola was in bad health ; but he at once
replied, "Whilst she is in danger, and till she is out of
it, I feel that I have no spirits for an engagement of
any kind."   Some years afterwards when she became
well, and was about to be married, Lamb writes. " I
am about to lose my only walk companion," whose
mirthful spirits (as he prettily terms it) were " the
youth of our house." "With my perfect approval,
and more than concurrence," as he states, she was
to be married to Mr. Moxon. Miss Emma Isola,
who was, in Charles Lamb's phrase, " a very dear
friend of ours," remained his friend till death, and

became eventually his principal legatee. After her marriage, Charles, writing to her husband, (Nov., 1833,) says: "Tell Emma I every day love her more, and miss her less. Tell her so, from her loving Uncle, as she has let me call myself." It was, as I believe, a very deep paternal affection.

The particulars disclosed by the letters of 1823 and 1824 are so generally unimportant, that it is unnecessary to refer to them. Lamb, indeed, became acquainted with the author of "Virginius," (Sheridan Knowles,) with Mr. Macready, and with the writers in the "London Magazine" (which then had not been long established). And he appears gradually to discover that his work at the India House is wearisome, and complains of it in bitter terms: "Thirty years have I served the Philistines," (he writes to Wordsworth,) "and my neck is not subdued to the yoke." He confesses that he had once hoped to have a pension on "this side of absolute incapacity and infirmity," and to have walked out in the "fine Izaac Walton mornings, careless as a beggar, and walking, walking, and dying walking;" but he says, "the hope is gone. I sit like Philomel all day, (but not singing,) with my breast against this thorn of a desk." The character of his letters at this time is not generally lively; there is, he says, "a certain deadness to everything, which I think I may date from poor John's [his brother's] loss. Deaths overset one. Then there's Captain Burney gone. What fun has whist now?" He proceeds, "I am made up of queer points. My theory is to enjoy life: but my practice is against it." The only hope he has, he says, is "that some pulmonary affection may relieve me."—The success which attended the

" Elia " Essays did not comfort him, nor the (pecu-
niary) temptations of the bookseller to renew them.
" The spirit of the thing in my own mind is gone"
(he writes). " Some brains," as Ben Jonson says,
" will endure but one skimming." Notwithstanding
his melancholy humour, however, there is Hope in
the distance, which he does not see, and Freedom is
not far off.

It was during this period of Lamb's life (1823) that
the quarrel between him and his old friend Robert
Southey took place. Southey had long been (as was
well known) one of the most constant and efficient
contributors to the " Quarterly Review:" and Lamb
assigned to him the authorship of one of the Review
articles, in which he himself was scantily compli-
mented, and his friends Hazlitt and Leigh Hunt denounced Sir T. Talfourd thinks that Mr. Southey
was not the author of the offending essay. Be that
as it may, Lamb was then of opinion that his old
Tory friend was the enemy. In a letter to Bernard
Barton, (July, 1823,) he writes, "Southey has attacked ' Elia,' on the score of infidelity. He might
have spared an old friend. I hate his Review, and
his being a Reviewer;" but he adds, "I love and
respect Southey, and will not retort." However, in
the end, irritated by the calumny, or (which is more
probable) resenting compliments bestowed on himself
at the expense of his friends, he sat down and penned
his famous " Letter of Elia to Robert Southey, Esq.,"
which appeared in the " London Magazine," for
October, 1823, and which was afterwards published
amongst his collected letters.

This letter, I remember, produced a strong sensation in literary circles ; and Mr. Southey's acquaint-

ances smiled, and his enemies rejoiced at it. Indeed, the letter itself is a remarkable document. With much of Lamb's peculiar phraseology, it is argumentative, and defends the imaginary weaknesses or faults, against what (as he guesses) the "Quarterly" reproofs had been levelled. The occasion having gone by, this letter has been dismissed from most minds, except that part of it which exhibits Lamb's championship, on behalf of Hunt and Hazlitt; and which is more touching than anything to be found in controversial literature.

Lamb's letter was unknown to his sister, until after it appeared in the Magazine, it being his practice to write his letters in Leadenhall Street. It caused her a good deal of annoyance, when she saw it in print. It is pleasant to think, however, that it was the means of restoring the old intimacy between Southey and Lamb, and also of strengthening the friendship between Lamb and Hazlitt, which some misunderstanding, at that time, had a little loosened.

When I was married, (October, 1824,) Lamb sent me a congratulatory letter; which, as it was not published by Sir T. Talfourd, and is, moreover, characteristic, I insert here, from the MS.

"My Dear Procter,—I do agnise a shame in not having been to pay my congratulations to Mrs. Procter and your happy self, but on Sunday (my only morning) I was engaged to a country walk; and in virtue of the hypostatical union between us, when Mary calls, it is understood that I call too, we being univocal.

"But indeed I am ill at these ceremonious inductions. I fancy I was not born with a call on my

head, though I have brought one down upon it with
a vengeance. I love not to pluck that sort of frail
crude, but to stay its ripening into visits. In probability Mary will be at Southampton Row this morning, and something of that kind be matured between
you, but in any case not many hours shall elapse before I shake you by the hand.

"Meantime give my kindest felicitations to Mrs.
Procter, and assure her I look forward with the
greatest delight to our acquaintance. By the way,
the deuce a bit of cake has come to hand, which hath
an inauspicious look at first, but I comfort myself
that the Mysterious Service hath that property of Sa-
cramental bread, which mice cannot nibble, nor time
moulder.

"I am married myself—to a severe step-wife—who
keeps me, not at bed and board, but at desk and
board, and is jealous of my morning aberrations. I
cannot slip out to congratulate kinder unions. It is
well she leaves me alone o' nights—the d—d Day-
hag *Business*. She is even now peeping over me to
see I am writing no love letters. I come, my dear
—Where is the Indigo Sale Book?

"Twenty adieus, my dear friends, till we meet.

"Yours most truly,

"C. LAMB.

"*Leadenhall, Nov. 11th, '24.*"

The necessity for labour continued for some short
time longer.—At last (in the beginning of the year
1825) deliverance came. Charles had previously intimated his wish to resign. The directors of the
East India House call him into their private room,
and after complimenting him on his long and meri-

torious services, they suggest that his health does not
appear to be good; that a little ease is expedient at
his time of life, and they then conclude their conversation, by suddenly intimating their intention of
granting him a pension for his life, of two-thirds the
amount of his salary: "a magnificent offer," as he
terms it He is from that moment emancipated; let
loose from all ties of labour, free to fly wheresoever
he will. At the commencement of the talk Charles
had had misgivings, for he was summoned into the
" formidable back parlour," he says, and thought that
the Directors were about to intimate that they had
no further occasion for his services. The whole
scene seems like one of the summer sunsets, preceded
by threatenings of tempest, when the dark piles of
clouds are separated and disappear, lost and swallowed by the radiance which fills the whole length
and breadth of the sky, and looks as if it would be
eternal. "I don't know what I answered," Lamb
says, " between surprise and gratitude; but it was
understood that I accepted their proposal, and I
was told that I was free from that hour to leave their
service. I stammered out a bow, and, at just ten
minutes after eight, I went home—for ever."—At this
time Lamb's salary was £600 per annum. The
amount of two-thirds of this sum, therefore, would be
an annuity of £400. But an annual provision was
also made for his sister, in case she should survive
him, and this occasioned a small diminution. In
exact figures, he was to receive £391 a year during
the remainder of his life, and then an annuity was to
become payable to Mary Lamb. His sensations,
first of stupefaction, and afterwards of measureless
delight, will be seen by reference to his exulting

letters of this period. First he writes to Wordsworth of " the good that has befallen me." These are his words : " I came home—for ever—on Tuesday last. The incomprehensibleness of my condition over-whelmed me. It was like passing from Time into Eternity." * * * " Mary wakes every morning with an obscure feeling that some good has happened to us."—To Bernard Barton his words are, " I have scarce steadiness of head to compose a letter. I am free, B. B. , free as air. I will live another fifty years." * * "Would I could sell you some of my leisure ! Positively the best thing a man can have to do is— Nothing : and next to that, perhaps, Good Works." To Miss Hutchinson he writes, "I would not go back to my prison for seven years longer for £10,000 a year. For some days I was staggered, and could not comprehend the magnitude of my deliverance , was confused, giddy. But these giddy feelings have gone away, and my weather-glass stands at a degree or two above 'Content.' All being holidays, I feel as if I had none ; as they do in Heaven, where 'tis all Red Letter days."

Lamb's discharge or relief was timely and gra-ciously bestowed. It opened a bright vista through which he beheld (in hope) many years of enjoyment ; scenes in which his spirit. rescued from painful work, had only to disport itself in endless delights. He had well earned his discharge. He had laboured without cessation for thirty-three years, had been diligent and trusted—a labourer worthy of his hire. And the con-sciousness of this long and good service must have mingled with his reward and sweetened it. It is a great thing to have earned your meal—your rest,— whatever may be the payment in full for your deserts

You have not to force up gratitude from oblivious depths, day by day, for undeserved bounty. In Lamb's case it happened, unfortunately, that the activity of mind which had procured his repose, tended afterwards to disqualify him from enjoying it. The leisure that he had once reckoned on so much exceeded, when it came, the pains of the old count- ing-house travail. It is only the imbecile, or those brought up in complete lazyhood, who can encounter successfully the monotony of "nothing to do," and can slumber away their lives unharmed amongst the dumb weeds and flowers.

In the course of a short time it appeared that he was unable to enjoy so perfectly as he had anticipated his golden time of " Nothing to do," his Liberia. He therefore took long walks into the country. He also acquired the companionship of the large dog, Dash, much given to wandering, to whose erratic propensities (Lamb walking at the rate of fourteen miles a day) he eventually became a slave. The rambling, inconstant dog rendered the clear serene day of leisure almost turbid; and he was ultimately, (in order to preserve for Charles some little remaining enjoyment,) bestowed upon another master. Lamb was always (as I have said) fond of walking, and he had some vague liking, I suppose, for free air and green pastures; although he had no great relish spe- cially for the flowers and ornaments of the country. I have often walked with him, in the neighbourhood of our great city; and I do not think that he ever treasured up in his memory the violets, (or other flowers,) the songs of birds, or the pictures of sheep or kine dotting the meadows. Neither his conversa- tion nor writings afforded evidence that he had done

MEMOIR OF CHARLES LAMB.

So. It is not easy, therefore, to determine what the special attractions were that drew him out of London, which he loved, into the adjoining country, where his walks oftenest lay.

At the time of Lamb's deliverance from office labour, he was living in Colebrook Row. It was there that George Dyer, whose blindness and absence of mind rendered it almost dangerous for him to wander unaccompanied about the suburbs of London, came to visit him on one occasion. By accident, instead of entering the house door, Dyer's aqueous instincts led him towards the water, and in a moment he had plunged overhead in the New River. I happened to go to Lamb's house, about an hour after his rescue and restoration to dry land, and met Miss Lamb in the passage, in a state of great alarm : she was whimpering, and could only utter " Poor Mr. Dyer! poor Mr. Dyer," in tremulous tones. I went upstairs, aghast, and found that the involuntary diver had been placed in bed, and that Miss Lamb had administered brandy and water, as a well established preventive against cold. Dyer, unaccustomed to anything stronger than the " crystal spring," was sitting upright in the bed, perfectly delirious. His hair had been rubbed up, and stood out like so many needles of iron grey. He did not (like Falstaff) babble of " green fields," but of the " watery Neptune." " I soon found out where I was," he cried out to me, laughing; and then he went wandering on, his words taking flight into regions where no one could follow. Charles Lamb has commemorated this immersion of his old friend, in his (Elia) essay of " Amicus Redivivus."

In the summer of 1826 Lamb published in " Black-

2 P 2

wood's Magazine," a little drama in one act, entitled
" The Wife's Trial." It was founded on Crabbe's
poetical tale of " The Confidant ;" and contains the
germ of a plot, which undoubtedly might have been
worked out with more effect, if Lamb had devoted
sufficient labour to that object.

Amongst the remarkable persons whom Charles
became acquainted with, in these years, was Edward
Irving. Lamb used to meet him at Coleridge's house
at Highgate, and elsewhere ; and he came to the conclusion that he was (as indeed he *was*) a fine sincere
spirited man, terribly slandered. Edward Irving,
who issued, like a sudden light, from the obscure
little town of Annan, in Scotland, acquired, in the
year 1822, a wide reputation in London. He was a
minister of the Scotch Church, and before he came
to England had acted as an assistant preacher to Dr.
Chalmers. In one of Charles's letters (in 1835) to
Bernard Barton, (who had evidently been measuring
Irving by a low Quaker standard,) he takes the opportunity of speaking of the great respect that he entertained for the Scotch minister. " Let me adjure
you," (writes Charles,) " have no doubt of Irving.
Let Mr. ——— [?] drop his disrespect."—" Irving
has prefixed a dedication, of a missionary character,
to Coleridge—most beautiful, cordial, and sincere.
He there acknowledges his obligations to S. T. C.,
at whose Gamaliel feet he sits weekly, rather than to
all men living." Again he writes · " Some friend
said to Irving, ' This will do you no good' (no good
in worldly repute). ' *That is a reason for doing it,*'
quoth Irving. I am thoroughly pleased with him.
He is firm, outspeaking, intrepid, and docile as a
pupil of Pythagoras." In April, 1825, Lamb writes

to Wordsworth to the same effect. "Have you read the noble dedication of Irving's Missionary Sermons?" he inquires. and then he repeats Irving's fine answer to the suggested impolicy of publishing his book with its sincere prefix.—Poor Edward Irving, whom I always deeply respected, and knew intimately for some years, and who was one of the best and truest men whom it has been my good fortune to meet in life! He entered London amidst the shouts of his admirers, and he departed in the midst of contumely ; sick and sad, and maligned, and misunderstood ; going back to his dear native Scotland only to die. The time has long passed for discussing the truths or errors of Edward Irving's peculiar creed ; but there can be no doubt that he himself was true and faithful till death ; and that he preached only what he entirely believed. And what can man do more ? If he was wrong, his errors arose from his extreme modesty, his extreme veneration, for the subject to which he raised his thoughts.

In the last year of Edward Irving's life, (1834,) he was counselled by his physician to pass the winter in a milder climate—that " it was the only safe thing for him." Prevented from ministering in his own church, where " he had become an embarrassment," he travels into the rural places, subdued and chastened by his weakness,—to the Wye and the Severn—to the fine mountains and pleasant places of Wales. Sometimes he thinks himself better. He quits London (for ever) in the early part of September, and on the 23rd of that month he writes to his wife that he is " surely better, for *his pulse has come to be under* 100." He passes by Cader Idris and Snowdon—by Bedgelert to Bangor, a " place of repose ;" but gets wet whilst viewing the Menai Bridge, and had "a fevered night;" yet he is able to droop on to Liverpool. Thence (the love of his native land drawing him on) he goes northwards, instead of to the south. He reaches Glasgow, where " he thinks of organising a church," although Dr. Darling "decidedly says that he cannot humanly live over the winter." Yet still he goes on with his holy task; he writes " pastoral letters," and preaches, and prays, and offers kind advice. His friends, from Kirkaldy and elsewhere, come to see him, where, " for a few weeks still, he is visible about Glasgow. In the sunshine —in a lonely street, his gaunt gigantic figure rises feebly against the light." At last he lies down on " the bed from which he is never to rise;" his mind wanders, and his articulation becomes indistinct; but he is occasionally understood, and is heard murmuring (in Hebrew) parts of the 23rd Psalm, "The Lord is my shepherd : He leadeth me beside the still waters." And thus gradually sinking, at the close of a gloomy Sunday night in December, he dies.

Mr. Thomas Carlyle, his friend, (the friend of his youth,) has written an eloquent epitaph upon him ; not partial, for they differed in opinion—but eloquent, and very touching. I read it over once or twice in every year. Edward Irving's last words, according to his statement, were, " In life and in death I am the Lord's." Carlyle then adds :—" But for Irving, I had never known what the communion of man with man means. He was the freest, brotherliest, bravest human soul mine ever came in contact with ; the best man I have ever (after trial enough) found in this world, or now hope to find."

So Edward Irving went to the true and brave enthusiasts who had gone before him.   He died on his final Sabbath, (7th December, 1834,) and left the world and all its troubles behind him.

CHAPTER VII.

SPECIMEN OF LAMB'S HUMOUR—DEATH OF MR. NORRIS—GARRICK PLAYS—LETTERS TO BARTON—OPINIONS ON BOOKS—BREAKFAST WITH MR. N. P. WILLIS—MOVES TO ENFIELD—CARICATURE OF LAMB— ALBUMS AND ACROSTICS—PAINS OF LEISURE—THE BARTON CORRE- SPONDENCE—DEATH OF HAZLITT—MUNDEN'S ACTING AND QUITTING THE STAGE—LAMB BECOMES A BOARDER—MOVES TO EDMONTON— METROPOLITAN ATTACHMENTS—DEATH OF COLERIDGE—LAMB'S FALL AND DEATH—DEATH OF MARY LAMB—POSTSCRIPT.

WITH the expiration of the "London Magazine," Lamb's literary career terminated.   A few trifling contributions to the "New Monthly," and other periodicals are scarcely sufficient to qualify this statement.

It may be convenient, in this place, to specify some of those examples of humour and of jocose speech, for which Charles Lamb in his lifetime was well known.   These (not his best thoughts) can be separated from the rest, and may attract the notice of the reader, here and there, and relieve the tameness of a not very eventful narrative.

It is possible to define wit, (which, as Mr Cole- ridge says, is "impersonal,") and humour also ; but it is not easy to distinguish the humour of one man from that of all other humorists, so as to bring his special quality clearly before the apprehension of the reader.   Perhaps the best (if not the most scientific) way, might be to produce specimens of each. In Charles Lamb's case, instances of his humour are to be found in his essays, in his sayings, (already partially reported,) and throughout his letters ; where they are very frequent. They are often of the composite order, in which humour and wit and (sometimes) pathos are intermingled. Sometimes they merely exhibit the character of the man.

He once said of himself that his biography "would go into an epigram." His sayings require greater space. Some of those which have been circulated are apocryphal. The following are taken chiefly from his letters, and from my own recollections.

—In his exultation, on being released from his thirty-four years of labour at the India House, he says, "Had I a little son, I would christen him ' Nothing to do.'" (This is in "the Superannuated Man.")

Speaking of Don Quixote, he calls him " the errant Star of Knighthood, made more tender by eclipse."

On being asked by a schoolmistress for some sign indicative of her calling, he recommended "The Murder of the Innocents."

I once said something in his presence, which I thought possessed smartness. He commended me with a stammer· very well, my dear boy, very well; Ben, (taking a pinch of snuff,) Ben Jonson has said worse things than that—and—and b—b—better." [1]

---

[1] This, with a small variation, is given in Mr. Thomas Moore's autobiography. I suppose I must have repeated it to him, and that he forgot the precise words.

l   *D*

His young chimney sweepers " from their little pulpits (the tops of chimneys) in the nipping air of a December morning, preach a lesson of patience to mankind."

His saying to Martin Burney has been often repeated : " Oh Martin, if dirt were trumps, what a hand you would hold !"

To Coleridge, " Bless you, old sophist, who next to human nature taught me all the corruption I was capable of knowing."

To Mr. Gillman, a surgeon (" query Killman ?") he writes, " Coleridge is very bad, but he wonderfully picks up, and his face, when he repeats his verses, hath its ancient glory : an archangel a little damaged."

To Wordsworth, (who was superfluously solemn,) he writes, " Some d—d people have come in, and I must finish abruptly. By d—d, I only mean deuced."

The second son of George the Second, it was said, had a very cold and ungenial manner. Lamb stammered out in his defence that " this was very natural in the Duke of Cu-Cum-ber-land."

To Bernard Barton, of a person of repute : " There must be something in him. Such great names imply greatness. Which of us has seen Michael Angelo's things ? yet which of us disbelieves his greatness ?"

To Mrs. H., of a person eccentric, " Why does not his guardian angel look to him ? He deserves one—maybe he has tired him out."

" Charles," said Coleridge to Lamb, " I think you have heard me preach ?" " I n—n—never heard you do anything else," replied Lamb.

One evening Coleridge had consumed the whole

time in talking of some "regenerated" orthodoxy.
Leigh Hunt, who was one of the listeners, on leaving the house, expressed his surprise at the prodigality and intensity of Coleridge's religious expressions. Lamb tranquillized him by " Ne—ne—never
mind what Coleridge says , he's full of fun."

There were, &c., &c., " and at the top of all,
Hunger, (eldest, strongest of the Passions,) predominant, breaking down the stony fences of
shame."

The Bank, the India House, and other rich
traders look insultingly on the old deserted South
Sea .House, as on " their poor neighbour out of
business."

To a Frenchman, setting up Voltaire's character
in opposition to that of Christ, Lamb asserted that
" Voltaire was a very good Jesus Christ—*for the
French.*"

Of a Scotchman. " His understanding is always
at its meridian. Between the affirmative and the
negative there is no border land with him. You
cannot hover with him on the confines of truth."

On a book of Coleridge's nephew he writes, " I
confess he has more of the Sterne about him than
the Sternhold. But he saddens into excellent sense,
before the conclusion."

As to a monument being erected for Clarkson, in
his lifetime, he opposes it ; and argues, " Goodness
blows no trumpet, nor desires to have it blown. We
should be modest for a modest man."

" M.B. is on the top scale of my friendship's
ladder, which an angel or two is still climbing : and
some, alas, descending."

A fine sonnet of his (The Gipsy's Malison) being

refused publication, he exclaimed, " Hang the age !
I will write for Antiquity."

Once, whilst waiting in the Highgate stage, a
woman came to the door and inquired in a stern
voice, " Are you full inside ? " " Yes, ma'am," said
Charles, in meek reply, " quite ; that plateful of Mrs.
Gillman's pudding has quite filled us."

Mrs. K., after expressing her love for her young
children, added, tenderly, " And how do *you* like
babies, Mr. Lamb ? " His answer, immediate, almost
precipitate, was " Boi-boi-boiled, ma'am."

Hood tempting Lamb to dine with him, said " We
have a hare." " And many friends ? " inquired
Lamb.

It being suggested that he would not sit down to a
meal with the Italian witnesses at the Queen's trial,
Lamb rejected the imputation, asserting that he
would sit with anything, except a hen or a tailor.

Of a man too prodigal of lampoons and verbal
jokes, Lamb said, threateningly, " I'll Lamp-pun
him."

On two Prussians of the same name being accused
of the same crime, it was remarked as curious that
they were not in any way related to each other. " A
mistake," said he, " they are cozens german."

An old lady, fond of her dissenting minister,
wearied Lamb by the length of her praises. I speak,
because I *know* him well, said she. " Well, I don't ;"
replied Lamb ; " I don't ; but d——n him, at a ' venture.' "

The Scotch, whom he did not like, ought, he said,
to have double punishment ; and to have fire without brimstone.

Southey, in 1799, showed him a dull poem on a

rose; Lamb's criticism was, "Your rose is insipid: it has neither thorns nor sweetness."

A person sending an unnecessarily large sum with a lawyer's brief, Lamb said it was 'a fee simple.'"

Mr. H. C. Robinson, just called to the bar, tells him, exultingly, that he is retained in a cause in the King's Bench. "Ah," (said Lamb,) "the great first cause, least understood."

Of a pun, Lamb says it is a noble thing *per se.* It is entire. It fills the mind; it is as perfect as a sonnet; better. It limps ashamed, in the train and retinue of humour."[1]

---

[1] I fear that I have not, in all the foregoing instances, set forth with sufficient precision, the grounds or premises upon which the jests were founded There were, moreover, various other sayings of Lamb, which do not come into the above catalogue ; as where—when enjoying a pipe with Dr. Parr, that divine inquired how he came to acquire the love of smoking so much, he replied, "I toiled after it as some people do after virtue."—When Godwin was expatiating on the benefit of unlimited freedom of thought, especially in matters of religion, Lamb, who did not like this, interrupted him by humming the little child's song of "Old father Longlegs won't say his prayers," adding, violently, "*Throw him down stairs !*"—He consoles Mr. Crabb Robinson, suffering under tedious rheumatism, by writing "Your doctor seems to keep you under the long cure."—To Wordsworth, in order to explain that his friend A. was in good health, he writes, " A. is well, he is proof against weather, ingratitude, meat underdone, and every weapon of fate."—The story of Lamb replying to some one, who insisted very strenuously on some interesting circumstances being "a matter of fact," by saying that *he* was "a matter of lie" man, is like Leigh Hunt, who in opposing the frequent confessions of "I'm in love," asserted, in a series of verses, that he was " In hate."—Charles hated noise and fuss and fine words, but never hated any person Once when he had said, "I hate Z," some one present remonstrated with him, "Why you have never seen him." "No," replied Lamb, "certainly not; I never could hate any man that I have once seen."—Being

Lamb's puns, as far as I recollect, were not frequent; and, except in the case of a pun, it is difficult to divest a good saying of the facts surrounding it without impoverishing the saying itself. Lamb's humour is generally imbedded in the surrounding sense, and cannot often be disentangled without injury.

I have said that the proprietorship of the "London Magazine," in the year 1821, became vested in Messrs. Taylor and Hessey, under whom it became a social centre for the meeting of many literary men. The publication, however, seems to have interfered with the ordinary calling of the booksellers, and the sale was not therefore (I suppose) sufficiently important to remunerate them for the disturbance of

asked how he felt when amongst the lakes and mountains of Cumberland, he replied that he was obliged to think of the Ham and Beef shop near Saint Martin's Lane; this was in order to bring down his thoughts from their almost too painful elevation, to the sober regions of everyday life.

In the foregoing little history, I have set forth such facts as tend in my opinion, to illustrate my friend's character. One anecdote I have omitted, and it should not be forgotten. Lamb, one day, encountered a small urchin loaded with a too heavy package of grocery. It caused him to tremble and stop. Charles inquired where he was going, took (although weak) the load upon his own shoulder, and managed to carry it to Islington, the place of its destination. Finding that the purchaser of the grocery was a female, he went with the urchin before her, and expressed a hope that she should intercede with the poor boy's master, in order to prevent his being overweighted in future. "Sir," said the dame, after the manner of Tisiphone, frowning upon him, "I buy my sugar and have nothing to do with the man's manner of sending it." Lamb at once perceived the character of the purchaser, and taking off his hat, said, humbly, "Then I hope, ma'am, you'll give me a drink of small beer." This was of course refused. He afterwards called upon the grocer, on the boy's behalf. With what effect I do not know.

their general trade.   At all events, it was sold to Mr.
Henry Southern, the editor of " The Retrospective
Review," at the expiration of 1825, after having
been in existence during five entire years.   In Mr.
Southern's hands, under a different system of
management, it speedily ceased.

In 1828 (January) Charles Lamb suffered great
grief from the loss of a very old friend, Mr. Norris.
It may be remembered that he was one of the two
persons who went to comfort Lamb when his mother
so suddenly died.   Mr. Norris had been one of the
officers of the Inner Temple or Christ's Hospital, and
had been intimate with the Lambs for many years ;
and Charles, when young, used always to spend his
Christmases with him.   " He was my friend and my
father's friend," Lamb writes, " all the life I can remember.   I seem to have made foolish friendships
ever since.   Old as I am, in his eyes, I was still the
child he first knew me.   To the last, he called me
' Charley.'   I have none to call me Charley now.   He
was the last link that bound me to the Temple."

It was after his death that Lamb once more re-
sorted to the British Museum ; which he had been
in the habit of frequenting formerly, when his first
" Dramatic Specimens " were published.   Now he
went there to make other extracts from the old plays.
These were entitled " The Garrick Plays," and were
bestowed upon Mr. Hone, who was poor, and were
by him published in his " Every Day Book."   Subsequently they were collected by Charles himself, and
formed a supplement to the earlier " Specimens."
Lamb's labours in this task were by no means trivial.
" I am now going through a course of reading," (of
old plays,) he writes, " I have two thousand to go
through."

Lamb's correspondence with his Quaker friend, Bernard Barton, ("the busy B," as Hood called him,) whose knowledge of the English drama was confined to Shakespeare and Miss Baillie, went on constantly. His letters to this gentleman comprised a variety of subjects, on most of which Charles offers him good advice. Sometimes they are less personal, as where·he tells him that "six hundred have been sold of Hood's book; while Sion's songs do not disperse so quickly:" and where he enters (very ably) into the defects and merits of Martin's pictures, Belshazzar and Joshua; and ventures an opinion as to what Art should and should not be. He is strenuous in advising him not to forsake the Bank (where he is a clerk) and throw himself on what the chance of employ by booksellers would afford. "Throw yourself, rather, from the steep Tarpeian rock, headlong upon the iron spikes. Keep to your bank, and your bank will keep you. Trust not to the Public," he says. Then, referring to his own previous complaints of official toil, he adds, " I retract all my fond complaints. Look on them as lovers' quarrels. I was but half in earnest. Welcome, dead timber of a desk that gives me life. A little grumbling is wholesome for the spleen ; but in my inner heart I do approve and embrace this our close but unharassing way of life."

Lamb's opinions on books, as well as on conduct, making some deduction for his preference of old writers, is almost always sound. When he is writing to Mr. Walter Wilson, who is editing De Foe, he says of the famous author of " Robinson Crusoe :"—

" In appearance of *truth* his works exceed any works of fiction that I am acquainted with. It is

perfect illusion. It is like reading evidence in a court
of justice. There is all the minute detail of a log-
book in it. Facts are repeated in varying phrases
till you cannot choose but believe them." His liking
for books (rather than his criticism on them) is shown
frequently in his letters. "Oh! to forget Fielding,
Steele, &c., and to read 'em *new*," he says. Of De
Foe, " His style is everywhere beautiful, but plain
and homely." Again, he speaks of " Fielding, Smollett, Sterne,—great Nature's stereotypes " " Milton,"
he says, " almost requires a solemn service of music
to be played before you enter upon him." Of Shen-
stone he speaks as " the dear author of the Schoolmistress ;" and so on from time to time, as occasion
prompts, of Bunyan, Izaac Walton, and Jeremy Taylor, and Fuller and Sir Philip Sidney, and others in
affectionate terms. These always relate to English
authors. Lamb, although a good Latinist, had not
much of that which ordinarily passes under the name
of Learning. He had little knowledge of languages,
living or dead. Of French, German, Italian, &c., he
knew nothing ; and in Greek his acquirements were
very moderate. These children of the tongues were
never adopted by him , but in his own Saxon English
he was a competent scholar, a lover, nice, discriminative, and critical.

The most graphic account of Lamb at a somewhat
later period of his life appears in Mr. N. P. Willis's
" Pencillings by the Way." He had been invited by
a gentleman in the Temple, Mr. R—— (Robinson ?)
to meet Charles Lamb and his sister at breakfast.
The Lambs lived at that time "a little way out of
London, and were not quite punctual." At last, they
enter ; " the gentleman in black small-clothes and

gaiters, short and very slight in person ; his head set
on his shoulders with a thoughtful forward bent, his
hair just sprinkled with grey, a beautiful deep set eye,
an aquiline nose, and a very indescribable mouth.
Whether it expressed most humour or feeling, good
nature or a kind of whimsical peevishness, or twenty
other things which passed over it by turns, I cannot
in the least be certain." This is Mr. Willis's excellent picture of Lamb at that period. The guest places
a large arm chair for Mary Lamb ; Charles pulls it
away, saying, gravely, "Mary, don't take it ; it looks
as if you were going to have a tooth drawn." Miss
Lamb was at that time very hard of hearing, and
Charles took advantage of her temporary deafness to
impute various improbabilities to her, which however
were so obvious as to render any denial or explanation unnecessary. Willis told Charles that he had
bought a copy of the " Elia " in America, in order to
give to a friend. "What did you give for it ?" asked
Lamb. " About seven and sixpence." " Permit me
to pay you that," said Lamb, counting out the money
with earnestness on the table ; " I never yet wrote
anything that could sell. I am the publisher's ruin.
My last poem won't sell,—not a copy. Have you
seen it." No ; Willis had not. " It's only eighteen-
pence, and I'll give you sixpence toward it," said
Lamb: and he described where Willis would find it,
" sticking up in a shop window in the Strand." Lamb
ate nothing ; but inquired anxiously for some potted
fish, which Mr. R—— used to procure for him.
There was none in the house, he therefore asked to
see the cover of the pot which had contained it ; he
thought it would do him good. It was brought, and
on it was a picture of the fish. Lamb kissed it, and

then left the table and began to wander about the room, with an uncertain step, &c.

This visit must have taken place, I suppose, at or after the time when Lamb was living at Colebrook Cottage ; and the breakfast took place probably in Mr. Henry Crabbe Robinson's chambers in the Temple, where I first met Wordsworth.

In the year 1827 Lamb moved into a small house at Enfield, a " gamboge-coloured house," he calls it, where I and other friends went to dine with him ; but it was too far from London, except for rare visits.— It was rather before that time that a very clever caricature of him had been designed and engraved (" scratched on copper," as the artist termed it) by Mr. Brook Pulham. It is still extant : and although somewhat ludicrous and hyperbolical in the countenance and outline, it certainly renders a likeness of Charles Lamb. The nose is monstrous, and the limbs are dwarfed and attenuated. Lamb himself, in a letter to Bernard Barton, (10th August, 1827,) adverts to it in these terms, " 'Tis a little sixpenny thing ; too like by half, in which the draughtsman has done his best to avoid flattery." Charles's hatred for annuals and albumbs was continually breaking out, " I die of albophobia." " I detest to appear in an annual," he writes ; " I hate the paper, the type, the gloss, the dandy plates." " Coleridge is too deep," again he says, " among the prophets, the gentleman annuals." " If I take the wings of the morning, and fly to the uttermost parts of the earth, there will albums be." To Southey he writes about this time, " I have gone lately into the acrostic line. I find genius declines with me ; but I get clever." The reader readily appreciates the distinction, which the humorist thus cleverly (more than cleverly) makes. In proof of his subdued quality, however, under the acrostical tyranny, I quote two little unpublished specimens addressed to the Misses Locke, whom he had never seen.

To M L. [MARY LOCKE.]

Must I write with pen unwilling,
And describe those graces killing,
Rightly, which I never saw?
Yes—it is the album's law.

Let me then invention strain.
On your excelling grace to feign,
Cold is fiction. I believe it
Kindly as I did receive it;
Even as I. F.'s tongue did weave it.

To S. L. [SARAH LOCKE.]

Shall I praise a face unseen,
And extol a fancied mien,
Rave on visionary charm,
And from shadows take alarm!
Hatred hates without a cause.

Love may love without applause,
Or, without a reason given,
Charmed be with unknown heaven.
Keep the secret, though, unmocked,
Ever in your bosom Locked.

After the transfer to Mr. Southern of the " London Magazine," Lamb was prevailed upon to allow some short papers to be published in the " New Monthly Magazine." They were entitled " Popular Fallacies," and were subsequently published conjointly with the " Elia Essays." He also sent brief contributions to

the " Athenæum " and the " Englishman," and wrote
some election squibs for Serjeant Wilde, during his
then contest for " Newark."   But his animal spirits
were not so elastic as formerly, when his time was
divided between official work and companionable
leisure ; the latter acting as a wholesome relief to his
mind when wearied by labour.

On this subject hear him speaking to Bernard
Barton, to whom as to others, he had formerly complained of his harassing duties at the India House,
and of his delightful prospect of leisure.   Now he
writes, " Deadly long are the days, with but half an
hour's candle-light and no fire-light.   The streets,
the shops remain, but old friends are gone."   " I
assure you " (he goes on) " no work is worse than
overwork.   The mind preys on itself, the most unwholesome food.   I have ceased to care almost for
anybody."   To remedy this tedium, he tries visiting ;
for the houses of his old friends were always open to
him, and he had a welcome everywhere.   But this
visiting will not revive him.   His spirits descended
to zero : below it.   He is convinced that happiness
is not to be found abroad.   It is better to go " to my
hole at Enfield, and hide like a sick cat in my
corner."   Again, he says, " Home, I have none.
Never did the waters of heaven pour down on a for-
lorner head.   What I can do, and over do, is to walk.
I am a sanguinary murderer of time.   But the snake
is vital.   Your forlorn—C. L."   These are his meditations in 1829, four years only after he had rushed
abroad, full of exultation and delight, from the prison
of a " work-a-day " life, into the happy gardens of
boundless leisure.   Time, which was once his friend,
had become his enemy.   His letters, which were

always full of goodness, generally full of cheerful humour, sink into discontent. "I have killed an hour or two with this poor scrawl," he writes. It is unnecessary to inflict upon the reader all the points of the obvious moral, that obtrudes itself at this period of Charles Lamb's history. It is clear that the Otiosa Eternitas was pressing upon his days, and he did not know how to find relief. Although a good Latin scholar, indeed fond of writing letters in Latin, he did not at this period resort to classical literature. I heard him indeed once (and once only) quote the well-known Latin verse from the Georgics, "O Fortunatos," &c., but generally he showed himself careless about Greeks and Romans; and when (as Mr. Moxon states) "a traveller brought him some acorns from an ilex that grew over the tomb of Virgil, he valued them so little that he threw them at the hackney coachmen as they passed by his window."

I have been much impressed by Lamb's letters to Bernard Barton, which are numerous, and which, taken altogether, are equal to any which he has written The letters to Coleridge do not exhibit so much care or thought; nor those to Wordsworth or Manning, nor to any others of his intellectual equals. These correspondents could think and speculate for themselves, and they were accordingly left to their own resources. "The Volsces have much corn." But Bernard Barton was in a different condition : he was poor. His education had been inferior, his range of reading and thinking had been very confined, his knowledge of the English drama being limited to Shakespeare and Miss Baillie. He seems, however, to have been an amiable man, desirous of cultivating the

power, such as it was, which he possessed, and
Lamb therefore lavished upon him—the poor Quaker
clerk of a Suffolk Banker—all that his wants or ambition required; excellent worldly counsel; sound
thoughts upon literature and art; critical advice on
his own verses; letters, which in their actual value
surpass the wealth of many more celebrated collec-
tions. Lamb's correspondence with Barton, whom
he had first known in 1822, continued until his
death.

In 1830 (September 18th) Hazlitt died. It is unnecessary to enter into any enumeration of his remarkable qualities. They were known to all his
friends, and to some of his enemies. In Sir Edward
Lytton's words, " He went down to the dust, without having won the crown for which he so bravely
struggled. He who had done so much for the pro-
pagation of thought, left no stir upon the surface
when he sank." I will not in this place attempt to
weave the moral which nevertheless lies hid in his
unrequited life. At that time the number of Lamb's
old intimates was gradually diminished. The eternally
recurring madness of his sister was more frequent The
hopelessness of it—if hope indeed ever existed—was
more palpable, more depressing. His own spring of
mind was fast losing its power of rebound. He felt
the decay of the active principle, and now confined
his efforts to morsels of criticism, to verses for albums,
and small contributions to periodicals, which (excepting only the " Popular Fallacies ") it has not been
thought important enough to reprint. To the editor
of the " Athenæum," indeed, he laments sincerely
over the death of Munden. This was in February,
1832, and was a matter that touched his affections.

" He was not an actor " (he writes) " but something
better." To a reader of the present day,—even to a
contemporary of Lamb himself, there was something
almost amounting to extravagance in the terms of his
admiration. Yet Munden was, in his way, a remarkable man; and although he was an actor in farce, he
often stood aloof and beyond the farce itself. The
play was a thing merely on which to hang his own
conceptions. These did not arise from the drama;
but were elsewhere cogitated; and were interleaved,
as it were, with the farce or comedy which served as
an excuse for their display. The actor was to all in-
tents and purposes *sui generis*.

To speak of my own impressions, Munden did not
affect me much in some of his earlier performances;
for then he depended on the play. Afterwards, when
he took the matter into his own hands, and created
personages who owed little or nothing to the play-
wright, then he became an inventor. He rose with
the occasion. *Sic ivit ad astra*. In the Drama of
" Modern Antiques," especially, space was allowed
him for his movements. The words were nothing.
The prosperity of the piece depended exclusively on
the genius of the actor. Munden enacted the part of
an old man credulous beyond ordinary credulity, and
when he came upon the stage there was in him an
almost sublime look of wonder, passing over the scene
and people around him, and settling apparently somewhere beyond the moon. What he believed in, improbable as it was to mere terrestrial visions, you at
once conceived to be quite possible,—to be true. The
sceptical idiots of the play pretend to give him a
phial nearly full of water. He is assured that this
contains Cleopatra's tear. Well; who can disprove

it ?   Munden evidently recognised it. "What a
large tear!" he exclaimed. Then they place in his
hands a druidical harp, which to vulgar eyes might
resemble a modern gridiron.   He touches the chords
gently : " pipes to the spirit ditties of no tone ;" and
you imagine Æolian strains.   At last, William Tell's
cap is produced.   The people who affect to cheat
him, apparently cut the rim from a modern hat, and
place the skull-cap in his hands ; and then begins
the almost finest piece of acting that I ever witnessed.
Munden accepts the accredited cap of Tell, with confusion and reverence.   He places it slowly and
solemnly on his head, growing taller in the act of
crowning himself.   Soon he swells into the heroic
size, a great archer ; and enters upon his dreadful
task.   He weighs the arrow carefully ; he tries the
tension of the bow, the elasticity of the string ; and
finally, after a most deliberate aim, he permits the
arrow to fly, and looks forward at the same time with
intense anxiety.   You hear the twang, you see the
hero's knitted forehead, his eagerness ; you tremble ;
—at last you mark his calmer brow, his relaxing
smile, and are satisfied that the son is saved !—It is
difficult to paint in words this extraordinary performance, which I have several times seen ; but you feel
that is is transcendent.   You think of Sagittarius, in
the broad circle of the Zodiac ; you recollect that
archery is as old as Genesis : you are reminded that
Ishmael, the son of Hagar, wandered about the
Judæan deserts and became an archer.

The old actor is now dead ; but on his last performance, when he was to act Sir Robert Bramble, on the
night of his taking final leave of the stage, Lamb
greatly desired to be present.   He had always loved

the actors, especially the old actors, from his youth;
and this was the last of the Romans. Accordingly
Lamb and his sister went to the Drury Lane; but
there being no room in the ordinary parts of the house,
(boxes or pit,) Munden obtained places for his two
visitors in the orchestra, close to the stage. He saw
them carefully ushered in, and well posted; then
acted with his usual vigour, and no doubt enjoyed
the plaudits wrung from a thousand hands. Afterwards, in the interval between the comedy and the
farce, he was seen to appear cautiously, diffidently, at
the low door of the orchestra (where the musicians
enter) and beckon to his friends; who then perceived
that he was armed with a mighty pot of porter for
their refreshment. Lamb, grateful for the generous
liquid, drank heartily but not ostentatiously, and returned the pot of beer to Munden, who had waited to
remove it from fastidious eyes. He then retreated,
into the farce, and then he retired—for ever.

After Munden's retirement Lamb almost entirely
forsook the theatre; and his habits became more solitary. He had not relinquished society, nor professedly narrowed the circle of his friends. But insen-
sibly his visitors became fewer in number and came
less frequently. Some had died; some had grown
old, some had increased occupation to care for. His
old Wednesday evenings had ceased; and he had
placed several miles of road between London (the
residence of their familes) and his own home. The
weight of years indeed had its effect, in pressing down
his strength and buoyancy: his spirit no longer possessed its old power of rebound. Even the care of
housekeeping (not very onerous, one would suppose)
troubled Charles and his sister so much, that they

determined to abandon it. This occurred in 1829. Then they became boarders and lodgers, with an old person (T. W.) who was their next-door-neighbour at Enfield; and of him Lamb has given an elaborate description :—T. W., his new landlord or housekeeper, he says, is seventy years old; " he has something under a competence;" he has one joke, and £40 a year, upon which he retires in a green old age; he laughs when he hears a joke, and when (which is much oftener) he hears it not. Having served the greater parish offices, Lamb and his sister become greater, being *his* lodgers, than they were when substantial householders. The children of the village venerate him for his gentility; but wonder also at him, for a gentle endorsation of the person, not amounting to a hump, or if one, then like that of the buffalo, and coronative of as mild qualities."

Writing to Wordsworth (and speaking as a great landed proprietor), he says, " We have ridded ourselves of the dirty acres; settled down into poor boarders and lodgers; confiding ravens." The distasteful country, however, still remains, and the clouds still hang over it, " Let not the lying poets be believed, who entice men from the cheerful streets," he writes. The country, he thinks, does well enough when he is amongst his books, by the fire and with candle-light; but day and the green fields return, and restore his natural antipathies; then he says, " In a calenture I plunge into St. Giles's." So Lamb and his sister leave their comfortable little house and subside into the rooms of the Humpback. Their chairs and tables and beds also retreat, all except the ancient bookcase full of his " ragged veterans." This I saw, years after Charles Lamb's death, in the possession of his sister Mary. "All our furniture has faded," he writes, "under the auctioneer's hammer; going for nothing, like the tarnished frippery of the prodigal." Four years afterwards (in 1833) Lamb moves to his last home, in Church Street, Edmonton: where he is somewhat nearer to his London friends.

Very curious was the antipathy of Charles to objects that are generally so pleasant to other men. It was not a passing humour, but a lifelong dislike. He admired the trees and the meadows and murmuring streams in poetry. I have heard him repeat some of Keats's beautiful lines in the Ode to the Nightingale, about the "pastoral eglantine," with great delight. But that was another thing: that was an object in its proper place: that was a piece of art. Long ago he had admitted that the mountains of Cumberland were grand objects "to look at," but (as he said) "the houses in streets were the places to live in." I imagine that he would no more have received the former as an equivalent for his own modest home, than he would have accepted a portrait as a substitute for a friend. He was, beyond all other men whom I have met, essentially metropolitan. He loved "the sweet security of streets," as he says: "I would set up my tabernacle there."

In the spring of 1834, Coleridge's health began to decline. Charles had written to him (in reply) on the 14th April; at which time his friend had been evidently unwell; for Lamb says that he is glad to see that he could write so long a letter. He was indeed very ill, and no further personal intercourse (I believe) took place between Charles and his old schoolfellow. Coleridge lay ill for months; but his faculties seem to have survived his bodily decay. He died on

the 25th July, 1834; yet on the 5th of that month he
was able to discourse with his nephew on Dryden and
Barrow, on Lord Brook, and Fielding and Richard-
son, without any apparent diminution of judgment.
Even on the 10th (a fortnight only before his death)
there was no sympton of speedy dissolution ; he then
said, " the scenes of my early life have stolen into my
mind, like breezes blown from the Spice Islands."
Charles's sorrow was unceasing.   " He was my fifty
years' old friend " (he says), " without a dissension.
I cannot think without an ineffectual reference to
him."   Lamb's frequent exclamations, " Coleridge is
dead ! Coleridge is dead !" have been already noticed.

And now the figures of other old friends of Charles
Lamb, gradually (one by one) slip out of sight.   Still
in his later letters are to be found glimpses of Wordsworth and Southey, of Rogers and Hood, of Cary,
(with whom his intimacy increases,) especially may
be noted Miss Isola, whom he tenderly regarded, and
after whose marriage (then left more alone) he retreats
to his last retreat, in Church Street, Edmonton.

From details let us escape into a more general
narrative   The latest facts need not be painfully
enumerated.   There is little left, indeed, to particularize.   Mary's health fluctuates perhaps more frequently than heretofore.   At one time she is well and
happy ; at another her mind becomes turbid, and she
is then sheltered as usual under her brother's care.
The last Essays of Elia are published ;—friends visit
him ;—and he occasionally visits them in London.
He dines with Talfourd and Cary.   The sparks which
are brought out are as bright as ever, although the
splendour is not so frequent.   Apparently the bodily
strength, never great, but sufficient to move him

pleasantly throughout life, seem to flag a little. Yet
he walks as usual. He and his sister "scramble
through the Inferno," (as he says to Cary,) "Mary's
chief pride in it was that she should some day brag
of it to you." Then he and Mary became very poorly.
He writes .—"We have had a sick child, sleeping, or
not sleeping, next to me, with a pasteboard partition
between, who killed my sleep. My bedfellows are
Cough and Cramp ; we sleep three in a bed. Don't
come yet, to this house of pest and age." This is in
1833. At the end of that year (in December) he
writes (once more humorously) to Rogers, expressing
amongst other things his love for that fine artist,
Stothard : " I met the dear old man, and it was sublime to see him sit, deaf, and enjoy all that was going
on, mirthful with the company. He reposed upon
the many graceful and many fantastic images he had
created." His last letter, written to Mrs. Dyer on
the day after his fall, was an effort to recover a book
of Mr. Cary, which had been mislaid or lost, so
anxious was he always that every man should have
his own.

In December, 1834, the history of Charles Lamb
comes suddenly to a close. He had all along had a
troubled day : now came the night. His spirits had
previously been tolerably cheerful ; reading and con-
versing as heretofore, with his friends, on subjects
that were familiar to him. There was little manifest
alteration or falling off, in his condition of mind or
body. He took his morning walks, as usual. One
day he stumbled against a stone, and fell. His face
was slightly wounded ; but no fatal (or even alarm-
ing) consequence was foreboded. Erysipelas, however, followed the wound, and his strength (never

robust) was not sufficient to enable him to combat successfully that inflammatory and exhausting disease. He suffered no pain; (I believe;) and when the presence of a clergyman was suggested to him, he made no remark, but understood that his life was in danger, he was quite calm and collected, quite resigned. At last his voice began to fail, his perceptions became confused, and he sank gradually—very gradually, until the 27th of December, 1834: and then —he died! It was the fading away or disappearance of life, rather than a violent transit into another world.

He died at Edmonton; not, as has been supposed, at Enfield, to which place he never returned as to a place of residence, after he had once quitted it.

It is not true that he was ever deranged, or subjected to any restraint, shortly before his death. There never was the least symptom of mental disturbance in him, after the time (1795-6) when he was placed for a few weeks in Hoxton Asylum, to allay a little nervous irritation. If it were necessary to confirm this assertion, which is known to me from personal observation and other incontrovertible evidence, I would adduce ten of his published letters; (in 1833 and several in 1834;) one of them bearing date only four days before his death. All these documents afford ample testimony of his clear good sense and kind heart: some of them indeed being tinged with his usual humour.

Charles Lamb was fifty-nine years old at his death; of the same age as Cromwell; betweem whom and himself there was of course no other similitude. A few years before, when he was about to be released from his wearisome toil, at the India House, he said

exultingly, that he was passing out of Time into
Eternity. But now came the true Eternity; the old
Eternity,—without change or limit; in which all men
surrender their leisure, as well as their labour ; when
their sensations and infirmities (sometimes harassing
enough) cease and are at rest. No more anxiety for
the debtor; no more toil for the worker. The rich
man's ambition, the poor man's pains at last are over.
Hic jacet. That " forlorn " inscription is the universal epitaph. What a world of moral—what speculations—what pathetic wishes, and what terrible
dreams—lie enshrouded in that one final issue, which
we call—DEATH.

To him who never gave pain to a human being;
whose genius yielded nothing but instruction and
delight, was awarded a calm and easy death. No
man, it is my belief, was ever loved or lamented more
sincerely than Charles Lamb. His sister (his elder
by a decade) survived him for the space of thirteen
years.

By strict economy, without meanness; with much
unpretending hospitality; with frequent gifts and
lendings, and without any borrowing; he accumu-
lated, during his thirty-three years of constant labour,
the moderate sum of £2000. No more. That was
the sum, I believe, which was eventually shared
amongst his legatees. His other riches were gathered
together and deposited elsewhere ; in the memory of
those who loved him, and there were many of them :
or amongst others of our Anglo-Saxon race, whose
minds he has helped to enrich and soften.

The property of Charles Lamb, or so much as
might be wanted for the purpose, was by his will
directed to be applied towards the maintenance and

comfort of his sister; and, subject to the primary object, it was vested in Trustees for the benefit of Miss Isola—Mrs. Moxon.

Mary Lamb's comforts were supplied, with anxiety and tenderness, throughout the thirteen years, during which she survived her brother. I went to see her, after her brother's death; but her frequent illnesses did not render visits at all times welcome or feasible. She then resided in Alpha Road, Saint John's Wood, under the care of an experienced nurse. There was a twilight of consciousness in her, scarcely more, at times, so that perhaps the mercy of God saved her from full knowledge of her great loss. Charles—who had given up all his days for her protection and benefit,—who had fought the great battle of life so nobly, had left her "for that unknown and silent shore," where, it is hoped, the brother and sister will renew the love which once united them on earth and made their lives holy. Mary Lamb died on the 20th May, 1847; and the brother and sister now lie near each other (in the same grave) in the churchyard of Edmonton, in Middlesex.

POSTSCRIPT.

———

I HAVE thus told, as far as my ability permits, the story of the life of Charles Lamb.

I have not ventured to deduce any formidable moral from it. Like Lamb himself, I have great dislike to ostentatious precepts and impertinent lessons. Facts themselves should disclose their own virtues. A man who is able to benefit by a lesson, will no doubt discover it, under any husk or disguise, before it is stripped and laid bare—to the kernel.

Besides, too much teaching may disagree with the reader. It is apt to harden the heart; wearying the attention, and mortifying the self-love. Such disturbances of the system interfere with the digestion of a truth.

Even Gulliver is sometimes too manifestly didactic. His adventures simply told, would have emitted spontaneously a luminous atmosphere, and need not have been distilled into brilliant or pungent drops.

No history is barren of good. Even from the foregoing narrative some benefit may be gleaned, some sympathy may be excited, which naturally forms itself into a lesson.

Let us look at it cursorily.

Charles Lamb was born almost in penury, and he was taught by charity. Even when a boy he was forced to labour for his bread. In the first opening

of manhood a terrible calamity fell upon him ; in
magnitude fit to form the mystery or centre of an
antique drama. He had to dwell, all his days, with
a person incurably mad. From poverty he passed
at once to unpleasant toil and perpetual fear. These
were the sole changes in his fortune. Yet, he gained
friends, respect, a position ; and great sympathy
from all; showing what one poor man of genius
under grievous misfortune, may do, if he be courageous and faithful to the end.

Charles Lamb never preached nor prescribed ; but
let his own actions tell their tale and produce their
natural effects ; neither did he' deal out little apoph-
thegms or scraps of wisdom, derived from other
minds. But he succeeded , and in every success
there must be a mainstay of right or truth to support it ; otherwise it will eventually fail.

It is true that in his essays and numerous letters
many of his sincere thoughts and opinions are
written down. These, however, are written down
simply and just as they occur, without any special
design. Some persons exhibit only their ingenuity,
or learning. It is not every one who is able, like the
licentiate Pedro Garcias, to deposit his wealth of soul
by the road-side.

Like all persons of great intellectual sensibility,
Lamb responded to all impressions. To sympathise
with Tragedy or Comedy only, argues a limited
capacity. The mind thus constructed is partially
lame or torpid. One hemisphere has never been
reached

It should not be forgotten that Lamb possessed
one great advantage. He lived and died amongst
his equals. This was what enabled him to exercise

his natural strength; as neither a parasite nor a patron can. It is marvellous how freedom of thought operates: what strength it gives to the system; with what lightness and freshness it endues the spirit.— Then, he was made stronger by trouble; made wiser by grief.

I have not attempted to fix the precise spot in which Charles Lamb is to shine hereafter in the firmanent of letters. I am not of sufficient magnitude to determine his astral elevation—where he is to dwell — between the sun Shakespeare, and the twinkling Zoilus. That must be left to time. Even the fixed stars at first waver and coruscate, and require long seasons for their consummation and final settlement.

Whenever he differs with us in opinion, (as he does occasionally,) let us not hastily pronounce him to be wrong. It is wise, as well as modest, not to show too much eagerness to adjust the ideas of all other thinkers to the (sometimes low) level of our own.

London   Swift & Co., 55, King Street, Regent Street   W.

L   D

l   ꝰ

ι   ϸ

l   D